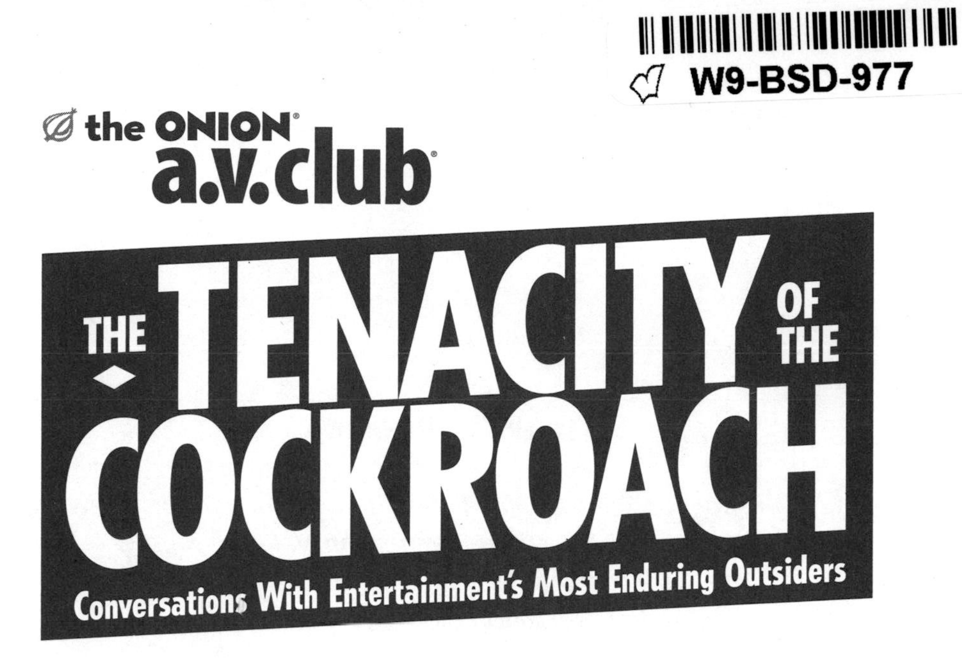
W9-BSD-977
the ONION
a.v.club
THE TENACITY OF THE COCKROACH
Conversations With Entertainment's Most Enduring Outsiders

ALSO FROM THE ONION

Our Dumb Century: 100 Years Of Headlines From America's Finest News Source
The Onion's Finest News Reporting, Volume One
Dispatches From The Tenth Circle
The Onion Ad Nauseam: Complete News Archives, Volume 13

EDITOR
Stephen Thompson

ASSISTANT EDITORS
Keith Phipps
Tasha Robinson

DESIGNER (INTERIOR)
Andrew Welyczko

DESIGNER (COVER)
Scott K. Templeton

CONTRIBUTORS
Stephen Thompson, Keith Phipps, Nathan Rabin, Tasha Robinson, John Krewson, Joe Garden, Joshua Klein, Scott Tobias, Al Yankovic

COPY EDITOR
Andy Battaglia

MADE POSSIBLE BY
Peter Haise

SPECIAL THANKS
Ken Artis, Brian Belfiglio, Christine Carlson, Chris Cranmer, Rich Dahm, Scott Dikkers, Pete Fornatale, Jessica Gartner, Daniel Greenberg, Trisha Howell, Allison Klaas, Steven J. Krauth, Stephanie Kuenn, Annik LaFarge, Mike Loew, Rita Madrigal, David Miner, Josh Modell, Noel Murray, Chad Nackers, Michael O'Brien, Steve Ross, Robert Siegel, Dorianne Steele, Denise Thompson, Maggie Thompson, Dan Vebber, Al Yankovic

THREE RIVERS PRESS • NEW YORK

For Denise and Jonah

Published By Three Rivers Press, New York, New York
Member of the Crown Publishing Group, a division of Random House, Inc.

www.randomhouse.com

Printed in the United States of America

Design by The Onion

Library of Congress Cataloging-in-Publication Data
The tenacity of the cockroach: conversations with entertainment's
most enduring outsiders / editor, Stephen Thompson.
1. Entertainers—United States—Interviews.
I. Title: At head of title: Onion A.V. Club.
II. Thompson, Stephen, 1972–
PN2285 T46 2002
791'.092'273—dc21 2002028695

Original Trade Paperback ISBN 0-609-80991-1

10 9 8 7 6 5 4 3 2 1

First Edition

PHOTO CREDITS

p. 4, Henry Rollins; p. 96, Steve Albini: © 2002 Cynthia Connolly. p. 12, Harlan Ellison: Maggie Thompson/Comics Buyers Guide (www.comicsbuyersguide.com). p. 20, George Carlin: Randee St. Nicholas/Photofest. p. 26, John Kricfalusi: ©1998 Donya Fiorentino/Spümcø, Inc. p. 36, Jello Biafra: Jay Blakesberg/Alternative Tentacles Records. p. 42, Ralph Bakshi: Elizabeth Bakshi. p. 50, Tom Lehrer: courtesy of Tom Lehrer. p. 56, Opus: © 2001 by Berkeley Breathed. p. 64, Mr. Show: Bonnie Schiffman/courtesy of Baker Winokur Ryder Public Relations. p. 72, XTC: Steve Gullick/TVT Records. p. 78, Aimee Mann: Carlos Serrao. p. 84, Lloyd Kaufman; p. 92, Martha Plimpton; p. 102, George Romero; p. 158, Dr. Demento; p. 170, William H. Macy; p. 180, Ray Bradbury; p. 194, Robert Altman; p. 200, Ron Jeremy; p. 210, Alice Cooper; p. 214, Stan Freberg; p. 234, Elvira; p. 248, Mr. T; p. 254, Teller; p. 258, Penn Jillette; p. 284, Lemmy Kilmister; p. 316, Roger Corman; p. 322, Rick James; p. 328, Joan Jett; p. 332, Pam Grier; p. 348, Russ Meyer; p. 378, Michael McKean; p. 390, James Ellroy; p. 402, Robert Forster: Photofest. p. 106, Penelope Spheeris: Roger Jans/Photofest. p. 112, Mr. Show; p. 354, Mr. Show: Bonnie Schiffman/Photofest. p. 116, Fugazi: Cynthia Connolly/Dischord Records. p. 124, Tom Waits: EFE Photos (Newscom). p. 130, Grant Hart: Eric Johanson. p. 136, Gene Simmons bear; cockroach on cover: Scott Templeton/Onion Photos. p. 142, Merle Haggard: Scott Newton/Photofest. p. 148, John Waters: Henny Garfunkel/Photofest. p. 154, Rick Nielsen: Mike Graham/Graham Images. p. 164, Chuck Jones: Robert Zuckerman/Photofest. p. 176, Douglas Adams: Dan Callister/Online USA/Getty (Newscom). p. 184, Conan O'Brien: Edie Baskin/Photofest. p. 190, Elmore Leonard: Nancy Kaszerman/Zuma Press (Newscom). p. 206, Mr. Show: Janet Van Ham/Photofest. p. 220, Andrew W.K.: Anaka/IXO/Zuma Press (Newscom). p. 228, Tim Quirk: Jenn Morris. p. 242, some members of Negativland: Rose Whitaker/Negativland. p. 262, KRS-One: Frank Micelotta/Image Direct (Newscom). p. 268, Devo: Robert Matheu/Photofest. p. 274, Alan Moore: Leah Moore. p. 280, David Cross; p. 294, Andy Richter: courtesy of Baker Winokur Ryder Public Relations. p. 288, Bob Barker: David Keeler/Getty Images (Newscom). p. 300, Vanilla Ice: Mike Valdez/Zuma Press (Newscom). p. 304, David Lee Roth: Rick Diamond/Image Direct (Newscom). p. 310, "Weird Al" Yankovic: Johnny Buzzerio/Volcano Records. p. 338, Peter Frampton: Ed Rode/Vision 3. p. 344, Ronnie Spector: Debra Greenberg. p. 362, Quentin Crisp: © 2002 Phillip Ward/Quentin Crisp Archives (www.crisperanto.org). p. 368, Joss Whedon: Kevin Winter/Image Direct (Newscom). p. 384, Billy Barty: Jim Ruymen/UPI Photo Service (Newscom). p. 394, The Unknown Comic: courtesy of Murray Langston.

CONTENTS

INTRODUCTION

"I had 18 minutes instead of 15 because of tenacity, the will of the cockroach."

Henry Rollins

Over the course of the decade that interviews have run in the back of The Onion, *what started out as weaknesses—difficulty in attracting A-list stars, a lack of visibility behind pages of high-profile satirical content—soon revealed themselves as strengths. Most entertainment publications are forced, usually by market pressures, to profile stars with fleeting appeal, with an emphasis on pretty young faces. Celebrities over 30 rarely appear on magazine covers, and if they do, they tend to be so hardened by years in the limelight that they speak no candid words for public consumption.*

Through trial and error, The Onion A.V. Club *(the longstanding name for* The Onion's *entertainment section, referencing high-school audio-visual clubs) eventually discovered its interviewing niche: entertainers and storytellers whose long-term career accomplishments don't get much play in the media. From amiable retirees and passionate visionaries to bitter, jilted, eternally warring cranks, the interview subjects in* The Tenacity Of The Cockroach *offer fresh perspectives, colorful stories, and even sage advice.*

Collecting dozens of The Onion A.V. Club's *best and most timeless conversations—grouped by tone to segue from anger and resignation to joy and contentment—*The Tenacity Of The Cockroach *also features five stops on the career path of Bob Odenkirk and David Cross, the masterminds of the brilliant HBO sketch-comedy series* Mr. Show. *Documented chronologically to provide a sort of counter-narrative, their ever-evolving battles shed light on what happens when tenacious entertainers fight for their ideas. Plus, for added historical perspective, noted pundit "Weird Al" Yankovic periodically weighs in on his friends and heroes.*

Onion A.V. Club *interviews are presented in edited Q&A form to place emphasis on the subjects, and usually focus on the entirety of careers rather than projects being promoted. Those subjects' persistence, clarity of vision, and fierce independence—combined with the occasional smattering of delusion—connect them on the unique pop-cultural landscape that follows.*

Stephen Thompson
Editor, *The Onion A.V. Club*

"I'm just so sick of supplying high-quality art to deaf ears and blind eyes." CHAPTER 1

"It's disheartening to know that you live in a country that's just teeming with semi-literate, mediocre psychos. If they had better reading skills and laid off the Budweiser, I'd dig the psychosis. Now it just scares me... I'm just so sick of supplying high-quality art to deaf ears and blind eyes. Let 'em go have their fuckin' *Armageddon* movie, you know?"

Henry Rollins page 5

"Atavists and elitists like me who do read don't understand that they are surrounded by people who are bone-stick-stone stupid. Every time we have some lunatic run amok and shoot someone, when we have kids in schoolyards blowing each other's asses off, everybody says, 'What was the reason? What was the motivation?' There is no fucking motivation! The world is turning into a cesspool of imbeciles."

Harlan Ellison page 13

"There is no hope, because I think we're locked in by commerce. The pursuit of goods and possessions has completely corrupted the human experience, along with religion, which I think limits the intellect. With those two things in place as firmly as they are, I don't see any hope for getting around them short of some sort of interesting cataclysm."

George Carlin page 21

"There are no standards anymore. All you have to do is open up a magazine from the '30s or '40s and just look at the illustrations, and your jaw will hang limp. Every illustration—even the cheesiest ones, like the underwear ads—is drawn a thousand times better than the best fine art is today. It was a time of greatness... Now, you have the Age Of Amateurism."

John Kricfalusi page 27

"We have an entire audience of people who call themselves 'punk' because they've written the name of a British band that broke up 15 years ago on the leather jacket they bought the day before at the mall, who only want to hear one kind of music. They're as conservative as Republicans or fundamentalist Christians. I like to shock and torment those people."

Jello Biafra page 37

Henry Rollins

By Stephen Thompson

Originally Printed July 1998

"I had 18 minutes instead of 15 because of tenacity, the will of the cockroach."

Henry Rollins' long and storied career has included lengthy stints in the legendary noise-rock group Black Flag and his venerable Rollins Band, as well as numerous spoken-word albums and acting roles in movies ranging from Lost Highway *to* Johnny Mnemonic *to* Jack Frost. *He's run a record label, Infinite Zero, with Rick Rubin, focusing on reissues of out-of-print albums by Devo, Gang Of Four, and more, as well as new releases by his favorite obscure musicians. And he's carved out a career as an author and publisher, releasing books of essays and poetry through his independent 2.13.61 imprint. While preparing for the 1998 release of a book (*Solipsist*) and a spoken-word record (*Think Tank*), Rollins spoke to* The Onion A.V. Club *about his rocky past, successful present, and uncertain future.*

The Onion: ***What's the story with*** **Solipsist?** ***I haven't seen it yet.***

Henry Rollins: We didn't send out any copies for review, which made our press girl very angry. But I'm tired of critics and their opinions of me, good or bad. Not only do I not give a fuck, but it also gets me hostile at some guy who I could kill with my hands, who, like, gets to wield his fake verbal superiority over me. So I said, "Fuck 'em. Just save your money in printing up press copies, and take out other ads." But what I did was, in summer '93, I was looking through the dictionary, which I like to do a lot, and I saw the word "solipsist," which is one who thinks the world is an extension of himself. And I feel like that a lot, when I'm in album mode, when I'm making a record, or if I'm living in New York City. Everything tends to get very closed in. The only reason they make a subway train is to pack it full of people and stick you in it; that's how you feel at 7 a.m. on the train. "This hell has been created for me. It is my hell." It's easy to get in that kind of mindset, especially when you get... Like, in lyric-writing mode, songwriting mode, you get very self-involved. And cities kind of pack you into yourself. I've noticed that people get very insular, very isolated. So what I did was, I tried to write a book from that point of view, and it ended up being this three-year struggle with these very strange essays and these characters, some of whom are very tragic. It's a very strange book. Very extreme. It is an interesting book—in quotations, like when you have someone read your poetry, and they go, "Wow, that was... intense." "Thanks a lot. Don't come over soon."

O: *How do you feel about being called a poet?*
HR: That doesn't work for me. I respect good poetry, and we have a couple of great poets on our label, like Ellyn Maybe and Bill Shields. And, you know, I like [French poet Jean] Rimbaud and the good stuff, but my association with poetry is going to a place like Beyond Baroque in Venice, California, which is a real poetry place, and seeing these guys with their corduroy pants, looking like substitute teachers, wearing a scarf, reading this utter bullshit, and that's poetry. And it's so lame. I respect the idea of it, how you can render some heightened imagery and heightened intensity of a moment, but most of the stuff I see, and the pretension that goes around it... Anyone who would say, "I'm a poet"... I gotta run. "Well, then there's my poetry..." Running! I'm running out the door. It's brutal. In New York, you talk to these people, and they're like, "Well, I'm working here, but really I'm a poet." "Aieee!" Run! Out the door! Like Bukowski once said, not that I can quote him all that freely, "Most people who write shouldn't." You know, he was right. He had a point there. He could kick that stuff and make it sing all right. I'd much rather read good literature. I'd much rather find good poetry in literature. If you read Thomas Wolfe—not Tom Wolfe, the guy who did *Bonfire Of The Vanities*—he was your classic Southern writer, and his stuff was very lyrical and poetic. There's so much poetry in his work, and he's not even trying. He's just describing what's on the breakfast table, and it takes two pages, and it's just beautiful, you know? It makes you hungry. That's the kind of poetry I appreciate, when someone is inside a paragraph, and they're making it go.

"It's disheartening to know that you live in a country that's just teeming with semi-literate, mediocre psychos."

O: *Now that your Infinite Zero label is gone, are you planning to release any material yourself?*
HR: No. I'm looking at a couple of different labels. I'll take it to a good home and, yeah, if I can't do it there, I'll print up a thousand of everything and just do it myself. It's basically a thing where you get integrity, you break even, and you get to supply some good records to some good people. I'm really sick of the fact that the music industry has lost that. I mean, there are a ton of labels who haven't, and there are a lot of little labels who... I mean, like this book company: We're not making money. We're struggling, and there are a lot of record companies that are the same way. They get some cool stuff out, and it pays for itself some months, and then some months you eat shit. But then you have a rush and it'll catch you up. I feel for those labels—I'm one of them, and I'm usually a patron of those labels, because it's that kind of music that I'm interested in. I fully realize that the stuff I like doesn't sell. I've put out records I think are awesome, like Alan Vega's stuff, and Matthew Shipp, the great jazz pianist. No one buys 'em, and I go, "What the fuck? They're awesome." Even though Matthew's getting incredible critical acclaim and the cover of *Jazziz*, and all that stuff, people are too busy buying... I don't know what they're buying. You look at the *Billboard* Top 200, and you're like, "Gee, who's buying all those *Titanic* records? What kind of dummies are out there?" It's disheartening to know that you live in a country that's just teeming with semi-literate, mediocre psychos. If they had better reading skills and laid off the Budweiser, I'd dig the psychosis. Now it just scares me, because they're dumb enough to go out and buy guns and stuff. The older I get, the more I'll wake up some days and say, "Fuck it, I'm dissolving this company and giving everyone their books and records back, and I'm just gonna do my own thing, support myself..." I'm just so sick of supplying high-quality art to deaf ears and blind eyes. Let 'em

go have their fuckin' *Armageddon* movie, you know? And then I get one letter, like, "Dude, Alan Vega rules!" And I'm like, "That's it, I'm back in." All it takes is one. I'm so desperate to hear, "Oh, I got the new Ellyn Maybe poetry book. Thank you so much. She's wonderful." "I'm in. I'm back in. Full steam." It means so much.

O: ***Well, smart people are out there.***

HR: Oh, I know. The struggle is finding them, getting to them, connecting to them, keeping them.

O: ***You've worked in an ice-cream store. You've slept on 100,000 filthy floors. You've been beaned in the head with bottles and spit globs. Now, you're at a point in your life where you've acted in movies with Michael Keaton and Charlie Sheen. You run your own company. Is it difficult to maintain your intensity?***

HR: No. No, that's never a problem, believe it or not. And the irony of my life is never wasted upon me. Now, if someone wants to spit on me, I just roll up the window of my BMW 540i. I have a lot of money and all that stuff, and I'm sitting in the house I own right now, which also serves as an office for everyone here [at 2.13.61]. On that level, I've had some success, and to me, I approach the whole thing with a very wry smile. That lifestyle. It's not like I'm livin' large; I'm living adequately. If you amortize the last 18 years, it's been like $8.50 an hour, so God bless me. It's no problem at all, because my head is still in the same place. For me, the venues got bigger over the years. But you know what? Then they got smaller again. They're on their way down again. You come and you go, and attendance-wise, I'm probably on my way out. As far as creatively and everything, I'm holding just fine. It's not a problem maintaining intensity. A producer friend of mine made a really good point a couple years ago. He said, "Find any Frank Sinatra record that's not intense." He's fully focused; he's riveted on the topic like a laser beam. I play Frank's records a lot, and he's right. Even when he's like, [imitates Sinatra] "Hey...," he's doing "Hey..." within an inch of its life. That's just discipline and application. But where I might not be blue in the face yelling and screaming like I once was, I'm 37. I no longer feel the need to do that. I'm not a young man, and I can find intensity in a lot of different ways, sometimes without even raising my voice. When I was younger, it was all about how I needed three extra sets of lungs to get enough wind to get out the thing at the screaming level I need to. Now, I see that there's a whole lot of other colors on the palette. A lot of people never really lose their thing. A guy like Iggy Pop... Iggy's like 51. Iggy's like... Fuck, man. Where does it come from? He's like the fountain of youth or something. He's this self-recharging battery who just gets more crazed as he goes. You see this chemical change come over him when he hits the stage; it's like, "I don't know this guy." And then, afterwards, he's like, "Hey, man, how are ya?" He's this other animal. I think you just have to keep finding passion.

O: ***You talk openly about tragedies, about your past, about your dark side. Is there anything you still keep from people?***

HR: No. Not really. Everyone who knows me knows that I'm a hopeless romantic who listens to love ballads and doo-wop songs all the time. I can't be keeping it that secret, since I just told you. I like romance with women, not just grabbing them and fucking them and throwing them out the window. I like the idea of going out with a woman and not doing anything and just eating dinner and talking, and that's cool, too. So someone might look at me and say, "No way, man. He's just banging strippers." And I do that, but not all the time. Just once a year or something. That's one

"Now, if someone wants to spit on me, I just roll up the window of my BMW 540i."

thing a lot of people wouldn't know. But otherwise, yeah. Maybe I'm ego-tripping, but I don't find myself a particularly horrible person, so I don't think I need to hold back anything I think or feel. I've never raped or killed anybody, or hurt a kid. I've done all the more inept, high-volume stuff—like, "Whoops, sorry I came in your hair. Don't worry, I won't use your name when I tell this story on stage." Stuff like that is more what I've done: just your sort of boy-growing-up fuck-ups. I've made some great mistakes in my life, but, you know, they were honest mistakes. I've never tried to rip someone off and gotten caught. I went out on tour and played my hardest, and maybe no one gave a fuck that summer, and that's a failure in a way.

O: ***You have a new record coming out, right?***

HR: Yeah, it's a talking record. It's called *Think Tank*, not because my mind is some sort of huge intellectual engine; it's just that the original cover concept I had was a drawing of a bunch of kids in the '50s in a classroom. Kind of one of those wholesome, Wonder Bread images. And the collective thought balloon over their heads was going to be a tank. But I ran into a young man who did an amazing flyer for a speaking date in Montana; he drew this hilarious, overblown caricature of me—huge neck, little head, confused scowl, the testosterone has made me bewildered. It's just hilarious-looking, and it says, tattooed on my arm, "Spoken Word." It's great, so we bought the artwork for the cover. It looks like one of those monster-truck posters. It's like the record: totally over the top. And I'm working on a solo album with music, and there's a band I just finished producing called Mother Superior. It's not that I have a problem with the Rollins Band, or that we've broken up or anything, but I just wanted to give those guys a rest and give myself a rest from the Rollins Band ritual. It's been 10 1/2 years without a break. The new band is basically like Thin Lizzy meets The Stooges. It's real simple, real rock, not a metal thing. It's a blues-based alley-rock thing. With the Rollins Band, there are roadies and all that stuff, but these guys just haul it out of the van, whack it together, and it's, "All right, let's rock." We go into it with such lack of pretense, it's alarming. We get it done. We're practicing in the same room I practiced in when I first joined Black Flag. It's this really hellish little place, but it's still around. And it's 10 bucks an hour, so you've gotta go. It's so weird to walk in there and go, "Oh, yeah. I learned 'TV Party' in this room 17 years ago, and here I am again." So it's gonna be an interesting record, and the reason I can work with such abandon is that I know none of this is getting airplay, just like no one cared about my last record [Rollins Band's 1997 album *Come In And Burn*]. I never tried to write songs for radio, but I would have radio edits in mind. These songs end up being seven-minute, howling, "Rock on!" kind of songs. My manager came last night to listen, and I go, "What do you think?" And he goes, "Fuckin' awesome. No video, no airplay." And I'm like, "Hey, no video budget, no radio tour." No money, no money problems. I don't give a fuck, because it's not as if they play me on the radio anyway. A major label will spend tons of money trying to get you on the radio, because that's how they sell records. Dreamworks dropped a lot of money on me last year, video-wise and promo-wise, and, to their dismay, nothing happened. So this time around, I figured, "Fuck it. Let's make a record on one-tenth the budget, go get in a van, and do some shows here in town. Go fuck people up." This band will dance on people's heads. So I'm havin' fun in my old age with these guys.

O: ***Are you ready for another publicity onslaught? You were kind of everywhere for a long time, and then the record didn't do much...***

HR: Well, I came back from the tour, from Japan and Australia. I finished with the band in Osaka, then I went right to Australia and did a bunch of speaking dates. Then I came back here in November and basically hunkered down to winter out and work on the book company, which I do every winter. In December, I went out to England. I worked with Black Sabbath, helping them with the video press kit for their reunion shows, and from there, I went to Africa and Madagascar and hung out. That was fun. That was an eye-opener.

O: ***So you've just been sitting around on the couch watching TV this whole time.***

HR: Yeah, that's me. Then I did a bunch more speaking dates and lecture dates and, come spring, I started working on this record, editing down the talking record and the video, and finalizing this book. I have two books in motion now. I've been busy, but I've been mostly in L.A. This year, I did work on the soundtrack for *Small Soldiers*, the video that's on MTV now. That's me and the Bone Thugs guys [doing a cover of Edwin Starr's "War"]. I just wrapped up a part in the film *Desperate But Not Serious* with Claudia Schiffer and Christine Taylor and all these beautiful women. Very strange to be on the set with, like, 20 drop-dead women who have, besides a professional capacity, zero interest in you. And you're just sitting amongst them, and none of them are looking at you. None of them are talking to you. Claudia Schiffer has bodyguards with her. She's real nice; I mean, no one bugged her. She's mellow. I guess she gets enough crazoids running at her in airports that she kind of has to have her big Samoan man around her. So that was fun, and I just finished a film called *Jack Frost* with Michael Keaton. It's not like he and I worked together—I never met the guy—but I play his son's psycho hockey coach, so it was me and all these 12-year-olds. In the movie, I yell and scream, "Go kill 'em!" and everything, and they know I'm nuts, so none of them pay attention to me. It's great to have all these precocious Hollywood 12-year-olds blow me off at every opportunity. It's great to be in a kids' film, to be dissed by all these kids. I'm lovin' it. I'm the voice for GMC trucks, so I've been doing all the voiceovers for their TV ads. Nice work if you can get it. I've been pretty busy here, just not geographically intense. But then I go to Europe for press, come right back, start doing the talking shows in September, and then go back to Europe. I'll be in Europe until December, and then in January, I'm headlining this thing in New Zealand, and then I go to Australia for press. From there, I think I'm gonna go hike through Java. It's so close, and I'll have all these frequent-flyer miles. My next book is like a travel book that goes literally around the world two different times, from Russia to Japan to Bangkok to Africa, all over. I've got to take it to Indonesia now.

"Everyone who knows me knows that I'm a hopeless romantic who listens to love ballads and doo-wop songs all the time."

O: ***Did you ever think, when you were managing the ice-cream store, that you'd have a trip to Java planned?***

HR: No, but I do plan on having a job like the ice-cream store again before I die. I'm pretty survivalist: The money I make, I invest. With a lot of the books and records, I own the masters. I don't know what it's going to be worth, but I own 'em. I put away money every year, in the IRA thing and in stocks and all that. I've seen a lot of my peers... You know, one of the singers in Black Flag is a waiter at this really bad diner in Hollywood. He's salt of the earth, and he's a sweetheart, but he'll pour your coffee for $4.25 an hour, and that's how you can end up. There are a lot of people—big metal guys—who are now working at Blockbuster, but they still have the eyeliner and the dyed-black hair and the idiot stripper girlfriend, and they're waiting for the next deal. They didn't save the money. They didn't realize how quickly it'd all be over. For a guy like me, I had 18 minutes instead of 15 because of tenacity, the will of the cockroach. I realize that, 18 months from now, I could have pretty meager resources. So I'm always frugal, and I'm taking advantage of taking a shot while I've got the shot to take. Because in two years, all this may be a memory.

O: ***Well, music styles come and go, but you'll always be able to talk.***

HR: Yeah. As it is now, those audiences get exponentially bigger every year—like, up to 2,500 people a night. It staggers me. But you never know. Things come and go. At the end of the day, I would love to end up like a guy like George Carlin: ancient, still cool, still gets to work. I've hung out with him, and he's just the coolest. Zero burned out. He's a phenomenon. There's not many like him. I would still like to be able to talk to young people when I'm older. As it is now, I'm older than all those students on campus when I go to the universities, by 10 years or more, and I can definitely bring them something they're not getting from their parents. I'm not a peer. I am older. And I can definitely bring something positive, which to me is worth it right there: to give some young person a different perspective on smoking and drinking. Definitely attack kids' latent homophobia. I'd love to get in there and knock those motherfuckers around. And, hopefully, there'll be a chance for me to do that at some point. But my manager has said to me, sitting at his pool at his big house that's bigger than mine—the one I helped him get; the irony of that is like falling on your keys—he said, "Effectively, your career in music is over." I'm like, "Richard, don't say that. Dude, my brotha, how can you say that?" And I went, "Okay, well, if that's that, fuck it. Let's call the movie agent and start going on auditions again. Let's broaden another horizon."

"I love making money off Tristar and turning it into a poetry book or a CD. It's the shit. It's my kind of subversion."

O: ***There's plenty of work for guys who can play mean authority figures.***

HR: Yeah, right. Thanks a lot. That's all there is for me. All I get is the character-actor parts: "We need a nut job. Let's give Henry Rollins a call." Hey, if it's a cool script, I'll take it. I pass on the corny scripts, but if it's a good script, I go audition. Hollywood for me is just like the money train. I love corporate money. I love making money off Tristar and turning it into a poetry book or a CD. It's the shit. It's my kind of subversion. The money they spend... Even when Dreamworks sends me around, it's business class, nice hotels. They go, "Where do you want to eat today?" And I go, "Well, there's this steak place I like here in town." Boom! We're there. I'm like, "Goddamn. All right." To me, it's really fascinating on that level, knowing the distortion of reality and how you sit with these people and have these power meetings. They are so full of shit, and you talk the shit with them, and they're nodding, like, "This is synergy! We're happening!" And I'm like, "Oh my God, you guys are such assholes. Nine people live in a room and sweat to death because of people like you, you ponytail-having, Mercedes Benz–driving motherfuckers." And all I think is, "How can I get some of your money?"

O: ***Do you ever lie in your king-size bed at the Four Seasons and think, "God, I used to be on someone's couch"?***

HR: Nightly. And whenever I eat a full meal, I remember, like, 13 years ago, when this was once a year when I used to go visit my mom on tour, and she'd feed us, or I'd stay with the Misfits, and their moms would cook up a holy storm of food. None of that ever escapes me. It's one of the reasons I've been able to stick around, because none of it is taken for granted. When I'm driving this utter monstrosity of a car, it's hilarious. People double-take all the time in traffic. They go, like, "Oh my God! That's Hank Rollins in a Beemer with Sabbath pounding!" The best thing is to drive around in that thing with the new Slayer CD in it, and watch people's heads turn. I have cops wave at me, like, "No shit, there goes that Black Flag dude." Black Flag's old roadie from '82 saw me pull up in that thing at the wrap party for a movie, and he said, "Hank Rollins, punk rock has been very good to me!" Which is what I say all the time. It's hilarious. So whenever any of that happens—when I'm at the nice hotel—I'm laughing. Knowing it's temporary, but, oh my God, what a ride. ⌀

Harlan Ellison

By John Krewson
Originally Printed September 1998

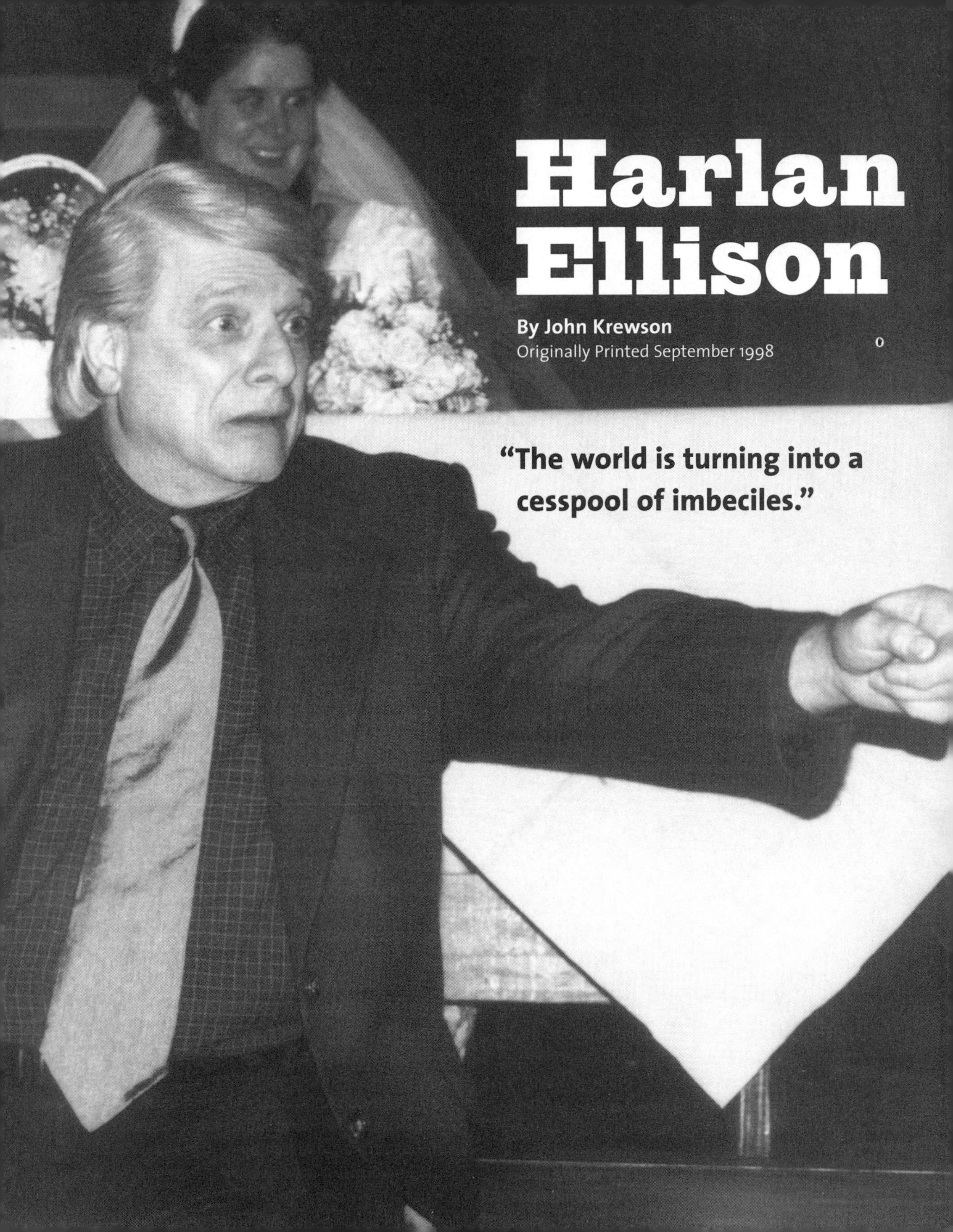

"The world is turning into a cesspool of imbeciles."

In a career spanning more than 40 years, Harlan Ellison has written or edited just about everything: 73 books, a dozen-odd screenplays, countless television scripts, treatments for dozens of different shows, a handful of graphic novels, a CD-ROM, a newspaper column, and more than 1,700 short stories. He's joined a Brooklyn street gang in order to write about juvenile delinquency, written award-winning stories while on display in bookstore windows, and been called the 20th-century Lewis Carroll. Ellison has managed to cultivate a strange double reputation, both as a champion of decency, truth, and compassion and as the world's oldest enfant terrible. *Those sorts of apparent contradictions run throughout his career, which includes two anti-television books (1970's* The Glass Teat *and its 1976 sequel,* The Other Glass Teat*) and frequent subsequent work in the television industry. But Ellison has always worked on his own terms, as discussed in this 1998 interview with* The Onion A.V. Club.

The Onion: ***What have you been doing lately?***
Harlan Ellison: [Laughs.] This is by you an interview question, right? Let's get a little more specific, since you and I both have a limited amount of life to live and I'd just as soon not turn this interview into a career. What am I supposed to say? That I'm working on a movie or working on a book? I'm always working on a movie or working on a book. What I'm doing lately... A month ago, I did nine days in Manchester, New Hampshire, 100-degree heat, mosquitoes the size of Stuka dive bombers, conducting a writer's workshop. First one I've done in about 12 years. I just got back from lecture gigs in London, England, and Atlanta, Georgia, where I did a live radio drama presentation and signed about 265,000 autographs. I'm doing a script for *The Outer Limits*. I'm going up to Toronto in October to play a role on the syndicated series *Psi Factor*. I optioned out about half a dozen other stories this week. It's the usual bullshit. That's just work. Is anyone going to be interested in reading about that? I wouldn't be. That's the silliness of late-night talk shows, where you have self-engrossed actors coming out to talk about how they're going to be in a revival of *Under The Yum-Yum Tree* at the Red Coach Grill in New Haven, Connecticut, next month; and this is supposed to pass for conversation in our time. I would rather we talked about... well, almost anything else.
O: ***As far as your writing goes, your*** **Edgeworks**

collection of reprinted writing continues to come out. Have you been working on new things at all?

HE: Kiddo, I had two books published last year. I've had at least two books published every year for the past 20 years. What does it matter if something is old? Charles Dickens said any book you haven't read is a new book. Yes, of course I'm still writing, but I'm 64 years old now, and I write more slowly, and I do a lot of other things, and my bones ache when I get the fuck out of bed in the morning, and I've got 73 books published. I don't understand what this lemming-like dementia is about constantly having new stuff. When was the last time you read the totality of Steinbeck or Faulkner or Katherine Anne Porter or Shirley Jackson? Everybody always wants something new, new, new—and that's what's killing life for writers. This dementia for "new" is ridiculous. It turns everybody into a back number. I don't mean to get cranky about it, but it's something that weighs very heavily, not only on my mind but on the mind of everybody who works in this kind of medium. We're dealing with a more and more illiterate and amnesiac constituency. It's impossible to get a readership that will follow you, because all they know is what they knew yesterday. And they've been so bastardized as an audience that there are actually average citizens out there who think William Shatner writes those idiot novels with his byline on them. It's like going to take a look at the Top 40 list; there's no point in remembering the names of the people on there, because they weren't here last week and they ain't gonna be here next week. There is a loss of memory. When they start naming the 100 greatest performers of the century, for Christ's sake, and Edith Piaf is not on the goddamn list and Bob Dylan is, then you say, "Wait a minute, folks, there's something wrong here." They don't remember Bert Williams, they don't remember Al Jolson, they don't remember fuckin' Glenn Miller. They don't remember Stevie Ray Vaughan! And so when I hear this what-are-you-doing-lately thing, or that the *Edgeworks* books are bringing back all of my older books, I say, "Yeah, they're real old books—like five years old!" See, I do go off on these things. And if you ask the wrong question, I get real cranky.

O: ***I'm sorry. But I'd like to hear more about the terrible—according to you—attention span of our society.***

HE: Like I'm all alone in thinking this, right? The guy who runs one of my web sites sent me a review that a very nice 18-year-old girl did of one of my books. She's a very nice kid—very smart, unlike most other 18-year-olds, who are dumber than ditchposts. She had a couple questions about several of the essays in the *Harlan Ellison Hornbook*. One of them is called "With Bloch And Bormann In Brazil." It was an anecdote about a time in 1967, or something like that, when I was down in Brazil with a film festival, and I was there in the company of Robert Bloch, the great fantasy writer. We saw a Nazi marching around in his apartment across the street with a swastika flag and a framed portrait of Hitler and all of that stuff. This was around the time when they didn't know if Martin Bormann, the escaped Nazi, was still alive and if he was in South America, or what was going on. So I wrote this piece. Well, she couldn't figure out what the hell was going on in this piece. So I called her, and she was a very nice young woman; we had a wonderful conversation and she was very embarrassed. She said, "I thought you would probably yell at me for being so stupid." I said, "You're not stupid at all! There's an enormous amount of things out there to know: Up until maybe 20 years ago, it was possible to have read pretty widely and know pretty much everything that was going on. But now, what with the Internet, the greatest disseminator of bad data and bad information the universe has ever known, it's become impossible to trust any news from any source at all, because it's all filtered through this crazy yenta gossip line. It's impossible to know anything. So you're not a stupid person or an ignorant person—you just aren't aware of these certain things." The horror of being a writer today, and the reason why we are a dying breed, and why the entertainment dollar goes to things like *Independence Day* and *My Best Friend's Wedding*, and crap like that which goes through you like beets through a baby's backside, is that the audience has been so completely dumbed down by the media, by tabloid scumbags, by the Christian right, by politicians in general, the schools, parents who are dumber than their parents were, and all of whom think that they can bring up a child just because they got down in bed and had a little sex. When we see the amount of child abuse and neglect and stupid people leaving guns lying around, well, frankly, here is an audience that knows more and more about less and less as the years go by. As a writer, you suddenly have a horrendous epiphany: "Wait a minute, I can't say, in a story, 'He had the eyes of a guard at Buchenwald,' or 'He had the stoic manner of a Dachau survivor.' They don't remember the names Buchenwald and Dachau. They don't know about World War II or the Holocaust. They simply don't know the history of the human race! Whether they weren't taught them at school, or weren't curious enough to read about them in books, they are absolutely tabula fucking rasa. We are talking about a constituency—and I do a lot of college lecturing—that knows nothing. This is terrifyingly, paralyzingly pandemic. Three months ago, I was doing an evening lecture at Cerro Coso College in California, and it was well-attended. The joint was jammed, maybe 2,000 people. I draw good crowds wherever I go, I guess because they don't have that many live human beings coming to scream at them. A guy in the audience raised his hand and said, "I saw you on *Politically Incorrect* and you got real mad at some black lady because of something about some film director." I said, "Yeah, it was [Elia] Kazan, and the subject was how he had been denied an award from a film critics' group because he had been a rat for the House Un-American Activities Committee." He said, "What?" I said, "HUAC! You know, HUAC?" And he said, "What?" So I had to spend half an hour explaining J. Parnell Thomas, and the Hollywood Ten, and "The Red Menace," and how *High Noon* was a protest film against the people who had ratted out others to the Committee, and how *On The Waterfront* was Kazan's apologia for being a narc, and also how that had nothing to do with the McCarthy hearings seven years later. And this guy wasn't an isolated case in that large gathering! They didn't know who Elia Kazan was, or what he had done that made him a pariah, or who Strom Thurmond is, or what a Hooverville was, or why we were fighting in Korea, or Wounded Knee, or... hell, they barely knew Nixon. They knew McCarthy's name, but not what it was he'd done. Someone asked if he hadn't done a good job ferreting out communists, and I said, "No! He never ferreted out anygoddamnbody! All he ever ferreted out was every bottle of booze in Congress!" So when you're dealing with people who know nothing, you find yourself suddenly turning into a fucking pedant instead of a storyteller. I have to educate them before I can use a trope

"These mooks expect a nobility of me that they themselves do not possess! They sit with their thumb in their mouth and watch television seven and a half hours a day, and yet they have the temerity, the audacity, the gall to accuse me of being a hypocrite because I went back to earn a fucking living!"

or a reference. Now, people who are going to be reading this are going to be saying, "Gee, I know who Strom Thurmond is. I know about Kazan." Well, that's them! So tell me how many ignorant jamooks you have to work with and deal with in the course of a day... You say this same kind of crazy rant yourself! The problem is that the intellectuals, the people who really do have some sort of education, the atavists and elitists like me who do read, don't understand that they are surrounded by people who are bone-stick-stone stupid. Every time we have some lunatic run amok and shoot someone, when we have kids in schoolyards blowing each other's asses off, everybody says, "What was the reason? What was the motivation?" There is no fucking motivation! The world is turning into a cesspool of imbeciles. The genetic pool has been so hideously polluted, and we have condoned all of it—every bit of stupidity from bad movies and cheap novels and shit fast food to rap music to pretending that the gun lobby is not an evil and insidious operation that serves the gun makers... All of this crap is part of our inability to deal with the size of our own brains. We've got technological wonders around us and we've used them to abrogate all responsibility for everything in our lives. You call someone on the phone; you don't get anybody. There's voice mail: That way, no one ever has to return a phone call. If they don't like you, or if they're so filled with arrogance and hubris that they think they don't need to respond, they just don't return your calls. That sort of thing produces a level of frustration that in turn produces people who run around with guns and shoot the shit out of everybody because they're just fucking pissed off. They watch television and see Leonardo DiCaprio being interviewed about fiscal responsibility and the International Monetary Fund, and no qualitative distinction is made by a Leno or a Letterman or a Larry King between an uninformed "celebrity" and some smart but tv-boring authority. [Ellison insisted that "tv" be in lowercase. —ed.] So we wind up with piss-ants like Limbaugh and Pat Buchanan and Falwell, who are so bloody damned mean-spirited and Ugly Elitist that the noise-to-signal ratio is overwhelming. Look, kiddo, I don't know you. I have no idea how smart, how dumb, how educated, how ethical, how moral, how courageous you are. You're a telephone voice. You call me to interview me, and I'm supposed to be cute, so the readers won't say, "Jesus, what a smartass mean fucker." But I don't know if you're as smart as I am. I like to think you're as smart as I am—I like to think everyone is. Probably a hell of a lot smarter, because I know how dumb I am, how much shit I don't know. So maybe what I'm saying is stuff that you yourself say, when you're sitting around with your pals at *The Onion*... Do you look at each other and say, "Goddammit! The world is just filling up with more and more idiots! And the computer is giving them access to the world! They're spreading their stupidity! At least they were contained before—now they're on the loose everywhere!"? You get tired of hearing your own voice. And you know you're preaching to the choir, which doesn't mean anyone is listening. I wrote a story once called "Silent In Gehenna" in which a near-future student revolutionary is in an air duct trying to get out of an administration building in which he's just planted a bomb. Suddenly there's this golden glow, and he's captured by a machine that brings people

"I never understand the chutzpah of people who can't write a coherent story themselves, but who always need to give you their fucking input. I don't want your input! You wanna input something, write your own goddamn story, moron!"

to the future, and he finds himself in this golden cage suspended over a street, and coming down the street are these great grotesque alien creatures, Jabba The Hutt kind of things, on palanquins dragged by yoked teams of human beings. This guy, being a revolutionary, stands up there and screams at them, "Throw off your chains! Fight for your humanity! This is evil, evil! They mustn't use others as slaves!" They stop beneath them and beat their breasts and say, "God, yes, this is evil, evil. It's not a good thing." But then they roll on past and forget the whole thing. And he realizes, as all revolutionaries do, that you're just a fucking clown shouting at people who are agreeing but not really listening. This is the most horrible way for him to end. He finds himself absolutely impotent.

O: ***Does that ever make you want to quit writing? I mean, if nobody's paying attention, why bother?***

HE: People keep saying that books will never die out. Well, books may never die out, but hundreds of thousands of individual writers will, and for them, it's as if books did die out. When they go, they're gone. The publishing industry will never die out. That's the difference. And it's the distinction that's almost never made. I make a decent living. Stephen King could buy and sell me a million times over, and he deserves it, he's a good guy, and that's fine—but I'm still more successful than most writers. I'm considered in the first percentile of moneymaking writers in the country. That's only because there's so little money to be made that being in the first percentile doesn't mean squat. Nonetheless, I have had to loan out vast amounts of money to my friends who are writers, because they're all starving. We've got about 85 grand out in loans, and we know we're never gonna see it again, but it's okay—you should never loan money unless you're prepared never to get it back. But I look around at my friends, at writers I admire and have admired for decades, and I see them fucking drowning! It's because they can't keep up with James Cameron and McDonald's and Nike and all this crap that is just draining the energy out of everybody. Boy, don'tcha just love a fragmented, hyperkinetic, bugfuck screed that makes no sense?! Gee, welcome to Jerry Springer World!

O: ***One of the things you've railed against, and that as a writer you compete against, is television. But you mentioned that you're writing for* Outer Limits. *You've had some bad experiences writing for tv.***

HE: That's true.

O: ***But you still do it, even though you seem to loathe the medium.***

HE: So what you're asking is, if I hate it so much, why do I do it? It's like people who complain about bad tv but still watch. Well... This is another one of those situations that's no-win. I stopped writing for commercial tv a lot of years ago. I went back in 1985—almost 10 years of doing only pilots and movies for television, and feature films—and I went back to work on *The Twilight Zone*. People would accuse me—in a less accusatory fashion than your question, but there's still an implied *j'accuse* there—"If you're always pissing and moaning about this, why do it?" Kiddo, you do it because first of all, it dominates the landscape. It is one of the most powerful forces that bestride the world today. You can't escape television. I did two books of tv criticism, *The Glass Teat* and *The Other Glass Teat*, in which I said, "Hey, folks! This sucker is gonna steal your souls and you're gonna turn into morons!" Well, it's come to pass. In fact, that's the next one of the *Edgeworks* books. You can go back and read those books, and they'll fit perfectly with tv today: Just change *Marcus Welby* to *ER* and *The Brady Bunch* to *Friends*. People who are now television critics come into town on their junkets and come to visit me as if they're paying obeisance at the altar of some ancient god. They come in with a battered paperback copy of *The Glass Teat* in hand, and they say, "I grew up on this and it sits on the shelf in my office at *The Miami Her-*

ald or *The East Waukegan Blat* or *The Onion*," and they want to meet me because I'm the oracle who can give them The Word. I absented myself from tv because I just couldn't take it anymore. I just couldn't fucking take it. You watch enough tv, and very soon the inside of your head has become a vast, arid plain, across which you cannot detect the passage of a thought. But I went back to do *Twilight Zone*, and people said, "Oh, man! You're back on television!" These mooks expect a nobility of me that they themselves do not possess! They sit with their thumb in their mouth and watch television seven and a half hours a day, and yet they have the temerity, the audacity, the gall to accuse me of being a hypocrite because I went back to earn a fucking living! Well, I didn't go back to work on television. I went back to work on *The Twilight Zone*. It was a different thing. That's like saying to somebody, "Would you like to take a ride on the *Titanic*? I got one ticket left on the *Hindenburg*. You wanna go?" Hell, yes! I mean, you know the damned thing's going down! But who could say no? You can't pass it up! I wanted to be part of history. I wanted to work on a show like *The Twilight Zone*. So I went back to it. I worked on the show for a year, and it was a terrific year; I had a wonderful time with wonderful people. And then I walked off the show because of the censors. They wouldn't let me do a show about racism that I wanted to do at Christmastime. I wrote about that in the new book *Slippage*. So I walked off the show, and the only people to notice were at *Time* magazine. I walked away from $4,000 a week and everyone said, "Nobody just walks away from $4,000 a week!" I said, "Just watch me," and I booked. But nobody who had accused me of being a hypocrite for going to work there noticed. Nobody said, "By god [Ellison insisted that "god" be lowercase, too —ed.], he still has his ethical moorings! He walked off the show the first time they wouldn't let him do what he wanted!" They pissed and moaned that I'd deserted the show, and, oh, how that inconvenienced their asses. As if being a tv viewer gave them the right to express an uneducated opinion about my behavior! No. If you get set up as some sort of a whited sepulchre, which is what keeps happening, then invariably you will get little pissants who want to drag you down and prove that you're actually morally turpitudinous, and no better a piece of human offal than they are. I've developed as curmudgeonly a manner as it is possible to wear, and I wear it like a badge of honor. It keeps a lot of the more egregious fools away from me, and with the ones who try to get through, it provides me with a way of saying, "Piss off and leave me alone." I'm expected to be mean and rude. In fact, I am neither mean nor rude. I was brought up by my mommy and daddy in Painesville, Ohio, to be polite, and those who know me will tell you—they'd better tell you, or I'll hurt 'em—that I only go after someone when they go after me. I'm like a snake sleeping on a rock. I won't bother you unless you poke a stick at me.

O: ***That's the reputation you have, certainly. I was somewhat intimidated by the idea of this interview.***

HE: And there was no reason to be. As you see, I am really very jocular, very pleasant, well-spoken, and sanguine. Anyway, if I had my druthers, I would not work in television at all, but again, it's a cultural medium from which most people derive their knowledge and education. For a writer today to stay in business, just to stay a writer, means that you have to have some kind of public profile. I've been doing this for a lot of years, and I've always been pilloried by writers who thought that it was an ivory-tower job: "You just write great things and everything will be fine." Well, that may have been the way it was in the days of Emerson and Thoreau, but unfortunately, we live in a time where if you want to be read at all, you have to outshout Danielle Steel and John Grisham and Tom Clancy and Judith Krantz and *South Park* and *Friends* and *Seinfeld* and everything else that's grabbing for attention. That means you have to do a lot of stuff that, if you had your druthers, you would not do. Now, I'm writing a script for *Outer Limits*. You may say, "Okay, it's different 'cause it's cable." No, cable's the same damn thing. There's not much difference. But! My contract with them is very simple. Nobody touches the script but me. If they don't like it, I give 'em their money back and I take my script back. So, in effect, what I'm doing is writing on spec, which is a dangerous thing to do. My hubris is that I write well enough, and they like me well enough, and my name is well enough known to them, that they aren't gonna do that. They're gonna have input; everybody always has input, but these seem to be smart, educated guys, so I'm crossing my fingers. I never understand the chutzpah of people who can't write a coherent story themselves, but who always need to give you their fucking input. I don't want your input! You wanna input something, write your own goddamn story, moron! One of the great quotes that I live by is from the French essayist Jules Renard, who said, "Writing is an occupation in which you must constantly prove you have talent to people who have none of their own." You do what you have to do to make a living in the world these days, but there are things that I will not do. I did a commercial—I was the on-camera spokesperson for Geo cars when they first came out in California. People at lectures would point at me and say, "You did a commercial! Why did you do a commercial?" I did a commercial for the most environmentally responsible car in the country today! I was not a prison guard at Dachau! There's no amount of money in the world that could get me to do a commercial for McDonald's toadburgers. I just wouldn't do it. There are things that I wouldn't go anywhere near! I can't be bought! I can be rented, but I can't be bought, because at the final tick, right at the core, money doesn't mean much to me. My wife worries about money because she's a normal human being. I don't and I never have. Making money is the easiest thing in the world for me. I've been earning my own living since I was 13 years old, and if I couldn't do it as a writer, I'd go back to bricklaying or driving trucks. I never do anything for money. Money's what they give me when I do my job right. It's what they give you to keep your mouth shut so you don't blow the whistle. It's a way for them to buy you and put you in their pocket. So I never, ever do a job for money. I earn a living doing mostly what I want to do, anyhow. I think everybody should be able to do that, but of course, not everybody has that luxury. Fortunately, my wife, Susan, trusts me implicitly, and when I say, "No, I can't do this one, honey; it's a bum thing," she'll say, "Fine, don't do it." I'm lucky. I've got a great marriage to an absolutely spectacular woman... after four shitty marriages, and hundreds of sexual liaisons over the years, always with women. I lead a very dull life, I don't use drugs, I don't drink, and as far as I know, I have never had anybody make a homosexual advance at me. I'm a very dull guy in that respect. I don't need to tie women up, I don't lie, I don't cheat. I just get in trouble every other way. See, there was no need to be nervous about interviewing me. Hell, kiddo, you're *The Onion*; I oughta be nervous about you. After all, an angry god's gonna strike both of us with a bolt of lightning, and we'll wind up side-by-side in hospital beds, silent and dumb as rutabagas, just for being such wiseasses. ⌀

"I've developed as curmudgeonly a manner as it is possible to wear, and I wear it like a badge of honor."

George Carlin

By Stephen Thompson
Originally Printed November 1999

"I don't see any hope... short of some sort of interesting cataclysm. So I root for a cataclysm, for its own sake, just as entertainment."

George Carlin has always straddled and blurred the line separating the mainstream from the counterculture, testing the boundaries of the First Amendment when he's not trying his hand at a Fox sitcom or MCI commercials. A successful author, recording artist, movie actor, and all-around icon, Carlin would remain famous even if he had stopped generating material after his legendary monologue about the seven words you can never say on television. Immediately following the release of a seven-disc box set, 1999's George Carlin: The Little David Years, *the comic spoke to* The Onion A.V. Club *about language, religion, hope, and the story behind his work as a phone-company pitchman.*

The Onion: ***Is anything shocking anymore?***

George Carlin: Um, no. It depends on who's receiving the shock. Obviously, there are people who constrict themselves and build walls around themselves, whether it's from a moral standpoint or a patriotic standpoint or just plain old conformity, and who therefore live in those little prisons, and when things breach those walls, it's shocking for them. But I think for my little segment of the public... I have broad recognition, and then I have a somewhat narrower following, and I fill up theaters of 2,000–2,500 seats about 100 nights a year, so I have a nice little niche. And to my folks, there are only degrees of surprise. I think of shock as kind of an uptown form of surprise. Comedy is filled with surprise, so when I cross a line... I like to find out where the line might be and then cross it deliberately, and then make the audience happy about crossing the line with me. In the case of the most recent HBO show, the *You Are All Diseased* show, it's children. This is one of the new sacred areas in our lives, one of the taboos, so I like taking on that whole parent/child culture that's developed—this insane, neurotic over-parenting. And then the God thing at the end has been an ongoing thing of mine, attacking religion in various ways. I try to get a little something in each show. But this time, I actually said He doesn't exist, and He should strike me dead if He does, and He doesn't strike me dead. So I like finding out where I can push it a little farther, even with my own people.

O: ***Do you get to the point where you run the risk of going too far where it's not funny anymore?***

GC: No, because the first obligation I have is to be funny; it's my first impulse and an instinct.

I like being funny and finding the jokes. I like big jokes. Secondarily, I like my jokes to be built on a foundation of ideas, or at least smart observations, and then if I can add stunning or spectacular—and I use the words advisedly—language... I don't necessarily mean dirty language, but rhetorical flourishes, things that have rhythm to them and have kind of a value of their own in just the way they sound. If I can add that, I'm really happy. So it's laughs first, but because my slant and my attitude are based on questioning values, there are ideas already in the work. I just make sure that I'm always funny. I know if I'm consistently funny, I can take a long stretch and get a little... not serious, not preachy, but where there aren't as many laughs. There's a little more tone to it.

O: ***A few of the seven words are actually on TV now, where you've got "shit" on* Chicago Hope. *How do you feel about that?***

GC: Well, it's always been kind of a false arrangement anyway. When I was a little boy, I was taught to look up to policemen, look up to military personnel, and look up to sports figures. We all know how they speak, so apparently the message was, "These people have not been corrupted morally. Therefore, I can derive from that that dirty language didn't corrupt them morally." There's no foundation for this language being harmful in any way. It's just rude to some people, less rude to others. So it's one of those fake barriers that's rooted in a fake morality about sex, the body parts that produce sexual experience—and, as it happens, bathroom experience—and an ultimate fear of the human body and sexuality. And, therefore, I don't honor those arbitrary demarcations, and that's that.

"The pursuit of goods and possessions has completely corrupted the human experience, along with religion, which I think limits the intellect."

O: ***Is there such a thing as a politically correct comedian? It's a pet peeve of mine: Every press release I get announces, "He's a politically incorrect comedian!"***

GC: Well, there shouldn't be, and one person's correctness is another person's incorrectness. Here we are, back at arbitrary standards. I understand the need not to unnecessarily insult or hurt people's feelings, but I also understand the need for an honest exchange of ideas, even in the form of entertainment and art—and especially, maybe, in the form of art. I use words that some people who didn't know me well enough, or didn't know my work well enough, could interpret as, well, "He's a complete anti-this or anti-that, he's phobic about this," or whatever. And my argument is that that's not who I am. I do not believe language has that kind of power. I do not believe the occasional use of a derogatory term, used in a non-insulting way, is harmful. So I use 'em, and I think it's up to the people and society to know the difference between hate speech and casual use of slang terms.

O: ***You've said, "If you think there's a solution, you're part of the problem." Do you really lack hope?***

GC: Well, they say, "If you scratch a cynic, underneath you'll find a disappointed idealist." So I would imagine that there's some little flame, however weak, that still burns, but I know time is against my seeing that. I think this world would need a long time, maybe a thousand years, to evolve to what may be a golden age, and in the meantime, there are all these very small, parochial struggles between peoples of different language and color and arbitrary political and national boundaries. And my understanding of it is that there is no hope, because I think we're locked in by commerce. The pursuit of goods and possessions has completely corrupted the human experience, along with religion, which I think limits the intellect. With those two things in place as firmly as they are, I don't see any hope for getting around them short of some sort of interesting cataclysm. So I root for a cataclysm, for its own sake, just as entertainment. I don't even care if it has a good result. We're circling the drain, and I just like seeing the circles get faster and shorter all the time.

O: ***I was reading your web site [georgecarlin.com], and you referred to George W. Bush as a fascist. But you don't vote. Why not vote against someone you think is a fascist?***

GC: Well, because it wouldn't make any difference. When fascism comes to this country, it won't be wearing jackboots; it'll be wearing sneakers with lights in them, and it'll have a smiley face and a Michael Jordan T-shirt on. They learned the mistake of overt control. They've learned how to be much subtler. No, I don't think my vote would mean anything, and at the same time, it would make me very untrue to myself to participate in what I really think is a charade.

O: ***Well, you more or less hate society anyway, don't you?***

GC: Um, I'm very disrespectful of it, and I'm contemptuous of it, but I don't think hate is in me, although we use that word the same way we use love: "Oh, boy, I love ice cream and I hate the Dodgers." But it is a distaste, a contempt, a dissatisfaction, a disillusionment, and a lot of qualities and feelings that come together and appear as anger onstage. I don't experience them as anger, I experience them as a deep distaste. I'm splitting semantic hairs here, but that's what they're for.

O: ***A lot of people like you seem to be running for president under the Reform Party.***

GC: [Laughs.] I know. Well, you see, there's another thing: The Reform Party should be a serious reform party. This culture won't allow that, and most likely the Democrats and the Republicans are feeding that clown aspect of the Perot paranoia, whatever quality about Jesse Ventura they don't like, Pat Buchanan... They just demonize people. This culture is set up to end the debate before it even begins. The boundaries of debate are decided long before *Nightline* goes on the air by who they've selected to sit there. You don't see the fringe people—they put on Perot and put on Jesse Ventura largely, they think, to expose them as clowns. It's just funny to watch the gyrations and the machinations and the gymnastics that this culture goes through to bullshit itself. It's fun. To me, it's all entertainment. I'm here for the show. Philosophers say, "Why are we here?" I'll tell you why: I'm here for the show. I love it, and they entertain me to no end.

"Even Ted Kaczynski, who hated technology, used a typewriter to type his manifesto. So who's a sellout?"

O: ***You mentioned before that you have wide recognition. Like it or not, you're part of mainstream society.***

GC: Sure, absolutely. That's one of the interesting and odd things about my own success: It's rooted in a distinctly anti-mainstream point of view. And yet, in order for me to project that, I have to put my foot in the stream. I wrote a thing for my web page called "The Big Sellout." A couple of people took issue with my doing a commercial for 10-10-220...

O: ***I was going to ask you about that.***

GC: Yeah, well, that will soon be on the web site in a very complete form. There's an explanation of first of all why I would make that decision—and it's always for money, of course, but why money was important to me at that moment. That's on there. And then, more important, an examination of this whole idea of selling out. It's uttered and spat at you as if it were an absolute; you did it or you didn't. And this person at home saying it probably has on a Gucci shirt or a McDonald's hat, and he has a telephone and he might even own a little bit of stock, and he has made some adjustments along the way himself. He doesn't live in the woods and eat bark and make his own clothing out of vines. No one is really pure. There is a continuum, and it's up to each person to decide what decisions are worth making to accommodate yourself to the system in order to do what you want to do. Even Ted Kaczynski, who hated technology, used a typewriter to type his manifesto. He rode buses to go to the post office to use a government agency to deliver his bombs, which were also a form of crude technology. So who's a sellout? That's what the whole thing is about.

O: ***Was it simply a matter of money?***

GC: I had 20 years of tax struggle, which I've talked about publicly before, and what I did in this thing on the web page is give the history of the development of that back-taxes debt, and how penalties and interest prevent you from chopping it down to size very quickly. It took 20 years. And what happened, the shorthand of it is, my wife died about two and a half years ago. I met a woman and we're very in love, and it's a magnificent experience that's going on between Sally and me. I just didn't want to get into this relationship with any vestige of that tax problem still lingering. I had it down to several hundred thousand dollars—maybe $350,000—and I said, "I need a quick source of unexpected income." I didn't go hunting: MCI had already approached me, and they made a lot of concessions to try to make it consistent with my personal approach to stand-up, and to make me seem less like a pitchman. Anyway, for whatever compromise there was, for my purposes it was a good one, and I think no harm was done to the culture or to myself.

"It's just funny to watch the gyrations and the machinations and the gymnastics that this culture goes through to bullshit itself."

O: ***You tend to shy away from topical humor, and it was interesting listening to the box set: It didn't feel that much like a product of its era, and it still seemed fairly fresh. Is that why you avoid topicality?***

GC: Yeah, that's the effect, and I welcome that effect, to have the stuff not be dated. But the purpose was to not be a slave to the headlines. If I'm going to do a show at 8:30 that night and something happens that afternoon that everybody knows about, I'm sort of obliged to have a few funny things to say about it if I'm known for some topical commentary. So, rather than do that and also have to throw things away that develop... Let's say a story is good for a month and you have a little routine, and it's getting better and better, and now it's up to about five minutes and it's really nice, and then the story is kind of dead and stale. Then you're stuck with five dated minutes, or you're throwing away something very nice that you've crafted. I don't like that feeling, so to avoid it, I just say, "Well, I'll be a little less timely and more timeless."

O: ***Do you still want to do TV?***

GC: No, I don't want to do commercial TV on any sustained basis. I like using the Lenos and Lettermans to promote my stuff, and HBO is my home and always will be. I've had my little forays and sidetracks into different parts of show business where I didn't have a good fit, but there was always some stupid local reason I had for trying it, and then I'd say, "Ugh, there I go again. Fuck 'em." That's where I am now.

O: ***The pace of your act has sort of accelerated over the years, even as you go through the box set.***

GC: Well, that especially happened in the '90s, as I realized I had to raise my voice literally and in a figurative sense, to raise the stakes a little bit on stage in order to compete with a very noisy culture. There's a lot of din in the culture, and to get attention, you have to raise your voice.

O: ***Aren't you supposed to be slowing down?***

GC: Yeah, that's the "old" deal, yeah. That's right. You know, I'm blessed with a great genetic package: Among the genetic qualities I got for free was this energy and stamina, as well as great enthusiasm and a positive, optimistic sense of self. My personal sphere is really positive. It's the world that I have my doubts about. ⌀

John Kricfalusi

By Tasha Robinson
Originally Printed April 2001

“Anything that’s corporate and large is doomed to be bad.”

Like his mentor Ralph Bakshi, native Canadian John Kricfalusi spent the better part of a decade drawing low-end studio television cartoons before his big break. Bakshi "rescued" Kricfalusi in 1987, making him an executive director on the chaotic and controversial New Adventures Of Mighty Mouse. *A year later, Kricfalusi and partner Jim Smith founded their own studio, Spümcø, and sold Kricfalusi's brainchild, the beloved gross-out cartoon* Ren & Stimpy, *to Nickelodeon. The series was a huge hit, but Kricfalusi and Nickelodeon clashed frequently, and the studio eventually booted him from his own show. Kricfalusi later took some of* Ren & Stimpy's *subsidiary characters to the Internet, where he produced online cartoons with the now-defunct icebox.com. He returned to television briefly with a couple of special features for The Cartoon Network, and continued to produce animated ads for companies such as Nike, Old Navy, and Quisp cereal. In 2001, while preparing to launch the Fox Kids series* The Ripping Friends, *Kricfalusi spoke to* The Onion A.V. Club *about why modern cartoons, film, music, education, art, and sexual politics are all disgraceful.*

The Onion: *When will* The Ripping Friends *air?*
John Kricfalusi: I'm not exactly sure. Summer or fall or something. It's about the world's most manly men, four guys who go around the world kicking ass and taking the law into their own hands and making the world a safe place in which to be manly. They're kind of the opposite of what men are brainwashed into being these days. They're like old-fashioned men, before political correctness. You ever see young guys now, where they're all hugging each other and shit like that? Trying to convince the girls that they're sensitive so they can get laid? Pile of crap.
O: *Are we talking men from the 1950s, or Neanderthal Man? How far back?*
JK: All men before the '70s.
O: *You've complained in interviews about classic cartoon characters becoming artificially nice throughout the '70s. Is this a society-wide problem?*
JK: Well, let's not call it "nice." I have nothing against being nice. Political correctness didn't invent nice. Political correctness is a mean-spirited Commie plot, if you ask me. But just one symptom of political correctness is men hugging men, and that's just a ploy anyway, like I said, to get laid, to convince girls that you're sensitive. No guy is really into that, unless he's gay. Which I'm not saying anything

against; I'm just saying that naturally, guys don't like to touch each other, except two ways. And one is really hard, with a clenched fist. My dad gave me this theory just last year. He was railing on and on. "I go down to the mall, and I see these young guys, you know the kind, they got the earrings and the long hair and those giant pants, looks like they're wearing a tent? They're down there hugging

"When you think about it, content online, on a widely known scale, is only about six months old. So it's kind of funny for people to doom something that just got started."

each other. They're disgusting." He was telling me about this guy on his dart team, one of these touchy-feely guys. "Got his hand on your shoulder, he's slapping your butt. One time I turn around and he slaps me on the butt, and I put both my fists in his face, and I said, 'You try that again, I'm gonna black both your eyes.' And this guy was, like, 30 years younger than me, and you know what he did? You'd think he would take a swing at me, right? No, he sat down and he started to cry! What kinda men are they makin' these days?" "You got me, Dad. I'm going to do something about it. I'm going to make a cartoon that cures kids."

O: ***After all your problems with networks, do you still think the Internet is the future of animation?***

JK: Oh, yeah. Internet animation is my favorite thing. Unfortunately, with this Internet crash, it affected everybody—people who were actually doing real businesses, as well as the people doing bogus businesses to raise money through stocks. So now, for the time being, a lot of people don't have very much confidence in the web. But I think it's only a temporary thing. When you think about it, content online, on a widely known scale, is only about six months old. So it's kind of funny for people to doom something that just got started. But it's the typical thing in the press.

O: ***Were your updates of Hanna-Barbara cartoons your idea, or The Cartoon Network's?***

JK: I've been doing it since I was a little kid, on my own. I loved all cartoons, but for some reason there was something about the early Hanna-Barbera cartoons, like *Yogi Bear*, *Huckleberry Hound*, and *Quick-Draw McGraw*. Those were my favorite cartoons at the time. I just sat there drawing them all day. And I went out and bought all the coloring books and all the comic books. In the comic books, they'd show you how to draw the characters. They'd have a grid with a character's head, and it would say, "Now you, Junior, can draw your own grid and fill it in, and then you get Lumpy Bunny!" So I'd do that, and that style became ingrained in me. For years, I would just draw my own stories with those characters. Even when I went to high school and got rebellious like everybody else, I just drew rebellious versions of Hanna-Barbera cartoons. I was a skinny kid, not athletic or anything, but I wanted to go to the parties with the football players and stuff. And to make sure I didn't get my ass kicked, I would have to be the life of the party. So I'd be telling jokes, or drawing this strip I called *CaveNewts* that I used to do in high school, which was dirty stories with the Flintstones. Meanwhile, on Saturday-morning cartoons they would make re-dos of classic cartoon characters. But they would take out everything that made them popular in the first place. Like, Yogi Bear was a rascal, right? He went around filching picnic baskets. He didn't want to get caught. So kids identified with him: "Oh, that's cool, he's getting away with stuff!" In the '70s, all of a sudden he's in charge of cleaning up the environment, which is the total opposite of his personality. They made Fred Flintstone nice, but when he first started, he was a complete asshole. So they basically destroyed all the characters. About... I don't remember what year it was, '95 or something like that? Fred Siebert started up this program at Hanna-Barbera, where they would do six-minute shorts like the old days, and he would look for new directors and new series that he could develop out of the shorts. I showed him my fucked-up drawings of Hanna-Barbera characters, and he thought that was funny. I said, "I don't know how radical you're going to be here at Hanna-Barbera, but if you really wanted to do something wacky, I would love to make cartoons in this style at Hanna-Barbera. And my cartoons would actually be a lot closer to the original cartoons than the recent Hanna-Barbera cartoons were, the ones where they were bastardizing the personalities, having everybody get along and share and all that stuff."

O: ***Didn't you start your animation career in the late '70s working for Hanna-Barbera and Filmation?***

JK: Yeah. They weren't doing those characters at that time, or at least I wasn't working on them. I was working on the really, really hideous stuff, like *Fat Albert* And *The Cosby Kids*. But actually, the first cartoons I worked on at Filmation were re-dos of *Mighty Mouse* and *Heckle & Jeckle*. So that was my introduction to ruining old characters that I loved when I was a kid. The next year we ruined *Tom & Jerry* and *Droopy*, and a few years later I got to ruin *The Jetsons*. I actually tried to save it while I was working on it, but it was pretty hard, because the whole thing was set up to ruin them. They sent me overseas, to Taiwan, to supervise the production of 15 episodes of *The Jetsons* there. I was kind of out of sight, so I did my best to make the drawings cool, at least.

O: ***Was that the series with Orbitty, the little white blobby...***

JK: Ahhhh! You see what I mean? They invent these characters in a completely different style that has nothing to do with [the original characters]. Orbitty was there because *E.T.* had just hit it big a couple-something years before, and they wanted to make sure that the kids liked *The Jetsons*. They figure the Jetsons would be too old-fashioned by themselves, so they say, "Let's get this ugly character in there! E.T.'s really ugly, but the kids loved him!" Every chance I got, I'd have Astro accidentally step on his head, get him crushed under the couch. Everything I could do to get that thing out of the way.

O: ***How did you make the transition from Filmation to working with Ralph Bakshi?***

JK: He saved me. He saved the business for cartoonists. I'd just finished the *Jetsons* thing. I came back, waiting to be hailed as... I thought they'd have a parade waiting for me. "John went and put jokes in our cartoons! He's going to be our hero!" I thought there'd be a big party for me, but instead, a lot of people were mad at me for putting jokes in the show and making it lively. I was out of a job when I got back. So I was getting depressed. Cartoons were getting uglier and uglier, and I was moping around the apartment. And one day I got a call from Hanna-Barbera that said, "Some guy named Ralph has been calling, wants your phone number. We don't normally give phone numbers out, but he says he's a friend of your dad's, and your dad is really sick, in the hospital. Should we give him your number?" "Uh, yeah, okay!" The only Ralph I've ever met is Ralph Bakshi, so I thought, "I bet this is Ralph Bakshi, pulling a fast one." Sure enough, I call his number, and it's Ralph. [Adopts deep, grav-

"They figure the Jetsons would be too old-fashioned by themselves, so they say, 'Let's get this ugly character in there! E.T.'s really ugly, but the kids loved him!' Every chance I got, I'd have Astro accidentally step on his head."

elly voice.] "Sorry about that message, but the only way I could get a-holda ya was to make up some story! You're not pissed, are ya?" "Nah, that's okay, I'm just glad my dad's not dead." Ralph had retired for a few years. He got disgusted with the business and had retired, maybe three or four years before. [Gravelly voice.] "I'm comin' outta retirement! I'm gonna start a TV cartoon studio this time—fuck features! We're gonna be partners, 50/50, you and me, buddy! 'Cause you're the funniest guy I ever met! All right, I'm comin' out." "Uh, okay." He goes, "Wait a minute. Describe yourself to me!"

O: ***You'd never met in person?***

JK: No, we had met! He wasn't sure he had the right guy when he called me. "Describe yourself to me!" "I don't know, I'm about 5'11", skinny, kinda pasty-looking..." "All right, all right, that's you, Johnny! I'm comin' over!" A couple days later, at seven in the morning, bang bang bang bang, an elephant knocking at my door. I come to the door in my pajamas,

"Movies are just a headache to me. You go to a movie and there's no organization, no planning of thoughts. Hand-held cameras, that stuff drives me insane. I keep expecting the camera to drop on the ground or something."

"Uhhh..." "Johnny, yeah, that's you! We're gonna be partners, 50/50! C'mon, let's go, put your clothes on, we're startin'!" So he rented a space down on Ventura Boulevard, above an old clothing store. We developed something like six Saturday-morning cartoons, wrote a script for a movie. It was really funny: It was called *Bobby's Girl*, a sort of '50s teen-comedy thing. Those were sort of popular in the '80s. Anyway, we couldn't sell anything. In those days, you couldn't sell a cartoon unless it was pre-sold. No matter how good the concept was, all the executives in the Saturday-morning cartoon business wanted to play it safe. And their idea of playing it safe was that you had to do a show based on a toy, like He-Man or G.I. Joe, or you did something based on a well-known property like Spider-Man or whatever. You couldn't sell anything original, and you couldn't sell anything cartoony. No one understood what cartoons were.

O: ***When you say "what cartoons were," what do you mean?***

JK: What makes a cartoon a cartoon is that it can do things that you can't do in any other medium. Just like any medium. What makes music music is melody and rhythm, and a million variations on those things—a pleasant melody, normally, unless you're talking about modern music. If you took those out, it wouldn't be music anymore. So in cartoons, what makes it cartoony is that you're doing things that are impossible to do. You have characters that have strong personalities, but they can do crazy things. If you watch a *Bugs Bunny* cartoon, they squash and stretch and make funny expressions, and they do all kinds of things that you laugh at, visually. You couldn't do anything like that in the '70s or '80s. It was against the law. They thought you were crazy if you did anything like that. They said, "The way you're drawing, the character looks weird!" Well, it's supposed to look weird. It's a cartoon. I swear, all the people in charge of cartoons had never seen a cartoon before except for the '70s ones.

O: ***Why do you think the industry changed so much in the '70s?***

JK: Well, a lot of things happened. The thing everyone blames is that TV cartoons are a lot cheaper than theatrical cartoons, and that's true, and that's obviously going to hamper the quality considerably. The characters still did impossible things; they just didn't do them with full animation and as many backgrounds. They just cut down on the production values.

That was because those cartoons were still made by cartoonists. By about 1964, [CBS network executive] Fred Silverman had invented the concept of doing Saturday-morning cartoons, where you had a whole block and ran cartoons back to back. And once he did that, the demand for cartoons rose considerably. They had to produce a million cartoons, faster and more than they had ever done before. And all the cartoonists who had done the classic cartoons were starting to get old, and there weren't enough of them to go around. So they just started hiring people off the street. There was a big dearth of writers. People who could draw at all were really valuable by that time. People who could write, nobody gave a shit about. They started giving writing jobs to people who were driving trucks the week before, gofers, film editors. And all of a sudden, hordes of complete amateurs are writing cartoons. And while that happened, we started getting these executives in the Saturday-morning cartoons that were basically somebody's secretary, because nobody really wanted to be in charge of Saturday-morning cartoons. Everybody wants to be in prime time, right? So you have people who didn't know anything about cartoons, about entertainment... They were just stenographers or something, they're in charge of the decisions, and we have people with no experience writing the cartoons. They take over. Now, the most imaginative art form ever created is the least imaginative art form. That killed creativity in cartoons. From about the mid-'60s until about 1990, it was the worst form of art ever created.

O: ***So cartoons have improved in the last decade?***

JK: Yeah, they've gotten considerably better since *Mighty Mouse*. That was what started the whole change.

O: ***What was different about how* Mighty Mouse *was produced?***

JK: It was the first series that was completely created by cartoonists. It was totally different from anything anybody had done. We broke every rule you could think of. I used to, once in a while, have characters turn to the camera and say something. They used to tell us, "You can't break screen direction. You'll lose the audience, and the kids won't believe in the characters anymore." I said, "Have you seen Bugs Bunny or anything, or Popeye, where he turns to the camera and says something funny before he pops his can of spinach open?" They said, "No, no, kids are more sophisticated today." Anyway, we did that once in a while on *Mighty Mouse*, and that spawned *Tiny Toons*. A whole bunch of things we did once or twice on *Mighty Mouse* became whole trends in other people's cartoons. Everybody copied it instantly. *Tiny Toons* was founded on not only the types of jokes we were doing in *Mighty Mouse*, but they also hired half our staff. *Tiny Toons* took everything we tried in *Mighty Mouse* that didn't work. They took all our mistakes, and created their own style around them.

"If you want a good story, read Hemingway. Some comic writer is going to write better than a real writer? I don't think so."

O: ***You've certainly gone on record before about not particularly caring for* Tiny Toons.**

JK: It's terrible. It's absolutely horrible. Producers were losing control, executives were losing control, because all the artists wanted to do their own thing, like we did on *Mighty Mouse*. So gradually all the writers sneaked back in... You should put quotes around "writers," because they're not real writers. People who write cartoons are not real writers. They'd all rather be writing movies or sitcoms, or something like that, but they're not good enough. These are people who can't construct a sentence, let alone a plot. And if you watch *Tiny Toons*, it's like watching an 11-year-old in front of the class on Red Cross Day, trying to tell a joke. Telling it badly and, when he gets to the punchline, saying, "Did you get it? You get it? Well, let me explain it to you, 'cause you didn't laugh." They do that in *Tiny Toons* all the time. Somebody will walk off a cliff, look down, and then fall. And when they hit the bottom, they say, "There is an unwritten cartoon law that if you don't see that you've stepped off a cliff, you won't fall, but as soon as you see that you've stepped off..." Shut up! You don't have to explain it! We got the joke when we saw it 50 years ago, when it was invented! It just drives you crazy, watching that stuff. It's so obnoxious.

O: ***Did you have to fight CBS to get* Mighty Mouse *done your way?***

JK: I had no contact with the network past the first week. It was really funny, because Ralph had convinced them that we'd developed *Mighty Mouse* as a show and we had the rights to it, and we didn't. He was in a meeting where we were pitching all the shows that we'd developed, and they told him, "I'm sorry, we really like all these shows, but we can't buy them because they don't have any marquee

"Education would be nice if it were real education, but that's gone out of fashion. Now it's hippie education, the everybody-is-creative theory."

value." And he blew up. He had one of his famous explosions. He spit out his cigarette at them and screamed at the top of his lungs, "Marquee value? You want fucking marquee value? You're talking to me, Ralph Bakshi, king of animation, about marquee value?" Scared the crap out of them. He's a very large guy, super-strong, and he's been known to hurl... I've seen him pick up desks and throw them across the room. And he has perfect aim, too, absolutely dead-perfect aim. You don't want to fuck with Ralph. So he starts screaming at them, and they were scared, right? They told him, "Honestly, Ralph, if you had a character that was safe, that everybody knew, we'd buy the show from you. We really want to buy one of your shows." He goes, "I'll give you fucking marquee value!" "Well, who you got, Ralph?" "Mmmm... *Mighty Mouse*!" He remembered the first job he ever worked on was at Terrytoons in the mid-'50s, and just spit out "*Mighty Mouse*." They said, "Okay, we'll take it, just please leave the room and don't kill us!" So he gets to the car, races back to the studio, and tells his partner, "Find out who the hell owns *Mighty Mouse*, quick!" Then he goes over to my house, because we'd finished all our development and were just trying to figure out whether we were ever going to get a job. And he pounds on my door on Saturday morning, again at like seven in the morning, yelling, "Johnny, get out of bed! I sold *Mighty Mouse*, let's go! We've gotta have a studio by next week! We need 35 people and 13 scripts!" So I got on the phone and called everyone I knew who hated working on Saturday-morning cartoons, all the disgruntled artists, and raided a bunch of studios. They left in droves, and by Monday we had a studio. We wrote, like, 20 stories in a week. And the following week we started production. It was a crazy, crazy time, with everybody working 15-hour days, all sorts of personality conflicts, everybody getting in each other's way, but somehow we pulled it off and made this weird show.

O: ***If* Mighty Mouse *was the start of cartoons being cartoony again,* Ren & Stimpy *set the standard for gross and confrontational humor.***

JK: That was a direct line through me. Everything that I did wrong in *Mighty Mouse*—and we did a lot of things wrong—I swore I wasn't going to do on *Ren & Stimpy*. I got rid of all the self-conscious stuff, the sporadic storylines, and not being able to stick to a character. I went off and said, "I'm going to pick some star characters and really develop their personalities and stick with them." So I stuck more to the stories on *Ren & Stimpy* and less to the anarchy of *Mighty Mouse*. *Ren & Stimpy* seems anarchic, but what holds it together is the definite conflict between the main characters. That didn't exist with *Mighty Mouse*, which was more like *Mad* magazine: Whatever we came up with that was weird, we'd do.

O: ***Were you just trying to push the envelope, or did you have a specific artistic goal in mind?***

JK: Depends on what you mean by pushing the envelope. Some people use that to mean push censorship. Other people just say it's creative, trying to do new things all the time. That's probably more what I like to do. I just like to experiment and not do the same plot over and over. The famous thing among writers on Saturday morning is, they say there are only seven plots, and you interchange the characters. I always thought that was the dumbest thing I'd ever heard. I'm always coming up with new things to try. If I'd doomed myself to seven plots, I would have quit a long time ago.

O: Ren & Stimpy *was where you seriously started incorporating '30s, '40s, and '50s styles into your art. How did you develop that visual style?*

JK: I don't know. Some of my influences... Bob Clampett, the greatest cartoonist of all time. Chuck Jones is a big influence, and Tex Avery. Then there are a lot of comic-strip and comic-book artists. Don Martin... not his drawing style so much as his humor. There are millions of influences. I loved Marvel Comics, though you probably wouldn't see much of that in *Ren & Stimpy*. If it shows up, it's probably subtle. I'm also a big fan of old movies, so a lot of my visual influences come from Fritz Lang and Billy Wilder and Hitchcock. And early Hanna-Barbera cartoons, which have the simplest, clearest staging in the world. That was really good for me to learn when I was a kid, because it was so clear: When I started my own comics and storyboards, I just used that. And then, as I was influenced by more sophisticated things, I added my live-action influences. Clampett has really sophisticated cutting, and that started entering into my staging. But I always had the solid basis of the simple three-shot cutting and staging of Hanna-Barbera, where they had a long shot, a medium shot, and closeups for reaction. That's the absolute basis of film language. It was admittedly a cheap system, but it also made it clear. Not very many cartoons do that. Particularly *Tiny Toons* and *Animaniacs* and all that stuff, where the staging choices work completely against what's going on. I mean, the stories aren't worth doing anyway, but it's just

"All you have to do is open up a magazine from the '30s or '40s and just look at the illustrations, and your jaw will hang limp. Every illustration—even the cheesiest ones, like the underwear ads—is drawn a thousand times better than the best fine art is today."

anarchy. You watch that stuff and go, "Oh, my eyes are sore."

O: ***What do you think about the MTV editing style that's taken over popular culture over the past couple of decades?***

JK: I think it's crazy. It's terrible, out of control. Movies are just a headache to me. You go to a movie and there's no organization, no planning of thoughts. Hand-held cameras, that stuff drives me insane. I keep expecting the camera to drop on the ground or something. Makes me dizzy. Nobody has any control over anything anymore. All the people I like were in the Age Of Thought. Everything was planned, organized, thought out, practiced, rehearsed. Perfectionism. Now, it's just like, "Throw a bunch of ideas up in the air. Where they land, that's what you get." Every time I go to a movie, I come away depressed. They all look like committee products. Nobody has any skill anymore.

O: ***What about music or television? Is anyone producing anything new that you enjoy?***

JK: There are cartoons that have elements of things I think are good. *Powerpuff Girls* has some really imaginative color in it, and that's a first for cartoons. Color has been pretty crappy for the longest time in cartoons. And it's controlled color, not random, very well thought out. A lot of the Cartoon Network cartoons are much better than in the previous decade, that's for sure. *Cow And Chicken* has absolutely beautiful drawings in it. Then there are some that are just... I'm not going to name them, but they look like 3-year-olds draw them. I don't have any interest in that stuff. They're holding back history.

"You ever see young guys now, where they're all hugging each other and shit like that? Trying to convince the girls that they're sensitive so they can get laid? Pile of crap."

O: ***Is there any future for network cartoons, or is the future of real cartoons all on the Internet?***

JK: The future of everything is on the Internet. Anything that's corporate and large is doomed to be bad.

O: ***What about something like* South Park*? Does that give you any hope for independent animators pushing their own vision on cable?***

JK: It's not their own vision. What vision? It's a bunch of used *Ren & Stimpy* jokes. It's the same stuff over and over again. It's all been done. And cartoons have to be drawn well. Every once in a while, people will say, "Hey, did you read this comic book?" "Ah, the drawings were really crummy in that one." "Oh, but the story was great!" I'm sorry, but I can't get past the ugly drawings. If you want a good story, read Hemingway. Some comic writer is going to write better than a real writer? I don't think so. It's not all about the drawings, but it's about the drawings first. I don't say story is not important. But without the drawings, who gives a shit?

O: ***What about Internet cartoonists? Are there any you think are moving in the right direction?***

JK: They're sort of in the same mold as the sitcom cartoons. They're all drawn really primitively, and they're not really about characters, the ones I've seen. They're all really random. We're at the amateur stage right now on the Internet. Anyone who can get online can make a cartoon. It's really easy to use Flash. We need to get to the point where professionals are doing it.

O: ***What professionals? If you hate everyone producing cartoons these days...***

JK: There really aren't many professionals these days. We need a medium that allows people to grow enough to become professional, like we had in the '30s and '40s and '50s. Because there are no schools that teach anybody anything useful anymore, as far as art goes, or storytelling, or anything like that. It's something that has to evolve like it did in the early 20th century. There are people who are good artists in animation. The storytellers have yet to rear their heads.

O: ***Do you think the presence of the Internet can make that possible, or is some kind of formal education or mentoring system necessary?***

JK: Education would be nice if it were real education, but that's gone out of fashion. Now it's hippie education, the everybody-is-creative theory. You just summon your creative soul out of the dust or something, instead of them sitting you down and teaching you, "Okay, here's how composition works. Here's how anatomy works. Here's how you incorporate your knowledge of composition and anatomy into the work you're doing professionally." There's no school like that today. There are no standards anymore. All you have to do is open up a magazine from the '30s or '40s and just look at the illustrations, and your jaw will hang limp. Every illustration—even the cheesiest ones, like the underwear ads—is drawn a thousand times better than the best fine art is today. It was a time of greatness. Everyone was really good at what they did in the '30s, '40s, and '50s. Now, you have the Age Of Amateurism. ⌀

Jello Biafra

"Arguing about what is and is not punk is not gonna feed the homeless person starving outside your front door."

By John Krewson
Originally Printed April 1997

Seminal California punk band Dead Kennedys left some listeners wondering whether its music or its politics came first, a question former frontman Jello Biafra was happy to leave unanswered. A San Francisco mayoral candidate even before the release of the group's first album, Biafra has long prided himself on never backing away from a challenge. In 1981, he formed the Alternative Tentacles label to counter the homogeneity of the music industry, and four years later, he faced an obscenity trial (and frequent police harassment) over the band's Frankenchrist *album, which included a phallus-intensive poster by H.R. Giger. Following Dead Kennedys' 1987 breakup, Biafra began dividing his time among the lecture circuit, recordings (both musical and spoken-word), Alternative Tentacles, and politics. In the 1990s, he survived both a near-fatal attack by skinheads and a lawsuit by his former bandmates while becoming one of the most outspoken members of the Green Party. Biafra would always rather talk about issues than himself, however, as illustrated in this 1997 interview with* The Onion A.V. Club.

The Onion: ***How's it going?***
Jello Biafra: Next question. I just did another long interview, so let's just draw a blank on a question like, "How's it going?"
O: ***Okay, I'll jump to the really tough stuff, then. Everybody wants to know the story about your legs getting broken by punks.***
JB: No, I'm not gonna answer that. That's boring, tabloid, O.J. Simpson shit. I'm not interested. Not gonna do it. Ask an intelligent question.
O: ***Then tell me the story of how you hosted that Make-A-Wish Foundation kid.***
JB: God! Umm... How'd you hear about that?
O: ***I'm not telling.***
JB: Well, basically, he came to visit, and we took him some places, and he enjoyed it and went home, and I hope he's okay. I was never quite clear from his condition whether he was somebody who was destined to live a short life or destined to be very ill a lot of the time. He went off and bought a guitar, he went to record stores. We mainly hung out at the label and went out to dinner, and I sort of gave him some tips on other places to visit around San Francisco: Avoid Fisherman's Wharf, go to the redwoods, and so on. A lot of people who visit from Europe or Japan or Australia go only to big cities and then wonder why they're not finding stuff that's as interesting as they'd hoped for.

O: ***Well, what's cool out in San Francisco these days? What's your take on the scene there?***
JB: I can't think of a good answer to that. There are 500 scenes in this town, just like any other town now, and they don't communicate enough with each other. There are lots and lots and lots of bands that want to sound like Green Day or get on Fat Wreck Chords or something, and there's lots and lots of bands that want to sound like Nirvana, and lots and lots of bands that want to sound like Pearl Jam, and lots and lots of bands that want to sound like R.E.M. And every once in a while, someone cuts through who sounds completely unique, and often they wind up on Alternative Tentacles because nobody else will touch them. The reward of AT is being able to put out some really cool music that wouldn't turn up or even be out there otherwise. That was the original goal when not enough of the great bands were being documented. It was just to get music out there that I liked, and to try and help out other people whose minds are similar to mine; that is, they want to operate totally outside the straight entertainment industry and not worry about major-label jackasses in satin baseball jackets telling them what to do and say, or to jump around and look stupid in a video, or to get on MTV or something like that. Contrary to what the commercial industry would like you to believe, there's plenty of room just to play music your own way because you want to, without having to worry about getting signed, making a video, doing a CD-ROM, or whatever.
O: ***And the state of punk these days?***
JB: I think that what's perceived as punk out in shopping malls or in chain stores or on MTV has almost nothing to do with what punk is about. Punk was originally about creating new, important, energetic music that would hopefully threaten the status quo and the stupidity of the 1970s. Now we have an entire audience of people who call themselves "punk" because they've written the name of a British band that broke up 15 years ago on the leather jacket they bought the day before at the mall, who only want to hear one kind of music. They're as conservative as Republicans or fundamentalist Christians. I like to shock and torment those people as much as I liked to shock fern-bar idiots and disco zombies when punk first began. I think the spirit of punk has almost completely evaporated from most of what's popularly thought of as punk music. The sound is a faithful imitation of earlier bands, but the very fact that it's a deliberate, faithful imitation is what makes it not punk anymore, in my mind. I mean, conservative, narrow-minded power brokers like *Maximumrocknroll* have played a major role in ruining punk as a forward musical force. People should all think alike, people should all sound alike—that's exactly the opposite of what punk means to me. I think the true spirit of punk has more in common with the spirit of the early Beats or the early hippies, when that was centered on stopping the Vietnam War and fighting for civil rights and cleaning up the planet. That's sort of where that spirit moves from movement-and-theme to movement-and-scene. For all its violence, sexism, and homophobic warts, I still think that rap, and gangsta rap in particular, is far closer to the true spirit of punk than all of the sound-alike pop-punk bands. I don't care how loud the guitars are. As soon as I hear a whiny voice that sounds exactly like The Eagles, it nauseates me as much as The Eagles did. I have very little tolerance for people whose entire lyrical focus is, "Boo hoo, my girlfriend left me, I feel so sorry for myself as a middle-class white kid in the richest country in the world. Oh, woe is me. Maybe I should die now." As far as I'm concerned, maybe those people should. I think punk is moving away from causes, except for two things: the punk scene as a cocoon where you hide from reality, and making money. I think they could stand to move much closer to things like environmental causes. I don't think it's too hippie to want to clean up the planet so you don't wind up dying

of some kind of cancer when you're 45 years old. It enrages me that these big cancer-research organizations can't be bothered to man the front lines of environmental protest. If you clean up the pollution that causes the cancer, maybe you won't need some magic cure after all. Of course, the corporations would much prefer to pour millions into trying to find a magic cure so they can then force their workers into even worse conditions than they already have, and not worry about making them all sick. There's even been open pipe-dreaming among corporate executives allowing themselves to be quoted in commercial pulp-fiction like *Newsweek*, saying that they're almost to the point where they think they can require some kind of genetic alteration or DNA work to be done on prospective workers so they don't have to clean up the damn factories. First the lie detector, then the drug test, now this. My latest spoken-word thing, *Beyond The Valley Of The Gift Police*, breaks some new ground for me in that I'm trying to offer some solutions to the stuff I complain about, as well as looking under rocks to show people why they should really be worried. Forget O.J. and whether Green Day sold out when they signed to Reprise; this stuff is really important, and it's affecting your lives. Arguing about what is and is not punk is not gonna feed the homeless person starving outside your front door. There are two solution pieces on the album. Both borrow liberally from my mayoral campaign platform, but, again, there's the wiseass solutions and others that are dead serious. For example, the California Green Party had a great idea about enacting a maximum wage. You have a minimum wage, so why not a maximum wage? Once a person starts getting really, really rich, it's like a narcotic. The most dangerous drug in America, much worse than crack, is money. Once people have it, they start getting obsessed with making more, and they become much more predatory and uncaring toward all those people they're screwing by accumulating so much wealth and property while other people go homeless. People whine about balancing the budget. Why not just cut everybody off after a hundred grand? There'd probably be enough money left over to bring all the poor up to the level of having a hundred grand just to see what they'd do with it. Unlike right-wing pop culture today, I'm all in favor of more taxes, especially on rich people, and also in favor of more welfare. I've been to enough other countries in the world to know what happens when you have socialized single-payer health care. It works. But here, some people are scared to see a doctor because they'll either

"Punk was originally about creating new, important, energetic music that would hopefully threaten the status quo and the stupidity of the 1970s."

lose their shirt or they'll lose their home 'cause they'll get deported back to Mexico 'cause their skin's the wrong color or something. There's actually cholera in this country again. There's reports of cholera all up and down the Texas/Mexico borders, especially in El Paso and Brownsville. There's tuberculosis sprouting up again in San Francisco, Los Angeles, New York, and other places. You'd expect this sort of thing to happen in Calcutta, but corporations and rich people are all too eager to let America turn into Calcutta, if they can squeeze a few more dollars out of it to go blow on Wall Street. I think one thing people need to start working on is a self-help organization called Democrats Anonymous for people who still think there really is an alternative in a Mexico-style one-party state, which in America's case masquerades as a two-party state. People could all go to meeting halls and get up sheepishly before a podium and say, "Hi, I'm so-and-so, I'm a Democrat. But now I've learned, and I've weaned myself from being lied to again and again and again by Nixonian corporate puppets like the Hill-Billarys and their religious-right Trojan-horse friends the Gores." What puts the spinelessness of Clinton in its place is, here he is getting bashed up and down over a non-scandal like Whitewater when the Hill-Billarys losing 60 grand is a drop in the bucket compared to George Bush's own kids making off with over a hundred million bucks and not going to jail. If you really want to turn the tables on Whitewater, why not

"Resistance should be fun. Resistance isn't some pain in the ass. It's not just good for the soul and uplifting spiritually, but it can also be a great kick in the ass."

start prosecuting all those savings-and-loan Crips who got away with murder in the Reagan-Bush era? We're still paying thousands of dollars apiece in taxes to bail out those assholes, when they should be locked up. You sure have to dig deep to find the good guys in this day and age, don't you? It was interesting that Ralph Nader ran for president [in 1996], but I think he should have openly campaigned more, or at least run some op-ed pieces and some ads. I'm sure they could have raised the money to do that. What good are a bunch of decent new ideas when you don't really tell anybody about them? I like Michael Moore, and believe it or not, this long after "California Uber Alles," I think some good ideas have come out of Jerry Brown. I have very mixed feelings about Jesse Jackson. He's very good about labor and human- and civil-rights issues, but not so good on cultural issues. He's been as anti-rock-music as any of the Tipper Gore types. He characterized it as child abuse in his 1988 campaign, all because he took his kids to see Funkadelic and the singer told the audience to light up joints. That was a reactionary response, but keep in mind that, for the many good things Jackson says, he's also a reactionary preacher. I think Noam Chomsky is a national treasure—make that an international treasure. I definitely think the farty old left is as much an enemy as the conservatives in power, as far as turning people off to activism and change. Resistance should be fun. Resistance isn't some pain in the ass. It's not just good for the soul and uplifting spiritually, but it can also be a great kick in the ass. Remember how much fun you had shooting spitwads at the teacher in seventh grade? Imagine applying that kind of attitude to actually fucking with Mitsubishi! A more mature, sophisticated version of that spirit was probably the driving force of my campaign for mayor, and now several other people's, too. I love torpedoing the illusions of people who think punk should be some cocoon of a scene where you can argue over bullshit and non-issues like Green Day and Rancid as a way of avoiding the real world. You can argue about whether Offspring sold out when they signed to Sony until you're blue in the face, but that ain't gonna feed the homeless person outside your front door. Or did I already say that?

O: ***That's okay.***

JB: But it's not going to do a damn thing to put a stop to the drug war. How's that? [Sound of splashing, paper rolling.]

O: ***Hey... Is that you? Are you taking a crap?***

JB: I just finished.

O: ***Ah, well, that's all right.***

JB: When you gotta go, you gotta go.

O: ***I respect that. It's fine.***

JB: It's not a matter of respect, it's a matter of, um...

O: ***It's necessity. It's hydraulic pressure.***

JB: Even somebody who knows very little about science can figure that one out. ⌀

"Fuck 'em. I made a few bucks and got out." CHAPTER 2

"Fuck 'em. I made a few bucks and got out. I don't want to spend the rest of my life with those people. They're disgusting people, and you can quote me on that. There's a lot of great talent there, but it's no place I wanted to spend much time."

"The last couple things I did, looking back, I think, 'I really did that? I went out there in front of 2,000 people and sang a song? I can't believe I did that.' I would never want to do that for a career, or even for fun."

"We're over-saturated with commentary and with absurdity, and we're numb because of it. Nothing shocks, so what's the fun? And irony, oh, the goddamned irony, that courses through the popular culture like a cancer. If nothing is serious anymore, then there's nothing to satirize."

"We're really very proud of what we've done, but the standard should be higher for us."

Ralph Bakshi

By Tasha Robinson
Originally Printed December 2000

"Sweetheart, I'm the biggest ripped-off cartoonist in the history of the world, and that's all I'm going to say."

Ralph Bakshi started working for the Terrytoons Animation Studio when he was 21, but he didn't come into his own as an animator until 12 years later, when he wrote and directed America's first X-rated animated feature, an adaptation of R. Crumb's Fritz The Cat. *Bakshi followed* Fritz *with a series of highly textured, idiosyncratic urban pieces (*Heavy Traffic, American Pop, *and* Hey Good Lookin'*) and three high-fantasy films (*Fire And Ice, *the tanks-vs.-elves cult favorite* Wizards, *and the animated screen adaptation of* Lord Of The Rings*). In the late '80s and early '90s, Bakshi worked on a variety of projects, including The Rolling Stones' "Harlem Shuffle" video and the* New Adventures Of Mighty Mouse *series for CBS. But after his last feature film, 1992's* Cool World, *flopped and his 1997 HBO series* Spicy City *was summarily canceled, he left animation to become a full-time painter. In 2000, as advance hype over Peter Jackson's* Lord Of The Rings *adaptations was escalating, Bakshi spoke to* The Onion A.V. Club *about his* Rings *movie, why some of his own work horrifies him, and why Hollywood is hell.*

The Onion: ***Have you paid attention to the hype over the new version of*** **Lord Of The Rings*?***

Ralph Bakshi: No, not really.

O: ***Are you interested in seeing what he does with it?***

RB: Why would I be?

O: ***Because your version has been the definitive one for 20 years, and this is the first new adaptation since your version.***

RB: It's hard for me to talk about, for reasons I'm not going to get involved in.

O: ***Do you think it'll work as a live-action movie?***

RB: I have no idea. I've always seen it as animation. I really don't know what's happening with the live-action version. I don't understand it at all. Do I wish it to be a good movie? Absolutely.

O: ***What do you mean, you can't understand it? Just the decision to make it live-action?***

RB: I'm not going to go into this. You've got to read between the lines. I'm sorry. I mean, I don't know the director. I have no idea what they're doing. I wasn't consulted. Certainly, I love *The Rings* very much, and I hope that my version stands up.

O: ***Well, let's talk about your version.***

RB: [Laughs.] Thanks.

O: ***Your films are sharply divided between site-specific, street-smart urban dramas and high***

fantasy. Why those two genres? Where's the connection?

RB: First of all, animation is a medium I grew up in. It was always fantasy-oriented, or child-fantasy-oriented to be more exact. I'm 62, and I grew up in the '40s and '50s, so we're talking about Disney, right? And [Max] Fleischer. So all the animation I ever saw was of a fantasy or fairy-tale orientation... I wanted to make films that were closer to my heart. I started with *Fritz*, went on to *Heavy Traffic* and *Coonskin* and *Hey Good Lookin'*. Those films were personal paintings, and I never thought I'd do more than one. The fact that some of them became hits startled me. I thought I had one shot at these earlier films and then I'd be gone, but I wanted to take the shot, because animation was my medium and I didn't want to ape Disney. So those films were very natural for me to do. But then, as I was a young cartoonist studying my craft, cartooning and fantasy always worked together. I'm a great reader of science fiction, and certainly I read *Lord Of The Rings*. So I had this other love that wasn't personal—though *Wizards* was very personal, and I could tell you why. So it was natural for me to sometimes take a break from this heavy philosophical soul-searching I was doing and just make a film that maybe the guys in the studio would enjoy.

"I go to the new guy and tell him, 'Danny and I were making *Lord Of The Rings*,' and he says, 'Lord of the what? We're not going to make this fucking picture, Ralph. We don't understand it. Danny's an idiot and we don't want to make it.' "

O: ***And what about* Wizards?**

RB: *Wizards* was a split difference. *Wizards* was about the creation of the state of Israel and the Holocaust, about the Jews looking for a homeland, and about the fact that fascism was on the rise again, I thought. That was way before the right wing made their appearance again, and I felt that things were shifting back. On that level, *Wizards* was a very personal film.

O: ***What drew you to* Lord Of The Rings *specifically?***

RB: Brilliance. Absolute brilliance. It's probably one of the greatest fantasies ever written. The language is perfect, the characterizations are perfect, the mood is perfect. There isn't a page of *The Rings* that you wouldn't want to re-read a hundred times. Then I heard United Artists was making this film, and John Boorman was writing the screenplay in live-action. I heard that Boorman was taking the three books and collapsing them into one screenplay, and I thought that was madness, certainly a lack of character on Boorman's part. Why would you want to tamper with anything Tolkien did? So I approached United Artists and told them the film should be made in animation, and it should be made in three parts, because there's no way you can take the three books and condense them into one film. It's a physical impossibility. And here comes the horror story, right? They said fine, because Boorman handed in this 700-page script, and do I want to read it? I said, "Well, is it all three books in one?" They said, "Yes, but he's changed a lot of the characters, and he's added characters. He's got some sneakers he's merchandising in the middle." I said, "No, I'd rather not read it. I'd rather do the books as close as we can, using Tolkien's exact dialogue and scenes." They said, "Fine," which knocked me down, "because we don't understand a word Boorman wrote. We never read the books." They owned the rights, but they'd never read the original books. "We ain't got time to read it. You understand it, Ralph, so go do it." So help me God. Now this is funny. UA and MGM were in the same building in those days; they occupied the same studio. And right across the hall from Mike

Medavoy at United Artists was MGM, who owned the rights. So I said, "Okay, wait here." I walked across the hall—you could do these things in those days, or at least I could; I was young and had good-looking hair, you know—and went to see MGM. Dan Melnick was running MGM, he was the president, and he had done some films, *All That Jazz* and everything, that were very good. So he came off as an intellect, and I thought he would understand what *The Rings* meant, because UA did not. Me and Melnick walk across the hall to Mike Medavoy's office and make a deal right there. Melnick gives Medavoy his money back—the Boorman script cost $3 million, so Boorman was happy by the pool, screaming and laughing and drinking, 'cause he got $3 million for his script to be thrown out—MGM now owned the rights, and I walked back with Mike Medavoy from UA, and he kissed me, because I had gotten him his money back and the books were clear.

O: ***Why was the second half of the trilogy never filmed?***

RB: Wait, I've got more to tell you about this. I'll tell you about the second half. To make a long story short, I'm making the film for Melnick at MGM, Melnick gets fired, the whole deal falls through, and this new guy takes over, I forget his name. I go to the new guy and tell him, "Danny and I were making *Lord Of The Rings*," and he says, "Lord of the what? We're not going to make this fucking picture, Ralph. We don't understand it. Danny's an idiot and we don't want to make it." So I remembered that Saul Zaentz made a fortune on *Fritz The Cat*. He was one of the quiet investors in *Fritz* when I was a young man, and *Fritz* was a $700,000 picture that made $90 million worldwide and is still playing. So I knew he had made a fortune, and he took it and made *One Flew Over The Cuckoo's Nest*. So I gave him a call and asked him whether he wanted to make *The Rings* with me. And he said absolutely. So now we were back at UA, and Saul and I made the picture. It was supposed to be called *Lord Of The Rings: Part One* on the marquee. When I finished the film, under tremendous deadline pressure, they said, "We're dropping the *Part One*. People won't come in to see half a movie." I told them they can't drop the *Part One*, because people are going to come in thinking they'll see the whole film, and it's not there. We had a huge fight, and they released it as *Lord Of The Rings*. So when it came to the end, people were stunned in the theater, even worse than I ever realized they would be, because they were expecting to see the whole film. People keep telling me I never finished the film. And I keep saying, "That's right!" That's what they cost me, United Artists and probably the producer... I'm not sure who made the final decision. I was screaming, and it was like screaming into the wind. It's only because nobody ever understood the material. It was a very sad thing for me. I was very proud to have done *Part One*. I certainly would have done parts two and three and four in animation, but that was out of my hands, maybe. This is where the whole thing stands. And suddenly I hear they're making a live-action version. I'm sure the guys doing the live-action version looked at my version awfully hard. I'm sure they're picking everything out that worked. I can't see them not. Why don't you ask the director whether he did, whether he ever looked at my version. If he says no, laugh in his face. Seriously, ask him. Because I heard reports that they were screening it every single day at Fine Line.

"The decision to leave painting to do a movie at my age is very major, because if I go back to animation, I'll be lost again. I know what will happen."

O: ***Do you do that yourself? Go back and screen your own films?***

RB: No. I can't stand to look at them.
O: ***Why?***
RB: First of all, the animation isn't that good. I always think I could do it better if I'd had enough time. It frightens me, what I could have done, what I should have done. I remember the hard times I had dealing with certain things—can I say this, should I say this, do I have a right to say this? It wasn't easy. When you're breaking through, you say, "Do you show the penis? How far do you show the sexual activity? What will work in animation and what won't?" It was all brand-new, and I had nothing to look at. It brings back those very difficult decisions I had to make with no one to turn to. I couldn't screen a Disney film to be shown how to do it right. Plus, some of it's so frank and so crazy that it embarrasses me. "I don't believe I said that. I hope people don't understand what that really means." I mean, they're up there killing God in *Heavy Traffic*, blowing God's head off. Without blinking an eyelash, I went out and did it. Those things scare me, frighten me.

"I don't want to sound pretentious or anything, but I'm very involved in painting pictures, which don't need committees and don't need screenplays and don't need titles thrown out in your face."

O: ***You've actually come around so far in a circle that your own work offends you?***
RB: I don't know. I'd like to make another film just to find out. I don't know if it offends me as much as that I could have done everything more artistically. I've learned a lot about art since then, painting. I've always liked to tell the truth as I see it, but I probably would say the same things with more grace now. [Laughs.] That's old age talking. I'm mellowing, don't you get it?
O: ***But you've considered going back to directing?***
RB: Yeah, I made a couple of moves in that direction, got some flashes of inspiration. But I'm very serious about my painting. I don't want to sound pretentious or anything, but I'm very involved in painting pictures, which don't need committees and don't need screenplays and don't need titles thrown out in your face. It gets a little quiet, but I do sell my paintings. And the decision to leave painting to do a movie at my age is very major, because if I go back to animation, I'll be lost again. I know what will happen.
O: ***According to your autobiography, you started painting seriously as far back as 1978.***
RB: I didn't take painting as a lifestyle until much later. But I've always tried to paint the picture. I love painters. Painters are amazingly free people. If you had to pin down what drives me, it's freedom. The right to make choices, the fact that no one tells you what to do. I hate committees. Going to MGM or UA to get money to raise a film is every director's nightmare. Having to talk someone else into making a movie without their stupid fucking suggestions on how they think it should... You bring a movie in to these people, you get your heart into it, and they start telling you, "Yeah, we'll do it, but this is how we see it." It's the most disgusting thing in the world.
O: ***Do you paint for the same people you used to animate for, or do you consider an audience when you create art?***
RB: I'm very selfish, or very lucky. I just make films I want to make. I didn't think anybody would go see it. You can't make a *Coonskin* or a *Heavy Traffic* and think that anyone's going to have any interest in looking at it. I just did it because I had to do it, and I had the power to do it. Let me be very clear: *Fritz* made a fortune. I was a hero, and no one said no to me, so I took the opportunity to do it. I could have gone on to do much more commercial things, and obviously been much wealthier, but I'm wealthy enough. I had the power to do it. They

were saying, "This kid"—and I was a kid, I was 24 or 25—"did a $750,000-budgeted movie and made $90 million. Not only that, the critics mostly liked it!" So no one said no to me. They said no to me later, once they saw the films. [Laughs.] Once I had to show them the films, they got pissed off at me, but in the beginning they all liked me.

O: *Coonskin* *was actually advertised as "the movie guaranteed to offend everyone." Did you ever actually set out to offend people?*

RB: No, that's how the studio... I didn't control the advertising. When they saw these films, they'd get up ashen and turn to me in the screening room, these executives from Middle America in their suits, and they'd say, "Well, Ralph, you offended everyone. Congratulations." I mean, they were horrified.

O: *What do you say to the people who are offended by your work?*

RB: That's cool. Like I said, I can't be friends with everyone. I want people to react. I respond negatively to what different people say and do. That's okay. They have their rights. Just don't tell me what to make.

O: *How much of your work is autobiographical?*

RB: In *Heavy Traffic* and *Coonskin*, a lot. Some sequences in *Fritz*. I mean, psychologically. That's why I hate to look at them again.

O: *Because you preserved the emotions of the time, and you don't like feeling those emotions again?*

RB: How I was feeling sexually, about my hang-ups sexually. There were things being said in there that I didn't think about until I saw them years later and said, "Oh, Jesus." I mean, in *Heavy Traffic*, Carol says to Michael—pardon me if I offend you here—she says, "Why don't you take your cartoons around to the syndicate? Why won't they buy them?" And Michael says, "Because I still jerk off." Well, that was a problem I was having at that age; I was still jerking off. It's things like that that blow me out of my seat. The films are filled with stuff like that, where they become not the character on the screen but the character that drew them. That's hard to look at. I'm 62 now, and I was twentysomething when I drew that.

O: *MGM has just reissued* Heavy Traffic*, so it's out there for a whole new generation.*

RB: Have they?

"Let me be very clear: *Fritz* made a fortune. I was a hero, and no one said no to me, so I took the opportunity to do it. I could have gone on to do much more commercial things, and obviously been much wealthier, but I'm wealthy enough."

O: *The DVD came out at the beginning of September.*

RB: No one tells me anything. Well, they're all making fortunes on it, so I wish them all the luck in the world. [Laughs.]

O: *You weren't aware it was coming out again?*

RB: Sweetheart, I'm the biggest ripped-off cartoonist in the history of the world, and that's all I'm going to say.

O: *Which of your movies are you happiest with? Which do you look back on with the most pride?*

RB: *Coonskin. Wizards. Heavy Traffic.*

O: *Why those three? What did you accomplish with them?*

RB: I broke the back of fantasy in animation, I got very personal, I spoke about political issues that were happening at the time. And I look at them today and they're still not lying. Even *Fritz*. You look at these films, and you can't point to any one and say, "That was all bullshit." They hold up as accurate timepieces, so I'm very proud of that. They're pieces of America at a certain time, which animation never did. I'll take that. *Rings* is great, but it falls into the fantasy/adventure genre.

O: ***Is anyone producing animation today that you think is living up to the medium?***

RB: John Kricfalusi.

O: ***He worked with you on* The New Adventures Of Mighty Mouse, *didn't he?***

RB: Well, he worked for me for a long time. I made him a director on *Mighty Mouse*. I've always thought he was sensational. I made him a director because no one else would, and he was ready to direct.

O: ***How did you sell a network on such an unconventional Saturday-morning cartoon?***

RB: You wanna hear more stories? [Laughs.] I left animation and came back. I had a car accident, I forget what happened, it's a long story, and you don't want to hear it anyhow. I needed a show to sell to get going again. So I pulled a small crew together, with John and a few different guys who worked for me before and who I really loved. We developed many shows, and *Mighty Mouse* was not one of them. I brought the shows up to Judy Price at CBS. She turned down all the ideas John and I had developed, including *Ren & Stimpy*. Then at the end I said, "I have another idea. I own the rights to *Mighty Mouse*." I didn't, but I had worked with Terrytoons as a young man on *Mighty Mouse*, and I knew *Mighty Mouse* wasn't around anywhere. She said, "I'd buy that show tomorrow. That's a perfect hit show." So I said, "Okay, call my agent, make a deal." And as she was calling, I was trying to find out who owned the rights to *Mighty Mouse*. I found out Viacom had bought all of Terrytoons' work, so I ran over to them, and they said, "Please, do something with this crap. We don't know what to do with it." So we made a deal just in the nick of time, as Judy was finishing with my lawyer. I told Judy the story and she said, "I knew you didn't have the rights, Ralph, but I knew you'd get them." And we did what we felt was right for Saturday morning. We didn't do anything wrong. We had a hit show.

"They'd get up ashen and turn to me in the screening room, these executives from Middle America in their suits, and they'd say, 'Well, Ralph, you offended everyone. Congratulations.' "

O: ***It's been more than a decade, and people are still debating whether Mighty Mouse snorted coke on that cartoon.***

RB: He never sniffed cocaine. I wouldn't have done that. John wouldn't have done that. I'm not going to alibi too much, but he sniffed a flower just like Popeye sniffed his spinach. There are scenes in all the Fleischer films of Popeye doing exactly the same thing, sniffing spinach up his nose because his hands were tied and he's trying to get to it, so it was an action we'd seen a million times before in animation. But he never sniffed cocaine. I mean, what for? Was there a cocaine inference? I don't know what John had in his mind, but it was not cocaine.

O: ***What finally prompted you to give up on moviemaking?***

RB: Sick of Hollywood, tired of fighting and selling out as an artist. I don't believe anyone should do the same thing for the rest of his life. We get a very short time on this planet. Challenging oneself is very important. It's not that I couldn't make other great animated films, but I'd done what I wanted to do, which was make animation an adult medium, if one wanted it to be. And I'd proven to myself that it could work, and it was time to move on to something else. When I sell a painting, I get very excited. I need one person to like what I do, not a million. It's a different structure here. Plus the Hollywood thing. I mean, Hollywood is no place to grow up, no place to live. It's no place to have any friends, no place to enjoy life. It's a disgusting, horrible, craze-driven town. It's only how much you make, or how fancy a car you have, that determines your status there. And everyone's lying so much that they don't even know they're lying anymore. I mean, fuck 'em. I made a few bucks and got out. I don't want to spend the rest of my life with those people. They're disgusting people, and you can quote me on that. There's a lot of great talent there, but it's no place I wanted to spend much time. I'd rather spend time with Rembrandt and Goya at home. They're better company than those schmucks who never read *Lord Of The Rings.* Ø

"You can't be satirical and not be offensive to somebody."

Tom Lehrer

By Stephen Thompson
Originally Printed May 2000

Tom Lehrer's creative legacy is far larger than his musical catalog: The singer, pianist, teacher, mathematician, and political satirist influenced countless humorists and remains a staple on Dr. Demento's radio show, but his body of work consists of only a few dozen songs. That material, most of it recorded and released between 1953 and 1965 (although he wrote a few songs for the children's TV show The Electric Company *in the early '70s) remains widely circulated, with more than two million albums sold. His work still sounds fresh today: "The Vatican Rag" makes fun of Catholicism, "The Old Dope Peddler" sings the praises of drug dealers, "Folk Song Army" chides self-righteous activists, "National Brotherhood Week" mocks racism and political correctness in one fell swoop, and so on. Whether he's dealing in the darkly absurd ("Poisoning Pigeons In The Park") or the politically pointed ("Who's Next?"), Lehrer's snide delivery remains a constant throughout his music, virtually all of which was compiled (along with three new songs) on Rhino's three-disc box set,* The Remains Of Tom Lehrer. *Since 1972, Lehrer has refrained from performing—he officially retired in 1967, but made a few appearances over the following five years—choosing instead to focus on his work teaching mathematics and a course on the American musical at the University of California at Santa Cruz. His limited musical output and private nature have added to the mystique surrounding his career, but Lehrer cleared up some of the questions and rumors in a 2000 interview with* The Onion A.V. Club.

The Onion: ***Is it true that you stopped performing as a form of protest, because Henry Kissinger won the Nobel Peace Prize?***

Tom Lehrer: I don't know how that got started. I've said that political satire became obsolete when Henry Kissinger was awarded the Nobel Prize. For one thing, I quit long before that happened, so historically it doesn't make any sense. I've heard that quoted back to me, but I've also heard it quoted that I was dead, so there you are. You can't believe anything you read. That was just an offhand remark somebody picked up, and now it's been quoted and quoted, and therefore misquoted. I've heard that I stopped because Richard Nixon was elected, or because I got put away in an insane asylum, or whatever. It was just a remark about political satire, because it was true. Not literally, but everything is so weird in politics that it's very hard to be funny about it, I think. Years ago, it was much easier: We had Eisenhower to kick around. That was much funnier than Nixon.

O: ***A lot of the political humor that followed you, stuff like Mark Russell, is very de-fanged.***

TL: Yeah, de-fanged is exactly right. It's very mild, and that's part of the problem. You can't be satirical and not be offensive to somebody. That was one of the problems with the TV show *That Was The Week That Was* [on which Lehrer's songs appeared]. They announced right at the beginning that they were going to be hard-hitting and biting and satirical, but that they weren't going to offend anybody. Well, that's a contradiction in terms right there.

"Years ago, it was much easier: We had Eisenhower to kick around. That was much funnier than Nixon."

O: ***Do you feel that you had any impact?***

TL: That's hard for me to say. I don't think this kind of thing has an impact on the unconverted, frankly. It's not even preaching to the converted; it's titillating the converted. I think the people who say we need satire often mean, "We need satire of them, not of us." I'm fond of quoting Peter Cook, who talked about the satirical Berlin cabarets of the '30s, which did so much to stop the rise of Hitler and prevent the Second World War. You think, "Oh, wow! This is great! We need a song like this, and that will really convert people. Then they'll say, 'Oh, I thought war was good, but now I realize war is bad.'" No, it's not going to change much.

O: ***Is comedy important?***

TL: Comedy is very important, yes. For one thing, it keeps you sane. But it's not really a conversion. I mean, it's marginally a conversion, because if people tune in or go to a nightclub or even watch television, and hear that a lot of other people are laughing at something you thought was not funny, at least it'll force you to reconsider. I know people who've heard "The Vatican Rag" and then converted, so to speak. They'd think, "Hey, wait. There are actually people who take that as funny. I'm not the only one." I've always done some good along those lines. Many people over the years have said, "Oh, 'The Vatican Rag' changed my life." It's not that they were convinced of something they weren't convinced of before; it's just that now they realize it's okay to laugh. They're not the only ones.

O: ***Why did you leave? Why did you give up?***

TL: I didn't really give up.

O: ***I didn't mean give up, like, "surrender."***

TL: I just lay down and let them trample all over me. No, it's the wrong question, really, because there wasn't really a career to speak of. I figure I wrote 37 songs in 20 years, and that's not exactly a full-time job. It wasn't that I was writing and writing and writing and quit. Every now and then I wrote something, and every now and then I didn't. The second just outnumbered the first.

O: ***Which is more important, being funny or making a point?***

TL: Well, to me, being funny is more important, but I don't know. Most politicians are so interested in making points that they don't... I'd rather be funny myself, and I'd rather listen to somebody with a little sense of humor. We used to have [two-time Democratic presidential nominee] Adlai Stevenson in my day, but I don't know if there's anybody like that now. Bob Dole could have been; he was the closest. He seemed to have a sense of humor, but he didn't show it in the campaign. I would have loved to have Bob Dole come out and really say stuff. But after a while they tamed him, I guess, so it didn't work. Not that he would have won anyway, but at least we would have had a fun campaign.

O: ***How did you deal with people who can't process satire? For example, you did "National***

Brotherhood Week," which has the line, "Everybody hates the Jews."

TL: Yeah, there were a few remarks about that, but I think most people understood what the song was about. There are people... I mean, there's a recent case in Amherst, Massachusetts, where they canceled a performance of *West Side Story* in the high school because they thought it was offensive to Puerto Ricans or something, missing the point of the whole show. Or they ban Huckleberry Finn because it has the word "nigger" in it. That's just silly. But what can you do? Except kill those people. People like that should be put to sleep. That's one of my favorite lines from *UHF*. I don't know if you know that movie, but it's full of wonderful things. I love when Kevin McCarthy says, "People like that should be put to sleep."

O: ***How much of that did you face, where people would, say, accuse you of anti-Semitism? I mean, people are really stupid.***

TL: [Laughs.] People are stupider than anybody. People rarely accused me, you see, because in those days I wasn't on television. Occasionally, late at night when nobody was watching, I would do a talk show. But, no, I was never in the public eye. I would do nightclubs and concerts—particularly concerts—and only people who already agreed with me would show up. People weren't going to come and inadvertently turn on their television set and find this offensive stuff coming out. So I was never subjected to that, personally.

O: ***Is there more danger to free speech from the PC left or the far right?***

TL: Ah, I don't know about that. I don't know if it's a matter of danger. That's the problem here: People on both sides take the other side very seriously. There are people who get really mad if you say "fuck" on the television, or they won't let you say it, or something like that. It's just minor when you look at what's going on in the world. So I don't know which is worse. I doubt there's any danger there. People claim First Amendment and all that, but I don't think these are really important issues as long as there's poverty and hunger and a lack of education and people dying and children starving. This is important, not political correctness. I tell people, "I'll call you women instead of girls, just so long as I get paid more than you do." That's the issue, not all that PC stuff.

"Weird Al" Yankovic On Tom Lehrer

Tom Lehrer is one of my two living musical idols, Stan Freberg being the other. Even though his lifelong recorded output was not what you would call voluminous, the undisputed brilliance of those songs has inspired hero worship among several generations of fans of satire and funny music. I've never met Mr. Lehrer in person, but we've exchanged a couple of letters and phone calls. (I was thrilled beyond words when he started quoting lines from my movie, UHF*!) I tried my best to get him to appear on my ill-fated CBS Saturday-morning kids' show, but he declined. I knew it was a long shot: Lehrer treasures his anonymity so much that he never allowed publicity photos to be taken for his albums, and he's managed to avoid the spotlight for more than three decades. I've always kind of considered him the J.D. Salinger of demented music.*

O: ***Did you ever face any sort of Smothers Brothers–style suppression?***

TL: No, and they only faced it because they were on network television on Sunday night, a major time, so they had a lot of people watching. A lot of people who didn't like it watched. But I think one of the problems—and one of the objections I had to the way they handled it—was that they kept sort of implying that they were being naughty and dangerous and threatening and subversive, whereas if they'd just done it, maybe it would be less objectionable. But I was never on major-network TV or on prime time. I mean, I did one song on *The*

Jack Paar Show, and that certainly didn't offend anybody. I did "Whatever Became Of Hubert?" on *The Merv Griffin Show* when Hubert Humphrey was well-known, and they were patting themselves on the back for being so open-minded. So I called them later and asked, "Did you get any objections?" Not a single letter or phone call came in objecting, so I don't think people get as upset as some people would like to think they do.

O: ***Why aren't comedy albums as successful as they once were?***

TL: I really don't know. I think part of the reason is that you can see the whole routine every night on HBO and other places. I really don't understand when I see, for example, Adam Sandler selling all these records. Why don't you just watch it, or tape it, or something? And why would anybody actually want a record of these things? In the old days, you couldn't just turn on and see Bill Cosby or Shelley Berman or Bob Newhart doing that stuff, so the records were popular. The other thing is that you could listen to most of those records more than once. With most of the [new] comedy records I know about, I don't think I'd want to hear them more than once. I mean, I can still listen to Nichols & May records, and I actually laugh out loud at Monty Python and some of these other things, because they're so carefully crafted. They're not just, "Here's a joke. Here's something funny." Once you've heard the joke, it's not funny anymore, but it's the way it's told. And I think that's the same with the music: The reason some of my songs have lasted longer is there's a lot of stuff packed in there. You want to hear them more than once, as opposed to, say, Mark Russell.

"I figure I wrote 37 songs in 20 years, and that's not exactly a full-time job."

O: ***What new comedy do you like?***

TL: I don't really keep up with it, I'm afraid, so I can't really name anybody. Eddie Izzard is wonderful, I think, but I've only seen that one HBO special he did. He's one of the few people who talk about stuff other than girlfriends and relationships and flatulence and genitalia. There are very few of them who actually talk about real stuff. I like Jon Stewart. He's not as obnoxious as Dennis Miller, whom I really can't stand. The people who are sort of, "Aren't I funny?" It's that Chevy Chase school of comedy. I hate that. Just do the job. We all know, without a doubt, that the funniest program on television is *The Simpsons*, but they're sort of in a class by themselves. I love them. I actually watch *Sports Night*, too, because it doesn't have a laugh track, and that's my main criterion. It's not so much the obnoxiousness of the laugh track, although that has a lot to do with it; it's the fact that they can sneak in a little joke every now and then without having to have the audience laugh at it and cut it out if the audience doesn't. You can put in all these marvelous little things that don't interfere with the flow of the show.

O: ***Have you given any thought to performing again?***

TL: I have given a lot of thought to it. The answer is always no. I've given a lot of negative thought to this question. My last public performance for money was in 1967. For free, it was 1972, with the exception of two little one-shot, one-song things. But that's just for friends, out of friendship for the people involved, and also because it was fun. But, no, I don't have the temperament of a performer, and I certainly couldn't do it every night.

O: ***I was thinking one big concert.***

TL: But then it becomes what I think of as the Lenin's Tomb phenomenon: People want to see the actual flesh of Lenin, but it doesn't matter, because he's dead. You see Richard Burton in *Camelot* or Zero Mostel in *Fiddler On The Roof*: They drag these people out because people actually want to see the flesh. People would go anywhere to see a famous person in the flesh, no matter what they do. I would just be doing an imitation of myself, so unless I had a totally new act with a little nostalgia thrown in—not much—I wouldn't do it. And I don't have that, so that solves that problem. Even then, I wouldn't want to do it. It would require a lot of rehearsal. The last couple things I did, looking back, I think, "I really did that? I went out there in front of 2,000 people and sang a song? I can't believe I did that." I would never want to do that for a career, or even for fun.

O: ***Why aren't there more photos of you?***

TL: There are a whole bunch of pictures, but they're old. Part of my contract with Warner Bros. was that they're not allowed to use my picture, so it's not on any of the records except taken from a long distance. I like that a lot. That was part of the deal. Now, I let it all hang out. I figure this is it, the box set, so we might as well put some pictures in it. There are pictures in there.

O: ***Did you keep those out of the public eye for a love of privacy? People use the word "recluse" a lot.***

TL: Yeah, mainly. There were pictures available, but it wasn't a big thing. There was no big photo spread. There were a few when Rhino put out *Songs & More Songs* in 1997. But pictures in newspapers and magazines don't count, as you know, because they go out in the garbage. But in books, and even on television, that is an invasion of privacy, definitely. I find that people can pass me on the street who've just seen my picture in the paper and they wouldn't recognize me. If they'd seen me on television, the heads turn. They say, "Wait a minute. I don't know who that is, but he's somebody." I've seen that in action. I've done some TV, and the next day I'll be walking along and people will kind of look at me. I don't like that, because I've seen it the other way around. If I see a movie star in the department store buying something, I'll kind of sidle up and see what they're saying, what they look like, how they sound. That's an invasion of privacy.

O: ***Do people ever enroll in your class because they're fans, but they suck at math?***

TL: Well, maybe one or two, but after the first class they realize that this is math. I don't know any funny theorems.

O: ***You won't be favoring them with a song.***

TL: Not at those prices, no. ⌀

Berkeley Breathed

By Tasha Robinson
Originally Printed August 2001

"If nothing is serious anymore, then there's nothing to satirize."

When Berkeley Breathed launched the newspaper comic strip Bloom County *in 1980, it was primarily an odd spoof on Midwestern life, but as the years passed, it veered into political satire, social criticism, and sheer whimsy. It was a success in every mode:* Bloom County *collections hit bestseller lists, and in 1987, Breathed won the Pulitzer Prize for editorial cartooning. In 1989, the cartoonist (or "stripper," as he dubbed himself) made national news when he announced he was ending* Bloom County*—a virtually unheard-of career move in an industry where syndicated cartoonists often kept doggedly producing the same strip until their deaths. Breathed followed* Bloom County *with the Sunday-only spin-off* Outland*, but in 1995, he retired that strip, too. He continued to write and illustrate children's picture books, and in 2000, he made his directorial debut with an animated version of his tall tale* Edwurd Fudwupper Fibbed Big. *While waiting for Nickelodeon to determine the cartoon's fate, Breathed engaged in a 2001 e-mail interview with* The Onion A.V. Club *about his "shmiberal" politics, his cartooning career, his new daughter, and Tom Cruise.*

The Onion: ***Tracking down background information on your career was a little difficult: Even your book-jacket bios were just strings of jokes. Was this out of a desire for privacy?***

Berkeley Breathed: It was out of a desire not to bore anybody. I happen to think nearly everybody—especially those one might find in the odd issue of *People* magazine, including me—is frightfully boring, especially me. And Tom Cruise. Tom and I are alike in only this way. I remember in 1987, a freelance writer for *Rolling Stone* came out and spent a week with me, then returned to his loft in SoHo, only to find that after he typed in the words, "Big-beaked Berkeley Breathed lives in Iowa with a flatulent mixed-breed lab and has trouble with deadlines," he couldn't find anything else to say. Years later, he tried to sell the piece to *Penthouse*—I'm not making this up—and their fact-checker called to confirm that the writer had watched me get seduced by a woman and her twin teenage daughters in the laundry room of the apartment complex. I'd driven the poor chap over the edge of biographical desperation with my stark boringness. I'm still working on becoming more interesting. This year, I started listening to Celtic music and collecting vintage ray guns. If you don't think that's more interesting, well, then, you agree with my wife.

O: ***Has privacy been an issue for you throughout your career?***

BB: Having an extra free can of aerosol canola oil thrown into one's grocery bag by a giggling grocery clerk who recognized my name on a check is a bonus, I won't argue. Being recognized in a Starbucks by a gaggle of college kids—as I was in 1991—after I had been to the dentist... They waved as I sat there holding a mocha grande, with hot coffee dribbling down my deadened chin, shirt, pants, shoes, across the floor, and under the pastry counter. Those experiences I'll leave to, well, Tom Cruise.

O: ***Did you originally intend to be a professional cartoonist all your life, or was it something you fell into in and after college?***

BB: I started as a news photographer at the University Of Texas' *Daily Texan*. They failed to see the marketing advantage in manipulating news photos (this is pre-digital, remember) to enhance the drama. I recall a dandy front-page photo of a community street preacher, in which I burned a halo floating above his head. I got fired and started writing stories for the campus magazine. I wrote about an unnamed student who secretly released hundreds of baby alligators into nearby Lake Travis, which would have been compelling if I hadn't made it up. Property values around the lake plummeted over $70 million the next week, which brought federal game agents into town. I was arrested, eventually—you think I'm lying again, but I'm not, check the records—and then the death threats and getting kicked out of my apartment complex and I won't bore you with the rest, except to add that some wise sage finally suggested that the cartooning desk might be where I belonged, as I could let my little imagination soar wherever it wanted, and federal agents wouldn't be needed. So I started copying *Doonesbury*, and you know the rest.

O: ***Did you start out hoping to change the world, or just tease it?***

BB: When pretty, fragrant paths of opportunity open before you—with teenage twins and their mother waiting in the Laundromat at the end—chances are, you just trot on down without really asking too much about where they lead. I had never read the comics before, so I looked at the American comic page. It needed a little kick in the ass, and nobody was doing it. *Doonesbury* was on a two-year vacation in 1980. The most daring humor that could be found was *Garfield* screaming for lasagna... as he still does today, that funny little consistent bastard. An envelope that needs stretching is a red flag to the little bull in me, so I charged.

O: ***You always strongly resisted being moved to the editorial page, even though that might have protected you from the shrinking-comics phenomenon and some of the outcry about the stances you took on political issues. Why was staying on the comics page so important?***

BB: Same reason it was for Garry Trudeau. Here, let me put it vulgarly and in caps: NOBODY THE FUCK READS THE OPINION PAGES.

O: ***Do you miss that daily public forum where you could address political and social topics that bothered you?***

BB: Oh, to hell with that, I miss the money. If I could have drawn a cat yelling for lasagna every day for 15 years and had them pay me $30 million to do so, I would have. But for a guy with a rather small mouth, I just have too big a mouth. I can't help myself. The truth: The blander you are, the richer you'll be. I tried, truly I did.

O: ***How do you react when you read the news these days?***

BB: I'm like you. Shocked, hurt, betrayed. How's Nicole going to go it alone without Tom? Take off the makeup, and poof, she disappears like the Cheshire Cat. And don't talk to me about Tom being gay. Don't. Oh, if only I were still cartooning.

O: ***Are there still political issues that incense you?***

BB: Nope. Bill Clinton just took all the fun out of this stuff. Even Trudeau, brilliant as he is, couldn't do anything much with the last eight years, really. It's like doing a parody of *The National Enquirer*. Can't be done. We're over-saturated with commentary and with absurdity, and we're numb because of it. Nothing shocks, so what's the fun? And irony, oh, the goddamned irony, that courses through the popular culture like a cancer. If nothing is serious anymore, then there's nothing to satirize. Look at George W. Bush. He knows the game. He knows he's a maroon, as Daffy Duck would say, and refuses to take himself seriously. He cut off our satirist balls. We're like a gaggle of eunuchs running around the palace, wishing we could hump the princess. The game's changed forever.

O: ***What's in your anxiety closet these days?***

BB: Middle age. Mitigated by a 1-year-old little girl named Sophie sleeping in the room next to me as I type this. As she's going to sleep, I can hear over the monitor that she's saying, "da da da da da," which most experts translate as, "I'll love my dad forever, even through adolescence," in baby language. So it's a draw.

O: ***Are there any plans to put your* Bloom County *and* Outland *books back into print?***

BB: Why bother? Do a search at Amazon. But then, they're usually a little mildewed from sitting at the base of all those toilets in all those bathrooms throughout America during the '80s. Appreciate how this sort of legacy sits with a serious writer like myself.

O: ***Do you think the political issues you addressed at the time have dated the strips, or are they still as relevant today?***

BB: That's why it'd be silly to reprint them. They have the half-life of a flounder laying on the back porch.

O: ***How have your politics changed since you started* Bloom County*?***

BB: Ah, the naïve clarity that accompanies youth. Cynicism comes with age, as sure as death, and I haven't missed it. As I look back at those old strips, I see some pretty dumb simplemindedness. What remains the same as now, however, is the frustration at the continuing path the world seems to be on in avoiding lessons about accountability. It's a constant line on the graph, this avoidance of blame and penalty for one's actions. Started at the Nuremberg Trials in 1946, I figure. I thought it peaked with O.J., but then Tom Cruise comes along and won't own up to his sins. I don't feel good about this.

O: ***Is the liberal stance of the early strips indicative of your own personal politics?***

BB: Liberal, shmiberal. That should be a new word. Shmiberal: one who is assumed liberal, just because he's a professional whiner in the newspaper. If you'll read the subtext for many of those old strips, you'll find the heart of an old-fashioned Libertarian. And I'd be a Libertarian, if they weren't all a bunch of tax-dodging professional whiners.

"I could let my little imagination soar wherever it wanted, and federal agents wouldn't be needed. So I started copying *Doonesbury*, and you know the rest."

O: ***Are there any positions you took back then that you disagree with now, or that you wish you'd addressed differently?***

BB: Positions, no. But many of the strips make me physically cringe in the dumb-headed way I went at them... most of which I'll lay at the feet of inexperience. One rule: The more pissed-off you are about something, the less funny you are. Never good to get involved. I couldn't, for instance, do justice to animal experimentation. Not funny strips. Effective, though: We got dear Mary Kay to stop squeezing her cold cream into the eyes of rabbits. But not funny. And if you're not funny, you're just whining, and you know what I think about whiners.

O: ***You seemed to make a conscious effort to keep* Bloom County *racially balanced, but you rarely engaged racial issues. By contrast, you***

discussed gender issues a lot, but seemed to have problems keeping female characters in the strip. Any theories as to why?

BB: I did some strips about this... and I want everybody to stop dribbling their mochas down their shirts for one second while I mention it again: Throughout cartoon history, there aren't any—repeat, ANY—primary animal cartoon characters that are females. If one was female, she was primarily a girlfriend to the main character. Minnie Mouse. Look at kids' TV. If there's a female character in a big furry suit on *Barney* or *Sesame Street*, she has long eyelashes and flits and flutters about like some nightmarish caricature from Jerry Falwell's wet dream. This isn't a conspiracy. It's just nearly impossible, and it has something

"I miss the money. If I could have drawn a cat yelling for lasagna every day for 15 years and had them pay me $30 million to do so, I would have."

to do with the metaphorical response that a talking-animal character somehow evokes in the reader. Everyone has tried. Interesting human female characters are there, of course—*Doonesbury* in the thick of it—but the risk is that they become an icon for their "group," and you're damned if you do and damned if you don't. I just never nailed it, not that I tried hard enough. There's a much longer discussion to be had about this, but I'm going to duck the issue, so I can explain why a white boy like myself didn't write about race: You can't. You couldn't then. You can't now. Don't touch it. Run. Hide. Smile and say you love everybody equally, and don't make any jokes as you back out of the room. Race and humor only work in a comedy club with exclusively black comedians. That's it. There isn't a shade of a chance for anything resembling a real discussion about race occurring publicly in this country for another... well, ever. Tirades, yes. Conversations that don't become tirades after the first sentence spoken? No. Clinton, the big idiot shmiberal, started tiptoeing down the path. Funny how we never heard about the big "National Discussion On Race" again. Once bitten.

O: ***One of the ironies of*** **Bloom County** ***was that the child characters were among the most mature, while the adult characters were prone to egregious silliness and elaborate fantasies. Did you think of yourself as a particularly mature child? Do you think of yourself as a particularly silly adult?***

BB: Yes. And, yes, you shrewd little imp. Hanging onto the silly as I sail toward my mid-40s is my current project. The middle-age temptation to get serious about everything is Satan's handiwork. My child may be my aging soul's salvation at the altar of silliness. That, by the way, is why they call us writers.

O: ***To some degree, that playfulness became childishness as the strip developed. The humor seemed to curdle. Can you identify a point where you decided that doing the strip wasn't fun, or that the end results didn't meet your standards anymore?***

BB: I see juvenile humor throughout the life of the strip. It's a flaw of my personality. It's also a result of missing deadlines. Juvenile is always the refuge of the late. Funny, as soon as a writer, cartoonist, or sitcom producer announces retirement, there is a universal assessment that suddenly emerges that the most recent work was obviously in its decline. Some of my most popular single strips were done in the last two years. But, all in all, I was getting spent, and no doubt that early erratic, chaotic bounce that my strip—or any TV show, musician, or film director—inevitably rides on, finally slows to a predictable rhythm. So you look for the new bounce again, happy that you ever found one to begin with. Most don't.

O: ***In a recent online interview, you said, "Most humor is cynical by its very nature." This seems***

odd in light of the fairly cherubic qualities of your work. Do you think humor has to be cynical to be funny?

BB: Satire is, of course. It's destructive in its essence. As is most effective humor. Somebody pays in most jokes. The funniest Monty Python shtick, silly as it is, is deeply cynical about England's culture during the '60s. When we laugh at anything, you can usually find cynicism toward something somewhere. Keep looking. It's why I'm deeply suspicious of humor as a life calling. My favorite films are deeply dramatic, not funny.

O: ***Would you consider doing a newspaper strip again?***

BB: Pity the poor modern comic page. Frames the size of thumbnails. It started as the first mass-market entertainment medium in a world that didn't yet know television, film, or even radio. Its comic heroes were America's first celebrities, known coast to coast. Now, it's just a page of inky blur that only a 10-year-old's eyes could focus upon. It's the buggy whips of this millennium: quaint and eclipsed, sad to say.

O: ***In an issue of* The Comics Journal, *you went into detail about what you thought newspaper comic-strip syndicates were really looking for: a situational strip drawn by a disaffected office worker who saw funny things going on around him, and who had no artistic experience and could only draw a little, which wouldn't matter, because of the shrinking size of the comics pages. A year later,* Dilbert *made its debut. Coincidence? Do you have a future ahead of you as the new Edgar Cayce?***

BB: You're kind. Art via marketing ain't exactly rocket science. This is how they greenlight movies now. This is how they greenlight everything. I could never get *Bloom County* started today, because it wouldn't make any sense as a marketing platform. And there you have the State Of The World. When they can figure out how to make a profitable marketing franchise out of the long-awaited "National Discussion On Race," we'll finally have one. We'll put Bill Clinton sitting there dressed and grinning like Regis, with a circle of people around him screaming at each other, and the one who sounds the most victimized goes home with the million bucks. That's the only way you could ever keep people from throttling each other long enough to have a second show. Which, as we all know, means a franchise! What's Edgar Cayce got to do with this again?

O: ***Care to theorize about what they're looking for now?***

BB: I haven't looked at a comic page since 1989. But I can tell you, they're looking for something that's legible when reproduced smaller than the ingredients label on that teeny-tiny box of Sun-Maid Raisins. That eliminates most everything.

O: ***Quite a bit of your work is still available on the Internet, so barring a barrage of lawsuits, readers will probably always have access to your strips. Is that comforting or annoying?***

BB: What the hell are you talking about? My strips are there? Is this that Napster shit people keep mentioning?

O: ***A lot of fan sites reprint* Bloom County *strips and art. Have you never seen any of the web sites devoted to your work?***

BB: It's a little eerie. I actually have avoided looking. It's difficult to explain, but it's as if all those 15,679 strips that were drawn were done by somebody else. I can't recall actually doing them, as most were done at 4 a.m. in a sleep-deprived fog. This must be what it's like to sober up after 20 years as an alcoholic and look back at the carnage, saying, "What numbskull did that?"

O: ***Your early strips often referenced* Star Trek. *Were you a fan of the original show? Do you still watch it?***

BB: Oh, don't go there. *Star Trek*. It's like discussing buggy whips. Or it's been whipped to death by buggy whips. Something. I can't actually bring myself to see *Star Trek* again. It's like trying to discuss the culinary virtues of a loaf of bread found in King Tut's tomb. Yeck.

O: ***People frequently compare you to [Calvin And Hobbes'] Bill Watterson, I think in part because both your strips centered on a sense of whimsy, but also because your work left them with few comparisons. Do you think there's a valid parallel?***

BB: No. He was the real thing. I was just scampering nude through the aisles before anybody could kick me out. Garry Trudeau was our greatest satirist in the second half of the century. Crazy ol' Bill Watterson created the purest comic strip, after *Peanuts*, probably. Or before *Peanuts* became a shadow. Bless him for quitting at the top. It's not easy.

O: ***Do you think your decision to retire from comic strips affected his decision to retire, as well?***

BB: Probably. I know that I encouraged him to win back his copyright to his characters—always owned by the syndicates—before quitting. I had to quietly, secretly threaten the comic page's first walkout in 1989 to win back

"That should be a new word. Shmiberal: one who is assumed liberal, just because he's a professional whiner in the newspaper."

mine. It had never been done before. Even Sparky Schulz never owned the *Peanuts* characters. Technically, they could have fired him and hired college kids to do the strip. Maybe they did, for those last 20 years. Good ol' Sparky. He was our Elvis, in his prime.

O: ***To some degree, a lot of the readers have a mental image of you, Gary Larson, and Bill Watterson sitting around a pool somewhere together, drinking cocktails and being hilariously funny.***

BB: I'm not going to say a goddamned thing to divest anybody of that particular picture. Except to add that we are all incredibly handsome. Handsomer than, for instance, Tom Cruise.

O: ***You suggested, shortly after winning the Pulitzer for editorial cartooning, that your win would open up the field to other types of entrants that hadn't been considered previously. Do you think that's been the case?***

BB: Hardly. In the world of hardcore editorial cartoons, there's a small, unpleasant fellow with a very little penis, the result of a sneeze during circumcision, named Pat Oliphant—himself a Pulitzer winner—who threatened a boycott when my prize was announced in 1987. Those were the days.

O: ***Do you feel like the flak from that time period affected your career in any way?***

BB: I was never asked to join the Editorial Cartoonists Of America. No fraternity would have me in college, either. I think they know something.

O: ***Do you ever go back and reread your old strips?***

BB: Never. Painful. Neither do I look at myself in the mirror, nude, at 5 a.m., under harsh fluorescent lights.

O: ***Is it true you didn't ever read newspaper comics when you were drawing one? Is there an ideological reason, or is it a matter of taste?***

BB: I made myself a cartoonist. I wasn't born one. Watterson was the latter. Schulz, too. That's why I departed.

O: ***Do you think that's a good way for other artists to work? Should novelists not read other people's books, musicians not listen to other people's music, and so forth?***

BB: No, no, no. Art is a synthesis of everything that came before it. Garry Trudeau told me that in 1982, just before he asked me to stop making my characters look like his, goddammit.

O: ***Do you still avoid newspaper comics?***

BB: Like buggy whips.

O: ***What do you read by choice?***

BB: No fiction, oddly. I love the great stories unembellished with fiction: the Second World War, for instance. The greatest story of the millennium. Its dramatic depths are bottomless, and I find myself reading everything and walking through every musty museum on the Normandy coast and weeping at the memorials like it was me who sat in a hole on Utah Beach at 20 years old instead of being a professional shmiberal on the comic page. In therapy, I always begin with that sentence, by the way.

O: ***Do you have any lingering personal attachment to, or fondness for, the comics medium?***

BB: Sort of a nostalgic twinge, occasionally. I may live to see Opus live in a film. Soon as they see a franchise, of course.

O: ***Where did Opus' name come from?***

BB: Opus was named after a Kansas song. If you're too young to know who Kansas was, to hell with you.

O: ***Your early* Outland *strips included a lot of visual experimentation—in particular, backgrounds that looked like a mixture of* Krazy Kat *and Dr. Seuss. But that aspect of the strip faded fairly early on, along with Tim the purple otter. Why?***

BB: Didn't work. I'd love to say it was more complex than that. Many artists, filmmakers, songwriters, and actors assume that their fans will follow them happily on whatever stylistic detours they choose to steer. We're always wrong. Okay, Madonna does it, but that's it.

O: ***Were you satisfied with the artistic aspect of the experiment? What about it didn't work for you?***

BB: I loved the look. But the comic page isn't the place to experiment with success. Neither is Top 40 radio. Or prime-time TV. Your audience drives the art. This is as commercial as art gets. Learn to love it.

O: ***What's the difference, for you, between writing for kids and writing for adults?***

BB: That's been a problem. Although I'm frightfully immature, I don't really know how children think. Knowing that Dr. Seuss actually was childless and could never stand being in their presence was of only slight comfort. So, purely for professional reasons, I knocked my wife up last year. Little Sophie has much to teach me. My future books will be different, no doubt. Fewer guns, probably.

O: ***How did you develop the three-dimensional painted look you've used in your children's books?***

BB: By not knowing how to mix colors and paint like a real painter. I cheated with an airbrush. I'm very ashamed of this.

O: ***Are there any children's authors you particularly admire?***

BB: Seuss is God. We thought Clapton was, but it was grumpy, weird, wife-dumping, flawed genius Ted.

O: ***Some of the original innocence, or whimsy, of your early comics work carries over into your children's books. Is that a sign that you're doing what you want to do with your life?***

BB: Bingo.

O: ***Have you decided what you want to be when you grow up?***

BB: Dad. The rest is frosting. Ø

Mr. Show, Part I

By Stephen Thompson
Originally Printed October 1996

"We're really very proud of what we've done, but the standard should be higher for us."

For the most part, contemporary television sketch comedy is not a bastion of high quality. With the exception of a few ill-fated, mythologized series like The Ben Stiller Show, *the shows have been mediocre at best: Failures have included* Saturday Night Special, The Edge, *and* The Dana Carvey Show, *while successes like* Mad TV *and the ever-beleaguered* Saturday Night Live *have been critically panned for years. But HBO's* Mr. Show, *a smart, funny, dark-hearted half-hour sketch-comedy series, was something special, achieving the sort of cultish permanence reserved for the likes of Monty Python. At the beginning of the show's four-year, 30-episode run,* The Onion A.V. Club *spoke to* Mr. Show *masterminds David Cross and Bob Odenkirk, both of whom had also worked on* The Ben Stiller Show.

The Onion: ***How does* Mr. Show *fit into the state of sketch comedy today?***
David Cross: Well, we're really proud of *Mr. Show*. It works the way we wanted it to work, and maybe even a little bit better, but what does that say about the state of sketch comedy? I think the state of sketch comedy is the same as it was before we did *Mr. Show*: It's kind of shitty. It always is. Once in a while, there's a good project, and hopefully, we're that.
O: ***Where do you see yourselves fitting in, though? If your show were on ABC, it would get killed. Critics would hate it. Hold up* The Dana Carvey Show *as an example: It wasn't as funny, but its first episode was pretty good.***
DC: You know, there's a difference, though: With *The Dana Carvey Show*, there seemed to be this sense that the media took, which was, "Okay, you've gotta prove to me that you're going to be funny." And I don't think anybody has that attitude with this. We're so unknown, and we're just this little experiment, and we're different enough and weird enough that we come out as a surprise. There was kind of a hype and predisposition to *The Dana Carvey Show* that we aren't getting.
Bob Odenkirk: You know what else, though? I worked on *The Dana Carvey Show*, and I agree that it was a pretty good show. It had some really funny moments. But it was not well-conceived. It wasn't sound in its presentation. And maybe it never had a chance to grow into what it could have been. But David and I have done a lot more work with this show in theaters over the last two and a half years. We've

done a lot more pre-production in preparation for it, so it's more of a whole show. You can say what you want about ABC, but they did give those guys a chance—I was there, and they had a lot of interesting ideas, just like you said. You know, people wanted it to work. I also sort of disagree with David: I think people like Dana, and they wanted it to work. They weren't being mean to the show.

DC: I didn't say that.

BO: Well, it sounded like you were saying that critics were being hypercritical and demanding of the show, and I thought they were pretty considerate. I just think it takes a lot to do a good sketch-comedy show: It's a lot of preparation, and you have to ease into it, and maybe on a network you'll never have that opportunity, really, unless you're late-night.

O: ***With* The Dana Carvey Show, *the quality fell off quite a bit after the first episode. But if* The Dana Carvey Show *had been brilliant through and through, it still would have been killed.***

BO: Well, that's quite possible...

DC: Why do you think that?

O: ***Because it was on right after* Home Improvement. *And while that guarantees a large audience when you compare it to most everything else, it still guarantees a letdown.***

BO: Well, they didn't want to be on after *Home Improvement*, and they were really kind of upset about that, but there's not much you can do about those kinds of choices a network makes. You can only fight it so much. But you're right: They shouldn't have, and that's the network's fault, and the network could have helped make that show a success, possibly, by giving it a quieter slot and letting it grow for a couple episodes. But one of the problems with doing a show on a network is that you raise the stakes so much. It costs more money to do it, and it becomes more high-profile, and you can't sit in the back and grow and find your show. Anyway, the point is that we developed this show, HBO worked with us, they gave us the time and the room to grow with the show and create it and make it become what it is, and I think it's a solid investment.

O: ***What has the reception been?***

DC: Really positive.

BO: Except for me. People don't like me. People don't like the character of Bob Odenkirk.

DC: Yeah, they like Baldy McJew, but not the other guy.

BO: [Clears throat.] When you write this article, before my name I would appreciate it if... You know how Michael Jackson gets "King Of Pop" before his name? I would like "The Handsome Midwestern Looks Of Bob Odenkirk." Or "Handsome Midwesterner Bob Odenkirk." Every time you use my name, you have to use that.

O: ***And for David Cross? Baldy McJew?***

DC: Baldy McJew David Cross.

BO: Thanks, that's contractual.

O: ***What do you think of what else is out there?***

DC: I haven't watched *Saturday Night Live*. How is it this season?

BO: Well, those guys are friends of mine, a lot of them, and they're really cool people who are having a good time doing the show. But I don't know what that translates to in terms of quality.

O: ***I hear it's funnier this season.***

DC: It's gotta be. But they have a very difficult job.

BO: They have to spend $2 million every week, and that's tough. We don't have that kind of a burden.

O: ***What would you do with $2 million a week?***

BO: We'd do the same thing they do: Give most of it to Lorne Michaels.

O: ***You have an advantage over* Saturday Night Live, *because you're a half hour instead of 90 minutes.***

BO: We have a lot of advantages over *Saturday Night Live*. In a way, if people are going to compare *Mr. Show* to *Saturday Night Live*, we have a lot more opportunities to score. We can go to video, we can go to live...

DC: And we have time. We have time to write; we don't have to work the skits out at a dress rehearsal a couple hours before the show. We can go to a theater and work them out a month in advance.

BO: We don't have to make Wayne Gretzky funny. We don't have to do something about the biggest story of the news week that no one is gonna give a shit about in a few days. We get time to rewrite our stuff and make it better, and we even get time to put it up in front of an audience in a theater and test it out and run it and get used to it.

DC: They really are two completely different shows.

BO: And we have all the advantages, so we'd better be funnier than they are. Really. That's the way people should watch the show: They should say, "This had better be funnier than *SNL*, because they have all the opportunities."

O: ***So you're basically saying, "Give* SNL *a break."***

BO: Yeah. I think so. Absolutely, give *SNL* a break. They'll come back. They'll score again. And you know what? Then they'll suck again. It's a killer show to do, and no one's gonna score all the time. We're really very proud of what we've done, but the standard should be higher for us.

DC: And that's how we want it. That's how we choose to do it. To us, this is the best way to get the best half-hour of comedy. It's a lot of work, and it's very time-consuming.

BO: And it costs a lot: We have to order our jokes from the services.

O: ***"We need something on O.J.!"***

BO: That's us, every week. Need something on O.J.

O: ***You actually did an O.J. thing.***

BO: Yeah, in a roundabout way, which is how we do everything. The Pope murdered a bishop, and then tried to get away in the Popemobile. And obviously it was him, because his Papal ring fell off at the scene.

O: ***Did you get complaints from angry Catholics?***

DC: Most of the people who would complain don't get HBO.

BO: We only got one letter last year that we're aware of. We got a letter faxed to us from an angry veteran who was pissed off about the shitting-on-the-flag thing. That's it. That's all we know about. We called him up and explained to him that we meant to make fun of performance artists, not the flag. Which is true; he had turned off the sketch because he thought the character David was playing was going to shit on the flag, but the joke of the sketch was that he was constipated and

"I think the state of sketch comedy is the same as it was before we did *Mr. Show*: It's kind of shitty. It always is."

wanted to, but he couldn't. So we explained to this guy that what happened in the sketch was that he doesn't shit on the flag. And he was a really nice guy. He listened to us, and he really didn't understand what we were saying, but he was very cool. That was the only problem we had.

O: ***You tape your shows well in advance, and that means a longer gestation period. Do you think that helps you or hurts you in terms of topicality?***

DC: Well, I don't think it's gonna help, but I don't think it hurts us too much.

BO: We try to do stuff in a different way, like the way we touched on the O.J. trial. Because that's *SNL*'s ground, the topical things. What we do is take trends or general stories that are always running or are more a part of our time in a general way. We create our own alternate universe. One thing I like about Monty Python is that they would do characters where you could tell from the laughter of the live audience that they were doing an impersonation of somebody in British TV or something, but it still was funny to us. It was a funny character anyway. I think they probably even touched on political things and topical events, but in a way that was more general, and more about the trends behind that, and about a deeper level of the story. The Pope thing was about how, if a person has enough money, you can't accuse him of anything. The Pope has more money than anybody, and he would win. He could walk around murdering people and get away with it.

DC: Yeah, "I think he's innocent even if he's guilty."

O: ***So, what happened with* The Ben Stiller Show*?***

BO: Well, the guy who ran Fox left and moved over to the film division. And the guy who took over for him despised the show.

DC: He had an awful, awful sense of humor, too, judging from what they picked up and what they opted not to pick up. Terrible sense of humor.

O: ***What did they replace you with?***

BO: Oh, shit, who knows? I don't fuckin' know. They fuckin' didn't replace us right away; they moved *The Ben Stiller Show* to 10:30. It wasn't even on in some cities, and it was on at 1 a.m. in others. You know, that was just asinine. That show would have probably succeeded if it had been given a spot where it could have grown. That's also, to a certain extent, the responsibility of the producers to at least ask for a spot and try to get in the position they want. If you want to do absurdist humor, you don't go to ABC and try to be on prime time. You take a pay cut and you go to HBO. It's a lot harder and you get paid less, and maybe you don't get to do it where you want to do it, and that's life. But then you get to do the stuff you want to do. Part of that is the artists' responsibility: to try to get their project in the place where it's going to do best, where it's going to get the best opportunity.

O: If The Ben Stiller Show *were on HBO, do you think it would still be on the air?*

BO: I don't know, because it cost a lot of money.

DC: I bet it would still be on. In fact, I bet you $20.

O: ***Bob, you worked on* Get A Life*. I've heard your experiences were less than positive.***

BO: Yeah, I'll try to be nice about the whole thing. I am a big fan of Chris Elliott. Adam Resnick and Chris created *Get A Life*, and David Mirkin, the producer, helped them get it on the air. And I joined it in the second season. I thought the first season was brilliant and hilarious and wonderful. I just thought it was great, and when I was offered the opportunity to write on it, it was a great opportunity to move from *SNL* to L.A. and start performing and writing for a show out here. And then I got there, and Chris Elliott seemed uninterested, and Adam Resnick seemed unhappy, and I don't know what happened. I don't know the specifics, but they were very unhappy, so as a result, the two primary minds behind the show were uninvolved, and it was really disappointing for me. Chris Elliott never talked to the writers. I think I talked to him three times the whole season. I'm not kidding you. And for the length of, like, six minutes. He was completely uninvolved, and the show was bad the second season—the season I worked on. It was not even half as good as the first season, very weak and broad in a dumb way. And I guess that's what happened. Adam Resnick later explained to me that they'd lost control of the show in a way that made them very unhappy.

O: ***So was that Fox's fault?***

BO: I don't know if it was.

O: ***Maybe it was that same guy who screwed up* The Ben Stiller Show.**

DC: I wouldn't put it past him.

BO: I don't know. I don't want to blame anybody. You've got to fight for control of your show sometimes, I guess. Like I was saying before, one of the sacrifices you sometimes have to make if you want to do the kind of material you want to do is to live where they do the show, or make it work out. We always attack networks and stuff, and say, "Why didn't they support that show?" Sometimes artists are unwilling to go the extra mile to do the work they want to do. It's not always the networks' fault. If you do all you can do, and then they shit out on you or mishandle your project, then that's their fault. But a lot of times the networks get blamed when it's not all their fault.

O: ***But HBO's not going to do that to you.***

BO: No way, man. They're way behind this show. They've been so great just down the line. We couldn't have asked for more. They've been partners in the show, really.

O: ***So what you're saying is that HBO is good, and that everybody should get a subscription to HBO.***

BO: As far as I'm concerned, if you've got cable, I don't know why you're not paying the extra few bucks to get *The Larry Sanders Show* and *Mr. Show* and Shannon Tweed movies. There's lots of great stuff on HBO. It's definitely worth the few bucks. ⌀

"Let us out of this deal, oh great Satan." CHAPTER 3

"I've spent a long time learning to be selfish about my music, but it's good for me. ... It doesn't worry me that we're not accepted."

Andy Partridge (XTC)

By Keith Phipps

Originally Printed June 1997

Since making its debut in 1977 alongside The Sex Pistols, The Clash, Wire, and other influential acts, XTC has labored in relative obscurity, surfacing with some regularity to produce masterful English pop music. From the nervy new wave of White Noise *to the elaborate orchestrations of later albums, XTC's music was adored by the group's cult following but ignored by the public as a whole. After the release of 1992's* Nonsuch, *the pattern changed, as the generally prolific band seemed to disappear. Upon the release of the 1997 best-of compilation* Upsy Daisy Assortment, *singer-songwriter Andy Partridge (who, with Colin Moulding, has been one of XTC's two constant members) explained the absence to* The Onion A.V. Club.

The Onion: ***Your last album came out in 1992. What have you been up to since then, and why haven't we heard from you?***
Andy Partridge: Because we've been on strike. Because we had the shittiest record deal on planet Earth. You hear about those old blues artists who sign away their estate for five dollars and a bottle of beer... Hey, I'm still waiting for that bottle of beer! I'll tell you how crap our record deal was: Although we made Virgin Records [the band's label in England] somewhere in the region of 35 million pounds profit, we were still in debt to them after 15 years on the label.
O: ***You must have been running up a big catering bill in the meantime.***
AP: Well, we had a very corrupt manager to start with, but I'm not supposed to talk about that because he made me sign a very uncorrupt manager's gagging clause. The sort of gagging clause that really nice people who don't have anything to hide make you sign. We had a very corrupt manager who kept taking money and putting us continually in the hole. We didn't know. He was setting himself up nicely. And, of course, we got shot of him and inherited this debt. And, as I said, they were doing fine out of us, and we were still in the red. I mean, things were getting really bad just before we did *Nonsuch*. Dave [Gregory, guitar] and Colin [Moulding, bass] were collecting Hertz rental cars, you know, for money. One of the best things we've ever put out as a single, "Wrapped In Grey," they withdrew after something like 3,000 copies. They got cold feet and said, "Oh, no, this isn't a single." And that murdered it. That really incensed me, because not only were they not promoting us, but they

weren't paying us, and they were actively stopping our records from getting played on the radio. That was it. I said, "Look, let us out of this deal, oh great Satan." And they wouldn't. So the only thing we could do was withhold the one thing we had, which was our songs, our musical services. So, from '92 until the end of last year [1996], we weren't able to record, because if we had, they would have owned it. So we've been storing up material. They finally

"I blew my eardrum out. Which was, I tell you, short of pushing a thermometer down the hole in your penis and gently bending until it snaps, the most painful thing I can imagine."

let us out at the end of last year, and we've been talking legitimately to other record companies since then, and it looks like we're very, very close to signing a sensible record deal. But, in the meantime, we've stored up one hell of a lot of songs. The last four years have been unbelievably difficult for me. Just a quick scrape of the violin: I got divorced... [singing] "I woke up one morning, found myself divorced." That was kind of traumatic, because I wasn't really expecting it. I had an ear infection and went deaf for about three months. I blew my eardrum out. Which was, I tell you, short of pushing a thermometer down the hole in your penis and gently bending until it snaps, the most painful thing I can imagine. It was, like, 2 o'clock in the morning, banging my head on the wall saying, "For Chrissake, call the doctor, something's wrong in my head." And then I felt all this wet on my neck, and it was blood pouring out my ear, 'cause my eardrum had broke. I was deaf after that for a while. So, things have been really kind of odd for me, what with, fuck me, my prostate... I decided to grow a prostate. I never even knew what one was. I think I drank mine to death. It decided it was going to do the old-man thing and enlarge itself. Which means you're up all night pissing. Because I used to drink quite heavily, and now I hardly drink anything.

O: ***So the next XTC album is going to be full of lyrics about deafness, divorce, and enlarged prostates?***

AP: Oh, God, no! I don't want to do one of those Phil Collins–type records—you know the kind of things, *Songs For Swinging Divorcées*, that sort of stuff. I've been really careful to watch the divorce, so there's no mention of divorce. There's just one bitter song called "Your Dictionary," which I feel very tricky about doing, but everyone says, "Fuck me, that's so strong. You should do that." It kind of "poetically weaves a fine web of innuendo." And, at the end of the song, it says, "Let our marriage be undone." And that's about it. That's really the depths of my revenge, I suppose.

O: ***When the next XTC album does come out, are we going to see something like Prince's last album, where it's three albums in one?***

AP: Yeah, we're releasing a 19-album box set and changing our names to The Artists Formerly Known As Having A Quality-Control Button. His is busted, I think. Certainly his quantity-control button is busted. No, I think there are four albums' worth of stuff that we've written. I mean, that isn't a lot over the four years that I've been writing. Four albums worth of stuff is going to be pruned down to two good albums. I really think there are two good albums there. And, you know, I could say that evil word that all record companies run from: double.

O: ***Which of your songs do you wish would have been a bigger hit?***

AP: That's a tough question, because I'm not especially ultra-proud of our singles. I think our best stuff, the chewier stuff, is usually left on the album. The entire singles industry seems to be geared down to immediacy and lower IQ rather than geared up to people making some effort to listen to music and chew it. Most of the singles market seems to be... They like the pre-chewed kind of nursing-home food. There's nothing wrong with catchy music: One of my favorite musical forms is instantaneous, disposable music, I suppose, but instantaneous in that you hear it two or three times and then want to bin it. I think our best stuff is inevitably stuff with bones in it that takes wrestling with.

O: ***Looking back over your career, is there any song you wish hadn't seen the surface?***

AP: Oh, Jesus, yeah. Virtually the entire first two albums, *White Music* and *Go 2*. But, you know, they have their appeal. But if you were me, and you're trapped inside those songs, and they're your spotty, kind of masturbatory youth, it's kind of tough that they're out there on display still. Imagine someone had a picture of you with a really bad haircut and wearing really bad flared polyester trousers, and you've got your dick out and you're covered in spots and this was like, you know, one of the most—how shall I say?—vulnerable moments in your life, and suddenly they've blown it up, and there it is on permanent display in Times Square... You know, I mean, how would you feel? Maybe at the time you might think, "Yeah! That's me!" But then, 20 years later, you think, "Jesus, it's still there." I still see that record in shops and I think, "That's a different person that made that record." But, you know, it's got a kind of naïve charm.

O: ***It seems like you're one of the few bands from the big class of '77 that's still actively around.***

AP: Yeah. Are there any other bands still around from then?

O: ***The Buzzcocks still surface, right?***

AP: Yeah, but they're kind of sad now, because they're doing the chicken-in-a-basket circuit, the cabaret, you know? "Here we have from Manchester, Port Cabaret! Settle down, ladies and gentlemen, we got The National Buzzcocks, and they might say a few rude words in between songs, but they promise to turn it down so you can hear the bingo." It's all kind of a bit sad. They're just going around playing old shit, and I wouldn't want to do that.

O: ***On the other, far end of the spectrum, you have The Sex Pistols.***

AP: Yeah... Actually, there was a strange paradox to them re-forming and people going to see them. The paradox is that you knew they were crap in the first place and you bought the records, and then when they split up and said, "Yeah, we fooled you," you said, "Oh, okay, I've been had." And then they re-form, and people go and see them again! Talk about a dog returning to his own vomit! I mean, there's a great kind of paradox in that, of all bands, it should have been them that re-formed. It's kind of perfect.

O: ***Do you find it bothersome that you're still best known for "Dear God," 10 or 11 years later?***

"We've been on strike. Because we had the shittiest record deal on planet Earth. You hear about those old blues artists who sign away their estate for five dollars and a bottle of beer... Hey, I'm still waiting for that bottle of beer!"

AP: Yeah, that's a tough one. I don't think it's one of the best things I've ever written. It's a very clumsy way of saying something enormous. I wasn't that keen on it: I feel that I failed to capture the subject in three and a half minutes, or whatever it is. It's such a vast subject! I mean, how the hell do you do that? It's like saying, "Human Belief: You've got three and a half minutes. Go." You're not going to get a fraction of it out, are you? So, yeah, it kind of worries me, 'cause I think we've got much better material than "Dear God," and it's a combination of human laziness and the fact that we haven't had the exposure, so people don't get to hear the other things we've done.

O: ***Are you troubled by the lack of recognition?***

AP: I was terribly to start with. It was like, "Ah, Jesus, I'm in a band that looks like it's not going to get above cult status." And now it doesn't worry me. I've spent a long time learning to be selfish about my music, but it's good for me. It's good for your art for you to be selfish about it, for you to just please yourself totally and not give a damn what anyone else thinks. It doesn't worry me that we're not accepted; it's more important that we just get to make this music. And if some people like it, fine. If they don't, I suppose I'll just have to go and get a proper job.

"I don't want to do one of those Phil Collins–type records—you know the kind of things, *Songs For Swinging Divorcées*, that sort of stuff. I've been really careful to watch the divorce, so there's no mention of divorce."

O: ***Do you think the next album will change things?***

AP: I always think the next album's gonna change things, but then again, I always think that each album we make will be our last, and I've treated every album that way, from *White Music* onwards. We finished *White Music* and the mixing was finished and it was all sequenced up, and I thought, "Well, that's it then. That's about what you get," after literally 10 years of buildup, wanting to make an album and be in a band and get a recording contract. I used to fantasize about being in a band when I was a schoolkid. I used to write essays about being in a group. I used to illustrate them with pictures. You know, I'd be 14 years old and I'd project ahead and draw me onstage there with a guitar, or draw me in the recording studio. And I'd write these elaborate fantasies about what I thought I was going to do when I grew up. Um... What were we talking about? I suddenly came over this funny little wash of nostalgia about me stuck there over exercise books in school, drawing. But with each one, you build up to making an album, and you have to mentally treat it like it's the last thing you're gonna do. If not, you're not going to put your best work into it, and you'd just be coasting. I treat each one like it's the end and we're not going to make any more after that. And that helps me to put intense—and I don't know how you're going to spell this—to put intense [grunts loudly] into each one.

O: ***Are you a little bit nervous about putting out a greatest-hits album?***

AP: Yeah, they wanted to call it *Greatest Hits* and I said no, because they're not greatest hits. You know, there's a selection of things that were popular on the radio; there's a few things that people bought. There's things on there that nobody will know what the fuck they are. Instead, I came up with the idea of doing it like a sort of box of chocolates or something. 'Cause I had this incredibly tacky picture of this serene-looking lamb, and I thought, "That is such a beautiful picture! We've gotta use it somewhere." And it was an excuse to do the chocolate-box kind of thing, using that chocolate-box lamb. But I said, "You mustn't call it *Greatest Hits*, because that's wrong."

O: ***And it's often a band's tombstone, when you put out a greatest-hits album and call it one.***

AP: Yeah, I just see that, and *Fossil Fuel*, as being part one of the career. You know, now there will be a short intermission and you can run out and have a piss and get some popcorn. Or piss in somebody else's popcorn if you want to make the second half really interesting. And then the second half of the film or play gets going.

O: ***So the best-case scenario for you at the moment is...***
AP: The best-case scenario is suddenly someone walks in the door and gives me a couple of dozen ingots. That'd be great. But, go on...

O: ***You record the album, and then what happens?***
AP: And then suddenly everyone in the world says, "Oh, Christ, we were wrong about them! They were marvelous all along." Ø

Aimee Mann

By Joshua Klein

Originally Printed November 2000

"I would have to sell a million records on a major label to break even. Literally. They're all fucking criminals."

As the voice (and oversized hair) behind 'Til Tuesday's inescapable 1985 hit "Voices Carry," Aimee Mann was lumped in with that year's crop of late-new-wave one-hitters. The Boston band couldn't catch a break from an industry and a listening public that had moved on to newer things, and it dissolved in 1989. Label difficulties stalled Mann's solo debut until 1993, when Imago released Whatever, *an album that began Mann's long and fruitful collaboration with producer Jon Brion, but failed to end her business problems. Unable to release her follow-up album until she severed her ties with the bankrupt label, Mann remained in limbo until Geffen released* I'm With Stupid *in 1996. Disaster struck again when Interscope (which acquired Geffen in a merger) demanded that Mann make changes to her third solo record,* Bachelor #2, *then reluctantly released her from her contract, finally forcing her to buy back the album's master tapes. But Mann's fortunes changed with the release of Paul Thomas Anderson's 1999 film* Magnolia, *which prominently featured her songs and earned her an Oscar nomination. In the wake of the positive press generated by* Magnolia, *Mann secured an independent release for* Bachelor #2 *in 2000 and spoke to* The Onion A.V. Club *about the problems with radio and major music labels, and about trying to get along without them.*

The Onion: *Now that all that record-company trouble is behind you, and you seem to be doing pretty well, do you think it was worth it to get where you are now?*
Aimee Mann: That's kind of hard to say. The last record-company trouble maybe was worth it, but there have been three separate incidents that have just... I think that's why I had come to the end of my rope so thoroughly. When I was at Epic, it was like, "We really like what you're doing, and we're not going to release you from your contract unless you completely change the kind of person you are and deny your personality." I was kept there without being able to release a record for three years. With that kind of thing, you sort of feel like... I can't really make a statement like, "It was worth it," because it goes over a 15-year period. I think that when you get so soured on something, it's hard to work your way back to feeling optimistic and positive about it again. There was a point where I just felt so wretched about everything—and this was even before the merger; this was when I was at Geffen—I

felt that even the fact that I cared about music had brought me trouble, and that the best thing to do was possibly just to stop caring altogether. Which is a pretty hard position to work your way back from. It was difficult. You harden into a cranky old kook.

O: ***Did the Internet-only system work out for* Bachelor No. 2*?***

AM: I think it made for a really good beginning. I mean, I don't think I could have made a living off of it, but it helped to springboard me. We sold 25,000 records just from mail order off the Internet. That's a lot of records, and it helped get us a distribution deal. It's pretty difficult to do anything that doesn't involve regular retail stores. And making enough money to finance your record and finance the operation... It's a pretty expensive little hobby.

O: ***It was an interesting experiment, but I bet it was corrupted by* Magnolia.**

AM: Oh, *Magnolia* was the plow that got the

"I've never made money selling records. Never. It doesn't happen."

three feet of snow off the ground, and then I came along with the broom. So that helped enormously. That was not only a major label working that record, but a major studio, so they really put some muscle into it. Obviously, that introduced me to an audience, helped market me to an audience, and I could never have done that on my own.

O: ***When you noticed that your songs on the soundtrack and in the movie itself were starting to resonate with people, were you worried that that might overshadow your own album?***

AM: Nah. I didn't really think about that. If it did, whatever. The movie was a really powerful experience, and if people are like, "We're not having the same experience now that we're not watching Tom Cruise crying," that's just the way it goes.

O: ***Since your new album is on your own independent label, was it tough to get it into stores?***

AM: You have to have a distributor to get into stores. I've heard from friends of mine that Tower Records, HMV, and Virgin actually have displays. The albums are sort of displayed up front with the new artists. I mean, I'm sure we're paying, but I'm also sure we're not paying that much. But that's the kind of thing you pay for: visual space in the store. People keep telling me, "Yeah, I walked in and saw a big display with your record," which is amazing. I expected that it would be a situation where you go to the record store, hunt around, and find one in the bin if you were lucky.

O: ***Do you ever wonder, "Where were you 10 years ago?"***

AM: Well, the stores take their cues from the distributors, and the distributors take their cues from the record companies. We have an independent distributor, and we've sold over 100,000 records. That's a big seller for a independent record.

O: ***It's big compared to most major sales, as well.***

AM: I think that for Interscope Records, if you're not shipping a million records, they're not even interested in hearing about it. They don't care about it, so you get lost in the shuffle.

O: ***How about radio?***

AM: [Sighs.] Radio is another thing that's bought and paid for. The payola burden shifted to the artists so the record labels would be ostensibly uninvolved. They would appear to have their hands clean. This is how my manager describes it: You have a radio station, and maybe artist number one and their label are doing this thing where they're in town and they give away tickets to a show, and they have a contest for those tickets. And then maybe artist two has a thing where they have a contest and then fly the winners to Hawaii for a show. And then artist number three, like Sting or Limp Bizkit, will give you a car. You know, we can give away tickets to a show, but we can't really compete with that. And that's the kind of thing that gets you on the radio. You have to agree to do deals like that. The most we could ever do is give away tickets to a show, and if we're not touring constantly, even that goes away. So you not only pay independent promoters to get your music on the radio, but you're also expected to be involved with each radio station in this way. It's just too much. Too difficult.

O: ***One advantage you have over the competition is that you're a good songwriter.***

AM: But nobody cares about that. I don't think radio stations care about content. I think there are isolated DJs or programmers to whom your music might mean something, but it's very few. They're all run by consultants, and they're all going for the 18-to-34 male demographic, so the consultants tell them what to play. In certain formats, I can pay to get my record played, but it kind of requires the aforementioned involvement that I can't necessarily do. I can't tour constantly, because it's too exhausting. So your hands are tied, and if it's me versus some other band that has lots of funding and can pay for the contest-winner trip-to-Hawaii giveaway thing, they're not going to play my record. They're going to play the other guy's.

O: ***There's always been crap on the radio, but it's pretty dire now.***

AM: I don't know. It seems that once upon a time, there was programming that reflected what people wanted to hear, or new music that DJs thought was really good or interesting. There was a place for that. It doesn't seem like there's a place for that now.

O: ***Do you think people are receptive to good music these days?***

AM: Yeah, but people who are in the position of second-guessing what the people want are the problem. That's the problem with record companies, too. You know, there are all these great bands that don't get supported at their record company because the people in charge have decided that the people would not come out in droves to buy them. It used to be, if you could sell 250,000 records, they would come out with guns blazing. But an assessment of 250,000 records, they don't even get out of bed for that now. It's got to be a million records, at least. It's really come down to that.

O: ***Since the vast majority of artists will never sell a million records ever, total, why do you think so many bands still deal with the majors when there are so many alternatives?***

AM: I don't think they know. I really don't think they know the reality of it. And also, if they're getting courted... If you're a young band and you've played a couple of shows and there's a big buzz about you, and somebody from Interscope is assiduously pursuing you, you're going to think, "They think I'm great, so of course they're going to promote it and make a big deal out of it." But in reality, from the record company's point of view, Mr. Big says, "There's a band out there getting a lot of buzz, and I want that band!" So the A&R guy goes out, comes up with a million-dollar deal, and signs the band in order to ensure that they get the band and no one else does. But once they've got the band, their job is done. It's over. Half of it is just like a competition with other labels to get the hot band. It's like competing for a girl you have no intention of marrying. You get the girl, and then, what, you're going to get married and have children? No, that wasn't your intention. You just wanted to get the girl from the other guy! At least these bands get a lot of money up front. The take-the-money-and-run aspect is helpful.

O: ***Unless they spend it all too fast and end up in debt to the record company.***

"It seems that once upon a time, there was programming that reflected what people wanted to hear, or new music that DJs thought was really good or interesting."

AM: They're always in debt to the record company. I've made record companies money, but I'm still technically in debt, because the way you pay back your debt is through your tiny little chunk of the percentage.

O: ***Steve Earle claims he never got a royalty check until he recorded his first indie album a couple of years ago.***

AM: Oh, I've never made money selling records. Never. It doesn't happen. I would have to sell a million records on a major label to break even. Literally. They're all fucking criminals.

O: ***What were you thinking when they were courting you?***

AM: I didn't really get courted that much. When 'Til Tuesday got signed to Epic Records, I didn't sense an enormous amount of excitement. Actually, they told me I couldn't sing.

"It used to be, if you could sell 250,000 records, they would come out with guns blazing. But an assessment of 250,000 records, they don't even get out of bed for that now."

O: ***That must have been encouraging.***

AM: Yeah. "Go take singing lessons." Our deal was fucking tiny. That was nothing. You couldn't even make a record on what our advance was.

O: ***Did they pay for the hairspray?***

AM: [Laughs.] Well, we were on the road, and from whatever we made on the road we were paid a salary, and we made $150 each a week. That's what we got. Our advance was $140,000, which is a very, very tiny amount to make a record on. There's no money left over. We never made money selling that record. It's pathetic.

O: ***On an indie, the opportunities for massive wealth are probably minimized.***

AM: The majors have a system in place, but on the indie route, you pay for everything. I pay for the publicists, I pay for the lawyers, I pay the independent promotion guys to get it on the radio, I pay the photographers to do publicity photos. Though in my case, a lot of people have donated time and services. Photographers just let me use pictures they have taken, and so on. People have been extremely nice. And it's totally worth it, because at least I can make decisions about what to spend money on. My decision was really easy, because I was not a favored player at Geffen. I was not a priority, so I wasn't giving up two videos that cost a million dollars each for each album. I didn't make videos. They weren't about to do that kind of thing. They put ads in magazines. They may have paid some indies to get some airplay, and you get tour support, which is helpful. We can't really pay our musicians what they usually get. But the upside is, in lieu of getting this big record-company support, you can come up with alternative ways to market your record. I mean, maybe they're small-scale, maybe they're little, but they're your ideas, and you can decide whether to implement them. When I was at Geffen, or Imago, or Epic, if you had an alternate idea, they were like, "We don't do that, that's not what we do." They just don't do it. "Well, it won't cost you anything, and people might..." "Nope, we've never heard of that and we're not going to do it." It's very difficult to get anything happening, and you couldn't really do it yourself.

O: ***What was your Oscar experience like?***

AM: Well, I had the whole Phil Collins thing. Did you hear about that? I was playing a show in New York with Michael Penn. It was part of the Acoustic Vaudeville tour, and we had a comedian come with us to do our banter. So it was that show, and at some point somebody yells out, "What's your Oscar speech going to be?" And I said, "Here's my Oscar speech: 'Phil Collins sucks.' How about that?" It was just a gag. And then I said,

"Wouldn't it be funny if he wins and I boo him?" I thought it would be so funny, not that anyone would do it, but I'm always waiting for someone to be a sore loser. That would be so hilarious. Anyway, some jackass from *Newsweek* takes that quote—"I'm going to be the first person to boo one of the winners; when [Phil Collins] wins, I'm going to boo him"—totally minus the sarcasm and irony, and reports it as straight reportage. Like I'm announcing that I'm going to boo this guy and that he sucks. Of course, it was like, "Well, that sucks, because I'm not a Phil Collins fan, but he does what he does and I don't want him to think that I think he's some kind of asshole. How creepy is that?" So I sent him a fax that said I was just joking, and that *Newsweek* is a bunch of morons. I ran into him backstage, and he was really nice. They had a little meeting, him and his people, and decided I was joking.

O: ***So the possibility of you two working together in the future is not completely ruled out?***

AM: Well, there was a big project pending, and I guess I just have to write it off. Ø

Lloyd Kaufman

By Keith Phipps
Originally Printed August 1997

"The battlefield is littered with the bodies of dead independent movie companies. Troma is just about the only independent movie studio remaining."

For more than 25 years, Lloyd Kaufman and partner Michael Herz have headed Troma Entertainment Inc., a low-budget movie studio responsible for producing and distributing such video and late-night-TV favorites as Class Of Nuke 'Em High *(1986),* Chopper Chicks In Zombietown *(1991),* Teenage Cat Girls In Heat *(1997), and* The Toxic Avenger *(1983) and its sequels. Over the years, the studio's satirical vision of the world—which includes scantily clad women, dismemberment, and vomit of many colors—has developed a cult following. Troma's more recent output, including the Shakespeare send-up* Tromeo & Juliet *(directed by Kaufman) and* Sgt. Kabukiman, N.Y.P.D. *(directed by Kaufman and Herz), has netted the company the greatest attention and best reviews in its history. Shortly before publishing his 1997 memoir,* All I Need To Know About Filmmaking I Learned From The Toxic Avenger, *Kaufman spoke to* The Onion A.V. Club *about his craft, his influence, and the importance of being independent.*

The Onion: ***How are things in New York?***
Lloyd Kaufman: In Tromaville, the sun shines. Unfortunately, it's a global-warming type of sun, and it's toxic. The UV count is very high. There are mutants being created.
O: ***How does your slogan, "Movies Of The Future," apply to the movies that come out of Tromaville?***
LK: Well, you may have noticed that the battlefield is littered with the bodies of dead independent movie companies. Troma is just about the only independent movie studio remaining, unless you buy the brainwashing propaganda put out by your government and the industry that companies like Miramax and New Line are independents. If you buy that, then I say you have a major problem. Troma has to be ahead of its time: Otherwise, like the other independent companies that have been gobbled up, crushed, intimidated, or blacklisted, the public would not embrace our movies. One of the few reasons Troma is still in business is because we are ahead of the game. Our movies opened the doors for other filmmakers. If you talk to Quentin Tarantino or Peter Jackson or Shinya Tsukamoto or Kevin Smith, they will tell you that they appreciated what Troma did with movies like *The Toxic Avenger* or *Class Of Nuke 'Em High*, and that we wedged the door open a little bit so they could use elements that we had pioneered to create world-class masterpieces.

O: ***You mean in terms of the content of the movies?***
LK: Content, subject... Yes, by all means. *The Toxic Avenger* is a perfect example. Here's a movie that is environmentally involved before the environment became the puppy-dog of the media.
O: ***And one example of Troma inserting not-so-subtle left-wing messages into its movies.***
LK: Well, we have always had the message. Every movie that I've written or directed basically takes the premise that there is a conspiracy of the labor, bureaucratic, and corporate elite, and that this conspiracy of elites is sucking dry the little people of Tromaville—sucking them of their financial and spiritual capital. And that is indeed the fact; that is the way the United States of America has evolved in my lifetime. And it is now happening on the last democratic medium, namely, the Internet.

"I've been directing movies since the early '70s. I've got twenty-some-odd movies. Not that I'm a talented director. I'm probably a footnote in history, but I'm a footnote that's influenced."

O: ***Yeah, I checked out your web site the other day, and it seemed to have very firm views about censorship on the Internet. Do you feel as if that censorship has at least been postponed lately?***
LK: I hope I don't sound like a pompous ass, and I apologize if I do, but it's so clear to me that Clinton and his elitist group are out... They've got millions of dollars from the Seagrams... The Hollywood elite has given Spielberg huge amounts of money. Why? There is a deal of some sort. And one of the deals, I think, is that they're going to put up tollbooths on the Internet. They're going to make it so people like you or me will not be able to get on. Or that, when we are on, the public won't be able to find us because Microsoft or Disney... No matter how you punch in, you're always going to get to a Microsoft web site or a Disney web site. Even if you want to get to the Troma web site, you won't be able to find it. It's the same way that Viacom owns Blockbuster, and they blacklist Troma, and Sony owns movie chains. Thanks to Reagan, the consent decree that Truman had prohibiting movie companies from owning movie theaters was done away with—so now you can have a liquor company owning not only Universal Studios, but cinemas, television networks, newspapers, and cable systems. And where they don't own them, they own them in partnership with other companies. They control everything, and they're gonna screw up the Internet. A little more than 10 years ago, video was actually a somewhat democratic medium. Now, it is totally owned and operated by the major studios.
O: ***It seems like the great days of straight-to-video releases has passed, except for a few cases like Troma.***
LK: You're absolutely right. The stuff that's coming out straight-to-video is $8 million movies made by Fox...
O: ***...starring Eric Roberts.***
LK: Yeah, exactly! So, meanwhile, *Tromeo & Juliet* came out last month with 10,000 rental video tapes. This is a movie that ran nine months in L.A., it's gotten great reviews from literally every major critic, and Blockbuster doesn't carry it.
O: ***How long has Blockbuster refused to carry Troma films?***
LK: Always.
O: ***Is it a question of content?***
LK: No, it's basically blacklisting.
O: ***That sounds a little bit conspiracy-minded.***
LK: I'd say it is. I mean, they've killed off... Who's left? There are no independent companies left. *Variety* is basically the house organ of the majors. The MPAA ratings board disemboweled any independent movie that came

along in the '70s and '80s. And in those days, you couldn't get into movie theaters unless you had an "R" rating. Movie chains would not play unrated movies. So, in order to get an "R" rating, they would totally disembowel your movie. But they would permit movies like *Die Hard* to get an "R" rating with kneecaps getting knocked off. They would permit heart-plucking scenes in *Indiana Jones And The Temple Of Doom* and give it a PG. Every once in a while, they would have a little problem where the public would get pissed off, so they'd create a new rating. To service Spielberg or somebody, they'd create a "PG-13" because *Gremlins* or *Jaws*, one of those movies, had a problem. I can't remember which one. So they'd create a new thing. More recently, Disney's subsidiary had a problem with a movie, so they created the "NC-17" category to give it some legitimacy—so it wouldn't have to carry an "X." The MPAA has been very instrumental in killing off independents.

O: ***Would you say it's a combination of a puritanical sensibility and a desire to get rid of independents?***

LK: I would say it is solely a desire to get rid of the independents. In my opinion, it is purely a movement toward a cartel system and an elitist system. The V-chip, again, has nothing to do with protecting children. It will be a double standard. Movies from abroad, or Troma movies, what have you, will get V-chipped so they will have to play at two in the morning, get no sponsorship, and therefore get no revenue. But the Schwarzenegger movies and the heart-plucking movies, they'll go on in prime time.

O: ***But you've been getting more attention lately than you have in a while, for* Tromeo & Juliet *and* Sgt. Kabukiman, N.Y.P.D.**

LK: Yeah, that's true. You know, it's possible that the pendulum is swinging back a little bit. We have a web site—somehow people are still finding our web site—and we get hundreds of thousands of people visiting it. It's conceivable that people are fed up with these $50 million movies that are like baby food. There may well be a growing dissatisfaction with this smugness and this worship of jewelry and women smoking cigars and all this disgusting celebrity-worship. The pendulum has to swing back to some extent. The public is much smarter than the media and the big boys think it is. The problem is that you can brainwash it. Look what Mao did. He never spent 50 million bucks. You know, they put up those big posters and allegedly brainwashed an entire country. Think of what Warner Bros. does with one *Batman* movie.

O: Sgt. Kabukiman, N.Y.P.D. ***was reviewed on*** **Siskel & Ebert,** ***which hadn't happened for a Troma production in some time.***

LK: Well, let me tell you something else, speaking of *Siskel & Ebert*. I'm upset that they ignored *Tromeo & Juliet*, because I've been directing movies since the early '70s. I've got twenty-some-odd movies. Not that I'm a talented director. I'm probably a footnote in history, but I'm a footnote that's influenced, and they're perfectly willing to say I've been an influence on major directors of the next generation. It would be interesting to call Joel Siegel at ABC—he has a policy where he doesn't review Troma movies, and the same with Gene Shalit. Even though we distributed a movie called *My Neighbor Totoro*, which is an

"Preston Sturges' satirical depiction of small-town America led me to create Tromaville, this little town that appears in many of our movies. And the characters in Tromaville are influenced by the mugs in Preston Sturges' movies. The only difference is that his mugs could act."

animated film by the world's greatest animator, Hayao Miyazaki—he is better than Disney, a major, major talent, and this is a G-rated movie—they refused to review it because it's a Troma movie.

O: ***Are you comfortable calling the movies you made in the '70s exploitation movies?***

LK: Everything is exploitation movies. Everything we've ever done. Again, it's a bit of an unfair practice that *Face/Off* is not an exploitation movie but *Tromeo & Juliet* is. That's what the bigger movies are all about. Exploiting Batman, exploiting special effects, whatever. We happen to exploit sex and violence.

O: ***Do you see yourself carrying on the great exploitation tradition of AIP and Roger Corman?***

LK: Well, Corman is a major influence on me, without a doubt. We're very close friends, and he loves the fact that we have taken the straight genres that he has pioneered and put them all in a Cuisinart. Our movies combine all the genres. Rather than have a straight horror or science-fiction or sex movie, we put everything in one movie. In 1986, when he was interviewed about Troma, that's what he stated. And that's the first time I was aware of what we were doing.

"Oliver Stone started with us. He acted in *The Battle Of Love's Return*, which was one of my first feature-length movies, and I think it's going to come out this summer on video. It's never been out on video. It stinks."

O: ***Your movies have been called parodies of B-movies. Would you agree with that?***

LK: I don't think that's their intention. I think there are numerous literary allusions in all of our movies, parodies not just of B-movies. From the start, we had this notion of creating a Troma universe. Preston Sturges' satirical depiction of small-town America led me to create Tromaville, this little town that appears in many of our movies. And the characters in Tromaville are influenced by the mugs in Preston Sturges' movies. The only difference is that his mugs could act.

O: ***It seems the difference between your movies and Roger Corman's is that yours are self-consciously humorous in a way most of his weren't.***

LK: Yes, and his are more commercial. Comedy is not commercial; it is risky, because what is funny in one place isn't always funny somewhere else. With comedy you take a big risk, and that limits our viability and our audience, because we insist on making movies that are supposed to be funny.

O: ***But dismemberment, bare breasts, and puking are pretty universal, wouldn't you say?***

LK: Well, not necessarily, because Germany, for example, has major censorship. They will not permit the kind of violence that we do, so it's not necessarily universal. There are parts of the world, India for example, where they don't get the humor. We have major followings in most of the world, but there are parts of the world where they simply don't get our humor. I think my masterpiece is *Troma's War*, and most of the international territories just didn't get it. They thought it was going to be a straight action film. Instead, they got this movie that has... It's a war picture, but it's got Siamese twins joined at the head, it's got comedy and slapstick, it's got sex. I think it's the best film, certainly among the best films, we've ever done. But a lot of people just did not get it. Or, if they did get it, they didn't like it. [Laughs.]

O: ***Has that made you shy away from riskier ventures?***

LK: No, the only thing we've done is drop our budgets a bit. The budget of *Tromeo & Juliet* was $500,000, which is incredible. That is less than the original *Toxic Avenger* made in 1983. So we can take more chances.

O: *Speaking of* Toxic Avenger, *do you still see that as a turning point in Troma's history?*

LK: Well, it certainly gave us a much wider audience. That movie, for whatever reason, appealed to an enormous audience, and I think we ended with 300 or 400 35mm prints. It led to sequels, it led to a cartoon show, and there were a hundred companies that made Toxic Crusader toys and merchandise. There's some kind of magic that Toxie's got, and that has certainly helped give us a broader audience. Troma has emerged as kind of a brand name, and every so often, big companies want to buy us or merge with us or acquire us or do something, and part of the reason is that we've got a brand-name perception. People will rent a Troma movie. We estimate that there may be 2,000 video stores around the country that have Troma sections.

O: *Individual sections dedicated to Troma films?*

LK: Yeah. One of the big newspapers did an in-depth article about five years ago where the point was that Troma... They would question people, and the only studio that people had an awareness of as a brand—other than Disney—was Troma. But the biggest problem is getting the product to the fans. We have a movie called *Cannibal: The Musical*. It's been out on video for months, but we could not get it into any of the giant chains, and it's a wonderful film. The film is terrific. And, again, I had nothing to do with it: The guys who made it are major Troma fans, and they obviously were influenced by Troma, but these guys are major talents. These are going to be world-class moviemakers. The director, Trey Parker, has already been hired by Comedy Central. They've just finished a series of cartoons called *South Park*. And Trey Parker's got a major movie that he's going to be doing for Paramount, based on *Cannibal: The Musical*, the movie we helped him with. Yet Blockbuster wouldn't take it, one or two other chains wouldn't take it, and it's very hard to find. And I know damn well that if Miramax had *Cannibal: The Musical*, it'd be in every store.

O: *Parker aside, it seems that, unlike Roger Corman, you haven't really produced a lot of people who have gone on to more high-profile things. Do you think there's a reason for that?*

LK: Well, if you look, we have 150 movies. I didn't direct them, but we have the first two Kevin Costner movies. We did turn down Madonna.

O: *When was that?*

LK: With *The First Turn On*, we turned down Madonna. She was begging, begging to be in the movie. Absolutely. She created a little costume. *The First Turn On* is about camping, and my partner just didn't feel she was right for the part. Then, about six months later, while our movie was underwhelming critics and audiences alike, Madonna was a shooting star, a giant supernova. [Laughs.] And I've never let my partner forget that. But Vincent D'Onofrio, he was in that movie. Marisa Tomei, Oliver Stone started with us.

"Steve Tisch, who produced that shit movie with the chocolates that I hated, *Forrest Gump*, he was a production assistant for us. There are a fair number of future stars in our movies."

O: *What was Marisa Tomei in?*

LK: She's in *The Toxic Avenger*. She's just an extra. Oliver Stone started with us. He acted in *The Battle Of Love's Return*, which was one of my first feature-length movies, and I think it's going to come out this summer on video. It's never been out on video. It stinks.

O: *What's it about?*

LK: It stars me, and it's an identity type of... It's part color, which is fiction, and part black-and-white, where the characters are interviewed.

Steve Tisch, who produced that shit movie with the chocolates that I hated, *Forrest Gump*, he was a production assistant for us. There are a fair number of future stars in our movies, but certainly nothing like Corman. Part of that is because we're in New York, and a lot of New York people don't stay in movies. They go on to theater and other things.

O: ***There's been talk of a big-budget remake of* The Toxic Avenger. *Do you feel that, by dealing with a major company, you're shaking hands with the devil?***

LK: No, because the only way we're going to do it is, they're either going to give me 100 percent control, which they won't, or they'll give us a lot of money. And if we get a lot of money, we can make more movies, and not only give me a chance to make a movie every once in a while, but also allow me to hire more Trey Parkers. There's no middle ground. Either you get a lot of money and you walk away from it, or you take control.

"The public is much smarter than the media and the big boys think it is. The problem is that you can brainwash it. Look what Mao did. He never spent 50 million bucks. You know, they put up those big posters and allegedly brainwashed an entire country. Think of what Warner Bros. does with one *Batman* movie."

O: ***What's your favorite tag line for any of your movies?***

LK: Well, we have a movie called *Macho Woman*: "Born to shop, she learned to kill." I sort of find that amusing.

O: ***What's the worst thing you've ever put out?***

LK: Well, I don't think that we've ever put out a movie that we can't stand behind; there's only one that I would have second thoughts about today. And this is a movie that we picked up, and we helped the director complete it the way he wanted to. It had sort of a false start, and we went back and re-edited it so he got his director's cut. It's a movie called *Bloodsucking Freaks*, and I do believe this movie goes too far.

O: ***In what way?***

LK: Well, it is extremely... In today's world, it's not very complimentary to women.

O: ***Which is a criticism you've been hit with several times.***

LK: Well, that's fucked-up, because our movies are right on politically. It's absurd. Anyone who's seen our movies—anyone who's seen the movies I've written and directed—can't possibly have that criticism. It's usually people who assume that, because we have some men and women in small clothing, that we are exploiting women or something. That's horseshit. *Squeeze Play*, which was a big hit for us in the late '70s: *The New York Times* understood it. Janet Maslin gave it a good review because she understood it. But the idiot in San Francisco said *Squeeze Play* was made on the garbage scow, and it abused women—totally misunderstood it.

O: ***How is* Bloodsucking Freaks *different?***

LK: It's very misogynistic. I mean, you will laugh when you see it. It's very funny, and you should see it, but it's evil. Nasty. But it has a huge following. And actually, the younger generation of women are a lot more relaxed; they don't immediately get offended when they see a woman in a bikini. They're having fun with it now. *Squeeze Play* was about the women's-liberation movement, and the public got it. It was a huge success—in fact, that's pretty much how we bought our building. It was about a women's softball team. Not to be confused with the much inferior *A League Of Their Own*, which came out 15 years later. In fact, Penny Marshall borrowed a print of

Squeeze Play when she was organizing *A League Of Their Own*. And I believe that I may have seen a bit of *Squeeze Play*'s influence in *A League Of Their Own*, but I may be arrogant in that respect. What *Squeeze Play* was all about was strong women who had enough self-confidence to understand that they could not defeat men physically, because men are bigger and stronger, but that they didn't have to stay cooped up in the house—that they could do what they wanted. We were ahead of our time. Movies of the future. Ø

Martha Plimpton

By Keith Phipps
Originally Printed March 1999

"Mainly what I do is turn down lots of crap until I get really poor. And then I start taking the crap."

One of the most consistently compelling actresses working today, Martha Plimpton hasn't followed the career path chosen by most of her contemporaries. The daughter of actors Keith Carradine and Shelley Plimpton, she first achieved fame as a member of the young cast of 1985's The Goonies. *Since then, she's alternated between high-profile roles (*Parenthood, Beautiful Girls*) and independent projects (*Eye Of God, I Shot Andy Warhol*). While conducting interviews in conjunction with the 1999 release of* 200 Cigarettes, *Plimpton spoke to* The Onion A.V. Club *about her place in the entertainment industry.*

The Onion: ***One movie of yours that I thought really got overlooked was* Eye Of God. *What happened with that?***

Martha Plimpton: Well, we couldn't get a real distribution deal. We'd gotten incredible reviews. We'd done really well at the Sundance Film Festival, though I'm not really sure if that means anything.

O: ***That's sort of a curse these days, I think.***

MP: I think in some ways it kind of is. I really don't even know what's happening at Sundance. It was supposed to be about filmmakers showing each other their work, and now it's just turned into the same old damn meat market every other festival is. I remember going there and trying to get into some party, and literally getting my face smashed into a doorjamb because of the crowds trying to get in. It was ridiculous. I think it's worth going just to see how easy it is for filmmakers who call themselves independent to get swallowed by this fucking swirling vortex of greed and status and... It's just a nightmare out there. Independent film is not only an oxymoron; it doesn't exist anymore. I think it existed for about five minutes, and it's just been swallowed by this dragon, this Hollywood machine that's trying to make its own sort of Hollywood independent films.

O: ***What goes into deciding whether you'll do a film?***

MP: Well, some people think I have a fear of success. [Laughs.] And they might be right. I've always been at a weird age. When the John Hughes thing was happening, I was too young for that. Now I'm seen as too old for a lot of these other things, these things that Claire Danes does and stuff. She's great. I like her a lot. I'm sort of out of the loop all the time. I'm either one step too early or one step too late. There's not one set of rules that I follow.

Mainly what I do is turn down lots of crap until I get really poor. And then I start taking the crap.

O: ***If you could take one of your movies back, which one wouldn't you have done?***

MP: Oh, God. There are so many of them, and I'm not sure I would say anyway.

O: ***Did any of them involve android children?***

MP: Android children?

O: ***Isn't that what* Josh And S.A.M. *is about?***

MP: Oh, right... Yeah, that's a good guess on your part, but I won't say. I'd love to be able to say, "Hey, man. I'm really proud of everything I've done, and I've learned so much." And I wouldn't be lying if I said that.

"I was reading an old issue of *The New Yorker* that did a review of this movie, and there was this great line that said these two actresses had 'high-powered but expendable careers.' And I just thought that was really astute. It sort of validated me. It made me feel that even though I have no power at all, at least I'm somewhat irreplaceable."

O: **The Goonies** ***has developed a cult following over the years. Has that affected your life in any way?***

MP: Yeah, in the sense that it's the only movie people consistently recognize me from, even today.

O: ***Even without the Cyndi Lauper haircut?***

MP: Yeah. I guess everybody has seen that movie. I feel like it's another lifetime, but I can't believe that... When it came out, it didn't do such great business. It wasn't a failure, but it certainly wasn't a hit. And it's gotten this incredible afterlife that's amazing to me.

O: ***As part of a large acting clan, do you find yourself caught up in rivalries with the Barrymore and Van Patten families?***

MP: Yeah, all the time. Constantly.

O: ***If the Carradines and the Van Pattens and the Barrymores were in a big act-off, who would win?***

MP: Well, it would probably be a draw between the Carradines and the Van Pattens. Because the Barrymores, you know, they're a little full of themselves. They kind of have this superior attitude. I don't know. I occasionally get calls, like, "Will you do a Carradine family reunion on the new *Love Boat*?" It just mystifies me, because I don't have the same last name. I did not grow up with that side of my family; in fact, I barely know them. I see my father maybe once every two years. Suddenly, now that I have a somewhat successful career, it's like we're all related and they're responsible for me. That's a bit of a stretch.

O: ***What else do you want to talk about?***

MP: I don't know. Do you want me to complain about something?

O: ***Yeah. What do you want to complain about?***

MP: Oh... Umm... I won't complain. I will say that last night I was reading an old issue of *The New Yorker* that did a review of this movie, and there was this great line that said these two actresses had "high-powered but expendable careers." And I just thought that was really astute. It sort of validated me. It made me feel that even though I have no power at all, at least I'm somewhat irreplaceable.

O: ***Do you think you have longevity on your side, then?***

MP: Absolutely.

O: ***Versus people who will burn out?***

MP: Exactly. Well, I'm not famous.

O: ***You're a little bit famous.***

MP: Well, some people know who I am. At this point, I don't get hired a lot because people don't think I could finance a movie. I sort of disagree with that. I think a lot of people out there really like my work. I'm constantly being reminded of that every time I walk down the street. But on the other hand, I've never been on the cover of any big fucking magazine or anything. I'm also not having a relationship with any famous-guy movie star, which means I'm not, like, cemented into everyone's brains. People don't really know who I'm fucking, so they can't really fantasize about me in that way.

O: ***That's probably for the best.***

MP: I think so.

Steve Albini

By Stephen Thompson

Originally Printed April 1996

"Peace of mind is worth more than a million bucks to me... I'm doing a job where the very least people can say is that they're getting their money's worth."

As a musician, Steve Albini was a creative force behind the legendary noise-rock monolith Big Black, and he's continued to record and tour as a member of Shellac, but his greatest fame stems from his prolific production work. As producer of Nirvana's In Utero, *he found himself at the center of undeserved controversy, while his work with bands like Veruca Salt and Bush placed him on the receiving end of hipster backlash. But Albini continues to work constantly on projects both big and small, always placing musicians' wishes ahead of commercial interests and producing records by hundreds of independent and unsigned artists. In 1996,* The Onion A.V. Club *spoke with the notoriously outspoken Albini about all of this and more.*

The Onion: ***How do bands like Bush contact you? Do their people call your people, or do their people call you, or...***

Steve Albini: Well, no, Bush called me. I mean, that's the way I usually do things. I try to speak directly to the people involved.

O: ***So it's not like some slick-haired industry goon calls and says, "We need Albini!"***

SA: Well, that has happened in the past, and those people are usually pretty easy to swat away. You know, somebody says, "I'm calling on behalf of this band," and you say, "Well, give the band my number. I'd be happy to talk to them."

O: ***And that usually swats them away?***

SA: Yeah.

O: ***Because I would imagine you get a certain number of industry types who are thinking, "We need some credibility. Let's send them to Albini and he'll make a rough-sounding record for us."***

SA: Well, the weird thing is that the actual industry-type people despise me, and they would never send business my way. The conventional music-industry way of doing things—that is, having somebody else's manager call my manager—is impossible because I don't have a manager. If somebody wants to talk to me about doing a record, they have to talk to me. There's nobody else. And I've been doing it that way for so long, I find it much more efficient than having to do some elaborate courtship dance with intermediaries. I don't see the advantage to buffering myself from the people who actually want to talk to me by putting someone else in between.

O: ***Why do the industry types hate you?***

SA: Well, I think the significant thing is that

I'm not part of their world. Sleazy industry people sort of like to think that they know everyone, and that they've done everything. I don't travel in those circles at all, so most of these people have never met me, never spoken to me or had any interaction with me whatsoever, whereas quite a few of the musicians that they like to feel superior to have had interactions with me. And that puts them at a disadvantage, because these people are sort of

"I don't really feel like I should be in the position of arbiter of propriety, saying, 'You have offended my sensibilities of cultural commerce, and I wash my hands of thee.' But there are people whose business entanglements are so troublesome that there's nothing that could make it worth the trouble."

expected to be more knowledgeable and more connected than the bands that they're shepherding. When a band says, "Well, we know this guy Steve, and we'd like to do a record with him," that inverts the power structure. Instead of somebody at the record label setting them up with some dream-date arrangement with a record producer, you've got the band calling the shots. That is not kosher in that world. It's as though a band told someone at their record label that they wanted to have this famous plumber work on their record. And the guy at the record company says, "A plumber? Why do you want to work with a plumber? I've got all these record producers you can work with." Whether or not the plumber can actually do the job means nothing.

O: ***You've got a reputation as one of the meanest men in rock music.***

SA: Right, and that reputation comes almost exclusively from people who have never met me and never spoken to me. So those people are welcome to hold those opinions, but they shouldn't pretend that they have any substantive basis.

O: ***So you've never actually assaulted anyone or shat on anyone or done anything horrible?***

SA: Well, shitting on somebody... We're getting into a whole different area there. [Laughs.] But, whatever, I've made a thousand or more records in my life. I've dealt with literally thousands of people. Ask those people what they think of me. The people who've never met me and don't know anything about me having an opinion about me doesn't really interest me.

O: ***What sort of criteria do you use when you're picking bands to produce? What do you say to a band that just sucks?***

SA: It completely depends on their station, on their position. If the band is an underground band that has no business interest in their career, I bend over backwards to try to make myself available to those people, just because I feel it's not really my place to establish a litmus test of coolness or greatness for every band to pass before The Great Steve Albini will deign to spend a couple of days with them. I think to behave that way would be crass. I like to make myself available to people who don't have that many other options, just because I like the idea of those people getting the chance to do something of substance early on in their careers. People with more options and more wherewithal, those people I feel have to prove themselves a bit. If there's a record label involved, that means it's going to complicate my job, because there are more people I'm going to have to deal with and likely to be more of a nuisance level in terms of the administration I'm going to have to contend with. I have to have some strong feeling about it to do something like that. And then the most restrictive scale would be the bands who have an enormous amount of clout and involvement in the industry, and I don't get approached by those people very often. When it does happen, I have to be quite careful about who I associate myself with: If their intentions seem genuine to me, and the music seems like something I would do a good job on, and if philosophically we're in harmony, then I try to make myself available for those people, but I can be much more selective about people like that without feeling guilty, because I know that they could go elsewhere if they wanted to. The business people are a pain in the ass to deal with, and if I have to contend with them, I want to make sure that it's going to be for something that's going to be worth the nuisance. But my sympathies are always with the bands, and I don't really feel like I should be punishing them. I don't really feel like I should be in the position of arbiter of propriety, saying, "You have offended my sensibilities of cultural commerce, and I wash my hands of thee." But there are people whose business entanglements are so troublesome that there's nothing that could make it worth the trouble. There are some record labels, for example, who are so fundamentally dishonest, so matter-of-fact about their sleaziness, that the experience is doubtless going to be so unpleasant that they don't print money big enough. And then there are some bands where approaching me stylistically would create more obstacles than it would remove—if it's a band whose style of music I just have no sympathy for. There's no reason for me to work on one of their records, because I wouldn't know whether I was doing a good job or not. I've been approached occasionally about doing dance-music records. I have no taste whatsoever for dance music—it means nothing to me. And for me to work on a record like that, just for a paycheck, would be crass and insincere and dishonest. I generally decline stuff like that, not because I think the people involved are evil, or because the music is horrible, but because it's an area that I'm not familiar with and that I have no expertise in. I've been approached by certain crass heavy-metal concerns and certain aggregations of has-beens who are doing sort of vanity projects at the dog-end of their career, and I'd rather spend my time with people who are dedicated and sincere about what they do.

O: ***What's the worst experience you've ever had dealing with a label or artist?***

SA: Well, by far the worst experience has to be my dealings with Nirvana, and I say my experience dealing with the label, although I had no dealings with the label. I was made uncomfortable and made to feel as though I were being an obstacle and as though I were letting people down. I was put on the spot continuously for about six months, and I was attacked in print in various underhanded ways—you know, where you have somebody like the vice president of the record label calling rock journalists and telling them off-the-record that I had ruined this album. I took a lot of shit for it, and the end result was that the band was made uncomfortable about a perfectly good record that they should have been proud of. That aside, there are little trends you tend to hear, that you tend to recognize after dealing with them for a while: things like, you'll be working on a record, and the band and the label will be pleading poverty to you, so you

"I like to make myself available to people who don't have that many other options, just because I like the idea of those people getting the chance to do something of substance early on in their careers. People with more options and more wherewithal, those people I feel have to prove themselves."

cut them as much slack as you can. And while you're working on the record, everybody seems into it and excited about it, and then months down the line when the record comes out, you realize that they've called in a bunch of remix jockeys at great expense to remix this record.

"When a band says, 'Well, we know this guy Steve, and we'd like to do a record with him,' that inverts the power structure. Instead of somebody at the record label setting them up with some dream-date arrangement with a record producer, you've got the band calling the shots. That is not kosher in that world."

You realize that this supposed poverty didn't really exist, and that it's a dreadful record with your name on it. That's happened more often than I like to remember.

O: ***Do you have a sliding scale?***

SA: With regard to how much I charge? No, I basically charge whatever the hell I feel like. It sort of works on the same principles as the triage about whose records I'm going to work on and whose I'm not. That is, people who don't have very much money at their disposal, I try to charge as little as I can possibly get away with and still cover the expenses. Whereas, people who have more money and more resources at their disposal, I try to make sure they pay something more like what it's actually worth.

O: ***Are you ever tempted to say, "Okay, Bush. One million dollars!"?***

SA: Uh, no. When it comes to bands of a larger scale, what I generally do—and I haven't really gotten burned on this too much—is I tell them to figure out how much they were expecting to pay, and then pay me that. Generally speaking, the bands see this as an opportunity to economize a little bit. And I'm fine with that, because what happens is, the bands end up spending far less money than they would under normal industry circumstances, and I feel good about giving them a bargain. I still get paid what I consider a reasonable amount of money, so it's a win-win situation. I'm not shy about telling people how much I get paid. I think it's really crass and creepy that people in the music industry like to keep the financial details under wraps to avoid embarrassing each other. I think that's crappy. It's just a cheesy way of behaving, and it perpetuates this sort of backroom boys-clubbiness of the whole thing. For example, for the PJ Harvey *Rid Of Me* album, I was paid $50,000. A conventional record producer would probably have been paid something on the order of $50–$100,000 as an advance against a royalty arrangement of, say, three percentage points of the retail sale price of the record. So every time a record sells, the producer's royalty account is credited three or four points of the price for which the record sold. So, if you assume a half a million sales on a record like that, and a mean retail price of $12, that gives you a gross of $6 million, and that [punches a calculator] comes to $180,000. So your average record producer would've gotten paid $180,000. Let's say the Nirvana album that I worked on: I got paid $100,000 for that. And let's say that your average record producer would have gotten an advance of $100,000 against a royalty of three points. Let's say it sold three million. That gives you $36 million in gross sales, so multiply that by three points, and that's $1,080,000. Your average record producer would have made $1,080,000 off that record. So you can see how much of a financial advantage it is for a band to work with somebody like me, because they only have to pay me once.

O: ***Do you ever say to yourself, "I could have had a million dollars and paid all my bills and given all my employees bonuses..."?***

SA: Yeah, I suppose, except that I wouldn't be able to get to sleep at night, and peace of mind is worth more than a million bucks to me, frankly. And for every record I do of that scale, where it pays $20,000 to $50,000, in that same year I'll probably do 30 records where I get paid between $500 and $2,000. And I'm not embarrassed by doing an album for a band and getting paid four or five hundred dollars for it. That doesn't bother me in the slightest. I feel good about that, because I'm doing a job where the very least people can say is that they're getting their money's worth. That's a rare thing in life. ⌀

George Romero

By Keith Phipps
Originally Printed August 1998

"I don't want to make another zombie film. I'd rather make a good action film involving zombies."

In 1968, Pittsburgh-based filmmaker George Romero released Night Of The Living Dead, *forever changing the face of horror movies—and arguably, the face of movies in general. Gory to a degree unseen outside of the work of Herschell Gordon Lewis,* Night *established a mood of unshakable dread and suspense. The film's sequels (1978's* Dawn Of The Dead *and 1985's* Day Of The Dead*) followed suit, brilliantly using zombies as free-floating metaphors for the social anxieties of their respective eras. Though the* Dead *trilogy remains Romero's best-known work, he's directed other compelling films, including 1978's* Martin *(a fascinating look at a vampire living in Pittsburgh during the impoverished '70s) and 1981's* Knightriders *(which updates the Arthurian myths, using motorcycles instead of horses). For the clever EC Comics homage* Creepshow *(1982), Romero returned to a major studio in the first of several uneasy partnerships, which yielded the interesting* Monkey Shines *(1989) and 1993's* The Dark Half, *starring Timothy Hutton. The years following* The Dark Half *found Romero in the midst of a dry spell, and in 1998, while trying to find a suitable cinematic project, Romero spoke to* The Onion A.V. Club.

The Onion: ***You haven't made a movie since*** **The Dark Half** ***in 1993. Would you say you're semi-retired?***

George Romero: Oh, no. I've been in development hell. I've got about four projects out there now, all with studios. They keep paying me to rewrite and do this and that. It's literally all the sad tales you hear about development. It's awful. We have a little film that we're trying to raise the money on now, which looks pretty good, and I have a project at Disney. I have two projects at Fox, one at MGM, one with a producer named Joe Wizan. They're all sort of genre things. One is a little softer, for children, a soft-horror thing called *Moonshadows*. I think somebody's going to probably make that movie. And I just got signed to do *Resident Evil*.

O: ***That's interesting, because the game seems so directly, not even subtly, inspired by your movies. How are you approaching that?***

GR: We've just had one meeting so far. I have a creative meeting in a couple of weeks. I'd like to just stick to the game and try to make a really good action film out of it. It's got to be scary, obviously, but I don't want to go crazy with it. I don't want to make another zombie film. I'd rather make a good action film involving zombies.

O: ***You've expressed discontent working with studios in the past. Was* The Dark Half *a difficult experience for you?***

GR: Only because Orion was having financial trouble. Orion was pretty good. We did *Monkey Shines* with them, and then *Dark Half*. I liked the guys, and it was a pretty comfortable place to be. I just hate this preview process. That's what happens with having to change endings and all of that shit, which really bothered me on *Monkey Shines* a lot. But we had a pretty good experience on *Dark Half*, except that they were basically out of money. We never finished the 12th reel. If you look at that film, the 12th reel wasn't even scored. The music there was lifted from other reels. That was frustrating, but that wasn't because it was a studio, per se. They were just in financial dire straits. So it was forgivable that way.

O: ***Test screenings seem to be something a lot of directors complain about, and they don't even seem to work that well. Why are they continued?***

GR: I think it's ass-covering. They're completely wrong so many times. Pictures that test great go out and go in the toilet. And pictures that test poorly, all of a sudden they'll come out of the pack and people like them, but they don't get a chance because a studio won't really get behind it if it tests poorly. It's a mess. People go to those screenings, and you don't get honest answers. You get wise-aleck answers, and you get this whole array of different personalities and people having something to say about what you should do. And so often, you have to test it before it's finished, with a temporary music score and no effects. I think it's an extremely unfair process, and I wish they would stop it. But I doubt they will.

O: ***At the same time, there's this recent resurgence of affection for or attention to the films of the early '70s, when the studios put out films that didn't go through that process and were unusual. You'd think they'd at least try.***

GR: I know, but it costs so damn much to distribute a film now. That's the problem. Nobody wants to take that risk. It's very, very frustrating. There's almost no such thing as a little movie. If you get lucky and Miramax wants to do one of your little projects, then maybe. Because those guys are great distributors, and they can really get behind a thing. But even if you make a film for two million bucks or under, in order for it to have a shot in the marketplace, somebody is going to have to risk $10 or $15 million minimum just to get it out there. It's almost harder to get a little film financed than a big film. Because they figure, "Well, all right, we'll hire stars, we'll do this, we'll do that, and we'll do whatever we can to cover our ass." It's a pretty frustrating business right now, with all of the expansion and the companies taking other companies over, and all that. It's a bigger business than it ever was, and everybody's shooting for the moon. There's almost no such thing as a middle-ground movie anymore.

O: ***A lot of your earlier movies thrived because of the midnight-movie tradition. But that seems to have died now.***

GR: I think video has killed that.

O: ***But* The Beyond *is being reissued in an attempt to revive that. Do you think there's any chance that it can be revived?***

GR: I really have no idea. I don't know what people want to do these days. It's so hard to read those tea leaves. The big tickets come from a much younger audience and a different audience base. The midnight moviegoers were, like, movie fans: people who were either into films or into particular films, and into them in either a sophisticated or a kind of quirky way. I think today's audiences, the audiences that make the big money for a studio, are out for whatever the latest event picture is, or the must-see stuff. I think it's a different crowd. Maybe with old films, small-theater owners could revive that trend and actually make money. But that wouldn't help the producers or the talent, because there's never going to be enough money there to pay anything back to anybody.

O: ***On the other hand, if you were to announce that you were doing a new zombie movie, there would be a built-in audience for it.***
GR: Well, I'm actually talking about that. I'd love to do a fourth one for the '90s and, you know, *Resident Evil* ain't it. It ain't mine. I'd like to do one. But you'd be surprised. There's very little receptiveness, because everybody says it's hard to release an unrated thing now. It's the exact same thing I ran into with the last one. But I think we'll get it financed. Probably European or Japanese financing. I've been scribbling on it already.
O: ***What would a zombie movie for the '90s be?***
GR: I think it's about ignoring the problem. [Laughs.] That seems to be what the '90s are. Living around it, you know? Enclaves where people are... They try to re-create life as normal and ignore it. Some kind of a situation like that, where humanity has reorganized, sort of like living with the plague, setting up fortresses or walled cities to separate themselves. But, of course, they can't, because people die. Another disastrous scheme on the part of the jerks. [Laughs.]
O: ***I watched* Day Of The Dead *and wondered how you got away with a lot of that stuff in 1985.***
GR: Well, again, it was unrated. The distributor was willing to put it out, but it didn't make money. That's the problem. Even then, you couldn't advertise in certain newspapers. It's very limiting to go out unrated with something. Even the European markets now, the markets that used to not worry about stuff like that, like Germany, now they're pretty concerned about it. Even on *Resident Evil*, they're very concerned about how far they can go. Because most of the European money now is off TV, and they're having a hard time now with anything that pushes the envelope.
O: **Day Of The Dead *is probably the least well-regarded of the trilogy. How do you feel about it now?***
GR: I like it a lot. I would say it is my favorite. I don't know why. There are so many factors when you think of your own films. You think of the people you worked on it with and somehow forget the movie. You can't forgive the movie for a long time. It takes a few years to look at it with any objectivity and forgive its flaws. I guess I've come around to that now, and I think it was pretty successful. I mean, I laugh like hell watching that film.
O: ***Well, there's the clown. If nothing else, the clown zombie.***
GR: Yeah, I love him. I'm probably going to have some of those guys in the new one.
O: ***It seemed like horror had been dormant for a long time, and then* Scream *comes along. But when you look at it, it's not even a horror film.***
GR: I love Wes [Craven, *Scream*'s director], and he's a good friend of mine, but I didn't like *Scream* too much. I thought *Scream 2* was better. I thought *I Know What You Did Last Summer* was better than both of them. But, you know, that's really sort of listing them in order of preference. It's just not my cup of tea. I never liked those kinds of movies, except for the original *Halloween*, which was almost an exercise—which I thought was fun and well-made and all that. I never liked the *Friday The 13th* movies or any of that. It's a genre that I guess current audiences haven't seen in a while, or haven't seen at all. I have a 14-year-old daughter, and the first one of those she ever watched, she only watched because of peer pressure. It's very hard. It didn't open any doors, because when you go out there and try to pitch something different, you know, "Well, we want another *Scream*. We want a franchise." It doesn't really indicate that horror is strong. Occasionally something pops. But the studios aren't going to credit the genre as much as they are, you know, the marketing of an individual thing, or whatever it was. They'll try to imitate it. They want something that has the same things, like young stars from TV. They think they have the formula worked out. I just think it's a fool's game. ⊘

"I tried so hard to do other kinds of movies after *Wayne's World*, but I couldn't. So I said, 'Fuck it. Let's take the money.' "

Penelope Spheeris

By Nathan Rabin

Originally Printed March 1999

Penelope Spheeris is probably best known as the director of 1992's mega-hit Wayne's World, *a smart, funny comedy that inspired a slew of* Saturday Night Live*–derived films that were neither smart nor funny. But that hit represents only one side of Spheeris' multifaceted, fascinating career, which began when she produced Albert Brooks' short films for* SNL *and his hilarious and prescient 1979 film debut,* Real Life. *Spheeris' own directorial debut was 1981's vastly influential L.A. punk documentary* The Decline Of Western Civilization, *which was followed by a string of low-budget independent films, including* Suburbia, Dudes, *and* Hollywood Vice Squad. *In 1987, Spheeris made a second much-loved* Decline *film about L.A.'s heavy-metal scene, but she spent much of the '90s directing mainstream studio comedies, including* Senseless, Black Sheep, The Beverly Hillbillies, *and* The Little Rascals. *In 1998, she returned to her roots to make* The Decline Of Western Civilization Part III, *a moving, empathetic, disarmingly funny documentary about L.A.'s largely homeless teenage "gutter punks." Shortly thereafter, Spheeris spoke to* The Onion A.V. Club *about her documentaries, her studio work, and why she made a film combining heavy metal with female mud wrestling.*

The Onion: ***How did you come to make the first* Decline Of Western Civilization *film?***

Penelope Spheeris: The first one? Oh, boy, that was a real tragic story. Did you get to see the film?

O: ***Yeah. I actually just went back and saw the first two films again.***

PS: Well, let me ask you a question. How did you see the second one?

O: ***I just rented a copy from a video store.***

PS: Who was on the front cover?

O: ***I think it was the guitarist from Megadeth.***

PS: I'm only asking because there are a bunch of bootleg copies out there.

O: ***There's not a regular distributor for the second film?***

PS: I have the rights now, but for a while there, they were all being bootlegged. I went to a swap meet a couple weeks ago, and some guy had copies of *Part II* spread out on the ground with the rest of his freaky videos, so I picked it up, and he said, "Well, if you like that one, maybe you'll like this one, as well." So he brought out the first *Decline*, which he obviously didn't have the right to distribute, either. So I grabbed four other videos that I wanted for my own personal collection and I left. And he goes, "Wait a minute, you forgot to pay me." And I said, "No, you forgot to pay me." Anyway, what was your question?

O: ***Oh, I was just asking how you came to make the first* Decline Of Western Civilization *film.***

PS: Okay. Way back then, I had a company called Rock And Reel, which was the only film company in Los Angeles making music videos. And I was totally disgusted with popular music at that point, because it was all, like, disco. When I first saw all these punk bands starting up, I said, "I have to document all this." So I just went for it. I was involved at

"Ozzy is just naturally hilarious. He's one of the funniest people on the face of the earth. You just put a camera in front of him and he goes on. It's hard to screw that up."

that time in mainstream film production; I had just produced a film for Albert Brooks, *Real Life*, and I had been given offers to produce stuff like *Private Benjamin*, so I could have been rich a way long time ago. But, no, it had to take me 20 more years.

O: ***After you made the first* Decline, *your first narrative film was* Suburbia. *How did that film come about?***

PS: I had a really difficult time getting distribution for the first *Decline*. It seemed like no one wanted to play a documentary in a movie theater, even though people were going to see them in droves. So I said, "Okay, I know this subject matter and I've learned a lot. And I love these kids, so I'm going to sit down and write a narrative picture about them." It turned out to be *Suburbia*. I got Roger Corman to pay for half of it, and some dude from Cleveland who had a furniture chain paid for the other half.

O: ***Why make the second* Decline *film about heavy metal?***

PS: It was this whole big scene here in Los Angeles. You couldn't even walk around in the mid-'80s, because the streets were so packed with these long-haired freaks. So then Miles Copeland of I.R.S. Records called me up and said, "Penelope, I think you're a cool filmmaker. Is there any movie that you want to make right now?" And I said, "Yeah, I want to make *Decline Part II*," and I wanted to make it about heavy metal, because, you know, it is part of the decline.

O: ***The interesting thing about the second film is that it looks a lot more like a music video than either the first or the third film.***

PS: Yeah, but the interesting thing about that is... It's something that I've never really talked about, because I've always felt that it would sound arrogant to say it, but the fact of the matter is that I did the first *Decline* and gave the world that editing style before MTV was even invented. So people say to me, "Have you ever noticed how your films kind of look like MTV?" And I say, "Let's just stop right there and take a look at the situation, pal."

O: ***Yeah, but the first and third films both have sort of a minimalist look to them, whereas the second film looks a lot glitzier.***

PS: That's because I paid for the third film, and I certainly wasn't about to go broke on it. The first film cost, like, $100,000, and the second film cost around $500,000. It's a matter of dollars, but it's also a matter of people looking over our shoulders and saying, "We've gotta make this look slicker!" I didn't really dig that. People think directors have more power than they actually do.

O: ***It wasn't an artistic choice to make the second film look glossier?***

PS: No. It was a choice of, "It's our money. You'll do what we say."

O: ***But it also seemed to fit the music, in that hair-metal is a much more visual style of music than punk.***

PS: Well, yeah. That's part of the reason I went along with the program, to a degree. When we were doing both films [*Decline I* and *III*], we'd occasionally look at things and go, "Geez, that stuff looks like crap." But it's good enough for punk rock.

O: ***Some of the most memorable scenes from the series are the ones in* Decline II *in which Chris Holmes of W.A.S.P. gets drunk in his pool, and where Ozzy Osbourne cooks breakfast. First of all, how did the scene with Chris Holmes end up happening?***

PS: With everybody I filmed, I asked them, "How do you want me to film you?" I gave them a choice. So Gene Simmons goes, "I don't want to do anything tacky. How about a lingerie store?" So I say, "Oh, yeah. Good idea. That won't be tacky." And then with Paul Stanley, I asked him, "How do you want to be filmed?" And he said, "How 'bout in bed with a bunch of women?" When I got to Chris Holmes, I asked him how he wanted me to shoot him, and he said, "How about drowning in a pool with my mother watching?" That was his idea.

O: ***How did Chris Holmes feel about the scene?***

PS: Well, he had already signed a release. He got all pissed off about it, but whatever. You know, I was in a bar one night and he started yelling at me, but whatever. I don't care.

O: ***What about the Ozzy Osbourne scene? How did that come about?***

PS: Well, that's not really Ozzy's house. And I faked the orange-juice spill. So there's two broken bubbles. But Ozzy is just naturally hilarious. He's one of the funniest people on the face of the earth. You just put a camera in front of him and he goes on. It's hard to screw that up.

O: ***The first project you worked on after* Decline II *was a film called* Thunder And Mud, *which involved heavy-metal music and female wrestling. How on earth did you end up making that film?***

PS: How about that for a flaming piece of crap? That was a matter of... God, how did that happen? Thank God nobody has ever asked me about that until now. There was a guy working with Miles Copeland, and he said, "Let's do a live show and tape it, and then put it out straight to video." And I said, "Like what?" It wasn't really my idea, I don't think, but he said, "How about doing heavy metal and mud wrestling and putting the two together?" I said, "Yeah." So I did it. I don't even think I got paid for it, which is kind of pathetic, don't you think?

O: ***And I guess that was the last thing you did before* Wayne's World.**

PS: I think the only reason I got to do *Wayne's World* was because I had done *Thunder And Mud*. No, just kidding. I think I got it because I had done *Decline II*.

"A documentarian has an obligation to tell the truth as he or she interprets it. And what I mean by that is that documentarians don't necessarily have the same sort of obligations that a journalist might have. A journalist might be called upon to be objective, whereas a documentarian is sort of forced to take sides."

O: ***And you had already produced some of Albert Brooks' stuff for* Saturday Night Live.**

PS: Yeah, I knew Lorne Michaels from back then, when I was producing films for *Saturday Night Live*. But back then it was such a boys' club that none of us chicks could do any directing. We had to clean the toilets and mop the floors instead. But years later, I think Lorne said to himself, "Didn't I tell her she could direct something? Oh, yeah, here, how about this little movie?" Then we turned it into a big old hit. Don't ask me how.

O: ***And then you did* The Beverly Hillbillies. *What attracted you to that project?***

PS: A million dollars. No, dude. I tried to do the films that I wanted to do after *Wayne's World*. Because I am not a comedy director. If you look at the rest of my work and ask, "Is she a comedy director?," the answer is no. What sucks is that if you do one hit, you can't get out of it. I tried so hard to do other kinds of movies after *Wayne's World*, but I couldn't. So I said, "Fuck it. Let's take the money."

"With everybody I filmed, I asked them, 'How do you want me to film you?' I gave them a choice. So Gene Simmons goes, 'I don't want to do anything tacky. How about a lingerie store?' So I say, 'Oh, yeah. Good idea. That won't be tacky.' "

O: ***So you feel typecast as a comedy director?***
PS: Totally.
O: ***What about* The Little Rascals*?***
PS: Well, you know, I shouldn't even talk that way about *The Beverly Hillbillies*. I did like *The Beverly Hillbillies*. I thought they were hilarious. Growing up, I always watched *The Little Rascals*, and I thought that it would be cool if the next generation got a *Little Rascals* movie. And by that time, I was getting really discouraged, because I just wasn't able to make the movies I wanted to make.
O: ***What kind of movies did you want to make?***
PS: Like, psychological thrillers or pictures that had at least a little depth to them. Films that no studio would let me direct.
O: ***Even though* Wayne's World *was a massive hit?***
PS: Especially because *Wayne's World* was a huge hit. All they wanted me to do was comedies.
O: ***You'd figure that directing such a successful film would give you some kind of clout.***
PS: No. That's what I figured, and that's why I got so frustrated. The only recourse I've had in this fucked-up town has been to make money doing these comedies. And I don't mean to complain, because at least I've got the bread, but that's the truth. I tried so hard to do other films.
O: ***How do you think your background in documentaries has affected your work in narrative films?***
PS: Oh, not so much, really. If I could make a decent living doing documentaries, I would. I don't really care about the other stuff so much. But you can't make a living doing documentaries. Although it has affected my work, in that I think I make fairly realistic-looking pictures.
O: ***A lot of the reviews of* Decline III *describe its subjects as victims. Do you think that's a fair description?***
PS: Yeah, I do. Some of them go out on the streets as a conscious choice and then become victims, but a lot of them are victims in their home situations, as well. I've seen the terrible conditions they live in, and you see a lot of that in the film. I don't know. Bottom line is, a victim would say, "I don't want to be in this situation," whereas a punk would go, "Fuck you guys! I'm here and so what?!" So maybe they're not.
O: ***The kids in* Decline III *look almost exactly the same as the kids from* Decline I*. Why do you think that is?***
PS: Yeah. They have a great respect for history. Also, it's just a totally cool look, in my opinion. [Laughs.] But there are differences. You know, there are a lot more tattoos and piercings. They've actually added to it. It's not so cutesy; it's more mean-looking now. Also, the other thing about it that's different is that it's sort of derived out of survival. If you look in the bag of a punk from the '70s, you'd probably find a .45 and whatever, but now they've got can openers. They're more road-ready. It's way more practical.
O: ***What do you think is a documentarian's responsibility to his or her subjects?***

PS: I feel that a documentarian has an obligation to tell the truth as he or she interprets it. And what I mean by that is that documentarians don't necessarily have the same sort of obligations that a journalist might have. A journalist might be called upon to be objective, whereas a documentarian is sort of forced to take sides.

O: ***What was your relationship like with the subjects of* Decline III*?***

PS: It was good. People always ask the stupidest question; they always ask, "Did they treat you like you were their mother?" And the answer is, "No, they didn't. You know, if they had treated me like their mother, I'd probably be dead." We were good friends. We still are good friends. They stay at my house. We're in touch all the time. If they need money, they can call me. They're my soulmates. ∅

Mr. Show, Part II

By Stephen Thompson
Originally Printed September 1997

"All that's happening in our lives is we're writing and working on *Mr. Show*. It's a fucking hellish bitch that won't get off our backs."

During the HBO sketch-comedy series Mr. Show*'s four-year, 30-episode run,* The Onion A.V. Club *took every opportunity to speak to the show's masterminds, David Cross and Bob Odenkirk. In the fall of 1997, at the beginning of their second season, both struggled with the brutal workload that accompanies creative control and the pursuit of excellence.*

The Onion: ***What's going on in your lives?***
Bob Odenkirk: Well, all that's happening in our lives is we're writing and working on *Mr. Show*. It's a fucking hellish bitch that won't get off our backs.
David Cross: A tempestuous shrew.
BO: And we will do anything, anything at this point, to finish it up, get a laugh as we're leaving, and run. Run, run from the studio.
DC: Not look back.
BO: We're working our asses off to do justice to the last few episodes we're working on, as much as we did the first few. That's the hard thing.
DC: It's really caught up with us, our lack of proper preparation time.
BO: As of now, we've done seven shows out of the 10 we have to do, and they're good. Every one of them is great, and I don't feel like we've dropped the ball yet. Now, we have three left to go, and I know the next two are really strong. With the last one, we're still struggling at this late date. We have to do it in the next week and a half. We have some good ideas to fix it up, but it's more last-minute than we would want.
O: ***Exhaustion is setting in at this point?***
BO: We're very tired.
DC: It is in, my friend. It's set up camp, and it's not going anywhere.
O: ***So you're out of ideas.***
DC: No, no. But to be totally honest, there is a marked difference in our energy level. It's different when you're in your seventh month as opposed to your third month.
BO: Not to be egotistical, but it asks a lot of you to be brilliant day in and day out, and to be as groundbreaking as we are. Have you ever tried to break the ground in a brilliant way? That is hard to do. We want to keep things up to the same level that we always have. You know, I worked at another big-name sketch show for a long time—I'm not going to say the name—but there was a real attitude of, "Yeah, we got our laughs. We got our three laughs. It's done. We filled an hour and a half."

And really, that was the attitude from the word "go," and we never, ever want to feel that way.
DC: *The Edge* was an hour and a half long?
BO: [Laughs.] We want to look at each show as if it were the only show we were doing.
DC: It's tough. It was a fear we had when we started: We knew the schedule was going to be very, very tight for us. Those fears were substantiated. You just have to make the last one as good as the first nine, and it's hard, because we're still dealing with rehearsing, and we still

"Not to be egotistical, but it asks a lot of you to be brilliant day in and day out, and to be as groundbreaking as we are."

have stuff to shoot. We have one week to do... Oh, it's fucking nuts. It's crazy. I can't fucking wait until it's over. I'm just going to cry a deep, weird cry—the kind of cry that's not happy or sad.
O: ***What made the process different this time around?***
DC: Well, HBO expected more shows this time around, in the same amount of time, so you're not gaining any time.
BO: But we still wrote these 10 shows the way we wrote the first batch of four and the second batch of six. We sat down and wrote a bunch of scenes that made us laugh—all different kinds of scenes. Then we started putting them in order and finding connections between them. So as far as the actual process of writing the show goes, we did the exact same thing we've done every time. I just think we've found a limit of how many shows we can do in this length of time. Fans of the show should look forward to a great season, and ideas that are going to come just as fast and be just as cool and interesting as any other.
O: ***How long are you guys going to do this?***
DC: Honestly, Bob and I have talked about this with numerous people involved with the show. It just depends on the time we get to do the next 10, if we do 10. This is not enough time to do it properly.
BO: It doesn't help that they make us sleep upright. We eat G.I. rations. Worms are eating away at the skin of David's feet. It's called Wormfoot. Chunks fall off. ⌀

"Part of our heart as a band has to do with running things ourselves." CHAPTER 4

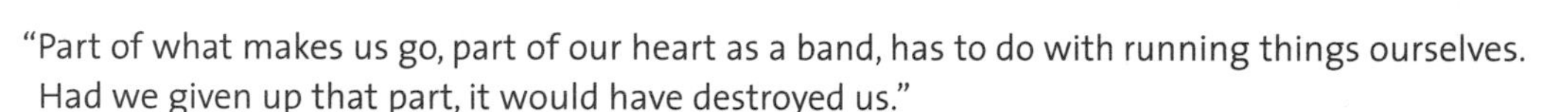

Ian MacKaye (Fugazi)

By Stephen Thompson

Originally Printed May 1999

"It's not that I'm out to smash the state. I'm just interested in building my own damn state."

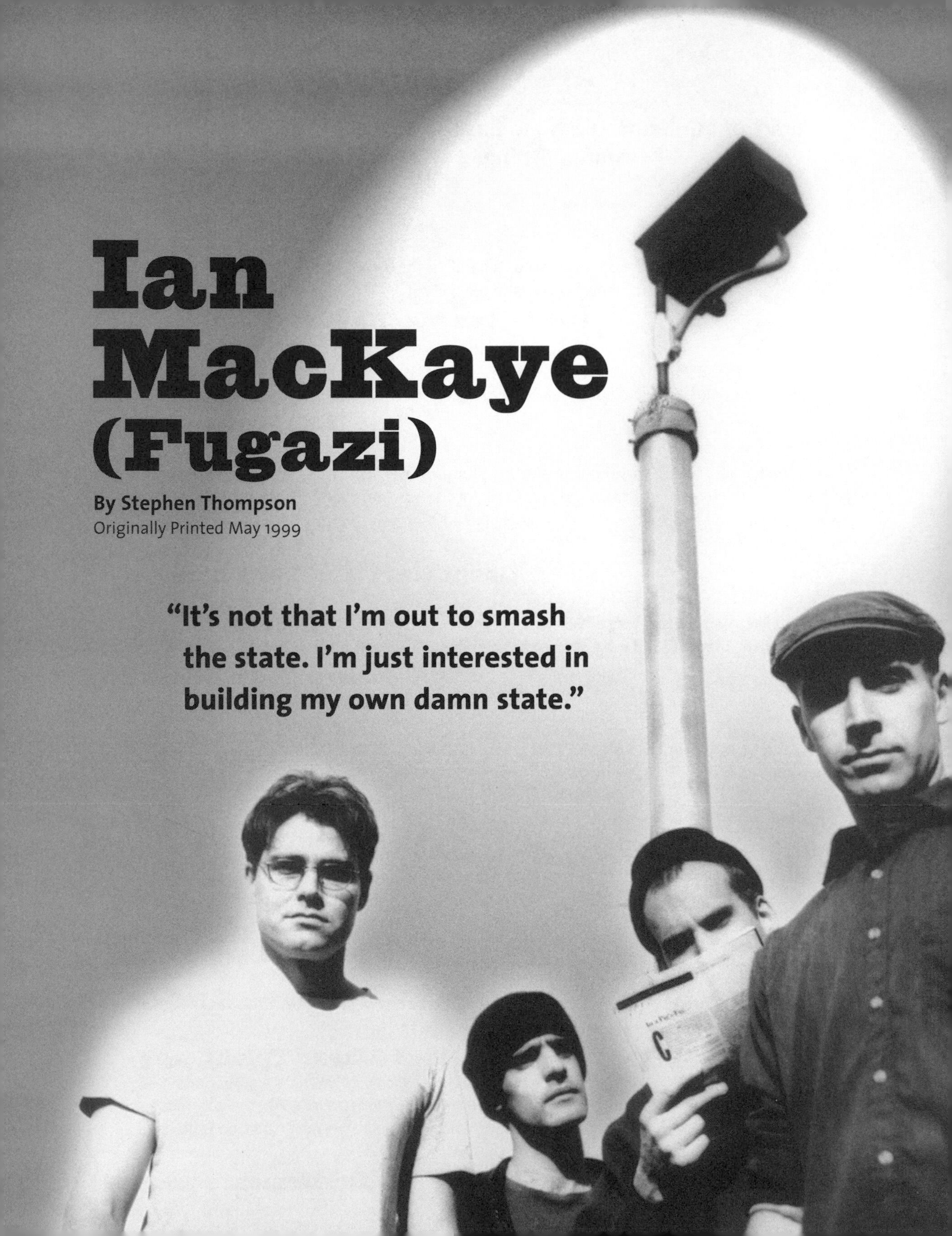

Since his early days in the late-'70s/early-'80s D.C. bands The Teen Idles and Minor Threat, singer, guitarist, and Dischord Records co-founder Ian MacKaye has never wavered from the ideals that first inspired him to play harsh, challenging punk. Fugazi, which features singer-guitarist MacKaye, drummer Brendan Canty, bassist Joe Lally, and singer-guitarist Guy Picciotto, has eschewed multimillion-dollar label offers and lucrative tours since its 1988 inception. To this day, the group still charges no more than $10 for CDs and no more than $6 for tickets to its strictly all-ages concerts. Of course, such ideological consistency wouldn't matter much if the music didn't remain vital, but it does. Shortly before embarking on a 1999 tour of Europe, MacKaye spoke to The Onion A.V. Club *about integrity and hope.*

The Onion: ***There's been a lot of talk about the impending collapse of the record industry, in light of all the mergers, the growth of the Internet, and what many perceive as the declining quality of the music being put out. At this point, do you sort of feel like, "I told you so"?***
Ian MacKaye: No. For a lot of my friends who signed to labels, I just feel bad for them. They worked really hard and were trying to make things work for their bands. Everyone has their own deals, their own realities to sort out, so I can't sit in judgment of them on that level. It's certainly not a surprise to me. It's just sort of depressing. Joe [Lally] and I were walking down the street maybe three or four years ago, and we ran into a friend of ours who we hadn't seen in a while. He's in a band. I asked him, you know, "How's the band?" And he's like, "Oh, we're getting fucked by our label." And he told us the story of how they were under contract but couldn't put anything out, and they couldn't put anything out anywhere else—the usual kind of stuff. So we said goodbye and continued walking, and Joe said, "How depressing is it that, for the next 10 years, we're going to hear that from so many of our friends?" Those exact words: "We're being fucked by our label." But it's sort of a peripheral thing for me, because I really stayed out of it. The mainstream industry is not something I have any involvement with whatsoever, so I'm just sort of hearing about it. It's sort of like when people complain to me about how their bosses suck, at their office jobs. I feel bad for them, but I'm not going to say to them, "Ha ha, I told you not to go work in an office." They made their own decisions.

It's not always a bad story: Sometimes things work out. It's just a little more hit-or-miss, and from my point of view, I was never really interested in even being a part of the record industry. I'm still not interested in it, and I think that confounds people, because in some ways my ambitions are so eccentric. I don't have an ambition, because for me, the idea is to document something. I don't want to put the cart in front of the horse, you know? There was music that was important to me, and there were people who were important to me, and there was a community that was important to me, so I kind of felt like that was what I was doing: documenting that. And the fact that other people were interested enough to help me realize it is amazing. I never, ever had it in my mind that I wanted to be in the record industry, because I still contend that the record industry is an insidious affair. It's this terrible collision between art and commerce, and it will always be that way. It has to be, because the people who run labels... No matter how on-time they were in the beginning—no matter how much they love music—at some point, if you just turn a label into its own entity, its sole purpose is to profit. And once that is established, you know that people are going to be mistreated, ideas are going to be mistreated, and the art is going to be mistreated. It has to be. But I also think a lot of people misunderstand me: I'm psyched for people when they work hard and are successful. I think what most people don't understand about my situation is that we worked hard in creating an infrastructure that can distribute our music, and within it, we've been very successful. With a lot of bands, they've never had this infrastructure, so for them, they're left high and dry. I've had people call me from bands that are very popular, and they're like, "What do we do? We want to do what you do." It's almost impossible to do what I do, because you would have had to start in 1980. You can't just do it. It has to grow. So I'm excited when people who work hard are successful. Regardless of all the crap with lawyers and managers and all that shit, if they worked hard and created something that was unique and not just commercially angled, and it was so good that it couldn't be denied, that makes me happy. I'm always happy when I hear about people selling records or selling books or selling movies. It makes me proud of them. My principles are not based on hatred; it's not about hating. I don't hate things. It's not that I'm out to smash the state. I'm just interested in building my own damn state.

"The record industry is an insidious affair. It's this terrible collision between art and commerce, and it will always be that way."

O: ***Do labels still make offers?***

IM: No. You've got to figure that A&R people are always, like, 20 years old for the most part, and a lot of them are either fully knowledgeable or they just don't give a fuck about us. And also, I think the labels were sort of excited about us because we were a much more proven quantity than most of the bands they were signing, so I think they felt like we would have been a safe return. There used to be this sort of theory, where people used to say, "You can sell twice as many records on a major label as you do on an independent." So I guess by that reckoning, if someone sold 5,000 on an independent, they could sell 10,000 on a major, no problem. So if we were selling 200,000, they're thinking, "We could sell half a million." I don't really know if that's true, and in fact, I think it's a bit of a legend. For a lot of people who sign, they forget that with independent labels—at least in the underground punk community—you had longevity. You had a community in which you continue to sell records. So you may not get the big, "Ta-da!," where you sell 30,000 records in the first week, but you may well sell 40,000 records in a year. All I can tell you is that our best-selling record is probably our first record [*13 Songs*], and that came out in 1988. And it still sells better than the other records. The Minor Threat CD [*Complete*] still sells ridiculous amounts to this day. It's just insane. The problem with the majors is that the records come out, and what sells in the first month is it. By the time your record comes out, people are already working on something else. That's it. They have to, because it's all about hustle. This may well change, but you've got one shot: You put a record out, and if the first single hits, bam, they'll work on it, and if it doesn't, they've got to get on something else. They're not going to sit with it for a while. No time! It's all microwave ovens now, baby. They're not gonna let it simmer. When people talk to me about majors, a lot of the time I tell them to think about it like the lottery: They buy up all these bands like they're at a 7-Eleven buying up lottery tickets. You only need one to hit, and that pays for all the other ones easily. Most bands end up torn up and on the floor. I can't criticize those bands; in fact, I've always leveled most of my criticism at the mid- to late-'80s independent music labels and distributors, who I feel behaved really poorly. They had a unique situation, and they obviously were going to sell fewer records than the majors, but what they had going for them was a different way of doing business, of interacting with people in a way that allows you to give them more attention. And instead of that, I feel like a lot of the large independent labels kind of took the major-label template and just acted like regular labels, except that they weren't selling as many records. You end up thinking in terms of, "Hey, I could be treated like an asshole and sell 10,000 records, or I could be treated like an asshole and sell 100,000 records, so I'm gonna sell 100,000 records." It seems totally clear to me, and I just feel like those labels fuckin' blew it. But even that end of music commerce is outside of our domain, because from the very beginning, this label was created to document music here in Washington—our friends' bands. I've never wavered from that, and there never was a moment when I considered branching out or looking for exciting new acts. If you look to the history of this label, there were years when we put out 20 records and there were years when we put out one. It really depends on the flow of what was happening here. Right now, we have three bands on the label, and who knows? Maybe next year there'll be none.

"Weird Al" Yankovic On **Fugazi**

I've definitely heard of them.

O: ***No one has contracts.***

IM: No. It has to do with the community that I feel I'm connected to, and it's a challenge. We're getting close to Dischord's 20th anniversary. But I like it, because I've always kept these parameters on this label. I've never had to be concerned about what was going on anywhere else. And I don't really care if Seagram's buys everybody. I'm not surprised about it. I feel bad for my friends who got sort of crushed up in the merger, because they're my friends, but I'd feel bad if they worked at a cannery that got shut down. The thing is, people can't complain about profit-oriented moves if they're only interested in profit themselves. You can't have it both ways. If they're willing to polish up a gift and sell it to make money, they can't really complain about the fact that somebody above them has sold them down the river. That's the way it goes.

O: ***How do you maintain the energy? Is there a point at which it just becomes too exhausting?***

IM: Well... In this interview, you'll hear me use the word "community" about a thousand times. But for me, it's always been about a collection of people who were really marginalized for whatever reason. And here in

Washington, because it's such a non-industry town, there was no music scene, and because we weren't taken seriously by anybody, we decided that we would have to take each other and our community seriously. And we were able to create something that had an incredibly lasting effect on us. The people I've been running with, I've been running with for many, many, many years. I'm not a religious person, and I'm not too interested in being part of a religion, but I do like having some sort of communal gathering and having some sense of peoples. It gives me a lot of energy to have the chance to be around my friends and family, and the people here at Dischord, and the bands—all these people who have donated their time and energy and commitment to be a part of this. And I feel like I have a responsibility to represent them in a good way, since they have all entrusted me with that. Keep in mind that I don't see Dischord as something that's happening today; I see it as almost a library. Over the years, all these bands, all these people, all these artists have committed their work to Dischord. So I feel that it's very important to continue to represent them in the best way possible. I guess that's a good enough reason for energy, and also, I'm a bit of a fighter, and I feel like there's stuff that can be done. A lot of the problems I encounter on a local level—which, to me, are kind of indicative of the world's problems—are easily solvable with a little bit of work. It's not so much that I have this incredible amount of energy; it's just that it takes so little energy to fix things that it's a shock when people don't even want to expend that much, because they're so concerned about their own well-being. One of the most disappointing aspects of American society is that people put their own wants, needs, and desires so far above the simplest of problems. They're not interested in dealing with those things. So as a label and an operation and a mission, a lot of good has come of it—and I'm not talking about just for me, or for Fugazi, but within the people I count as my friends in my collective group. There are so many people doing such good work in this world that people never know about, people who are working at youth centers and hospitals and homeless shelters, people who are doing outreach work, people who are doing all kinds of good stuff. These people aren't on any records, but they are lynchpins of this community—people who grew up here—and they've said to me, "Well, Dischord has been a big part of our inspiration." And I'm like, "Well, fuck, man. You guys have been a big part of mine!"

"They buy up all these bands like they're at a 7-Eleven buying up lottery tickets. You only need one to hit, and that pays for all the other ones easily. Most bands end up torn up and on the floor."

O: ***Do you ever get cynical?***

IM: I don't think so. I'm not a very cynical person.

O: ***I mean, this is a very cynical view, but it's often expected in society that if you're idealistic, that idealism will fade. You'll...***

IM: You'll get real. Again, that's part of the American culture—that sense of, "You're a kid until you grow up. You can play around until you get real. You're on a farm team until you get called up to the majors. You're an apprentice until you become a professional." There are all these stages, and in music, people don't take you seriously unless you're marketed by a major label. The only stamp of validity has to come from these heinous corporations. And it just seems so strange that people like Sony would have that special stamp in art. "This is an artist, and everyone else is not real because they're not willing to make money." Which is fucking utter bullshit. When I first wanted to play music, I thought I'd never get to, because it seemed like music—and the whole industry surrounding it—was really for professionals only. And, therefore, there was no point in me even trying. And punk rock was... I first started hearing about it in 1978 or '79, and it was like I had discovered this portal, this small window into a world that I knew must exist but could never find. Suddenly, here it was: this place where you could explore all sorts of unconventional ideas and approaches. People were just fucking around with good, creative things, and there are bad and good things going on. But it's important that you can have a place where bad things can be done. This world is not just about the good, and any time you're in a place where only good is being offered, you know that something very evil is working somewhere else. To get things right, you have to be able to make mistakes, and you can't be ashamed of that. That kind of thing can't really work in an arena that is completely predicated on profit. If you only have rock clubs, they won't book bands unless they draw, and a lot of new ideas can never be floated because people are never initially attracted to them. With bands like Minor Threat, people are like, "Oh, what a legendary band." But Minor Threat played in front of 20 people! Any band, like The Germs or anybody, that played in the beginning, played to nobody. Punk rock was a place where you didn't need to make money, because the music was the point, or the community was the point. People were like, "Fuck money." The first band I was in, The Teen Idles, played for a year in Washington, and because we were white kids from Washington in a punk-rock band, all the anarcho-yippie guys who ran the commune we used to play at called us things like "suburban white-boy punk-rockers" and "capitalists." God knows why, because every penny we made went into a cigar box. We never split our money up. We saved everything, and that money is the money we used to start the label. For us, it was never about making money; it was always about trying to create our own scene, because we wanted something to do. We were bored as fuck. So finding this sort of thing made me realize that there is an area that is not about getting real. It never occurred to me that you would have to get real sooner or later. People were saying, "Well, if you want to be in a punk band, you'll have to move to New York." And that's ridiculous. This is for real! In 1979, in Washington, D.C., not only if you wanted to be in a punk band, but if you wanted to be a punk, you had to live in New York. And I thought, "How could this be geography-based? Since when are anger and boredom and frustration limited to one city?" It just doesn't fuckin' make sense to me. So we were like, "Fuck that. We're just going to start it right here." We just did it. In the early years, there was this sense of always proving to people that they were full of shit. Even in the early

"Someone could say, 'Well, you could have sold a million records.' Who knows if that's true? But more importantly, who knows if that's important? Who cares?"

days of Fugazi, for the first year, people used to say, "Well, you can do this $5 deal now, but you're going to have to raise your cover prices when you get into bigger rooms." Well, it's 12 years now, and granted, some of our shows are $6, but for the most part, I think the point is pretty clear that those people were incorrect. They were wrong, and they were wrong because the limits they were drawing were their own. They didn't ever test the waters. So we're in a weird place as a band. People say, "Well, if you ever want to go any farther with the band, you're going to have to sign to a major label." Well, they're wrong! They're just wrong! Now, someone could say, "Well, you could have sold a million records." Who knows if that's true? But more importantly, who knows if that's important? Who cares? If you can continue to work, and you can still feel challenged... We're talking about 12 years, and we still practice three or four times a week. We like each other. We still work hard, we're still doing things that are creative and interesting, and apparently somebody else thinks so, too. So maybe people shouldn't always think in terms of escalation. Maybe they should think in terms of consistency.

O: ***The flip side of that is the desire to have people hear your music—the idea that if you were on a major label, you could reach a lot of people. Do you ever feel that way?***

IM: A lot of people have said to me, "It's criminal that more people don't hear your music." But our position is that our music is available to anybody in the world who wants to hear it. Now, that doesn't necessarily mean it's easily accessible, but good things aren't always easily accessible. I mean, if you want some food, you can walk over to the 7-Eleven and get some microwave whatever-the-fuck—you can get the food—but if you want something good, you're going to have to walk a little farther. You might have to walk to a restaurant that actually gives a fuck about what they're feeding you. You could just buy some frozen pizza and stick it in the oven, or you could make your own dough. It's going to be a hell of a lot better if you make your own pizza. Just because it's more accessible, that doesn't mean it's good, and it's usually quite the opposite. There are certainly good examples of incredibly brilliant, beautiful music that has been made commercially available and sold everywhere. But I would say that, for the most part, quantity certainly does not speak well for quality. And I think that part of what makes us go, part of our heart as a band, has to do with running things ourselves. Had we given up that part, it would have destroyed us. Of course I'd be happy if a million people bought the record. I'd love that, and it would make me feel even more justified in a lot of ways. I feel like it could happen. The problem is that there is a certain point where there is a cut-off, a chasm you can't get across. When we're playing gigs, we can handle up to about a 2,000-capacity room, as far as expenses are concerned. But after 2,000, the costs just go insane, and it is impossible for us to play those rooms. Even if we sold them out, at our ticket price we wouldn't be able to pay the janitors, because they're all union. So I realize that that does exist. The same thing happens with record sales: I think we have maxed out as far as initial sales—at least as far as the network we can operate within is concerned—because the majors hold the lock and key to the super-widespread stuff. But so what? It doesn't deter us from continuing, and we can still play shows. It's a weird thing, but, then, it's supposed to be weird. It was always about doing something interesting. We already know the trajectory of bands that have started out, worked hard, created their own scene, signed to a label, gotten huge, and then stopped. We've seen that trajectory in various forms of success many times. But it's not very often that you hear about a band that starts on its own terms and carries it out to the very end. It's more unusual. That's why I sometimes feel a little lonely, because I don't think there are a whole lot of other bands in our position. In punk rock and rock 'n' roll, I don't really know if there are any bands. There may well be.

"Our music is available to anybody in the world who wants to hear it. Now, that doesn't mean it's easily accessible, but good things aren't always easily accessible."

O: ***Do you wish you hadn't called that record* End Hits?**

IM: No. Why would I?

O: ***Well, it sort of fed into this perception that the band was breaking up.***

IM: Ah, but we knew that. It wasn't like it was

a surprise to us, because we talked about it. It's more about the end of the century and the slow-moving apocalypse, so it was sort of like, "Here are some last words from the world." But whatever. We were aware of the fact that people would construe that as a possible thing, but at the same time, it was sort of a joke. It has that sort of notion, but also we were just sort of fuckin' around. That's one thing about the band that people don't know: Most of our time, our best moments are always laughing. I don't know if you've seen our movie [*Instrument*] or not, but we just finished this movie, and a lot of people who've seen it are surprised that we're not sitting around a table plotting. I'm a great, funny guy, but people think I'm this scary asshole. I mean, we don't actively promote ourselves as easy-going, because who gives a fuck? We're not that easy-going! We mean business. It's just that we're funny. ⌀

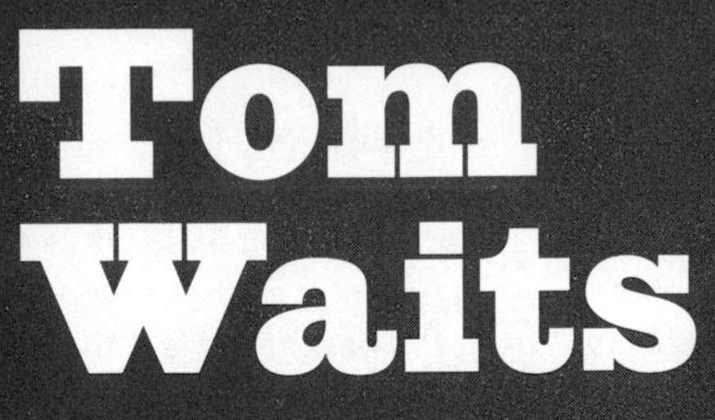

Tom Waits

By Keith Phipps
Originally Printed June 2002

"I don't cut the ribbon at the opening of markets. I don't stand next to the mayor. Hit your baseball into my yard, and you'll never see it again."

Tom Waits began performing Beat-inspired songs in clubs around the time he reached legal drinking age, though his gravelly voice seemed incongruous with his youth. Experience and albums followed, as he became a sort of hipster outsider cousin to the '70s California music scene. After meeting frequent collaborator Kathleen Brennan, who eventually became his wife, Waits adopted a more experimental approach only suggested by his previous work. His cluttered, clamoring new style, first fully developed on 1983's Swordfishtrombones, *led him to a new audience and a new label. Around the same time, Waits began curbing the lifestyle detailed in his gutter-trolling songs, tried his hand at acting, and found new collaborators, most notably director Jim Jarmusch and Robert Wilson, a longtime fixture of avant-garde theater. After a six-year silence following 1993's* The Black Rider, *Waits returned with* Mule Variations, *then disappeared again. From a carefully guarded location somewhere in rural California, Waits spoke to* The Onion A.V. Club *shortly after the simultaneous 2002 release of* Alice *and* Blood Money, *both soundtracks to Wilson works.*

The Onion: ***You've said before that the stories behind songs are less interesting than the songs themselves. Have you ever written a song where the opposite was true?***

Tom Waits: Oh, gee. I don't know. Most songs have meager beginnings. You wake up in the morning, you throw on your suspenders, and you subvocalize and just think. They seem to form like calcium. I can't think of a story right off the bat that was that interesting. I write things on the back of my hand, usually, and sing into a tape recorder. I don't know.

O: ***Many of your albums are filled with references to sailors and the sea. Is there a reason for that, beyond growing up in San Diego?***

TW: I think all songs should have weather in them. Names of towns and streets, and they should have a couple of sailors. I think those are just song prerequisites. [Laughs.]

O: ***For yours, or for all songs?***

TW: Oh, all songs. Most of them fail miserably. I go looking in other people's songs for their sailors and their towns. I don't know, everybody has things that they gravitate towards. Some people put toy cars or clouds or cat crap. Everybody puts something different, and it's entirely up to you what belongs and what doesn't. They're interesting little vessels of emotional information, and you carry them in your pocket like a bagel.

O: ***When*** **Mule Variations** ***came out, it seemed like the first question most people had for you was, "What took you so long?" Does that annoy you?***
TW: Well, I submitted myself to the questions, so it's hard to be annoyed. But, yeah, when people want to know what you've been up to, how can you possibly explain to a stranger what you've been doing for seven years? Would they truly be interested? [Laughs.]

"It's not like I'm one of those expensive, high-powered pop groups on the road eight months out of the year, talking to *Teen Beat*. I finally discovered that my life is more important than show business."

O: ***It seems artists with a devoted following are under pressure to turn out albums regularly. Does that pressure ever get to you?***
TW: Not really. It's not like I'm one of those expensive, high-powered pop groups on the road eight months out of the year, talking to *Teen Beat*. I finally discovered that my life is more important than show business. But, yeah, people are curious about all kinds of things, which takes your mind off that which is really important. They usually ask questions about things that don't matter—to them, or to me, or to anybody else. Just to take up time, I guess, and distract them from the important questions, like "Who won the World Series in 1957?" or "Who said, 'Today you will play jazz, tomorrow you will betray your country'?"
O: ***Is there an answer to that one?***
TW: It was on a Soviet propaganda poster in the '30s. Did you know that honey is the only food that won't spoil? They found it in King Tut's tomb. Jars of honey. They said it was just as fresh as it was on the first day.
O: ***Did they actually try it?***
TW: They tried it, yeah. Wouldn't you? If you found a jar of honey in a thousands-of-years-old tomb, would you put your finger into it and taste it?
O: ***So, why did it take you so long to record the songs on*** **Alice?**
TW: The songs were written around '92 or '93, 'round in there. It was done with Robert Wilson in Germany. We stuck 'em in a box and just left 'em there for a while. They were aging like the honey. And we locked in the freshness. They were hermetically sealed. You move on to other things, you know? And then you go back and say, "Well, this was okay."
O: ***It was kind of developing a reputation as the great lost Tom Waits album.***
TW: I bought a copy of the bootleg on eBay. 'Cause I didn't know where those tapes were.
O: ***How does the bootleg hold up?***
TW: Okay. There was stuff that didn't make it onto the record.
O: ***How many songs are usually left over on any given record?***
TW: Oh, there's always a bunch of them that don't make the boat. That's normal. You just stick 'em all together later and put 'em out by themselves. Those *Alice* songs were all in a briefcase that got stolen out of the back of my car, and they were ransomed by these radicals who thought they really had something. We had to pay a couple grand to get the briefcase back, but I think they copied the tapes.
O: ***What was the exchange like? Did you get to meet them somewhere?***
TW: Yeah, some dark café, you know, everybody was wearing sunglasses, it was really cold. They said, "We're gonna leave the briefcase by the trash can. Put the money in a bag..." It added a little intrigue to the whole project.
O: ***What's your collaborative process like with Kathleen Brennan?***
TW: [Chuckles.] Oh! Well, you know, "You wash, I'll dry." It all comes down to making choices and a lot of decisions. You know, are we gonna

do a song about our cruise ship, or a meadow, or a brothel, or... just a rhapsody, or is it a parlor song or a work song or a field holler? What is it? The form itself is like a Jell-O mold. It's like doing anything that you would do with someone. "You hold it right there while I hit it," or the other way around. You find a rhythm in the way of working. I trust her opinion above all else. You've gotta have somebody to trust, that knows a lot. She's done a lot of things. I'm Ingrid Bergman and she's Bogart. She's got a pilot's license, and she was gonna be a nun before we got married. I put an end to that. She knows about everything from motorcycle repair to high finance, and she's an excellent pianist. One of the leading authorities on the African violet. She's a lot of strong material. She's like Superwoman, standing there with her cape flapping. It works. We've been at this for some time now. Sometimes you quarrel, and it's the result of irritation, and sometimes it comes out of the ground like a potato and we marvel at it. She doesn't like the spotlight. She's a very private person, as opposed to myself. [Laughs.]

O: ***You have kind of developed a reputation as a recluse. Does that bother you?***

TW: Hell, no. I think that's a good one. It wards off strangers. It's like being a beekeeper. No, if people are a little nervous about approaching you at the market, it's good. I'm not Chuckles The Clown. Or Bozo. I don't cut the ribbon at the opening of markets. I don't stand next to the mayor. Hit your baseball into my yard, and you'll never see it again. I just have a close circle of friends and loved ones—the circle of trust, as they say.

O: ***There's a section on your web site about fans who have spotted or encountered you in public. Do you have a problem going out?***

TW: I go where I feel like. Funny little story... I drove on a field trip once, to a guitar factory, to show all these little kids how to make guitars. So we're standing there, and I'm looking around, and folks are looking over at me, and I'm just waiting for someone to recognize me—you know, "Hey, aren't you that music guy? That singer guy?" Nobody. Nothing. We're there for, like, two hours, watching them put the frets on and all that, and I'm waiting and waiting. A week later, I took the same group of kids on a field trip to the dump, and as I pulled up, don't ask me how, but my truck was surrounded by people that wanted an autograph. It was a dump, for Christ's sake. I guess everybody knows me at the dump.

O: ***It kind of proves that you never know who your audience is.***

TW: You don't really know. I guess one should not even assume that one has an audience, and allow it to go to your head.

O: ***Your early stuff is influenced by the Beats, and your later stuff seems equally influenced by older, harder-to-define influences. Do you think you're slipping further back into the past as you get older?***

TW: I don't know. I hope I'm not slipping at all.

O: ***I don't mean that in a negative sense. I mean, do you think you're drawing on older influences as you get older?***

TW: I really don't know. What you rely on... I think you kind of take the world apart and put it back together. The further you get from something, the better your memory is of it, sometimes. Who knows how that works? Those are big questions about the nature of memory and its influence on your present life. I don't know. Consider this: The number of cars on the planet is increasing three times faster than the population growth. Three times faster. I mean, there's eleven and a half million cars in Los Angeles alone.

O: ***What are you driving these days?***

TW: Oh, I got a beautiful 1959 Cadillac Coupe DeVille four-door. No one will ride in it with me.

O: ***Why's that?***

TW: It's unsafe. But it looks good. I take it to the dump. We spend a lot of time in our cars. You know what I really love? The CD players in a car. How when you put the CD right up by the slot, it actually takes it out of your hand, like it's hungry. It pulls it in, and you feel like it wants more silver discs. "More silver discs. Please." I enjoy that.

O: ***Do you have one in the Cadillac?***

TW: No, I have a little band in there. It's an old car, so I have a little old string band in the glove compartment. It's grumpy. You know the average person spends two weeks over their lifetime waiting for the traffic light to change?

O: ***Really? I would actually guess a little more.***

TW: I would guess more, too. I'm thinking, two weeks, you know...

O: ***That sounds like a bargain.***

TW: During your whole lifetime, though. You know mosquito repellents don't actually repel anything? They actually hide you because they block the mosquito's sensors. They don't know that you're there. It's like blinding them.

O: ***It used to be that, like you, a lot of musicians took a hard-line stance against having their music used in advertising. That seems to have shifted. Why do you think that is?***

"When you put the CD right up by the slot, it actually takes it out of your hand, like it's hungry. It pulls it in, and you feel like it wants more silver discs. 'More silver discs. Please.' I enjoy that."

TW: I don't know. They're all high on crack. Let's just say it's a sore subject with me. I went to court over it, you know... You know, you see a bathroom-tissue commercial, and you start hearing "Let The Good Times Roll," and the paper thing's rolling down the stairs. Why would anybody want to mortify and humiliate themselves? It's just business, you know? The memory that you have and the association you have with that song can be co-opted. And a lot of people are really in it for the money. Period. A lot of people don't have any control over it. I don't own the copyrights to my early tunes. So it is unfortunate, but there are a lot of people that consciously want their songs exploited in that way, which I think is demeaning. I hate it when I hear songs that I already have a connection with, used in a way that's humiliating. I mean, in the old days, if somebody was doing a commercial, you used to say, "Oh, gee, too bad, he probably needs the money." But now, it's like hocking cigarettes and underwear with rock 'n' roll. I guess that's our big export. It's like how a good butcher uses every part of the cow. I don't like hearing those Beatles songs in the commercials. It almost renders them useless. Maybe not for everyone else, but when I hear it I just think, "Oh, God, another one bites the dust."

O: ***I still can't hear "Good Vibrations" without thinking of Sunkist.***

TW: Oh, wow, yeah. That's exactly what they want. They want to plug your head into that and change the circuitry. While you're dreaming about your connection with that song, why don't you think about soda or candy or something? It's too bad, but it's the way of the world. They love to get their meat hooks in you.

O: ***Your kids are old enough to have their own musical tastes now. Do you approve of what they listen to?***

TW: Oh, sure, yeah. As long as they're listening. You know, what happens is that as you start getting older, you get out of touch. I'm like a turtleneck sweater. And then your kids kind of enlighten you: "Dad, have you heard Blackalicious?" I take 'em to the show, but I drop them off. I'm not allowed to go in. It'd be too embarrassing.

O: ***Do you have a favorite cover version of one of your songs?***

TW: Johnny Cash did a song called "Down There By The Train," Solomon Burke did one. But, you know, cover versions are good. I used to bark about it, and then I said, "Oh, it's good." If you write songs, you really do kind of want someone to hear it and say, "Hey, man, I could do that." So if they're not doing your songs, you wonder, "Why aren't they doing my songs?" If it's too individual, too personal, then it can't be re-imagined.

O: ***What's the most outrageous lie you've ever told a reporter?***

TW: That I'm a medical doctor.

O: ***Did the reporter buy it?***

TW: I started talking anatomy with the guy, and I think I strung him along pretty good for a while. But then I realized... He told me his dad was a doctor, and he tripped me up on something. I mispronounced "femur" or something. I do like books on anatomy. I have to say I'm an amateur physician, I guess.

O: ***You've never practiced.***

TW: I practice at home, on the kids. Interestingly enough, there are a lot of musicians who are also doctors, or a lot of doctors who are also musicians. There is a connection. Surgeons work in a theatre, and they call it a theatre. All medical procedures require two hands, so in a sense it's like when you play an instrument. That's what they call things that they use in their work: They call them instruments. I've played with a lot of musicians who are also doctors. I worked with a bass player who was a doctor. You know, I suppose there is a connection. A lot of people start out majoring in medicine and drop it and change their major to music. I don't know, it's just one of those things.

O: ***Any last words for our readers?***

TW: Famous last words? Lemme think here. All right, here we go. Umm... Never have I waltzed to "My Country 'Tis Of Thee," nor met anyone who did. Still, it's a waltz, for it's written in waltz time. ⌀

Grant Hart (Hüsker Dü)

By Joshua Klein

Originally Printed July 2000

"The way my life has been puffed up, I offer everything to people in terms of sex, drugs, and rock 'n' roll."

One third of Hüsker Dü, a group whose marriage of punk thrash and pop hooks proved influential long after its less-than-amicable 1987 breakup, Grant Hart was frequently overshadowed by bandmate Bob Mould. One look at the Minneapolis band's catalog proves the value of Hart's contributions, both as a drummer and as a singer-songwriter: Hart gave Hüsker Dü some of its most memorable songs, including "Green Eyes," "She's A Woman (And Now She Is A Man)," and "She Floated Away." But both alone and as the former leader of Nova Mob, Hart has found it difficult to attract as much attention as Mould has. Not long after the release of his second solo album, 1999's Good News For Modern Man, *Hart spoke to* The Onion A.V. Club *about sex, drugs, and the tangled history of Hüsker Dü.*

The Onion: ***Starting at the beginning, how did Hüsker Dü form?***

Grant Hart: I was working at a record store, and it was probably 1978 or so when I met Bob. He just breezed in as a customer one day. He had been acquainted with Greg [Norton, Hüsker Dü's bassist] for probably a year or two before that.

O: ***When you started playing together, what were some of the musical tastes you all had in common?***

GH: All the classic punk stuff: The Ramones, The Sex Pistols. Pretty much the non-regional stuff. A lot of what brought us together was what we didn't have in common, like the records that, say, Mould could get on the East Coast that never made it to the middle of the country, and vice versa. It was kind of hipping each other to our respective local music. Of course, there was CBGB and all that happening in New York, so it seemed like there was a lot of Heartbreakers and this band from Canada, The Diodes, that covered The Cyrkle's "Red Rubber Ball." That was an early common territory. Bob was a student of the guitar player from The Suicide Commandos, which was kind of like the first Minneapolis punk band. When they started, they would not have used the word "punk," but they were doing the same thing a lot of people were doing at the time. It was kind of a more shorthaired rock 'n' roll. They moved into that quite well, and they kind of brought their whole scene with them. In the early days, most of the punks were well into the second half of their 20s at least, because it wasn't the populist movement that it became later on. Or tried to become later on. It was a lot of spoiled art students and rich babies that had the opportunity to travel and be in the places where this stuff was taking place.

O: ***A lot of the hardcore bands at the time were all about, "How fast can we go?" or "How aggressive can we be?" At what point did you know that Hüsker Dü was going to develop beyond that?***

GH: Well, this is where it starts being a little bit divisive, because I didn't enjoy playing hardcore. At the time, while I was drummer for Hüsker Dü even though I played other instruments, it was just such a damn boring job for a drummer. [Mimics fast, repetitive drum beat.] I saw it as part of a whole set of possibilities for expression, but I found the hardcore thing very limiting and very dumb. It was just, you know, "Let's be super politically paranoid on the surface, and let's jump into a more stringent set of rules than what we're supposed to be rebelling against." I've never really enjoyed that macho, "Here are the rules, here's how you conform" stuff. There's this hard-ass stuff that didn't do anything for me. The compositions I had that could be classified as hardcore were already moving away, occupying a different topical ground. The first song that really comes to mind is from an early EP that we did: The song is called "What Do I Want?" and it was simply that. The questions, "What do I want? What will make me happy?" repeated over and over, ad nauseam. That's all I could really express with that genre of music. Starting off in '82, late '81, before we really worked our way into *Metal Circus*, my hair got long again. All of a sudden, all these great, liberated people were "not digging it." These people who were supposed to be about throwing away all the rules were suddenly getting caught up in their own hypocrisy. They're singing about how people "don't like me because I've got short hair" or whatever, "because I stand out in the crowd." They ended up doing the same thing, so I was kind of delighted surfing on that iconoclasm. Originally, it became apparent to me that there was more rebellion in bringing the music back into... the first term that comes to mind is "a thing of beauty." Not that there's not a place for some of that ugliness, because a lot of it is a component of my work to this day. But a steady diet of nothing but that... [Mimics the drum beat again.] I don't know if you're familiar with *Land Speed Record*, but the next album we made after that was pretty much a studio version of the same damn thing. I just started interjecting more of my material into the balance of things. You'd have to ask Mould this, but I'd assume that writing hardcore was fairly easy for him. Maybe he hadn't written enough different kinds of things to really know where songwriting could challenge you. Around the time of *Zen Arcade*, he started really blooming as a songwriter, even though he'd been in the band for a while. Things like "Chartered Trips" and "Celebrated Summer," these songs are associated with him to this day as the finer points of his musical upbringing. I'm certainly not taking credit for anything he's written, but I really started the ball moving in the other direction, as far as the band was concerned.

O: ***Did you have to fight for that?***

GH: Well, I had to take a lot of snide shit. Bob would be in camouflage fatigues from head to toe with a skinhead haircut, I would walk in, and he would ask me, "Oh, are you a surfer now?" I turned and thought, "Where did this question come from? From someone looking like an ersatz G.I. Joe?" I thought, "Okay, let's not be throwing any sort of mandatory identity around." One of the biggest frustrations I ended up having as I continued with that band was the mandatory-identity part. It went from that to "the barefoot drummer." And from there, it was, "Oh, he's the long-haired drummer now." I'd have people coming up to me at concerts and saying, "I know how it is, man. My girlfriend doesn't want me to cut mine off, either." Sorry, guys, it's got nothing to do with no girlfriend. [Laughs.]

Particularly with the way the media in general need to describe something, or classify it point-blank really quickly, I looked upon all these little categorizations as being real negative. Not so much frustrating, but it was certainly, "How shallow do people want to get?"

O: ***Toward the beginning, were you and/or Bob out of the closet? How did people treat you in hardcore punk circles?***

GH: Well, I had toured with male companions. When you went to the Longhorn, the original punk palace in town, it was three doors away from a bar that for 50 years has been called "The Gay '90s." It became a gay bar, conveniently. Especially in the early days of the pre-hardcore American punk thing, there was pretty consistent gayness coming through there. I'm the first one to use that word in the conversation, and it's not one that I really like the identity of, especially the way homosexual culture has moved in the post-AIDS days. I think it's gotten to be more about making money and wearing the right clothes. But I had toured with male companions very early on, and my partner at the time was posed with the question, "What does it feel like being the boyfriend of this famous man, blah blah blah?" And my friend was pretty unsophisticated, and he told her something that was rather crude, but it never seemed to be... You know, when you're dealing with a very small orbit, it doesn't seem like such a big thing. Then, by the time it would be a big thing, the people you're dealing with have dealt with it. Take Joan Rivers: Here's a person who's no stranger to gay people, and by the time we were appearing with her [on her TV show in 1987], it wouldn't be the kind of question or topic that the big industry moves you to discuss. You know what I mean? They accept it, they're cool with it, and they're doing it themselves, but we can't let the people in Topeka think that's the case. And really, it didn't define much about the band. If anything, it would have been just another question mark, because we were so unlike the stereotype du jour. With Bob, for instance, there was this apparent cross he was bearing about the thing for so long. He belabored making any kind of announcement about it, because other people were saying he was closeted and stuff, which was certainly not true, if anybody from Minneapolis would have asked, "What side is Bob's butter on?" There was no question. But he belabored this "coming out" thing, by which time the culture itself had become so unappreciative. I remember reading something in a Los Angeles gay paper, where it was like, "Big deal, Bob," you know? I think that kind of hurt him. I think he expected other gay people to be more supportive when in this day and age they're off doing their own thing. No real common ground, you know? I think maybe part of the hurt for him was that a little part of him wanted to be a spokesman. And, of course, I read some very cruel things that I didn't feel happy about when that happened for him. I've had a more strangely balanced relationship with the public and the media. I realized when the band broke up—and before then, for that matter—that a couple of vicious people shooting their mouth off can brand you with one topic. In my case, it was the breakup of the band and all the allegations that were thrown around then. It's just one part of the business that you have no control over. If somebody decides they're going to burn you, they're going to burn you.

O: ***Let the record show that I did not ask you about the breakup of Hüsker Dü.***

GH: It's been belabored. It was by no means... Well, I can safely say I was certainly not the biggest drug abuser in the band. But what's the point? The cow can't scratch off its brand, you know?

O: ***How early did the drugs start?***

GH: Well, there was amphetamine use throughout the early days. Around the time of *Metal Circus* I had stopped taking speed, because I did not appreciate the tension: I liked the momentum, but I didn't like the tension. Then, alcohol for me was out the window throughout the making of that record and *Zen Arcade*. Greg and I, in our very early days, kind of experimented together in a kind of late-'70s LSD renaissance, where there was some really, really good Owsely out there. It's certainly not anything I recommend, but that time of the decade was a crucial time for that. There was just tons and tons of superior LSD out there. There were all sorts of promoters who tried to pay bands off with whatever. As far as the breakup of Hüsker was concerned, without sounding like a paranoid freak, my contribution to the songwriting in numbers had grown so much, and, to be quite frank, Warners was making inroads to me personally, as it was expressed to me... Okay, Hüsker was this great do-it-yourself band, right? And I would have people coming up to me saying, "You guys' time would be much better spent concentrating on your art." Which was true. There was no reason that the band members themselves, at their peak, should be faxing their rider to people or making sure the cones are set up in the parking lot. Stupid minutiae shit like that. If anything, it just demonstrated our control-freakiness. By that time, a lot of time had gone on with the band, too. When we signed with Warners, we had been together for something like seven years, and by that time I had pretty much identified things I liked and didn't like. There was this control to deal with. Point blank, Mould told me when we were working on *Warehouse*, "We're not going to finish this song and this song because that would make the album equal: 10 songs Bob, 10 songs Grant. And that is never going to happen in this band." And then, two months later, I'm being told, "These side projects are not really impressing anybody. If you're going to put time into music, it's going to be put into this band." So, okay, I'm limited in what I can achieve inside this band, and I'm limited in what I can do outside this band. It's really no wonder that my personal results were what they were. But only one of three drug-abusing people was crucified about it. I read a review Friday, and this guy starts out, "If Grant Hart's drug addiction and contribution to the breakup of Hüsker Dü is true as alleged, then he probably has deserved the lack of success over the past 10 years." What the fuck does that have to do with music?

O: ***Greg Norton has managed to avoid all the post-Hüsker politics. You don't hear a lot from him.***

GH: No, but you hear a lot about Greg in different culinary magazines. Good for him, good for eaters.

O: ***Do you know why he decided to give up playing music?***

GH: I haven't discussed this theory of mine with him. You have a guy who wasn't the biggest songwriting force in the band, who, in his first post-Hüsker outings, musically was kind of stung by people who wanted to use him for his name and reputation but really didn't want to share the artistry and accolades. I think that hurt Greg, even in the last couple years of Hüsker Dü. Let me relate a story: Toward the end, when *Warehouse* came out and it was nine of my songs, eleven of Bob's songs, Greg had written one song, which became the B-side of the very last single. Now, after however many years that I'm fighting to get my songs across, Greg writes one song and immediately Bob's party line is, "We all three compose equally." After having never acknowledged my writing, when Greg writes this one song, it turns into, "We all three write equally." Before that, we would get, "I write most of the songs, and Grant contributes now and then." He couldn't deny it. It would turn from "he did it" to "we did it" to "I did it" with two simple retellings of the story. He's always looking backwards with his own Bob-colored glasses.

O: ***I'd heard some story about you and a gun in the Twin\Tone offices.***

GH: Oh, mercy! That would be apocryphal. Well, let's hear it.

O: ***I just heard that you came into the Twin\Tone offices waving a gun around once.***

GH: Tom Merkl from Nova Mob, who was also a lover of mine pretty much throughout the tenure of that band, would have people come up to him at family functions and say, "So, have you heard any good Grant stories lately?" And when you analyze it, the way my life has been puffed up, I offer everything to people in terms of sex, drugs, and rock 'n' roll. There's this apparent outlaw lack of remorse on my part that further stimulates the speculation. I've never even owned a firearm, which leads me to an interesting sidebar here. A friend of mine at the time of the breakup was posed with this question from Bob, who asked him, "Does Grant own any guns?" And, without batting an eye, my friend responded, "You'd be the first to know." [Laughs.] But it's one of two things: Either I'm completely innocent of such things, or I've done a great job of hiding the bodies. Ø

"The rest of the guys with guitars around their necks want credibility. I don't want credibility. That means nothing."

Gene Simmons (Kiss)

By Nathan Rabin

Originally Printed March 2002

Born Chaim Witz in Haifa, Israel, Gene Simmons grew up to be one of the most successful, notorious, and influential American rock stars of all time. As Simmons himself eagerly points out, the music, imagery, and showmanship of Kiss have seeped into nearly every corner of American culture, and not just because the sheer volume of its merchandise rivals any pop-culture phenomenon this side of Star Wars. *Since forming in 1973, Kiss has been an ultra-profitable institution, selling millions of albums, making untold millions through merchandising, and regularly ranking among the most popular live acts in the world. Though Simmons has remained in the group, he's also branched off into other arenas, including acting (*Wanted: Dead Or Alive, Red Surf*), producing, and even managing other artists' careers. Three decades into his career, he continues to make waves, obscene amounts of money, and headlines. The Kiss merchandising machine shows no sign of abating, either, with Simmons' 2002 autobiography (*Kiss And Make-Up*) hitting the bestseller list and numerous projects following in its wake. While promoting the book's release, Simmons spoke to* The Onion A.V. Club *about sex, money, his plans for further world domination, and why he's too rich to care.*

The Onion: ***After you immigrated to America, you spent some time in a yeshiva. Did that make much of an impact on you?***
Gene Simmons: No, not really. The biggest influence on me was television, which opened up all these worlds to me that I had only imagined. People were flying through the air. I saw people like Liberace going, "My brother George." I didn't know who these creatures were or where they came from. Everybody was bizarre. There were costume dramas and little kids with mouse ears on their heads. All that stuff opened up the possibilities visually for me. It was kind of like, "Why not?" You have to dream big. Television and comic books are, and continue to be, probably the biggest influence in my life. It's the biggest influence on everybody's life.
O: ***When and where did you develop the idea for what would become Kiss?***
GS: It happened gradually, over time. First, when I was 12, I saw a Spanish girl jumping rope. I never saw her face, but it was still the most beautiful sight I'd ever seen. And I thought, "Gee, this beats being a rabbi." That

was the first piece of the puzzle, and then the next piece of the puzzle was watching The Beatles on *The Ed Sullivan Show* and watching guys who thought The Beatles were cool and girls who wanted to have their babies. I thought, "Wow, that looks like a lot of fun." They were also from another country and spoke kind of weird, and so did I, having an accent at that point, so one thing led to another. Girls, The Beatles, horror, and science-fiction movies were the gruel that Kiss came out of.

O: ***Do you think that all rockers are motivated, at least initially, by a desire to meet women?***

GS: Sure. The straight ones, sure.

O: ***So you don't buy into that whole "It's all about the art" philosophy?***

GS: No. None of these guys ever took any music-theory lessons or anything, and that includes me. None of us ever took the time to go to music school, and we can't, to this day, read or write musical notation. We never took music lessons to learn about that. So the deluded notion that we're making anything other than sugar is nuts. I'm not saying that sugar doesn't taste good, but it burns fast. It's not meant to last. This is not classical music. It's modern, popular music, and for somebody who isn't really qualified to call himself a musician to claim he's making art is, at the very least, delusional.

O: ***What led you to decide to pursue music full-time?***

GS: Well, the band was always going on, but again, it was a social tool. It was a chance to get laid more often than not, because being in a band has its fringe benefits. It's a lot more exciting than saying, "Oh, yeah, I'm a dentist." If you're in a band, there's a kind of sexuality inherent in the clothes and what you're doing.

O: ***Were there always a lot of groupies around?***

GS: Well, if you're not famous, they're not groupies, because they know you. And they give it up a lot faster. Once you become famous, they become groupies, and groupies want to have sex with you because you're famous. That, by the way, is okay with me. However you get to the honey.

O: ***What were the first few Kiss shows like?***

GS: We did three club shows and then we got a recording contract. It happened that fast. Within a year and a half, we were playing Anaheim Stadium, and a year or two after that, we were the number-one band in the Gallup poll, above The Beatles and everybody. For three years in a row.

O: ***Why do you...***

GS: Wait, I'm not done tooting my own horn. Thirty years later, we are the number-one American group gold-record champions of all time. No other American group even comes close.

O: ***Why do you think Kiss took off so quickly?***

GS: Who cares? Just as long as we did. You know, if you win a race, you don't ask how you did it, as long as you do it. There are all sorts of notions I could throw back and forth about being in the right place at the right time, but I'm not gonna fool myself into thinking this is classical stuff, because if Kiss was around in the 1800s, people wouldn't have gotten it. You know, [sings] "Roll out the barrel / We'll have a barrel of fun," and John Philip Sousa, and then here comes Kiss. I just don't think Kiss would have worked then. But guess what? Beethoven worked then, and continues to work now.

O: ***It seems like Kiss was inspired by the more theatrical aspects of...***

GS: No, you said that. Kiss is not theatrical at all.

O: ***You don't think of yourself as theatrical?***

GS: No. We're not playing characters. In theater, you're playing characters. You believe you're somebody else, and you're acting.

O: ***And you don't feel like you're acting when you're onstage?***

GS: I think you should ask the millions of people who see us. They call out, "Hey, Gene!" It's clear to me you've never seen the band. See, Alice Cooper is theatrical. He says he plays a character. He's acting.

O: ***You're not playing a character?***

GS: No. You should ask the fans. In Alice's show, there are characters. There's a girl in a toothpaste outfit and dancers that come out. It's theater. We just get out there and play. Nobody else gets out there onstage. I mean, we dress interestingly, but so do football players.

O: ***Have you always played a major role in how Kiss is merchandised?***

GS: Sure. Of course, the more the better. Immediately, I saw that we were a rock 'n' roll brand, not just a rock 'n' roll band. See, the rest of the guys with guitars around their necks want credibility. I don't want credibility. That means nothing. Remember, none of these guys learned how to play their instruments properly. They all did it by ear, the lazy man's out. So a big word like "credibility" coming out of a guy who's unqualified to say anything other than "Do you want fries with that?" is delusional. I've never deluded myself about what this is. Kiss appears in comic books and puzzles and condoms and anything else we damn well please. I'm happy that the rest of the bands are afraid of merchandising themselves. They should all be afraid of it, and leave it to Kiss to do everything.

O: ***Was there ever a point where you said, "Gee, maybe this time the merchandising thing went too far? Maybe this is something that we don't want Kiss' name on?"***

GS: Oh, this is just the beginning. As far as I'm concerned, Christianity is next. I'm going to build my own shrine, and then every dollar I get is going to be tax-free. What do any of the other religions have that we don't have? It's all smoke and mirrors, anyway.

O: ***Why do you think fans remain so devoted to Kiss?***

GS: Kiss seems to be the anomaly. We completely and totally avoided all movements, including bowel movements. So, if hip-hop is around, we're not a part of hip-hop. If disco's around, we're not a part of it, although we'll do a disco song. If it's heavy metal, well, we were out before heavy metal. So you can't quite figure out what that thing is. We dress sillier and wear higher shoes than anybody. We wear more makeup and high heels than your mommy does, and we completely disregard all notions of what the rules of proper behavior are. The rule of proper behavior for a hip-hop artist is, you're supposed to be a criminal. You know, the more criminal stuff you have in your past, the higher your credibility. There goes that word again. You wear cowboy hats to get more credibility if you're a country star. If you're a punk kind of guy, well, it's more about how you are: spit-in-the-face, that type of attitude. Each and every one of these genres has rules. And I say, in the nicest possible way, "Fuck them all." The rules are made to be broken, as far as I'm concerned, because the original spirit of rock 'n' roll was, "There are no rules." And so, by definition, it's a contradiction in terms if you're a punk guy and you refuse to do a ballad. You're a slave to your own rules. That's why Kiss very bravely did a disco song. We have no problem doing ballads or selling merchandise.

"For somebody who isn't really qualified to call himself a musician to claim he's making art is, at the very least, delusional."

O: ***Kiss did a concept album [*****Music From "The Elder"*****] in the early '80s. What led you to pursue that kind of an album?***

GS: Delusional behavior. I fell into it because it was based on my story, "The Elder." We thought, "What we need to do is turn the critics around, because the fans don't count." And here we are, outselling everyone, outselling the Stones two-to-one and all that, breaking every attendance record set by The Beatles and Elvis. I thought, "Oh, we need to turn the critics around and make them like us." So we did a concept record. The Who had *Tommy*, The Beatles had *Sgt. Pepper*, Kiss needed *The Elder*.

You know what? I was wrong, because *The Elder* doesn't stand up to those records, and at the end of the day, why are we trying to court the favor of critics? If you think about it, critics are an unnecessary life-form on the planet Earth, and here's why: because it's a job without credentials. You don't have to go to school. To be a journalist, of course, you need to get a journalism degree, and there's such a thing as journalistic ethics. You know, if you print news, your opinion is not important. A critic has no credibility whatsoever. He doesn't even need a license to be a critic. He just sort of says, "I'm a critic." And then you are.

O: ***Couldn't the same be said of rock stars?***

GS: That's right. Except we're more famous and everybody likes us. Everybody hates critics. A long time ago, David Lee Roth—whom I discovered, I discovered Van Halen—said something that I found very apropos. He said, at the height of Van Halen's popularity, "You know why critics love Elvis Costello and hate Van Halen? Because critics look like Elvis Costello." And you know what? He's right. Critics look like the people who never got laid in high school.

O: ***Do you think it's a matter of getting revenge?***

GS: No, it's a matter of little people sitting in dark corners that nobody cares about.

O: ***Do you think people resent you because you have lots of money and have sex with lots of women and are a rock star?***

GS: Yes. I resent me for having lots of money and having sex with lots of women.

O: ***Earlier, you mentioned being involved in the business aspects of Kiss, and in the '80s you actually managed other artists. How did that come about?***

GS: I'm from Israel, so America has no limits. I started a record label, and then I started managing other artists, like Liza Minelli. I don't know. You want to see if you can do it. I figured out the Kiss rat-maze pretty quickly—I saw that I could get to the cheese pretty quickly—so I thought to myself, "Maybe there's another maze over there that I can get through, too." Life is all about the hunt, not the kill.

O: ***Is it true that Eddie Van Halen wanted to join Kiss at one point?***

GS: Yes. He came down while we were recording *Creatures Of The Night*, and he had had his fill of Roth, and he said, "I'm leaving. Are you guys looking for a guitar player?" That was back in '82. I told him to stick with his band.

O: ***How did the television movie* Kiss Meets The Phantom Of The Park *come about?***

GS: Well, they came to us. Kiss was so enormously popular back in the days when rock bands just played onstage, because we pervaded other areas. You know, every Halloween, you'd see an army of Kiss people walking around. I mean, if you're the Foo Fighters, God bless 'em, you tour and you make albums, and that's it. Kiss somehow pervaded Christmas and Halloween, and you saw people walking around who wanted to be like us. It was kind of a combination of Superman, Batman, Santa Claus, and a rock band. It wasn't just, "I like your records." They wanted to buy the toys and the games, and they wanted to look like us. When they approached us about the movie, the wacky idea came up of "Kiss meets Dracula and Frankenstein." It was kind of cheesy at the time, and in retrospect, maybe it's kind of retro-kitsch.

O: ***Is that how you caught the acting bug?***

GS: Nah. I want to do everything. I want to be the president, I want to learn Tae Kwan Do, I want to climb mountains. I'm always bugged by the notion that I can't do everything.

O: ***As a kid, I heard a lot of wild stories about Kiss, that their blood was in their comic books and...***

GS: That's true. I don't remember if it was my idea or Marvel Comics', but it just kind of came up. Stan Lee, the original head and creator of a lot of the characters, flew us up to Buffalo to their printing plant, and we literally withdrew blood from our veins and added it to the red ink. So, point of fact, there are actually comic books out there with our DNA in it.

O: *Another rumor was that Kiss stood for Knights In Satanic Service.*

GS: The Southern states, below the Mason-Dixon line, are still in the 1800s. There, the church, and particularly the far-right portion of the church, has a big hold on politics and perception. It started there, that whole bizarre notion. Especially that "Gene Simmons is the devil" thing. I go, "What do you mean by that?" And people say, "Well, you look like the devil." I want to meet the person who's actually met the devil. What does he look like? Especially past the Bible Belt, there are always people marching near our shows with crosses on their backs. It's always struck me, how come you never see Jews with the Star Of David on their backs? Or Muslims with the crescent moon? No, it's always the Christians with the cross. It's such bizarre behavior. It's almost like they're stuck back 2,000 years ago.

O: *Earlier, you mentioned performing ballads while in makeup. Does the makeup ever make you feel self-conscious?*

GS: I'm too rich to care. It always strikes me as a bizarre question. I don't even know what that means.

O: *When you took off the makeup, initially, were you anxious that you were making a mistake that you'd later regret?*

GS: I wasn't sure whether it would work, but we had to do it to maintain the integrity of the original makeup, because as more and more new members came into the band, it became silly. You know, "Here's Giraffe Boy and here's Hawkman." Less is more sometimes. By the way, even without the makeup, we did pretty well. We still filled up arenas and kept getting platinum records. It was not a problem.

O: *Is there a period of music that you regard as Kiss' golden age?*

GS: Maybe the beginning, the first few records. But that seems to be the case with most bands. There are very few bands like The Beatles, where they have this grand catalog and anything you pick up by them is a gem. Clearly, the Stones' early albums are more impressive than their later ones. I didn't like the '80s records very much in retrospect, although while I was doing them, I liked them a lot. I mean, everybody has photos of themselves at 14, where if you looked at them now, you'd think, "God, what a dork." But at the time, you didn't think you were a dork. You only have clarity in retrospect.

O: *You appear in the movie* Porn Star *with Ron Jeremy. What's your relationship with him like? What do you have in common with him?*

GS: Girls. Or, more specifically, the hunt for more rather than less. One ejaculation kicks out a billion sperm. We're designed to want more than just one. One woman is not going to be able to have all those sperm. The reason we can ejaculate more than once—well, those who are healthy and attractive and powerful like myself—is for multiple partners.

O: *Looking back on your life, do you have any regrets?*

GS: No. I think perhaps I'd try to do more. When you feel like you've done enough, you should just dig a hole, jump in it, and say, "Thank you and goodnight." That's the time to say, "Okay, I'm done." While you're alive, the notion is to do more. ⊘

"I started playing guitar in clubs back when America was still free and you could go out at night."

Merle Haggard

By Keith Phipps

Originally Printed March 2001

Merle Haggard was left fatherless at 9, taught himself to play guitar at 12, and became a runaway at 14. After run-ins with the law and a stint in San Quentin, he found his way into the then-burgeoning Bakersfield scene, quickly becoming one of the most popular country artists of the '60s and '70s. He didn't write many of his early hits, but his blue-collar roots came to the fore in the songs he did write, including "Mama Tried," "I Threw Away The Rose," "The Bottle Let Me Down," "Big City," and "Hungry Eyes." But when the new Nashville sound arrived in the late '80s, Haggard and many of his contemporaries became victims of industry indifference. His flagging career was further complicated by drugs and financial problems, and he didn't get his life back under control until the early '90s. Even then, Haggard came into conflict with his record label, which he accused of intentional sabotage. (His Curb albums, released without promotion and with nondescript covers, seem to justify that claim.) In 2000, Anti Records released his sonically spare, stylistically diverse, and thoroughly winning If I Could Only Fly. *That album showcased a reflective mood that extended into Haggard's 2001 interview with* The Onion A.V. Club.

The Onion: ***A lot of people were surprised to see you signed to the Anti label. How did you end up there?***
Merle Haggard: Maybe by accident. They called, and then somebody... It was their design. They came to me and asked me what I'd been doing, and was I fixing to sign with somebody or was I gonna stay with my own label. I had my own label, and they knew that. I said, "You know, it depends on what people offer. I'm just not really interested in a bad contract right now." I liked the fact that they were associated with punk rock and all that, because really, at the time I signed with 'em, I was really pissed off at country music. Not because they wouldn't play my music on the radio, but I was pissed off at the music they were playing. It doesn't make a difference whether they play me or not.
O: ***If they weren't playing you, but they were playing good music, that would be okay?***
MH: Yeah, if there was something better than what I had being played, I'd be happy, but there ain't. They don't even give the public a chance to decide. We're turning into the society that is accepting the force-feed. I don't quite understand why we're going for the things we're going for. There's no process of

elimination anymore in music. They have these grooming schools, and they're turning out these clones, and the music is sounding so refined that it's not even interesting.

O: ***I couldn't tell you what country music is at this point.***

MH: I wouldn't have a clue. I wouldn't know if a guy was a country artist or where to classify him. And there are so many conditions to programming in America, where it's dominated by these people that own 800 stations that have no idea who to play and who not to play, and they listen to somebody or read somebody else's programming sheet. Eight hundred stations are controlled by some guy that doesn't have a clue as to what to do about music.

O: ***It could be argued that when you first came on the scene, country music was in kind of a crisis, too. There was a refined countrypolitan sound that...***

MH: I don't think it's ever been in the crisis it's in now. The city of Nashville, Tennessee, as far as music, is kaput. There's no music industry down there. The Grand Ole Opry is on the verge of closing its doors, and they've been in existence since 1925 or so. The city of Austin is becoming the maverick center of music on the climb, but Nashville is really at its lowest moment right now. I hate to even pick on 'em and bring it to the public's attention, but it is a fact. And it's all because of 10 years of force-feeding the public instead of giving them what they want. The radio stations are in trouble, and the people that buy the talent and whatnot, that make a living buying talent, have all went broke. Promoters aren't going to buy music this year at the fairs; they're gonna buy tractor-pulling, because they spent millions of dollars in the last decade buying talent that nobody'd heard of. They'd spend $150,000 on some guy that had one hit, and he'd come out and do a medley of his hits, and it just didn't sit well with people.

O: ***You've said that one big draw in signing with Anti was they didn't want to make any changes to what you've done. Was that a big problem at other labels?***

MH: [Curb Records head Mike] Curb, for example, had an idea. He wanted me to record with what he called "a hot Nashville band." That hot Nashville band was collectively put together from everywhere, New York to L.A., but it was funny. Anyway, that's the way he put it. So I'd been there and done that, and I didn't want to do that again, and that's sort of what I meant by what I told them, that I'm not interested in anybody that wants me to record. What music I have has already been recorded, and it's either good or it's bad and it lays there, one way or the other. In other words, you take what I got to sell. I've already recorded. I'm not going to go somewhere and record.

O: If I Could Only Fly ***was recorded at your home studio, right?***

MH: Yeah. We just... I've had my own studio for 20 years, and I've made a lot of hits, and when the Garth Brooks thing happened in '89, it was sort of like they said, "Hey, let's get rid of the rest of the old cocksuckers and get them out of here, too." It was like the whole business turned around and went in another direction. Guys like me were pitched out to pasture.

O: ***Would you say*** **If I Could Only Fly** ***is more autobiographical than most of your albums, or less?***

MH: It's mostly always that way. If I write the songs, it's something about me, something I've done. I find that more successful than writing poetry. Putting melody to poetry is sort of what they do a lot of times. I try to come up with a concept and have a real thought that makes the difference, or some sort of a lesson or something, that's married to a good melody that's enjoyable to hear.

O: ***Is it easier to write songs about getting wasted, or to write songs about staying sober?***

MH: There's songs... I don't sit down and sweat out songs. I'm not a sweater. I don't get up in the morning and say, "Okay, I'm gonna try to write two lines by noon." I just try to keep the channels open. Things I write are impulsive, and I have stacks of songs all over the house, and it's just a very impulsive thing that I do. They come, I write the whole thing in a matter of minutes, and then I may improve upon it, but usually it's verbatim what will happen at the session. People say they want to get together with me and write, and I say, "I don't know how you could do that, because I don't know when I'm gonna write, and I'm not gonna sit around and wait. When I get an idea to write, I'm gonna call you up and say, 'Hey, I'm ready to write'? I'm not gonna do that, so how in the hell are we gonna write together?" It's just sort of silly, the way they go. They meet at 9 in the morning, pair off in pickups, and come back at 5 in the afternoon and see what they've written. That's exactly what the music sounds like to me, like they wrote them in pickups. There's never any credibility involved in that. It's just copy this and copy that, steal this and steal that.

O: ***You've cut tribute albums to Jimmie Rodgers and Bob Wills. How important is it for artists to pay dues to their inspirations? Do you think enough people today do that?***

MH: I don't know. It was enjoyable for me. I've just sort of stumbled through my career enjoying it, rather than... If I had a choice, and there was a "Y" in the road, I would always take the one that was more fun, as opposed to the one that might make me more money. In some ways, that was not agreeable in most cases to the people in charge of my money. There was a lot of maverick in me and my career. I just didn't do things the way I was supposed to do them. I don't really fit any mold. I grew up playing music in a beer-joint band, playing guitar to make some extra money, and I was an electrician. I worked five days a week, and I started playing guitar in clubs back when America was still free and you could go out at night. You could have a fistfight outside the beer joint and no one was carrying a gun. Back when I was living my life.

O: ***Since the '70s, you've been writing nostalgic songs like "That's The Way It Was In '51." Do you find that you get more nostalgic or less nostalgic as you get older?***

MH: Oh, I think you get more nostalgic, because the things that you'll do in life... The margins of success are set at some time in your life, and you peak out maybe around 42 or somewhere between there and 50. I think I probably did. Then you start looking back on your own life, on the records you've broken and whatever. I'm sure that great golfers look back on a better score, and it's no different with entertainers. We're probably more like sports figures. There's a certain amount of reserve energy that has to be available for me to perform and do it the way it's right. When I get to the age that I can't hit the stage with that sort of fire, then I'm gonna leave. That's where I'm gonna call it off.

O: ***But for now you're happy to stay on the road, right?***

MH: Well, I'm really happy to stay off the road, but I can't afford to do that, because if I let the chops get too far down, I wouldn't be able to sing and play guitar and do what I do, and then what the hell good would I be?

O: ***How do you stay in touch with your working-class roots?***

MH: I just follow my nose, and instead of letting someone run my affairs and probably make me wealthy within a matter of years, I've just kept the board of directors down to zero. I make all the decisions, and they can't all be right, and my lifestyle is very expensive, so that means I have to work a lot. It's the opposite side of the coin from sinking back into the recliner and becoming somebody they bury.

O: ***If you had to choose three songs to be remembered by, which three would you choose?***

MH: "Working Man Blues," "Big City," and "Mama Tried."

O: ***Why those?***

MH: I don't know. I guess that was just an impulsive answer. I wanted to be honest.

O: ***How do you feel about being closely identified with the politics of "Okie From Muskogee" and "The Fightin' Side Of Me" now?***

MH: Oh, I must have been an idiot. It's documentation of the uneducated that lived in America at the time, and I mirror that. I always have. It's pretty easy to lie to me. They had me in a film called *Wag The Dog* because of "Okie From Muskogee" and my close scrutiny of the people that are being shitted. I've become self-educated since I wrote that song. But it still has a very timely description.

"I have a shot of George Dickel within heart-attack range at all times, for reasons of being 63 years old."

O: ***You were expressing how a lot of people felt.***

MH: That's what I'm saying. That's the collective demeanor of America at the time.

O: ***Do you feel that those songs and the controversy over them limited your audience?***

MH: I'm sure it did. And there, again, I made mistakes, because I didn't have anybody saying, "Well, you shouldn't do this. You shouldn't do that. You know, you might not should do that, because you've got this good career going, and you've got this flow. Step out here and make a political opinion, and you're gonna be classified an idiot." I probably could have avoided a lot of this, had I had someone managing me that... I had a manager, but he didn't really try to get involved in my feelings on things. He always let me go.

O: ***Did you vote in the [2000] election?***

MH: Yeah, yeah, I did. And I don't know, I wasn't happy with the count myself. I thought it was pretty damn obvious that we had a situation there where it made no difference what the American public thought. They intended to be in office, and they are in office. That's the bottom line, and we've been manipulated. I feel really violated as a citizen.

O: ***You put out stuff through your web site, right?***

MH: We're doing our best to have the most desired web site in the world and sell all of our goods like everybody else is trying to do. And, of course, the competition is great, but the opportunity's vast. I'm not educated about computers, and I don't have any business talking about them, but they're upon us, and it looks like they're gonna make us educate ourselves to deal with them. I guess a guy like me has to talk about hiring a roomful of people to look at one of those computers. You see these rooms where somebody, some guy, some entrepreneur has got a bunch of people in there watching the computers. It's kind of funny to me, actually. Then they'll have on a cell phone at the same time. They'll be reading e-mail and talking to somebody on a cell phone and getting paid, by God.

O: ***I saw on your web site that you're selling a picture of you with Smokey The Bear. How did that come about?***

MH: They just came to me and found me to be a real live patriotic American that they wanted to take a picture with, and I was honored. I was one of about 100 celebrities. There were a lot of different people—John Wayne, people like that—that they took pictures with. They took everybody from John Wayne to Mickey Mouse, so Merle Haggard was somewhere in between that.

O: ***Are you still a spokesman for George Dickel whiskey?***

MH: No, George Dickel sold to a big conglomerate, and they're not interested in doing things like they used to. Another one of those sad stories.

O: ***Actually, that was probably a better endorsement deal than George Jones'. I never quite understood why he endorses dog food.***

MH: Well, 'cause they wrote him a check, bottom line.

O: ***You and George Dickel just seemed like a more appropriate match.***

MH: Well, whiskey, I really believed in what I was selling. I really... I think George Dickel is absolutely the best Tennessee mash whiskey. It's my understanding that Jack Daniel's was an attempt to try to take the recipe of George Dickel to a commercial state of reproducing it. Whereas they couldn't do that with George Dickel, because, in order to make it the way they make it, they would have had to repeat too many different formulas. It would have been impossible. They did certain things at certain temperatures in a certain kind of water. So I went down there and looked at their distilleries and saw what they were doing, saw the difference between that and Jack Daniel's, and I couldn't believe it. You take George Dickel and you pour it over ice and hold it up to the light, and it won't separate. But if you take Jack Daniel's and do that, hold it up to the light and you'll notice that the corn oil starts separating from the whiskey, because it hasn't been married at the correct temperature. When you go down and have this education thrown upon you, and then you drink it... Everybody got drunk when we was taking pictures. It was about 20 girls and about 20 guys, and we're all down in this creek drunk with two fists of George Dickel apiece, and we all stayed over and had breakfast together, and not a one of us had a hangover.

O: ***That's an endorsement right there.***

MH: I thought, "Man, I was meant to see that for some reason." It was true. And since then, I have a shot of George Dickel within heart-attack range at all times, for reasons of being 63 years old.

O: ***You must like somebody who plays country music now. Do you like anyone out there?***

MH: Oh, shit, I like a lot of them. I'm just kidding you. I like these Dixie Chicks. I like them a whole lot. I'm more into Dwight Yoakam than I would be into somebody younger than that. I've heard a couple things I really liked on the air by new artists in the last year. I don't know what their names were, but there was a delightful improvement in creativity in the couple records I heard this year.

O: ***Do you think country music will turn itself around?***

MH: I don't think so. I think this particular music is gonna die just like rock 'n' roll died, and something else moved in. Something else will overtake it. There'll be people that will last who came out of this decade, but there won't be many. Garth Brooks is about all they'll remember 50 years from now. Let's be honest: This is the Garth Brooks period, and we're still recovering. There hasn't been anybody who really went out there and grabbed the mic in the last couple years. There's been a couple of groups, like The Backstreet Boys... What's this other one?

O: ***'N Sync.***

MH: Yeah, 'N Sync. But who the fuck is 'N Sync? What guy are you gonna remember? Will there be a Ringo Starr in that group or not? I don't know. I wonder about it. Ø

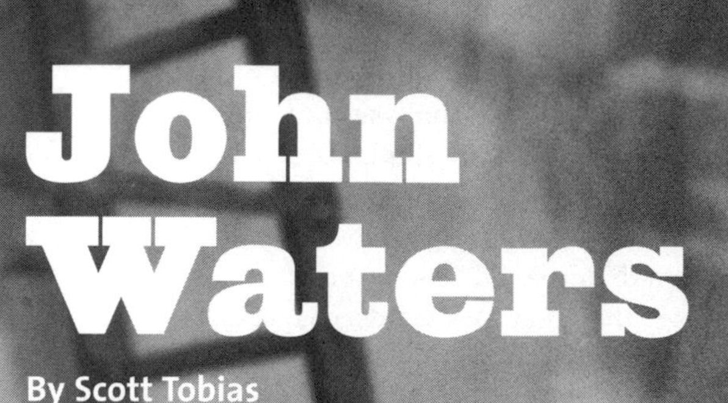

By Scott Tobias

Originally Printed August 2000

"They're all in the Battle Of Filth and they're duking it out. I've retired. I'm a filth elder."

It's been more than 30 years since writer-director John Waters and his friends first terrorized the streets and makeshift screening rooms of Baltimore with their underground assaults on decency and good taste. After pushing the boundaries of no-brow comedy with such crude early efforts as 1969's Mondo Trasho *and 1970's* Multiple Maniacs, *Waters caused a sensation on the midnight circuit with 1972's* Pink Flamingos, *a triumph of gross-out one-upmanship. His cult status continued to swell with 1975's* Female Trouble, *1977's* Desperate Living, *and 1981's Odorama-enhanced* Polyester, *but he surprised audiences again with 1988's PG-rated hit* Hairspray, *a bright nostalgia piece about television's early-'60s teen dance programs. He also found time to write his essential autobiography,* Shock Value, *and to publish a collection of humorous essays,* Crackpot: The Obsessions Of John Waters. *In the '90s, Waters made a smooth transition into studio projects, still thriving as his brand of comedy seeped into the mainstream via projects like* Cry-Baby, Serial Mom, *and* Pecker. *Just after the release of 2000's* Cecil B. Demented, *Waters spoke to* The Onion A.V. Club *about irony, filth, subversion, and censors.*

The Onion: ***In some ways,* Cecil B. Demented *seems as close to autobiography as you've gotten yet.***

John Waters: But that's what people said about *Pecker*. That's what they say about every movie, so I don't really agree with that statement. I get why you think that. Some of the things that happen in *Cecil* happened to us: We ran from the police, I didn't know how to ask permission to do anything, and I've used regular people on the street as extras and they didn't know it. But I didn't kill people, so that's certainly exaggerated. And Cecil is much more handsome than I was. Also, I had a much better sense of humor. Because he's a fascist, a real cult director—but like Waco, that kind of cult.

O: ***But the film does hark back to your earlier work. What was your relationship to the underground during that period?***

JW: I had no relationship, I just made the movies. In those days, early films like *Mondo Trasho* were never shown in New York, and that's really the only place underground films were at the time. It was totally a New York chauvinist thing. They didn't even look at my movies, because I was from Baltimore. Nothing played there until *Pink Flamingos* became a hit. In those days, I didn't know any directors. And no one said my films were any good, either, except the hippie audience that were really punks and didn't know it yet. My audience was about a third gay, a third angry hippies, and a third bikers. Bikers loved my movies. They used to come to my sets and try to eat shit—after *Pink Flamingos* was made. So it was an angry audience that hated peace and love and was sick of it. That was my core audience in the beginning, but no one said my

"Every person was on drugs in the audience, every person was on drugs in the movies themselves, and I was on drugs when I thought them up."

films were good except for Fran Lebowitz in an interview, and she was a cab driver. The only other good review we got was from *New York* magazine, which called *Pink Flamingos* "beyond pornography." [Laughs.] So nobody was saying they were good, and they never played in real movie theaters, but the audience was rabid. Every person was on drugs in the audience, every person was on drugs in the movies themselves, and I was on drugs when I thought them up. And [the exhibitors] would put down sawdust on the floor because of all the puking.

O: ***I remember you saying that if a person throws up at one of your movies, it's akin to a standing ovation.***

JW: Oh, sure, I would take credit for it. But they weren't puking because of the movie; they were puking because they were drunk.

O: ***Your films received a mixed reception in prison, didn't they?***

JW: Yeah. Later, when I showed them in a class I taught at prison during the '80s, the reaction was racially divided. Oddly enough, when I showed *Pink Flamingos* to my class—and I had a good class, because the warden gave me the smartest and the worst, the smartest people who had done the worst crimes—every black person left when Divine ate dog shit. They never came back, dropped the course. And every white person stayed. It was so weird.

O: ***Do you have any theories about that?***

JW: I don't know to this day. "Fuckin' white people are crazy," that's all I can think of. [Laughs.] That's what they must have said. Later, when I taught in prison another time, I walked in and my class was all black Muslim, with the hat and everything. At first, it was tense, but then I made them do improv and pretend like they were on a plane that was crashing. After that, we got along all right.

O: ***How do you feel about your sort of lowbrow humor crossing over into the mainstream?***

JW: I don't feel any connection to it. I'm not against it—I like those movies—but I don't feel like I'm part of it. I get asked that question all the time, and I get why people ask it, but it's only made it easier to get my films made. It hasn't hurt me in any way. But I did those films so long ago, and I don't really do them anymore. I'm not in this contest, this Battle Of Filth. I won! [Laughs.] Now, they're all in the Battle Of Filth and they're duking it out. I've retired. I'm a filth elder. I'm the Henry Cabot Lodge of filth. I don't think that many directors who started out making weird films in the '60s are still working, because you have to change. There are still kids who see my movies for the first time who want me to make *Pink Flamingos* over and over, but if I did, it wouldn't work. It would be too calculated. *Pink Flamingos* was made as a crime, almost. Nobody sent me head shots to make that movie. The guy with the singing asshole just came over and showed me. Incidentally, he went to the re-release 25 years later—he's like 50 years old—and he sat in the theater. When his scene came on, he would look over at the person next to him and whisper, "That's me." And people were shocked. It was like *Candid Camera*: It was terrorism all over again. People would be really uptight, because what could you say when you're sitting there in the theater and the guy with the sphincter is right next to you? Movie manners. He just did it on his own, which I thought was really a good star appearance.

O: ***Considering the extreme material that people are willing to accept as mainstream entertainment, it's surprising that the*** **Pink Flamingos** ***re-release still has the power to repulse people.***

JW: Yeah, it does, because it's real. The chicken got fucked and we ate it. Divine really eats dog shit. I mean, no one really shot a load into Cameron Diaz's hair. That's different, plain and simple.

O: ***Did you enjoy carting it out again for critics and the ratings board to revisit?***

JW: Well, no, because I was afraid they would take it out on me with *Cecil B. Demented*. I enjoyed the fact that it was the number-two best-selling video in the country. Number one was *Jerry Maguire* and number three was *The Rock*. How could that be? Blockbuster won't even carry it, so I don't know how that happened. In L.A., in certain neighborhoods, it was in supermarket checkout lines. I loved that. So I'm proud of the fact that when it came out again, a new audience showed up that hadn't been exposed to it before. And it didn't mellow. It got worse in a way, because of political correctness. It scared people, because it was so badly made that it looks like a documentary. It looks like *Blair Witch*. I think Rex Reed said it best, about *Female Trouble*, when he said, "Who are these people? Where do they go when the sun goes down? Isn't there a law or something?" People thought that was real. They thought we were those characters. I mean, we were pretty scary, I suppose, but not harmful. Eating the shit was nothing, really. It was worse when Divine had to shit in a box, gift-wrap it, and bring it to the set the next day. When I think back on it, that's much weirder. "Hey, could you shit in a box for me?" was said about as casually as, "Learn your lines."

O: ***What were your experiences with the Maryland Censor Board like?***

JW: We had a lot of trouble with the woman from the censor board. She still hates us to this day. I mean, she was my best press agent, but I hated her. She would actually hand me a pair of scissors, which is something I can laugh about now, but it wasn't funny to me at the time. She couldn't cut the dialogue, but she would make suggestions like "rear entry." Rear entry? I had never heard it said that way in my life. And she would also say, "Don't tell me about sex. I was married to an Italian!" I mean, what do you say to that? She said, "You can't show that vagina!" and I'd say, "That's a man." And she really wanted to cut that dog doo-doo. It made her so mad, because there were no laws. She couldn't find a law that said you couldn't eat shit. There's still no law, though people have horrified me over the years by coming up to me and saying, "Man, your movie turned me on." [Laughs.] I wasn't counting on that.

"*Pink Flamingos* was made as a crime, almost. Nobody sent me head shots to make that movie. The guy with the singing asshole just came over and showed me."

O: ***Do you get frightened of your fans sometimes? I remember a story about you having to sign a used tampon.***

JW: Oh, yeah. I've signed tampons. I signed a colostomy bag. This girl tattooed my autograph on her. But, no, I'm not really scared of them. They're really loyal and they send me great presents. Every year, I have to do an article about things I want for Christmas, and I always get them. Things that aren't expensive but are hard to find, like collectible things you can find in a thrift shop.

O: ***Other than the Odorama cards [scratch-and-sniff cards for strange odors in*** **Polyester*****], have***

you been able to pull off any large-scale William Castle gimmicks?

JW: Well, eating shit is a gimmick. I think Tab Hunter, in a way, is a gimmick, to have him with Divine [in *Polyester*]. Stars are gimmicks, aren't they? Odorama was a joke that worked, but I don't think I'd do anything like it again. They were expensive, too. And then it got politically correct: They wouldn't let me do "sniffing glue," so they reprinted them. And nobody paid us for them, either. Imagine collecting on your Odorama bill. It's hard enough to get rentals from independent theaters. "Hmm... What should I pay, my gas bill or my

"Why would you want to see teenagers unless they're nude? And stupid. I like stupid, nude teenagers."

Odorama bill?" What am I going to say? "You'll never get Odorama again!" There was absolutely nothing we could do about it.

O: ***There seems to be a perception that your tastes are exclusively cultish, which isn't necessarily true.***

JW: No. I liked *Magnolia*, which was my favorite movie of 2000. *Happiness* and *Magnolia* are two from the last couple years that I really, really liked. I liked *Rosetta* a lot. Something about an ugly girl who lives in a trailer with her alcoholic mother and can't get a job... That's my kind of movie! I love a feel-bad movie. That's what I like best: a minimalist, foreign, low-budget, feel-bad movie.

O: ***What was your experience on* The Simpsons *like?***

JW: It was great. You do a table reading with the whole cast and then you're all behind microphones, sort of like *The Fred Waring Show*. You do a page or two at a time, in order. It took a day and I loved it. And *The Simpsons* is a great, radical show. That there could be a show for the whole family, at that hour, about that... This never could have happened when I was in grade school. It's a subversive show in the best sense, because parents don't realize what their kids are watching. It's like a sneak attack.

O: ***Were you disappointed with the way Randall Kleiser's career turned out? [Waters wrote about Kleiser, director of* Grease *and* The Blue Lagoon, *in his book* Crackpot: The Obsessions Of John Waters. *—ed.]***

JW: No, not at all. He told me recently that he was going to do another movie along the lines of *Summer Lovers* or *The Blue Lagoon*. He's doing nude teenagers again, which makes me happy.

O: ***The problem now is that there are plenty of teenage movies...***

JW: But they're not nude. They should be nude. What's the point? Why would you want to see teenagers unless they're nude? And stupid. I like stupid, nude teenagers. Randall likes rich, stupid, nude teenagers. I like them poor. There's this new show on The WB called *The Young Americans*, which is very Randall Kleiser-ish. Only they should be nuder.

O: ***In* Pecker, *there's a key point in which a character calls for the death of irony. Do you have any struggles with it?***

JW: Not really, because that's my trade. I'm an irony dealer. I mean, that was an ironic statement. Irony is what I deal in from the moment I wake up until the moment I go to sleep. I am weary of it, though. To me, irony is snobbery in a way. There's no irony in Bangladesh. What's so-bad-it's-good if you're hungry? [Laughs.] Baltimore is very unironic, and they're not impressed with anything. People who like irony are impressed. People who don't could give a shit. They don't care if you like them, and they're not "with it"... With what? They think you're an asshole! I like to be around people like that sometimes. I don't want to be around witty people all the time. I know enough of them.

O: ***So this ends up being the New York-vs.-Baltimore problem?***

JW: Yes. I live in both for that exact reason. I'll ask myself, "What do I feel like doing this weekend? Do I feel like going to a redneck biker bar in Baltimore that I love, that totally accepts me, and where anyone else who went there would get beat up? Or do I want to go to an art opening in New York?" I love doing that, too. It's just a train ride. And I never go in the middle. That's my success, because I never have to be in the middle. I never have to be around assholes. The middle is people who want to be just like everyone else, and I've never understood that, even when I was 3 years old. It wasn't until I started reading and found books they wouldn't let us read in school that I discovered you could be insane and happy and have a good life without being like everybody else. I don't begrudge people who are "normal" like that. I like my family. I like kids. I like my nieces and nephew, though I have no desire to have a kid myself. I have no desire to be married or join the Army or anything like that. I'm not one bit like everybody else. And proud of it! ⌀

"We were influenced by so many other people that it's a compliment when someone's not ashamed to admit they like us."

Rick Nielsen (Cheap Trick)

By John Krewson

Originally Printed March 1997

*During the first half-decade after its 1975 inception, Cheap Trick became the consummate opening act, slowly growing in popularity while setting the stage for the likes of AC/DC, Santana, Kiss, and The Kinks. During the '80s, the band released everything from T&A soundtrack fodder ("Up The Creek") to a Top 40 power ballad ("The Flame") that could almost have passed as a parody of the genre. But with so many acts citing its wide-open power-pop as an influence, Cheap Trick seemed due for a renaissance in the '90s, when it released a box set (*Sex, America, Cheap Trick*) and a well-regarded comeback album (1997's* Cheap Trick*), returned to frequent touring, and performed the theme for Fox's* That '70s Show. *Shortly before the release of* Cheap Trick, *guitarist and chief songwriter Rick Nielsen examined his group's highs and lows in an interview with* The Onion A.V. Club.

The Onion: ***You have a detail-oriented reputation, as far as your music goes. Have you ever produced anything besides Cheap Trick's records?***

Rick Nielsen: I've been asked to do quite a few things, but when business was good I was always too busy. When business was lousy, I was still too busy. I'm going to start taking more projects, because I enjoy it. I produced and engineered stuff for *Stars On Ice* with Scott Hamilton, and I just did something for some modern-dance people who are with Baryshnikov and the Joffrey Ballet in New York. It played for three days three weeks ago. Reviews were such that it warranted more play, as they say.

O: Stars On Ice *to the Joffrey Ballet to Cheap Trick is quite a range.*

RN: Yeah, well, you know. I did an interview last week for *TV Guide Online*—I was like, "What in the world?"—and I was telling them basically the same story. Anything on ice to the Joffrey is not a direct line in most people's minds. And the editor says, "I'd love to have you for my other magazine." I say, "Oh, yeah? What's that?" And he says, "*Interview.*" "Oh!" I say. He says, "Yeah! I met Andy Warhol years ago." I thought, "Man, this is cool!" Telling people something they don't know rather than the normal ordinary boring bio baloney that's usually wrong anyhow. When I do interviews, I always go in with the attitude that something good can happen from it. You try to get something positive out of the whole situation. Otherwise, why do these dumb things?

O: ***You've enjoyed renewed popularity lately.***
RN: We have?
O: ***You played at Lollapalooza, didn't you?***
RN: Oh, yeah, we did! The bands asked us, and we didn't say no.
O: ***Who in particular asked you?***
RN: Soundgarden and Metallica, The Ramones, Everclear... I think they all wanted to see if we still knew how to play. And we got up there and just kicked their ass. We did. We just played and played well. It was fun.
O: ***Do you see a lot of Cheap Trick's influence in other bands?***
RN: I never really do. But with the ones I do see it in, we've never been bright enough to sue 'em. Besides, we stole it from somebody else. We were influenced by so many other people that it's a compliment when someone's not ashamed to admit they like us. Plus, the cool thing is that I don't like everything we do. At the time, you mean it to be the best, but I'm still critical of every record Cheap Trick has made, and I hope I continue that way. It's healthy.
O: ***What would you take back?***
RN: Oooh... Well, sonically and mix-wise, stuff on almost every album.
O: ***There's nothing in particular you're going to mention?***
RN: Nah. By me saying it, it influences somebody else.
O: ***What about "Up The Creek"?***
RN: Now that was a bad song! I co-wrote that... No, wait, let's see... I can't remember. Maybe I actually wrote that whole thing. Man! I must've been high. Put it this way, [*Up The Creek*] was one of the worst movies that's ever been out. Song-wise, it fit right in with the movie. Our video was the worst video we've ever done. We've done some bad ones, but that took the cake. The worst... [Background talking, laughter.] Hey, my wife, who wasn't even listening, heard me say "worst" and said, "Up The Creek"? Hey, at least we weren't standing there looking at each other trying to fake some ballad.
O: ***What was the crowd like at Lollapalooza? Were they good to you?***
RN: Well, at first, they were like, "My older brother knows those guys, my sister used to like them, my mother once, well, who knows?" It was 105 degrees in the sun, and here goes! At first it was like, "I don't know why they got you moes on stage here," but after a while the guys in Metallica, the guys in Soundgarden... Chris Cornell helped write the song list for us, although we were going to use the songs he suggested anyway, and I just gave a false sense of security to that guy. They were all real nice. And then Joey Ramone came up and sang "Surrender" with us, and the guys in Everclear came, and it was cool. And these bands are all onstage watching us. If they didn't want to be there, the stairs went the other way, too, but they stayed for the whole set, and by halfway through, people started to get it. Sure, we've been around, but we still know how to play. We've still got some cool songs.
O: ***And two weeks after that, you played The Casino Bar in Waupaca, Wisconsin.***
RN: Now, that was good. The reason some of that stuff happened—and every job is important—is we got asked. The only act that asked us to play with them last year was Boston. And we thought, "Well, we don't want to go out with them," but it was the only offer, and our box set was coming out. We didn't feel too bad about going out with them. And then they canceled right before Lollapalooza, and Lollapalooza had asked us to play more shows, too. We couldn't do it, because we were gonna play this Boston deal. So now we can't do Lollapalooza stuff and we're not doing the Boston thing, and we need to work. So we scrambled, and for two weeks we played some places that we normally wouldn't play, but so what? If we hold a grudge, the audience will know it for sure. I'm sure the Casino is acoustically not the finest pace, but what is? After all, Madison Square Garden sounds like crap. Uh, hey, I gotta get the other line. [Pauses, returns.] Sorry.

O: ***Hey, you're at home.***

RN: Yeah, and my kids don't give me messages too well. I'd rather be a better example to them than, well, the normal example. Although I'm quite an example. I have four kids, all from the same wife, all from the same husband, I think. I've been home four times in my career, and my wife was high or something each time. I'm a good, solid family man. I don't say I'm a good solid man, but, you know. They always love me. They don't always like me, and I deserve that.

O: ***Do you ever get crap from your kids for being a rock 'n' roller?***

RN: They don't give me crap about that. My daughter, who's only 8, is always, "When's Daddy coming back from vacation?" Vacation? Out on the road for months and months? It's not the hardest job in the world, but it ain't vacation. Ø

Dr. Demento

By Stephen Thompson
Originally Printed May 1999

"The fact that the show appeals to a large range of people and not just one narrow demographic is both a blessing and a curse."

For more than 30 years, Barry Hansen has hosted The Dr. Demento Show, *an internationally syndicated weekly radio broadcast highlighting the best and most popular novelty songs of the past and present. The show has been a part of life for millions of people—particularly teenagers, geeks, and teenage geeks—and it launched the decades-long career of pop satirist "Weird Al" Yankovic. Today, in addition to acting as titular host of his popular show, Hansen writes liner notes and books about rock history and assembles CDs celebrating the greatest novelty recordings of all time. In the wake of 1999's* The Very Best Of Dr. Demento, *which distills those works into 17 classic songs and radio skits, Hansen spoke to* The Onion A.V. Club *about his archives, his unique job, and the past and future of novelty songs.*

The Onion: ***Looking at* The Very Best Of Dr. Demento, *almost nothing is from the last 10 years. Was there a golden age of novelty songs?***

Barry Hansen: Well, *The Very Best Of* was intended to be things that have been popular on the show for a long period of time, so that influenced the selection. I could have included more recent things, but they just haven't piled up the long-term track record that, say, "They're Coming To Take Me Away, Ha-Haaa!" has. But, no, I like to think the golden age of funny music is still going on, as far as the underground goes. In terms of massive popularity, the golden age would have been from about 1956 to 1965. Stretch that to '66 to bring in "They're Coming To Take Me Away." That was the time when funny records could be regularly heard on Top 40 radio, which is what most young Americans listened to at that time. We didn't have the multiplicity of rock formats we do today.

O: ***Why do you think it's harder to make a successful comedy record today?***

BH: Well, rock music started taking itself more seriously. You can kind of see the whole thing in the career of The Beatles, from the bright, upbeat singles they did early in their career to the much more serious stuff they did toward the end. We started getting these groups like Yes and Pink Floyd, and a little later Asia, Emerson, Lake & Palmer, and all those people. *The Dark Side Of The Moon* is as serious as a symphony. That was not an atmosphere in which funny short songs flourished, and people got to think of rock as more profound. They got to turn up their noses at the silly little songs. Then "Weird Al" Yankovic brought it back, of course. But at some point around the mid- to late '80s, there was a decision that funny songs, if played at all, ought to be played only in the morning, which they certainly are on a good many morning shows. However, *Billboard* does not count airplay if it's only in the morning. That has led to less visibility, in terms of the charts, for funny songs.

O: *It's interesting that, "Weird Al" aside, there haven't been more eras in which novelty songs take hold. In rock, you tend to have the pendulum swinging back and forth, and most trends seem to be reactions to other trends.*

BH: Who knows? It may come back again. In the meantime, the underground is flourishing and my show is doing okay. Even if you can't hear us in your city, you can pick us up on the Internet.

O: *You listen to everything that's submitted to you. For every "Weird Al" Yankovic you've found, you must spend thousands of hours of your precious life listening to excruciating material.*

BH: That is true. Actually, the really bad stuff I can usually identify pretty quickly, and sometimes the bad ones are really fun. The most excruciating ones are the ones that are in-between. They're good, they're kind of funny, there's something going on, and there's some talent there, but it's just not quite making it. That's when I have to decide, "Is this something I should be playing?" I can't just look up in the music trades and see what other stations are playing, the way most program directors do. If they're on the edge about whether to play the new Goo Goo Dolls, they'll see who else is playing it, but I can't do that.

O: *As a rock historian, you're a pretty generous judge of music.*

BH: I try and give everything its due.

O: *But what do you hate?*

BH: Boring music. I don't hate rap music, but I don't listen to it. I just don't devote any enormous amount of time to it, simply because I'm so busy hearing other things.

O: *How do you find the time to listen to everything?*

BH: I don't watch a whole lot of television. I listen in my car when I drive somewhere, and since I'm in Los Angeles, I spend a fair amount of time doing that. As soon as we finish, I'll be going to get the mail, which is actually a 45-minute drive because we moved. We want to keep the same post-office box, because people have known that box number for 20 years and we don't want to give it up. That gives me a chance to listen to a couple more new CDs.

O: *You must have a warehouse or a basement that's a cavernous...*

BH: It's up to about a half-million records from

"Weird Al" Yankovic On Dr. Demento

If it hadn't been for the Good Doctor—that kindly purveyor of all things demented on the airwaves—I almost assuredly would have had to find a real job by now. As has been well-documented, Barry Hansen discovered me back in the mid-'70s when he decided to give airtime to a gangly 16-year-old accordion-playing nerd who happened to send some unsolicited tapes to his nationally syndicated radio show. The Doctor and I have been close friends ever since, and I'm told that to this day I hold the enviable title of being his most-requested artist. The Dr. Demento Show *has been on the air for more than 30 years now. It is a bona fide American institution and a national treasure. In an era when pop music sometimes took itself a tad too seriously, Dr. Demento kept the art form of the novelty song alive by introducing a new generation to Stan Freberg, Tom Lehrer, Allan Sherman, Spike Jones, and a plethora of other warped geniuses. His show is an oasis of insanity in a desert of drab conformity. Thank God for Dr. D.*

my career over the years, and also tons of stuff that arrived new that wasn't necessarily for the show. Especially in the '70s and '80s, I was usually employed locally by a radio station that played what was then current music, which meant there'd be 15 or 20 LPs in my box every week.

O: ***Do you have a staff that helps you?***

BH: No. I have hired people in the past on a temporary basis to help sort stuff and store it, but, no, it's just me.

O: ***It brings to mind this sort of Dr. Seussian vision of you running around in a top hat, carrying teetering stacks of reel-to-reel tape.***

BH: That's not far from the truth. An ongoing project over the last couple of years has been... Reel-to-reel tapes are not holding up over time. Cassettes, actually, have lasted longer. But I've been transferring my old reel tapes to CD. Of course, we'll see how long the home-made CDs last, but so far, so good.

O: ***How much trouble do you have getting the show to the largest possible audience?***

BH: Well, it's not always easy to clear it on radio stations. That's the technical term for getting a station to agree to carry a show. It's not easy, because the fact that the show appeals to a large range of people and not just one narrow demographic is both a blessing and a curse. Many program directors absolutely love it, but others say, "Well, I'm running an active-rock station for males 18 to 30, and here you are playing something by Spike Jones. How can I justify that?" On the other hand, we're on a good many active-rock stations. It all comes down to how the program director feels.

O: ***There aren't a lot of syndicated free-form radio shows.***

BH: Well, there aren't any like mine. I'm not competing with some other guy who's just like me. On the other hand, there are a lot of syndicated shows out there. It is a competitive area. There are lots of weekend features they can draw from.

O: ***Have you ever launched the career of someone whose music you don't like?***

BH: No, because I'm fairly easy to please, I'll put it that way. There are songs where maybe five or ten hearings was enough for me, but I don't mind. It's like a rock group that has a hit. If they have that hit, they'd better get used to playing it at every show, or have a good reason not to. ⌀

"You have to know what's going on in each 24th of a second."

"You have to know what's going on in each 24th of a second... If you look at any craft, you've got basic tools that you use. With writers, it's words and syntax, and with us, it's timing and drawing. Unless you can do that, you'd better find another occupation, like grave-digging."

Chuck Jones page 165

"That's my philosophy of acting. The emotions will take care of themselves. ... All that backstory stuff doesn't help. What you get paid for is to stand toe-to-toe with the other actor and get him to do your will."

William H. Macy page 171

"I think the most interesting work is done in fields where people don't think they're doing art, but are merely practicing a craft and working as good craftsmen."

Douglas Adams page 177

"I deal in metaphors. All my stories are like the Greek and Roman myths, and the Egyptian myths, and the Old and New Testament. If you speak in tongues, if you write in metaphors, then people can remember them."

Ray Bradbury page 181

"The trick is not to become a funny guy. You have to just be that from the beginning. The trick of these shows is figuring out how to be the person you always were in an unnatural situation."

Conan O'Brien page 185

"I want my books to be very readable. I want you to start reading and be pulled into the story and not be aware of me."

Elmore Leonard page 191

"Film, to me, is all based on literature and reading. But film isn't that; it's more like painting. They should be more like murals."

Robert Altman page 195

"Soft lighting, all of a sudden they think it's artwork. If it's hardcore lighting, then all of a sudden it's pornography."

Ron Jeremy page 201

"It has begun to really bother me how few people know about the show."

Mr. Show, Part III page 207

Chuck Jones

By Stephen Thompson
Originally Printed April 1998

"I hope that when I'm buried, they'll leave a place for my arm to come out so I can make a drawing."

Chuck Jones is one of the greatest animation directors of all time. He's worked on hundreds of classic Warner Bros. cartoons, from What's Opera, Doc? *to* Duck Amuck *to* One Froggy Evening. *He directed the animated Dr. Seuss masterpiece* How The Grinch Stole Christmas! *And he personally created or co-created Road Runner, Wile E. Coyote, Marvin Martian, Pepe Le Pew, and Gossamer, among other characters. Jones kept a busy professional schedule up until his death at 89 in 2002, but his cartoons from the '40s, '50s, and early '60s have taken on lives of their own, and still continually air on network TV and cable. While promoting a 1998 theatrical reissue of his best-known cartoons, Jones spoke to* The Onion A.V. Club *about animation's past and present, modern depictions of Michigan J. Frog, and his characters' personalities.*

The Onion: ***Have you been at this for 60 years now?***

Chuck Jones: Well, yes. As far as drawing is concerned, I've been at it for longer than that. I've been directing for 60 years, but I started in animation in 1931, so we're getting close to 70 years. As far as drawing is concerned, I've been drawing since I was big enough to hold a pencil, or a burnt match; I didn't care.

O: ***Do you ever plan to retire?***

CJ: I don't know what I'd retire from. I had a splendid uncle... If you've read my book [*Chuck Amuck*], you know who he is. I'm not suggesting you do so, because I'd hate to suggest things that might bring evil into your life. But anyway, he told me an old Spanish proverb: "The road is better than the inn," which simply means that, when you receive an Academy Award [Jones has three, plus an honorary award in 1996] or anything, you're at the inn, but then you've got to go outside and start up the road again. There's no end to it. And another one you might find useful: He said, "No artist ever completes a work. He only abandons it." It's true: Nobody ever completes anything. The great American novel can't be written, because somebody is going to write a better one. So my feeling is that the question of retirement is absurd. I hope that when I'm buried, they'll leave a place for my arm to come out so I can make a drawing.

O: ***You said that someone will always top the great American novel. Who do you feel is carrying on your legacy?***

CJ: Well, I don't really know. Animators today have technical and electronic tools that I wouldn't know how to use. We proceeded as all artists did before us: with pencil and paper. Nevertheless, if anybody wants to be an animator, they should learn to draw the human figure. That sounds strange, doesn't it? You don't want to copy Bugs Bunny or anything like that. If you learn how to draw the human figure, you will learn something that will stand you in good stead, because practically everything you will be doing throughout your life—whether you're an illustrator or an art director, or whoever you may be—will be based on the vertebrates, all the animals that have backbones. You see, anything from a shrew to a dinosaur has the same bones we do. If you draw a dinosaur or a shrew, all you have to do is look at it and compare it to your own anatomy, and you'll soon learn that a shrew is simply a very diminished vertebrate. The big difference, and I don't know if this is really what you want to talk about, is in the skull. If you think about it, our bodies aren't that much different from those of alligators. But our heads are quite different. So, anyway, I'm sure you want to talk about other things.

"Personality is what counts. The reason Bugs Bunny and the rest of them endure, I think, is that when you wrote lines for Bugs Bunny, they wouldn't ever work for Daffy or Yosemite Sam. Each one of them had a personal way."

O: ***Who do you feel is carrying on your legacy?***

CJ: Well, for one thing, a legacy is what somebody else says about your work; you can't say it about yourself. My wife objects to the term "legend," because she says, "Legend is what somebody has done." She wants to know what I'm going to do.

O: ***Well, that was my next question.***

CJ: What am I going to do? Well, I just continue on. People come in and ask me to do things, and I do them. But mainly I've been painting and drawing, oil paintings of beautiful women and beautiful rabbits and beautiful ducks, whatever. I'm not sure that I have time to direct a feature, and I'm not sure I want to. I did one once, called *The Phantom Tollbooth* (1971), when I was at MGM. I had that experience, but mainly I'm a cartoonist and an animator. And I'm an animator of short-subjects: I've done three or four hundred of them in my lifetime—I've never counted them carefully—and that's my field. You go back to the great essayists, like Samuel Johnson and people of that caliber, and they didn't make any excuse for being essayists. I make no excuse for being an animator. I came up that way, and all the great directors—and I don't mean to include myself, but those who surrounded me... Every one of them had been an animator first, in order to learn how to time, because we had to time our pictures before they were animated. It's very different from live action. That's why Steven Spielberg and George Lucas and Martin Scorsese can't believe that you can make a picture by timing it out to 540 feet, or six minutes. They don't understand how you can do that, because their idea is to take 25,000 feet of film and then cut it down to feature length. Well, we had to figure all that out before we even started. It's a curious craft, but as in all work, the most important thing is to have discipline and a deadline. A lot of people figure that, when you start writing, you don't have to have discipline. Well, oh, yes, you do. And when Scorsese starts cutting down a picture, he's tearing bits of his heart out and throwing them on the floor. Because his first inclination is to shoot the thing the way it should be shot, which is probably about six hours. And then he has to go chopping away at it, and that hurts. At least we're chopping beforehand.

O: ***As far as pacing goes, you must have to know what's happening in each individual second.***
CJ: Yes, you do. You have to know what's going on in each 24th of a second. We had to time our pictures down to that. But if you look at any craft, you've got basic tools that you use. With writers, it's words and syntax, and with us, it's timing and drawing. Unless you can do that, you'd better find another occupation, like grave-digging. [Laughs.] And that's rewarding work, because people are always dying. It's probably a good thing to learn.
O: ***What do you think of some of the other cartoons being produced today?***
CJ: Well, I have a lot of respect for *The Simpsons*, but it's in the same tradition as *Rocky & Bullwinkle*: They're very clever scripts, and they had no intention of animating them. Animating goes back to that basic term that Noah Webster wrote in his dictionary—"animation: to invoke life." Last night, when I was signing some cels, this deaf girl came up. She could read my lips, and she said that the thing she likes about the Warner cartoons and the Disney cartoons is that she could tell what was happening without hearing the dialogue. And that's what we tried to do: We always ran the pictures without dialogue, so we could see whether the action of the body would somehow convey what we were talking about. And she said that she'd watch *Rocky & Bullwinkle* or *The Simpsons*, and she couldn't tell what was happening, because so much of it is vocal. It's what I call "illustrated radio." The thing has to tell the whole story in words before you put drawings in front of it. A great artist once said—in describing lines, which is really what we work with—that respect for the line is the most important thing. He described the line: "My little dot goes for a walk." You must have an equal amount of respect for any point on the line. You don't zip from one place to another like you're likely to do when you're young. When you watch your little dot go for a walk, it has to be carefully done, and thoughtfully done, and respectfully done.
O: ***How do you feel about Michigan J. Frog becoming a corporate logo for the WB network?***
CJ: I had no control over it. They own all the characters, so there wasn't anything I could do about it. I could spend my life lamenting it, or I could continue to draw. I prefer to draw. See, the thing that makes all these characters is personality. *The Three Little Pigs* is one of the first pictures to use three characters that look alike and act differently; therefore, they had personality. A pretty woman isn't pretty because she's pretty. She's pretty because of the way she moves—her eyes, her mouth, and everything else. That's what makes beauty.

"Each character represents a part of me. You never find a character outside of yourself, because every human being has all the evil and all the good things, and it's how you use them, how you develop them. Those who enjoy Daffy obviously recognize Daffy in themselves."

Sure, it helps to have the proper features. But I remember someone asking Alfred Hitchcock what he required from actors, and he said, [imitating Alfred Hitchcock] "Well, I prefer them to have a mouth, and two eyes, hopefully on opposite sides of the nose..." He didn't care whether they were great actors or not. He could make them great actors by the way he directed them. So personality is what counts. The reason Bugs Bunny and the rest of them endure, I think, is that when you wrote lines for Bugs Bunny, they wouldn't ever work for Daffy or Yosemite Sam. Each one of them had a personal way, when you wrote dialogue for them, in the same sense that you'd never write dialogue for Chico Marx that you'd write for Groucho. The whole point here is personality, individuality—the character of each one—and this goes for the Disney people who worked on the early pictures, too. The same thing is true of them. You knew how Donald would act, and you knew how Daffy would act, and they're very different. You move your hands a certain

"You go back to the great essayists, like Samuel Johnson and people of that caliber, and they didn't make any excuse for being essayists. I make no excuse for being an animator."

way and move a certain way, and if you sat down with an animation director for two hours, he would be able to move a character the way you move. We not only have to figure out what a character looks like, but we have to find out what those little differences are. Moving your hands a certain way, or chopping your hands like Harry Truman did... That made him Harry Truman. That's the way he moved.

O: ***And Michigan J. Frog didn't talk, or rap...***

CJ: No, no. He only sang, and his personality was pretty flamboyant. But I didn't know who the hell he was. All I knew is, he could sing. I was as puzzled by him as anybody else is. [Laughs.] But I did know that he didn't talk, and shouldn't talk. And the only person who could ever hear him sing would be the man who uncovered him, and the audience. They shared that, but nobody else in the picture could hear him. Those are the disciplines. You know that in writing, you've got to have disciplines. And so, when you work with a character like Bugs Bunny, at first, he was crazy. And then we soon discovered that pretending like you're crazy is a much better way to develop personality. It's like Groucho Marx: He wasn't crazy, he was pretending to be. Daffy is a blatant loudmouth, and that's his personality. With Yosemite Sam, for example, which [animation director] Friz Freleng did, he took a grown man and had him act like a baby. If anything displeased him, he'd bellow and scream. My father was kind of like that, so I pushed him into a few characters of mine. Fortunately, he only saw them after... [Laughs.] I was going to say, "He only saw them after he was dead." I guess that's true.

O: ***Your relationship with your bosses influenced some of your Warner work, right?***

CJ: Well, I had a boss who came to Warner to run our operation when they bought us out in 1945, from Leon Schlesinger. This guy went through life like an untipped waiter.

O: ***He was the origin of the bullfighting cartoon [*Bully For Bugs*], wasn't he?***

CJ: Yeah, yeah. [Writer Michael Maltese] and I were sitting there looking at each other across the table, and suddenly here's this furious little man standing in the doorway, yelling at us. He said, "I don't want any pictures about bullfighting! There's nothing funny about a bullfight." And he walked out, and Mike and I looked at each other in wonderment, and he said, "My God, there must be something funny about a bullfight." We'd never even thought about doing a picture about a bullfight, but since everything he ever said was absolutely wrong, we were certain that we had to pursue it. We worked our asses off making that picture; I even went to Mexico City to see a bullfight. I figured that if we were going to do it, I might as well have fun with it and do it the way it should be done. If you're doing a takeoff on something, make sure you're doing it in an honest way.

O: ***What characters are most enduring for you?***

CJ: All of them. It's like somebody saying, "What's your favorite child?" Are you married?

O: ***Yes.***

CJ: Do you have children?

O: ***No, not yet.***

CJ: You know how to get them, don't you? When you have them, if you have more than one, you will have a favorite. But if you value your sanity, you will never mention it to anyone. The same thing is true here: Each character represents a part of me. You never find a character outside of yourself, because every human being has all the evil and all the good things, and it's how you use them, how you develop them. Those who enjoy Daffy obviously recognize Daffy in themselves. And with the heroes, like Bugs Bunny, what you have there is that that's the character you'd like to be like. You'll dream about being like Bugs Bunny, and then you wake up, and you're Daffy Duck. Ø

William H. Macy

By Scott Tobias

Originally Printed May 2001

"What you get paid for is to stand toe-to-toe with the other actor and get him to do your will."

When David Mamet made his directorial debut with 1987's House Of Games, *his former student and longtime collaborator William H. Macy appeared in a memorable cameo role. It was the first of Mamet and Macy's many screen collaborations, which include* Homicide, Things Change, Oleanna, *and* State And Main. *In the early '90s, Macy earned acclaim for his recurring appearances on the television series* ER, *as well as for his supporting parts in* Mr. Holland's Opus *and* Searching For Bobby Fischer, *among other features. But his career didn't truly take flight until his astonishing lead performance in 1996's* Fargo. *In the years since, Macy has landed substantial roles both in Hollywood features (*Pleasantville, Mystery Men, Jurassic Park III, Boogie Nights, Magnolia*) and in independent films (*Wag The Dog, Panic, Happy Texas*). In 2001, between takes on the set of the independent heist comedy* Welcome To Collinwood, *Macy talked to* The Onion A.V. Club *about the trials, pleasures, and craft of acting.*

The Onion: ***How difficult was it to make the initial transition from stage to screen?***
William H. Macy: I guess there was a transition, but in all honesty, acting is acting is acting. It's all the same. Seventy-five percent of the skills are the same in both media. There are a few differences. One of the things I did early on in film was over-enunciate and talk too loud. But, when you get right down to it, the acting problems are really just the same.
O: ***Doesn't the broken-up shooting schedule make it hard for you to maintain a continuity of character?***
WM: It's more frightening from the outside than when you're actually doing it. First of all, they have a continuity person who's there to help you with the mechanics of the thing: what you're wearing, which direction you were walking. This helps, because sometimes you'll do a scene and then come back a week later to finish it. Generally speaking, they try to shoot in order as much as they can. I think that, truly, the unit of measure for an actor is the moment, the tiny little moment. The continuity is not as large a problem as you'd think, because what you get paid for is that tiny little moment when you're looking at the other actor and you want X, and he wants Z, and it's just you guys fronting off and bringing your will to it.
O: ***What makes a good "actor's director"?***
WM: A good actor's director, first of all, is pre-

pared, so there's not an exorbitant amount of wasted footage. In other words, it's hard on an actor when you have to do a scene 45 times and you know damn well that three of the angles a director is shooting will never make it into the movie. If you use this angle, you can't use that angle. A good director is very well prepared and knows exactly how he's going to cut the film, so the shooting is as efficient as possible. Second, I love directors who talk action as opposed to emotion. I've always found it completely useless when a director comes up and says, "Okay, you're upset and you're desperate and you hate this guy." That's shit you can't act. That will lead you down the garden path to nowhere. What's good is when he says, "Okay, you've got to get this guy to do your will," or "You've got to get this guy to back down," or "You need a big favor."

O: ***That gives you more room for interpretation or improvisation?***

WM: Yes, because essentially, that's all that counts. That's my philosophy of acting. The emotions will take care of themselves. You don't have to prod them along. As a matter of fact, you get in trouble when you prod them along. Emotions are the natural result of striving for something. Every single scene has two or more people in it, and nobody wants the same thing, so they are negotiating this one way or another. The result of that negotiation will bring out all kinds of emotional stuff in you. The best thing for an actor to do is take your attention off of how you feel about it and put it on striving to obtain a particular objective. The happy result is that it brings out all this unexpected stuff in yourself.

O: ***You've been quoted as saying you're not a fan of independent films.***

WM: Here are the good things about independent films: They do the more interesting, chancy scripts. They're run by love. The only reason an indie gets made is because someone has a burning passion to do it and won't take no for an answer, as opposed to a big film, which is like a train that starts rolling down the tracks and nothing can stop it. But the reason I said that is, if I had my choice, I would do the same little independent films, but they would have $100 million budgets, so I could get paid a fortune and hang out in a huge trailer. [Laughs.] I'm not a fan of roughing it, per se.

O: ***So it's more taxing to work on an indie production.***

WM: Oh, yeah. With this film, *Welcome To Collinwood*, we'll do eight pages [of script] on a good day. On *Jurassic Park III*, we would do a quarter-page—some days, an eighth of a page. And that would be a full 12-hour day.

O: ***Aren't those conditions more frustrating?***

WM: It has its benefits and its frustrations. Working at that glacial pace, it's very hard to keep your spirits up and your energy up. With these indies, all of us are going to be acting all day. At the end of the day, what actors really want to do is act a lot and not wait around in the trailer.

O: ***Do you feel that projects of a large scale diminish the contributions of the actors?***

WM: Actually, no. I don't think *Jurassic Park* would get off the ground if it was just dinosaurs. Nope, it's got to have people in it. I feel very secure about the role of the actor in the future. They need us, because stories are about people.

O: ***Did you have to do a lot of acting against blue screens?***

WM: There was a bit of that, but Stan Winston's puppets were in almost every scene. Almost every scene involved puppetry and CGI and some blue-screen, so there was always something we could react to. And the puppets were beyond belief. I wish everybody could see them up close. They just boggle the mind.

O: ***Do you spend time on a set even when a scene doesn't involve you?***

WM: No, not so much. Perhaps I did when I was younger, but these days, that's like a postman taking a walk.

O: ***I'm thinking of something like the Paul Thomas Anderson films or the David Mamet***

films. There's a sense that you're part of a troupe, which makes it seem like people would be watching each other's work.

WM: It's not unheard of for your fellow actors to show up to watch a particular scene, or see a big stunt or a great gag. But you're right: There's a great sense of camaraderie in Paul's movies or David's movies, because we've worked together so much. You'd much rather act with a pal, someone you know really well. That way, you can cut all the niceties and go right to insulting each other. [Laughs.]

O: ***David Mamet is always mentioned first as a writer, but little is said of him as a director. What's he like in that capacity?***

WM: He's a strong director. He knows exactly what he wants. I think some actors probably find it frustrating, because he likes things clean as a whistle, unadorned, and unemotional, generally speaking. But I've always enjoyed his demeanor on the set. He's such a gentleman, and so kind. I've seen David greet a dozen extras at 7 in the morning, and 12 or 14 hours later say goodbye to them, thank them for being in the movie, and call them all by name. Mamet is a walking, talking genius. He's just about the smartest guy I've ever known.

O: ***Like the Coen brothers, he has a reputation for wanting his dialogue spoken in a very specific cadence. Is that constricting? What does that leave an actor to do?***

WM: It may seem that way, but their dialogue is not written for a particular cadence. It's just the way they write. If you learn it verbatim, it does have a natural cadence and a rhythm to it, and that's what you hear. It's not them. As a matter of fact, both the Coen brothers and Mamet are quite loose on the set. I've often seen David, when an actor screws up a line three or four times in a row, say, "Well, I must have written it wrong." He will change it on the set. So they're improvisatory, and they don't hold their writing as precious at all.

O: ***What do you see as the hardest thing about acting?***

WM: I'm not being smart-alecky here, but showing up is the roughest part. I think what all actors share is this fear that you're not going to be able to come up with the goods, that this is the one movie where you're going to look like a fool, and they should have cast someone else. And you feel ugly, and you've got three chins, and you've gained too much weight, and you're losing your hair, and there are so many better actors who could do this.

"Throughout the entire history of filmmaking, every year there have been about two really wonderful movies, about 10 others that are pretty good, and a whole pile of garbage."

But if you've got chops, what you realize is that everybody feels that way, so just show up and do the job.

O: ***What makes it a fruitful profession for you?***

WM: For me, it's that two or three minutes of the take when everybody has to step back, and I'm looking at the other guy and I'm talking to him. It's the actual acting. For some strange reason, it's the time that I'm the least self-conscious in my whole life. It's the time when I really feel like I fit in my skin.

O: ***How do you prepare for that point, so you won't feel that self-conscious?***

WM: Well, you've got to know the lines cold. You have to do whatever you can to limit the things that could make you feel insecure. There's very little you can do, really. But you should know the lines, be prepared, get sleep, and have the script analyzed so you're ready to rock and roll. And the final step is to say to yourself, "Are you nervous? Are you ill-prepared, still? Well, fuck it. Do it anyway. 'Cause you're the man."

O: ***So you're not of the Method school.***

WM: No, I've studied Stanislavsky, and Mamet

taught Stanislavsky, and I studied with Sanford Meisner. But the part of the method that I think is the most fruitful is the method of physical actions. It all comes down to your objective: Nothing else counts except what you want. How you feel will take care of itself. All that backstory stuff doesn't help. What you get paid for is to stand toe-to-toe with the other actor and get him to do your will.

O: ***It seems like the prevailing wisdom is that now is a bad time for movies, but a good one for acting. Would you agree with that statement?***

WM: I don't know. I've seen some movies recently that I loved. Last year, I thought if there had been nothing but Steven Soderbergh's movies [*Erin Brockovich* and *Traffic*], it would have been a great year. And I saw a bunch of films that I really, really liked. It seems to me that throughout the entire history of filmmaking, every year there have been about two really wonderful movies, about 10 others that are pretty good, and a whole pile of garbage. That seems to be consistent year after year, and I think acting is getting better and better. Actors are embracing a new aesthetic, which is leaning more toward truthful and simple and direct, as opposed to what we would normally call sitcom acting. I feel like a lot of the young actors that are just coming up are really good. I think directors are directing better. So, yeah, I agree with that statement.

O: ***It seems like the one lesson from Gus Van Sant's* Psycho *remake was just how much acting has changed between then and now. Acting is much more naturalistic now, and not so theatrical.***

WM: I thought *Psycho* was sort of a misguided adventure from the very beginning. But the great joy for me was getting to work with Gus Van Sant, and if there's a God, I will get to do another movie with him, because I think he's one of our great directors. But the film didn't really work. I hear you, though. Just speaking personally, I love what I did in *Psycho*, and Martin Balsam was awfully good [in the original role], too. But it was an interesting contrast in styles, I guess.

O: ***Did you have an idea going into* Boogie Nights *that it was going to be a sensation?***

WM: I knew right away. All modesty aside, I think I'm good at reading scripts. The way I read a script is as fast as I can, all in one sitting, and I don't read many of the stage directions. I only read enough stage directions to let me know where I am, because they're always so verbose and mostly horseshit. So I only read the dialogue, which allows me to see the movie in my mind's eye in real time. Many times, I like to read the script before I even know who they want me to play, so I can read it and really enjoy it as an audience member. I think that's given me the ability to ferret out the really special scripts from all the rest. On reading *Boogie Nights*, like everybody else, I was intrigued and shocked and outraged and all of those things. It was such a wacky world, such a novel approach. The film, I felt, was ultimately about family values. [Laughs.] It was about family, and to set it in the world of pornography was a stroke of genius. And it was such a loving look at that world. I've always felt that, no matter where you go, people are just people.

O: ***It seems your eye for good scripts leads you to try a lot of unproven talent.***

WM: You're right, I'm drawn to a lot of first-time directors. One of the great common denominators in these small independent films is that there's a person, or two people, who have an absolutely monomaniacal passion to get these films made. Sometimes, it takes years and years to finally get it done, but by never backing down, by never giving up, they get these films to the screen by hook or by crook. Many times, it's the director, and often a first-time director. It can be good sometimes, and it's rough many times, because they're untried and they make mistakes. And when a director makes a mistake, people suffer. People suffer horribly sometimes.

O: ***How do you mean?***

WM: Making a mistake means overshooting a scene, shooting too many takes, for instance. Long after you've got it, you just keep shooting. Sometimes, directors are afraid to stop shooting, because the second you stop and say "We got it" and move on, you'll never get another chance. And they're terrified to get in the cutting room and not be happy. So they just keep shooting. Ultimately, a more experienced director realizes that you've got to stop sometime and just move on. They're braver about that. Another mistake a director can make is not to be prepared, so you get there on the day to shoot the scene, and they don't know how it should be blocked, and they're not clear on how they want to do a scene. Many times, anarchy breaks out. Everyone is chipping in his or her two cents. Sometimes, craft services is telling you how to shoot the fucking scene. The result is that, when you could have gotten the scene in four different set-ups, you shoot eight. With an inexperienced director, a lot of times the days go on to 14, 15, 16 hours. It goes horrendously overtime, and because of the lack of money, they just keep you there, regardless of the hours.

O: ***Do you believe in rehearsals?***

WM: To a certain extent. I'm a fan of rehearsal on the day of the shoot, more than getting together a week beforehand. For the only film I've ever directed [1988's *Lip Service*], I did rehearse a great deal, but it was only because I had a very limited time to shoot it. I could only shoot what I had already directed, if you follow my reasoning.

O: ***And the worry with rehearsal is that it won't seem fresh in front of the camera.***

WM: No, it's not that. It's that it's a grand waste of time. You spend two hours rehearsing, and nothing gets done. The only thing that gets done is you get to know each other, smoke cigarettes, and lie about women. But I'm famous for pulling the cast together, not so much to formally rehearse, but just to run the lines. My theory of acting is that it takes all your attention just to stay in the moment, and keep your attention on the other person, and get him to do what you want him to do. I don't have any attention left over to try to remember, "What's the fucking line?" or "What's the blocking?" I like to get that stuff down by rote, so I can do it automatically and not devote any brain cells to the technical aspects.

O: ***Do you want to direct another film?***

WM: No, not in the foreseeable future. I'm just vaguely looking for a script. Directing is a huge amount of work with very little payoff and a quarter of the money and nine times more time spent. [Laughs.]

O: ***You've been so prolific, with upwards of 60 films and TV shows over the course of 20 years. You seem like an old-school character actor.***

WM: Well, some of it was because of the amount I was paid. There's no choice: If you want to earn a living, you've got to do a lot of this stuff. Many of those 50 or 60 films, I'm in a scene or two scenes. I worked a week or three days, so it's not as much work as it seems. I'm slowing down now, though. I'm getting bigger roles, and I'm on location more, and I have a wife and family. I'd rather work less, and I've started to implement that. It was either that or my wife would break my heart. ⊘

“I think the idea of art kills creativity.”

Douglas Adams

By Keith Phipps

Originally Printed January 1998

Douglas Adams is best known as the creator of The Hitchhiker's Guide To The Galaxy, *an absurdist science-fiction radio play that over the last two decades has been adapted into a series of books, a television show, and a computer game. After publishing a pair of unusual earthbound novels (1987's* Dirk Gently's Holistic Detective Agency *and its 1988 sequel,* The Long Dark Tea-Time Of The Soul*) and the fifth* Hitchhiker's Guide *installment, 1992's* Mostly Harmless, *Adams stopped writing fiction. But he remained busy until his death at 49 in 2001, exploring the possibilities of the Internet and CD-ROM games. In 1998, shortly before the release of his elaborate* Starship Titanic *game, Adams spoke to* The Onion A.V. Club *about his busy life.*

The Onion: ***Do you feel concerned that people won't treat the* Starship Titanic *CD-ROM with the gravity of, say, a movie or a book? That they won't treat it as an art form?***

Douglas Adams: I hope that's the case, yes. I get very worried about this idea of art. Having been an English literary graduate, I've been trying to avoid the idea of doing art ever since. I think the idea of art kills creativity. That was one of the reasons I really wanted to do a CD-ROM: because nobody will take it seriously, and therefore you can sneak under the fence with lots of good stuff. It's funny how often it happens. I guess that when the novel started, most early novels were just sort of pornography. Apparently, most media actually started as pornography and grew from there. This is not a pornographic CD-ROM, I hasten to add. Before 1962, everybody thought pop music was sort of... Nobody would have ever remotely called it art, and then somebody comes along and is incredibly creative in it, just because they love it to bits and think it's the greatest fun you can possibly have. And within a few years, you've got *Sgt. Pepper's* and so on, and everybody's calling it art. I think media are at their most interesting before anybody has thought of calling them art, when people still think they're just a load of junk.

O: ***But, say, 20 years from now, would you like to be recognized as one of the earliest practitioners of CD-ROM as art?***

DA: Well, I would just like a lot of people to have bought it. One, for the extremely obvious reason. But the other is that if it's popular and people really like it and have fun with it, you feel you've done a good job. And if somebody wants to come along and say, "Oh, it's art," that's as it may be. I don't really mind that much. But I think that's for other people to decide after the fact. It isn't what you should be aiming to do. There's nothing worse than sitting down to write a novel and saying, "Well, okay, I'm going to do something of high artistic worth." I think the most interesting work is done in fields where people don't think they're doing art, but are merely practicing a craft and working as good craftsmen. Being literate as a writer is good craft, is

"I think media are at their most interesting before anybody has thought of calling them art, when people still think they're just a load of junk."

knowing your job, is knowing how to use your tools properly and not to damage the tools as you use them. I find when I read Literary novels—you know, with a capital "L"—I think an awful lot is nonsense. I tend to get very suspicious of anything that thinks it's art while it's being created. As far as doing a CD-ROM is concerned, I just wanted to do the best thing I could and have as much fun as I could doing it. I think it's pretty good. There are always bits that you fret over for being less than perfect, but you can keep on worrying over something forever. The thing is pretty damn good.

O: ***You've got the movie, too. I've heard rumors of a*** **Hitchhiker's Guide** ***movie kicking around for decades.***

DA: Although it sort of bubbles under, there have been two previous sources of rumors. One was when I originally sold the rights about 15 years ago to Ivan Reitman, who was not as well-known then as he is now. It really didn't work out, because once we got down to it, Ivan and I didn't really see eye-to-eye. In fact, it turned out he hadn't actually read the book before he bought it. He'd merely read the sales figures. I think it really wasn't his cup of tea, so he wanted to make something rather different. Eventually, we agreed to differ and go our respective ways, and by this time the ownership had passed from him to Columbia, and he went on to make a movie called *Ghostbusters*, so you can imagine how irritated I was by that. [Laughs.] It sat there owned by Columbia for many years. I think Ivan Reitman then got somebody else to write a script based on it—which is, I think, the worst script I'd ever read. Unfortunately, it has my name on it, and the other writer's, whereas I did not contribute a single comma to it. I've only just discovered that that script has been sitting in Script City, or whatever it is, for a long time, and that everyone assumes I wrote it and am therefore a terrible screenwriter. Which is rather distressing to me. So then, a few years ago, I was introduced to Michael Nesmith, who has done a number of different things in his career. In addition to being a film producer, he was one of The Monkees. Which is kind of odd when you get to know him, because he's such a serious, thoughtful, quiet chap, but with quiet reserves of impish glee. His proposal was that we go into partnership together to make this. He's the producer, and I do the scripts and so on. We had a very good time working on it for quite a while, but I just think Hollywood at that point saw the thing as old. It's been around the block. And basically, what I was being told an awful lot was essentially, "Science-fiction comedy will not work as a movie. And here's why not: If it could work, somebody would have done it already." So what happens, of course, is that *Men In Black* came out this past year, so suddenly somebody has done it already. And *Men In Black* is... How can I put this delicately? There were elements of it I found quite familiar, shall we say? And suddenly, a comedy science-fiction movie that was very much in the same vein as *Hitchhiker's* became one of the most successful movies ever made. That kind of changed the landscape a little bit.

Suddenly, people kind of wanted it. The project with Michael... In the end, we hadn't gotten it to take, so we parted company very good friends, and still are. So now, the picture is with Caravan, which is one of the major independent production companies, but it's kind of joined at the hip to Disney. It's been very frustrating not to have made it in the last 15 years, but nevertheless, I feel extremely buoyed by the fact that one can make a much, much, much better movie out of it now than one could have 15 years ago. That's in technical terms. Obviously, the real quality of the picture is in the writing and the acting and the directing, and those skills have neither risen nor sunk in 15 years.

O: ***Which version of*** **Hitchhiker** ***are you happiest with?***

DA: Not the TV version, that's for sure. In different moods, I will feel either the radio or the book, which are the two other versions left, so it's got to be one of those, hasn't it? I feel differently about each of them. On the one hand, the radio series was where it originated. That's where the seed grew. Also, that's where I felt that myself and the other people working on it—the producer and the sound engineers and so on, and, of course, the actors—all created something that really felt groundbreaking at the time. Or rather, it felt like we were completely mad at the time. I can remember sitting in the subterranean studio auditioning the sound of a whale hitting the ground at 300 miles an hour for hours on end, just trying to find ways of tweaking the sound. After hours of that, day after day, you do begin to doubt your sanity. Of course, you have no idea if anybody is going to listen to this stuff. But, you know, there was a real sense that nobody had done this before, and that was great. There's a great charge that comes with that. On the other hand, the appeal of the books to me is that that's just me. The great appeal of a book to any writer is that it is just them. There's nobody else involved. That's not quite true, of course, because the thing developed out of a radio series in the first place, and there is a sense in there of all the people who have contributed, in one way or another, to the radio show that it grew out of. But there is a this-is-all-my-own-work feel about a book, and I'm pleased with the way it reads. I feel it flows nicely. It feels as if it were easy to write, and I know how difficult that was to achieve.

O: ***Do you ever get tired of*** **Hitchhiker's Guide To The Galaxy*****?***

DA: There was a period where I got heartily sick of it, and I really never wanted to hear anything more about it again, and I would almost scream at anybody who used the words to me. But since then, I went off and did other things. I did the *Dirk Gently* books. My favorite thing that I've ever done was a thing I did about 10 years ago: I went around the world with a zoologist friend of mine and looked for various rare and endangered species of animals, and wrote a book about that called *Last Chance To See*, which is my own personal favorite. *Hitchhiker* now is something from the past that I feel very fond of. It was great, it was terrific, and it's being very good to me. I had a conversation a little while ago with Pete Townshend of The Who, and I think at that point I was saying, "Oh, God, I hope I'm not just remembered as the person who wrote *Hitchhiker's Guide To The Galaxy*." And he kind of reprimanded me a little bit. He said, "Look, I have the same thing with *Tommy*, and for a while I thought like that. The thing is, when you've got something like that in your history, it opens an awful lot of doors. It allows you to do a lot of other things. People remember that. It's something one should be grateful for." And I thought that was quite right. ⌀

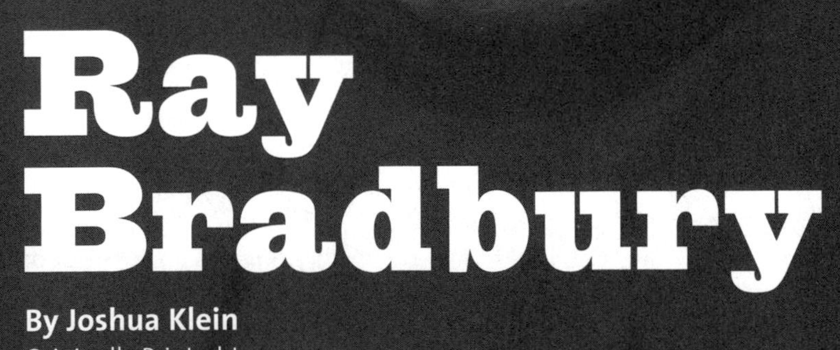

Ray Bradbury

By Joshua Klein
Originally Printed June 1999

"We're not teaching kids to read and write. So there is the danger that you raise up a generation of morons."

Now in his 80s, Ray Bradbury still maintains the busy writing schedule that has produced hundreds of short stories and half a dozen enduring, classic novels over the course of the past 60 years. From the anti-intellectual dystopia of Fahrenheit 451 *to the dark Americana of* Something Wicked This Way Comes *to the poetic blend of futurism and nostalgia in* The Martian Chronicles, *Bradbury has worked in a wide range of the colors on the science-fiction/fantasy palette, often inventing shades of his own. But Bradbury's greatest contribution may be the lyricism that drives his work. Without shying away from the bug-eyed monsters and gleaming spaceships favored by his peers, Bradbury describes his subjects with a knowing grace that has raised the bar in his genres of choice. In 1999, Bradbury's original projected date for the colonization of Mars, the author discussed his career and his none-too-rosy take on the present with* The Onion A.V. Club.

The Onion: ***How does it feel to be canonized?***
Ray Bradbury: I don't think about it. Just get your work done and never think about that sort of thing.
O: ***Still, it must be exciting to know that students are required to read your books in school.***
RB: Yeah, occasionally. I was at a ceremony yesterday to give an honorary degree to Ray Harryhausen, my old friend, the animator of dinosaurs. The two of us get one heck of a lot of love and affection from people.
O: ***There are so few authors who are actually on reading lists. Isn't that a validation?***
RB: It's amazing. I never thought it would happen. I wrote stories to please myself, and it's very gratifying to see that *Fahrenheit*, or *The Martian Chronicles*, or *Something Wicked* are in schools all over the country.
O: ***It's also relatively unusual for a science-fiction writer.***
RB: I'm not a science-fiction writer. I've only written one book that's science fiction, and that's *Fahrenheit 451*. All the others are fantasy.
O: ***What's the distinction for you?***
RB: Fantasies are things that can't happen, and science fiction is about things that can happen.
O: ***You set* The Martian Chronicles *in 1999, which then was a long way off. For all you knew, what you wrote about was not completely out of the realm of plausibility.***
RB: My Mars is fantastic, you see. It's not real, so it's a fantasy. I've just had to change all the

dates for the new edition. [Laughs.] I've set our colonization of Mars ahead to 2050.

O: ***Why did you originally estimate 1999?***

RB: Well, it seemed like a long way off. It was 50 years ago! The space age was nowhere in sight, and I thought that that gave it enough time. At least we got to the moon.

O: Fahrenheit 451 ***is one of the definitive anti-censorship books. What do you think of the renewed efforts to restrict or regulate the content of books, movies, music, and the like?***

RB: That's not censorship. You have to have taste. You know, there's a hell of a lot in movies that doesn't have to be there. I'll give you a good example: Mel Gibson is doing a new version of *Fahrenheit 451*. There are nine screenplays—nine screenplays! Now, if you know the book, you can just shoot the book off of the page. It's an automatic screenplay. I gave them one screenplay, and there are eight more by various screenwriters. And to give you an example of what should not go into a film—and it's not censorship, it's taste—there's one of the scenes by this other screenwriter. The fire chief comes to visit Montag, and Montag's wife, Mildred, says to him, "Would you like some coffee?" And the fire chief then says, "Do bears shit in the woods?" Do you want that in a film? It's not in the book. It's not me. So that's not censorship. It's just their bad taste.

"I've been writing every day of my life for 65 years. It's not discipline, it's passion. Passion is the discipline."

O: ***Is it hard to watch people changing what you wrote?***

RB: Oh, sure. Once you sell those things to the studio, they can do anything with it that they want. You have the privilege, of course, of not selling it to them. But Mel Gibson is a fine director and a fine actor, and I trust him to do a good job. But at the right moment, when they start production, I'll make a list of things that don't go into the film. If he doesn't listen, I'll call a press conference.

O: ***Compared to a lot of films out there, the example of bad taste you brought up is pretty mild.***

RB: There are a lot of "fuck" words in there, too!

O: ***I guess it's just a business, and that stuff sells.***

RB: They think they need it, but I have a new film out now, *The Wonderful Ice Cream Suit*. It's the best film I've ever made, and there's not one curse in the whole film. And it's about people who could very easily curse, you see? But you don't need those swear words.

O: ***Do you think screenwriters are just too lazy to write without profanity?***

RB: Oh, they're just trying to show off. It's just male macho crap.

O: ***But that sells tickets.***

RB: No, it doesn't. At least, I don't think it does. They imagine it does. It all started with *Saturday Night Fever* about 20 years ago. In the very first scene, the guys drive up and call him a "fuckhead." That's the point where I got up and left the theater with my wife. I said, "I don't need that." That's where it all started, about 20 years ago.

O: ***It's one thing if it's a matter of personal taste, but isn't it bad if someone else imposes their own tastes? Isn't that a dangerous direction to go, or can the task be handled responsibly?***

RB: I'll handle it for them. If they want, I'll kick 'em!

O: ***Well, you complained that you don't have control over the rights to your book...***

RB: But I can take a press conference, though. I'm a danger to them if they're not careful.

O: ***You've always written about people first and foremost. Do you think that accounts for the longevity of your stories?***

RB: Also, I deal in metaphors. All my stories are like the Greek and Roman myths, and the Egyptian myths, and the Old and New Testament. If you speak in tongues, if you write in metaphors, then people can remember them. The stories are very easy to recall, and you can tell them. So it's my ability as a teller of tales and a writer of metaphors. I think that's why I'm in the schools.

O: ***Are you always working?***

RB: Are you kidding? I've got six new books coming out in the next two years. I've been writing every day of my life for 65 years. It's not discipline, it's passion. Passion is the discipline.

O: ***Do you think contemporary writers have a similar passion?***

RB: Of course they do. You just have to look around for it, though. There are people writing in every field: essays, poetry, plays. But you have to search them out.

O: ***Do you think the average person these days has enough passion for reading to search these things out? It seems as if everybody winds up reading the same things.***

RB: Well, there's a lot of junk around: Barbara Taylor Bradford, Judith Krantz, and what have you. They sell in the millions. It's always been true. There have always been soap operas and summer-reading books. Look at *Gone With The Wind*. That was a big bestseller 60 years ago. But, you know, it's very shallow. It's a woman's book, and they read for the adventure of a woman trying to make do with these beasts called men.

O: ***Do you find it inspirational that people are still attracted to your writing through all the changes in fads and tastes?***

RB: Nope. I write just for myself. My tastes are the same. I've always loved *Tarzan*, I've always loved *John Carter Of Mars*, and I still collect *Buck Rogers* comic strips. I still love *Prince Valiant*. It doesn't change.

O: ***Is it difficult to weather cultural changes?***

RB: But you can cut it all off. You don't have to turn on the TV set. You don't have to work on the Internet. It's up to you. Everything is generated through your own will power. You don't have to do anything you don't want to do. This is a democracy.

O: ***On the subject of computers, I found a quote from you that says, "I don't understand this whole thing about computers and the superhighway. Who wants to be in touch with all those people?" That's from 1995.***

RB: That's right. And I haven't changed my mind. Bill Gates was at the library ahead of me two years ago. He signed in the guest book, and I wrote underneath his name, "I don't do Windows."

O: ***Have computers been a benefit? They are a good way for people to share certain passions.***

RB: That's a lot of nonsense. Go out and meet people! Don't get on a machine and do it.

O: ***You have written a good deal about the future—or what was then the future. Do you find it interesting that some of your predictions have come true?***

RB: *Fahrenheit* is full of them. A lot of things are unpleasant, like local television news. I'm sorry I predicted that. But here it is. It's all crap. At least we don't have a totalitarian government like what they had in the book. But through lack of education, we're not teaching kids to read and write. So there is the danger that you raise up a generation of morons. ⌀

By Keith Phipps

Originally Printed May 2001

"It's never over. You never really feel like you've made it."

Few would have predicted it from his 1993 debut, but Conan O'Brien has quietly become a late-night staple over the course of Late Night With Conan O'Brien*'s run. After a relatively low-visibility career writing for* The Simpsons *and* Saturday Night Live, *O'Brien took on the high-profile job of hosting* Late Night *after David Letterman switched networks. The show endured many troubles in its early years, but audiences eventually came around to its sensibility, a mix of self-aware talk-show conventions, absurdist humor, and relaxed interviews. Having weathered the departure of longtime co-host/sidekick Andy Richter,* Late Night *seems as strong as ever. In this 2001 interview with* The Onion A.V. Club, *O'Brien reflected on the odd course of his career and discussed what makes* Late Night *work.*

The Onion: ***Some people believe that everything on a talk show is planned.***

Conan O'Brien: Things are planned to a degree. To me, if too much is planned and it all goes according to plan, it's not fun to do. You've got to have some idea of what's happening. You don't want Matt Dillon to come out and no one's ever talked to him, and we have no idea what we're gonna talk about and just go fishing, because too often the result is going to sound like a conversation you'd have with some stranger on a bus. Maybe there are interesting moments over 25 minutes or half an hour, but when you're talking to someone for seven minutes, you want to have some idea of where the interesting areas are. Like, say Matt Dillon was a male prostitute in the late '70s, and that's how he earned money. If I know that in advance, and I know he's willing to talk about it, that's a good thing to have in your back pocket, because it's something we would have in common.

O: ***When you find a bit like Triumph The Insult Comic Dog, at what point do you know you've got a keeper?***

CO: It's the first night. You don't know how long it's gonna last, but you know the first night, "Oh, that's coming back. We'll be seeing more of that." We were always real concerned about running things into the ground early on, so we would phase things out. Like, we phased out PimpBot pretty quickly. I used to walk around New York, and all these college kids would be yelling out, "More PimpBot! Where's PimpBot?" and I would think, "What did we phase that out for?" We were too worried about running it into the ground. We were so worried that I think sometimes we almost did ourselves a disservice with some things. I think there are a lot of shows where, if they had found something like Triumph, he'd be a feature every night. "It's quarter to one, so it must be Triumph Time." I think that's when people are like, "Forget it. I'm tired of it."

O: ***Have you gotten tired of any bits that are too successful to get rid of?***

CO: We're aware at the show of the things that are less interesting and creative than some of our other bits. There are things like "If They Mated," which, we're not kidding ourselves: We know that it's just funny pictures. But we make a lot of shows. Not every night can just be a grab bag of new characters, or something that involves actors and camels in flames, because it's just too expensive, and it grinds everybody into the ground. We do a lot of jokes about how the show is low-budget. But we do occasionally, and actually not so occasionally, put a lot of effort into something that's just seven minutes between 12:40 and 12:47. Like movie reviews, or bits like "Guests We'll Never Have Back," where we're staging really complicated scenes, and we're using firearms and squibs, and we're rigging blood packs, and we're shooting it all day long, or we're shooting it for like four days before we do it. You put all this work into it, and then you get it just right and it's seven minutes long. A hardcore fan of our show, if such a thing really exists, maybe sees us twice a week. That means they're gonna miss that bit, probably. That's the kind of thing that's always eating at you.

O: ***On the other side of the coin, do you ever repeat a bit that didn't work the first time, and hope it might go over better a second time?***

CO: Yes. Yes.

O: ***Does it work?***

CO: No, never seen it happen. We did this bit once where we just said, "Ladies and gentlemen, please welcome Rev. Otis K. Dribbles," and in the performance area we cut to a guy dressed as a priest and wearing a dog mask dribbling while "Sweet Georgia Brown" played. It made us all really laugh at rehearsal for no reason, and we did it, and people didn't laugh. But the writers brought it back, and I don't think people laughed again. And then I think they were like, "No, we've got to try it a third time." I think we tried it a third time and it didn't work. On the show, there's this really delicate balance between pleasing ourselves and making the audience happy. You have to hit this balance, because you can't just completely appeal to the audience. Another one we tried a few times was "Seven Foot Groucho." We got a black guy who was seven feet tall, and we dressed him up as Groucho Marx, and we'd introduce him, and he'd come out and go, "That's the craziest thing I ever hoid!" He'd have a Groucho moustache, but we picked him solely for his physical presence, because he was seven feet tall. And he did a horrible Groucho, and no one got the... There was nothing to get. But it's not all just about jokes. Some of the best stuff we've done has been visually strange, and people laugh, but they don't quite know why they're laughing, because it just hits some nerve. So you always have to be willing to try. I think the quality about the show that I like, that I like about the writers and the spirit of the show, is that we do try stuff. When you demand that things work 100 percent of the time, you end up with a mediocre show. Whereas if you take a chance and do some strange stuff, and use puppets and animation, or let there be weird moments or try things, it's not always going to work. But when it does work, it has such a big payoff that you get people to come back, because that's the kind of thing that people talk about the next day. "Did you see that last night? That was really weird." That's the theory, anyway.

O: ***Do you think the studio audience is always the best gauge for what the TV audience...***

CO: No. There are nights when the audience reflects the core audience at home. Sometimes the audience is a pretty good representative, and if something is too mean or crass, or just too lame, they won't go for it. Then there are some nights where you're doing stuff you really like, but there's an audience that's not very demonstrative, or you don't know what their problem is. I've seen audiences sit there and not really laugh at anything, and then, after the show, they're all waving at me and smiling as I walk out the door, [saying] "Oh, man, that was great." And they're just not... They're intimidated, because it's this TV show, and they don't know what they're supposed to do. There are other audiences that are too frat... I get depressed if I do a joke that has something to do with alcohol or pot or something, and a whole audience of 20-year-olds with backwards baseball caps goes, [adopts low voice] "Yeah!" I feel my soul leaving my body. There's this phenomenon now in America of just, "Yeah, woo!" People go "Woo!" If you ever watch *Total Request Live*, everybody does that. It's a phenomenon that depresses me. I think it's partly daytime talk shows like *Jerry Springer* and stuff. It's encouraged on so many shows. "Woo!" It's kind of not why I got into comedy. If I wanted that, I'd have become a jai-alai player or something. I like an audience that's listening and then laughing or not, because if they listen and then don't laugh, I can usually have fun with the fact that they didn't laugh. That's fun, because that's just reality that people respond to. "Oh, look, the professional comedian/talk-show host is in a little bit of trouble out there." I think people like to see me work my way out of a situation. But when you're out there and they just hear, "I don't know if you heard, but a woman in San Antonio was arrested with 800 pounds of marijuana in her truck..." "Yeah! Woo!" I get sad, because I think, "Oh, I'm just the host of *American Gladiators*." The ladies of *The View* get a standing ovation every day on their show, and I think, "How much have we devalued the standing ovation? That's just ridiculous." Johnny Carson got one standing ovation, the last night he did his show, and it was really cool. It was like, "Wow, he did 30 years and then ended it on a classy note, and he got a standing ovation." And then you realize that Maury Povich is getting a standing ovation every day on his show. If I wanted to get "Woos," I'd have become the dictator of a South American country.

O: ***At what point did you decide to bring in Abe Vigoda?***

CO: It's called making your weaknesses strengths. David Letterman on CBS, back in '93, was such a big deal that he could have Tom Brokaw run out and throw crackers at the audience. He could have anybody walk on. He could have J.D. Salinger come out, pour fudge on himself, and do a dance, you know what I mean? And we were a new show, so we would have to sort of be creative about finding people. At the time, Abe Vigoda was the guy you didn't really see. So we had him on the show as a guest, and then we started using him, and we realized he's got this great face and really good comic timing. It was a happy surprise. He became this person of ours, so we started developing our own repertory company of Nipsey Russell and Abe Vigoda and the Masturbating Bear. It became our own over time, and became part of the identity of the show.

"The ladies of *The View* get a standing ovation every day on their show, and I think, 'How much have we devalued the standing ovation? That's just ridiculous.' "

O: ***Do you think people have forgotten the difficulties you had early in your career?***

CO: You know what, it's funny. Definitely. Four or five years ago on the show, I could have still gotten a laugh from, "Oh, my early days were a piece of cake." Everyone would laugh, because they would still kind of remember. What's fascinating is that young fans have no clue. I spoke at U Penn a couple years ago, and I started telling the kids about our early reviews, and reading really mean things they said about me and Andy, and the audience was like, "What are you talking about?" They weren't around, and to them the show is this established old chestnut. There are kids who started watching it in high school, and now they work for me. I gave this speech at Harvard last year that got sent all around the Internet. It had a lot of jokes in it, and then I tried to make a point by reading them the meanest review that anybody wrote of me, because I wanted them to understand: Once people get established and have success, people tend to think they were always like that. The most important thing you can tell young people is that there's this process, and it's never over. You never really feel like you've made it. I'm always feeling like, "Okay, now we've got to get this show to the next place, whatever that is." If tonight was not a good show, I'm depressed. I'm as depressed as I was seven or eight years ago when we had a bad show.

O: ***Do you think you brought the show around, or that people came around to the show?***

CO: I think it's both, because I think with the writing, it's people coming to us, because the writing was always there and always, I thought, pretty strong. If you go back and look at a tape of the first show on Sept. 13, 1993, it's a good show, but I hadn't figured out a way to be myself on TV yet. If you went back and looked at an old show, you would see, "Oh, yeah, that's Conan, but he's a little more rigid." I was real earnest and trying to do a good job, which nobody really wants to see. I think people came around to our sense of humor, but initially, I don't think all the criticism was wrong. Maybe in the severity, but I wasn't nearly as good a TV performer as I am now. The trick is not to become a funny guy. You have to just be that from the beginning. The trick of these shows is figuring out how to be the person you always were in an unnatural situation, with five cameras staring at you, and with an audience sitting there, and lights, and celebrities you've never met coming out.

O: ***When you have someone on whose work you just don't respect at all, how do you deal with that?***

CO: We won't name names. You can usually tell. I'm just a little more reticent. I take the title "host" seriously. I'm there to try and show these people off at their best, not rip them apart. And we've invited them, so I'm not a big believer in, "Let's get Carrot Top in here and rip him a new asshole." If you have someone here, just find what you like about that person. I'm not a really good liar, so I'm not going to stand up there and say I think someone is the greatest genius in the world if I can't stand him. I'll just try and find what I like about that person. One of the best observations about me I ever heard was, "Conan's funny with people. He's not funny at their expense." That's not a moral choice; that's just how I've always been. If Fabio comes on, try and have a really fun time with Fabio. Yeah, I'll walk the line of giving him a hard time about his man-boobs or something, but... I don't actually feel better than these people. We're all making a living somehow. I think that's part of the mood of the show. It can be mean-spirited at times, but I don't think that's us at our best.

O: ***Did you always want to be a talk-show host?***

CO: It was more like process of elimination with me. I knew that I'm not an actor. It wasn't something I was ever that interested in, like going and getting a head shot and reading stuff that other people wrote. Stand-up comedy... I never wanted to just memorize a routine and tell it to people. I admire stand-up, but I always thought what I like is much more interactive than that. Which is why I did improv for years in the '80s. That's kind of the thing that got me into performing: It could use my writer's head, but I could also get up in front of people and be physical. I remember in the '80s, when I was in college, staying up late and watching Letterman, and just thinking, "Oh, that thing he's doing..." I didn't think I could ever be as good as him, but I remember thinking, "I could do that kind of thing," where you get to tell a couple jokes and do stand-up for a second, but then you can also present really weird comedy and talk to people, and improvise, and try and be spontaneously funny in an interactive way. You can have cool music on. It just hit some nerve with me. I used to talk about someday having a show, when I was in college. I'm sure a lot of people do that, and they seem delusional. But did I ever expect that Letterman would leave, and through 50 crazy events I would replace him? No, I wasn't that crazy. I've had certain people credit me with being a genius for manipulating events so I could get the show, and I'm not that smart. It was literally a series of events that could not be duplicated. I was very, very lucky. I think that I have some ability in this area, and I'm glad I got to do it, and I think I've done a good job, but to this day I still can't believe sometimes how I got the job. People ask me, "I want to do what you're doing. What advice can you give me?" And I just think, it's like you're asking someone who got hit by a meteor, "I want to be hit by a meteor. How do I do it?" I don't know. I was walking in a field and the meteor hit me. ⌀

"I want my books to be very readable. I want you to start reading and be pulled into the story and not be aware of me."

Elmore Leonard

By Keith Phipps

Originally Printed March 2002

Author Elmore Leonard is living proof that there are exceptions to F. Scott Fitzgerald's line about American lives having no second acts. As Leonard has gotten older, he's gained literary celebrity and indirect Hollywood clout, all by following the path he was on all along. Born in New Orleans in 1925, Leonard found a permanent home and a permanent nickname, "Dutch," upon moving to Detroit in 1934. After serving in WWII, he began writing Westerns, turning out novels and short stories like "3:10 To Yuma" while working for an ad agency and, later, Encyclopedia Britannica Films. In the mid-'60s, as the market for Westerns waned, Leonard switched to crime fiction with The Big Bounce. *In the following years, he alternated writing screenplays and novels, sometimes adapting his own work. In the early '80s, Leonard began to receive mainstream recognition for pairing humor and inimitable dialogue with convincingly gritty crimescapes; the combination carried over well into films like* Get Shorty, Jackie Brown, *and* Out Of Sight. *Following the 2002 release of* Tishomingo Blues, *his 37th novel, Leonard spoke to* The Onion A.V. Club *about his sense of humor, what to leave out of books, and making it up as he goes along.*

The Onion: ***What was it like making the transition from Westerns to crime in the '60s?***
Elmore Leonard: I had to make a transition. The Western market was gone, because of television. I felt I was through with Westerns anyway, even though I did three more. The last one was in '79, called *Gunsights*. I used to refer to that as if it were full of outtakes from the other Westerns.
O: ***Though it's one of your contemporary Detroit novels,* City Primeval, *which follows it, is still very much a Western, isn't it?***
EL: It is. It's an Eastern Western, and it's the only Western I ever wrote, Eastern or Western, that has the showdown at the end where they're facing each other and they're gonna go for their guns. I never did that in any of my stories, because if you want to shoot somebody, you don't meet them in the street and somebody counts to three.
O: ***A lot of readers see* City Primeval *as a turning point for your writing. Would you agree?***
EL: I think the turning point was in the '70s, with *Unknown Man No. 89* and *Fifty-Two Pickup* and those. That's when I finally got the confidence to let it go and have some fun with it. Before that, in the Westerns especially, there's no humor at all. There's no irony to

speak of, and that's all the humor is. It's my humor. Because all these guys are serious. They can be funny, but they're serious when they deliver their lines. It's just that they're kind of out of context with what they're talking about.

O: ***Do you think you always had that humor, or is it something you aged into?***

EL: No, I think I've always had it, but I learned... I studied Hemingway so closely, everything that he wrote, and I feel that I learned to write from him. But eventually I didn't detect a sense of humor with the man, and I had to look elsewhere.

O: ***You've said that one of your secrets is that you leave out the stuff that people skip. What's your litmus test for that?***

EL: Well, I think it's mostly a lengthy description. With certain writers, you want to read it because they know how to write, but 90 percent of the writers... They start describing something, and you see them trying to write and become perhaps even poetic, and I think it's a waste of time. I go back to Hemingway: What did he describe? What did he describe in a person? Very little. And then you get to John Steinbeck, with his... My first rule is, never open a book with weather, what it's doing outside. Second, don't open a book with a prologue, because you're wasting time. Most prologues, especially in fiction, are about the backstory, and you can put backstory in any time you want. But in Steinbeck's prologue to *Sweet Thursday*... I went back to that, because I remembered that he labeled a couple of chapters "Hooptedoodle." He warns you in his prologue, "This is where I'm really gonna do some writing, and you can skip it if you want, because I've put it aside so it won't get in the way of the story." He also has a character in his prologue from *Cannery Row* saying, "I don't want to read the writer's description of a person. I don't want the writer telling me what somebody looks like. I want to figure it out from the way he talks and the way he is." I've always remembered that. In fact, it's not so much memory. I thought that I made it up. I had forgotten that I read that in his prologue in '54 or '55. I want my books to be very readable. I want you to start reading and be pulled into the story and not be aware of me. So that's in my rules. I try to show rather than tell, though the literary writer has a tendency to tell. He's telling the whole thing from his point of view. He's the omniscient author, and he's telling it all because he has the language. Martin Amis has the language, Margaret Atwood has the language, Philip Roth has the language. I don't, so I have to have my character tell you what's going on.

O: ***You tend to let your characters describe each other, too.***

EL: Right. That's important, because it not only describes the characters to some degree, but it also tells what the one describing thinks of him. Even weather, for that matter. If somebody looks out the window in my book, he has an attitude about the weather.

O: ***Do you think your work as an advertising copywriter helped you...***

EL: No.

O: ***Not at all?***

EL: Not at all. Before I got a job as a copywriter, I was with an agency. I had already written and sold about 10 short stories and a book. And I knew what kind of sound I wanted to develop, but that takes a while. It takes 10 or 15 years to get confidence in the style that you want to develop. I saw Hemingway doing it, and I see other writers doing it. I was impressed by John O'Hara's dialogue, and I would learn from and imitate as many as I could. I think the best way to learn to write is to just read and imitate for a while, until you finally get your own voice.

O: ***What do you think is the most common misconception about criminals?***

EL: That they sound like and always talk and act like criminals. I think they're only criminals when they're committing a crime. The guy who devotes his life to crime and eventually ends up in prison, I think he'll have a certain sound that you can't miss. I hear from convicts, and they want to know how I know what they know—how I get into their head. You just learn from documentaries, or books about prison life, or a feature story in the newspaper about particular prisons. I've visited prisons. Angola in Louisiana, I went there and talked to convicts. But you make it up. And then the reviewer says, "Boy, he's got it dead-on. He's got that dialogue exactly the way they talk, but how does he know?" You can get by with it.

O: ***When your work broke through in the '80s, was it a relief to have respectability at last?***

EL: Yeah. Well, it surprised me. And I was fortunate that I had stuck to what I wanted to do. Because in '66 or '67, when we sent out my first non-Western, *The Big Bounce*, it was rejected by everybody. Everyone in Hollywood rejected it. Anyone who cared to say anything said, "Well, it's a downer. There's nobody you'd like to associate with." The main character is a former burglar and a migrant worker. In the movie, of course, he turns out to be a returned Vietnam War vet.

O: ***Your books touch on a lot of social and racial issues. But have you ever written a book with an agenda?***

EL: No. It just comes out in the characters' attitudes. And they talk about movies and talk about music, because that's what we do.

O: ***Do you find there's a subject you want to cover, or is that incidental to your work?***

EL: There's a time I want to do, and I probably will in my next book, and that's the 1930s. I was impressed by the '30s. I was 5 to 10 years old. In the mid-'30s, I was living in Oklahoma, Texas, and Memphis before coming to Detroit. This was the period of all these desperadoes that were robbing banks: Bonnie and Clyde, Machine Gun Kelly, Pretty Boy Floyd. And they were all heroes. The banks were foreclosing on everyone's homes and farms and everything. I want to develop a famous Oklahoma lawman out of the '30s and see what I can do with him. I'll use a lot of what I remember, of course, and do a lot of research.

O: ***In the early '70s, you used to write books and develop movies simultaneously. Are you happy to have left that process behind?***

EL: I am. I'm not going to ever write another movie, because it's just work. You're an employee, and you do what you're told and you get your money. I did that for about 15 years, and it did support the book writing. But I don't want to work that way. I don't know why anyone would want to be a screenwriter. If they don't like what you write, they just say, "Get another writer. They're a dime a dozen." There are 8,000 members of the Writers Guild. You can imagine how many are working at any given time.

O: ***You've written a lot of books over the years. Are there any you'd like forgotten?***

EL: No. There are a couple where I went with the wrong main character. In *Pronto*, I went with the character who, when I was writing it, was my age, 67. When he got about 100 pages in, he was in character, but I lost interest in him, because he was getting hard to get along with. He was drinking again, and it all added to the plot, but I didn't care that much for the guy anymore. I had to bring another character on, who wasn't introduced until page 40, this guy Raylan Givens, the federal marshal in Kentucky. I could write a book about him any time. I made him a lot more important and opened the next book, *Riding The Rap*, with Raylan. So I gave him his due.

O: ***I take it that you don't work from a tight outline.***

EL: I don't have even a loose outline. I just make it up as I go along. E.L. Doctorow says you write the book to find out what it's about. I sure agree with that. He says it's like following your headlights driving at night down a country road. You can't see where you're going, but you get there. ⌀

Robert Altman

By Keith Phipps

Originally Printed August 2000

"People consider me some kind of a failure. I'm not a failure. My films may not satisfy a mass audience, but they were never made to do that."

*For more than 30 years, Robert Altman has been one of America's leading directors, working at a near-constant pace that has produced, on average, a movie each year. Altman directed some films that have been heralded as the best ever made (*M*A*S*H, Nashville*), and others that should have been (*McCabe & Mrs. Miller*). His work has been underrated and overlooked (*Buffalo Bill And The Indians, Secret Honor*), interesting even in failure (*Health, Ready To Wear*), experimentally rooted in genre (*The Gingerbread Man, Popeye*), and outright bizarre (*Brewster McCloud*). But across this broad range, Altman's films are guided by an easy-to-identify style and a difficult-to-describe sensibility, and capable of containing, without contradiction, the barely tempered sweetness of* Cookie's Fortune *and the almost unqualified pessimism of* Brewster McCloud. *As* Nashville *reached its 25th anniversary in 2000, Altman spoke to* The Onion A.V. Club *about his most acclaimed film, among other topics.*

The Onion: ***The ostensible reason we're talking today is the re-release of* Nashville, *which is often cited as your best film. Do you agree with that assessment?***

Robert Altman: Oh, I think the last one I did is. Yeah, I like *Nashville*. I mean, I like 'em all. They're like children, you know, and you tend to love your least successful children the most. But I don't think there's a best any more than... I don't think things are best. In terms of my own assessment of my work, it's no better than any others.

O: ***What would you pick out as your most underrated film, by that logic?***

RA: I don't know. I can't do those things. Emotionally and intellectually, you have to look at these like you do your own children. You're so connected to them. What critics say, and general assessments of these films and this kind of work, is about popularity and what's going on at the time. Right now, there are more movie critics than film critics out there. In other words, they're trying to reflect—which is their job—the popular taste. There are very few critics who go beyond that and treat this stuff as any more than movies.

O: ***Did you follow the whole affair of James Cameron writing a letter to* The Los Angeles Times' *Kenneth Turan?***

RA: James Cameron, can he write?

O: ***Apparently, he wrote an extensive letter about how he felt Turan should be fired***

because he gave a negative review to* Titanic*, arguing that everyone loves* Titanic *and Turan was out of touch.

RA: He should get a negative review. It was a shitty picture. For him to criticize anybody for what they say about that picture proves he's as crazy as he advertises.

O: ***Getting back to* Nashville *just for a moment, do you see it as being prescient of the current political and celebrity culture?***

RA: It's 25 years old. We did that 25 years ago, and it's as politically valid today as it was then. It was the precursor of a combination of Jimmy Carter, who got elected, and Ross Perot, who didn't get elected. But those kinds of candidates weren't heard of at that time.

O: ***Do you think that movement has sort of died off? Did the Perot candidacy excite you in any way?***

RA: I know a lot of people responded to it, just because it was something that wasn't in the machine. But it became part of the machine just as bad as everybody else.

O: ***It seems like the worst elements of it took it over.***

RA: Yeah. Well, they always do.

O: ***The new DVD version, I noticed, didn't have any deleted scenes. There are supposed to be hours of footage from* Nashville *that weren't included. Did you want any of that to see the light?***

RA: There weren't any deleted scenes. Almost everything we shot is in that film.

O: ***Just in shorter versions?***

RA: No, that whole thing that has been said for 25 years—that we cut another two or three hours of film, that we could have cut another version—just isn't true. That all stemmed from when we went to network television, because the film was so long at that time. I said we could add footage and put it on two different nights: in other words, make two two-hour films out of it. Because if you're not seeing it all in one sitting, and it's going to be separated by a week, you can afford to do a little reprise and repeat some stuff a little bit.

O: ***But that never happened?***

RA: No, they chose not to do that. *Nashville*... There's nothing I would do to change it. I'd probably cut it a little bit, but that isn't what it is. Most of the time trimmed is music.

O: ***In an interview 29 years ago, you said, "Nobody has ever made a good movie. Someday, someone will make half a good one." Have you seen one since then?***

RA: No, not really.

O: ***That quote was in reference to the overemphasis on narrative. Is that something you'd still like to see movies move away from?***

RA: Well, yes. Film, to me, is all based on literature and reading. But film isn't that; it's more like painting. They should be more like murals. They're all too articulate, and everything is told to you too many times. You're not allowed to glean anything from it or get impressions. Once you tell somebody, "Okay, this is red," that's red to them forever. And if they say, "Is this red or orange?," you should say, "I don't know." Their own brain will work on that answer, because everything is perceived slightly differently by every single human being. No two people are ever going to receive anything exactly the same way. It all has to filter through all the information you have in your computer, your brain.

O: ***So, by your assessment, the better films are the ones that leave more up to the viewer?***

RA: Yeah. It's the same way with a painting. The worst thing I hear, and you hear it all the time, is when people say, "Oh, did you see this film?" "Oh, I've already seen that and I don't want to go again." But with paintings, you stand and look at them as long as you want, and every time you look at them, your own experience is bringing something additional to the information that you're looking at. Music is the same way. But the problem with film is that it attacks too many of your senses. It's become more of a tonic, an escape. It's, "Oh, let's go tune out and watch Charles Bronson." And it's fine—there's room for that kind of material—but we're all just pushed into the same category. If all books were pushed into the same category, it'd be pretty dreadful. And it's getting to be that way anyway. You can't read anymore. But I don't care about that, because I'm in the looking business.

O: ***Do you agree with the fairly recent notion that the '70s were the last golden age of American filmmaking?***

RA: Well, I think probably of film as we know it now, yeah.

O: ***Do you see that changing at all?***

RA: No. I think it's just become all corporate now, and it's mostly run and controlled and ordered by the bean-counters. These guys start a new studio, and they're turning out the same old crap. Except a few individual artists—and they can almost not get financing—nobody does anything dealing with cinema as an art. They deal with it as a money machine. They have to. Every picture is geared toward the 16-year-old mind, because by the time the grown-ups decide to see a film, it's not playing anymore, and they say, "Oh, I'll wait and look at it on video." Video is getting better, and the screens are getting larger, so people don't go out. The only people who go out are these kids who want to run up and down the aisle and see this stuff, like this Tom Cruise crap [*Mission: Impossible 2*] and that Travolta thing he just did [*Battlefield Earth*].

O: ***Well, no one saw that, though.***

RA: Oh, but they did. They're gonna make money on that film. As long as they do that, as long as they make money on 'em, they're gonna keep making 'em.

O: ***You discovered Shelley Duvall working in a mall. You've used a lot of non-actors over the years in films like* The Long Goodbye *and* Kansas City. *Do you feel that there's a fundamentally different approach to using non-professional actors?***

RA: By the time I use them, they're professional. Professional is just somebody doing it. How much experience they've had is a different thing. Sometimes that's the desirable thing, because their experience helps you. At other times, you want the off-the-wall kind of raw truth that comes out of some of these inexperienced actors. It's like any skill or art: When you get too good at it, you get too facile and the art disappears. I don't think any rule should be set down. You get the very best, most experienced actor, and you're also not going to get surprised as much. They're going

"The problem with film is that it attacks too many of your senses. It's become more of a tonic, an escape."

to do a great job because they're skilled at that, but you're not going to see anything that really makes you sit up and say, "Wow, that's truthful."

O: ***Do you feel that, outside of films like yours, actors are underutilized?***

RA: Well, I think their talent is underutilized. I think many of these people should have fewer reins on them.

O: ***Were you surprised to find yourself still fighting with the studios when you made* The Gingerbread Man?**

RA: Well, I didn't think that was a studio. I was fighting, yeah, and I was quite surprised at that. But those were a bunch of... What was that, Polygram? They went ahead and hired a bunch of guys who had been fired from other studios, or lost their jobs, and they came in and tried to develop these films. They go out and do these test screenings, and whatever the test screening says, they say, "Oh, this is what we have to do." Because then, when the picture fails, they can say, "This isn't my fault. I did my job." They're not interested in, say, how we get the film to the largest and most appreciative audience. They say, "How can I protect my job and not look like an asshole if it fails?" That's what they all do.

O: ***Your cut went out, but only after the studio tried its own. Is that the first time a film had***

been taken out of your hands and re-cut?

RA: Uh, like that it was. But, of course, I got it back, and what ends up on the screen is, in fact, my work entirely. But in the meantime, the company went out of business—they sold themselves off—and they wrote it off as a loss and never distributed it. They didn't make enough prints. This is as close as I came to getting people to go to court on a thing like this, because they acted maliciously. I mean, we had really strong evidence, and we had attorneys ready to go along with us on spec to sue

"The directors who've probably had the most influence on me were probably names I don't even know, because I looked at a film that was really bad and I would say, 'Hmm, I'm never going to do that.' "

them, because theater exhibitors called them and tried to get that film, and they said, "We only have 15 prints," or whatever the number is. They would send them a print and say, "You can only have it for a week." That film could have been commercially successful, *The Gingerbread Man*, and it wasn't.

O: ***Was that the worst conflict you've had with a studio?***

RA: Well, no, but it was one of 'em. It was as bad as any, and it was pointless and silly. They didn't have to go through what they went through. Many of the major studios in the '80s and back in the '70s... I looked at a new print of *Brewster McCloud* the day before yesterday, because they're doing a lot of retrospectives of my stuff right now in New York and L.A., and that film was... Jim Aubrey, when he had just taken over MGM, he just buried that film, because he was selling off assets. He was crashing the company. He couldn't care whether that was film or green socks.

O: ***Does the idea of digital video excite you at all? It seems like technology that might be compatible with your style of filmmaking.***

RA: I think it will replace everything. There's always this problem of whether the light comes through the film—is it illuminated that way, or is the light reflected from the film? They'll solve all the problems, and I think there will be a day when you don't ever see film anymore.

O: ***Some people have drawn a direct correlation between* Popeye *and the fact that you spent much of the '80s working on low-profile projects. Is that fair, or was that partially by choice?***

RA: I don't know what you mean.

O: ***When you made* Popeye*, did it close some doors for you for bigger-budget studio projects?***

RA: Yes, it did. But *Popeye* is probably my most seen film. Probably more eyes have seen *Popeye* than all the other films I ever made, because it's the perennial babysitter.

O: ***It gets played a lot on television.***

RA: They lock the kids up in a room and turn it on. I know 4-year-olds who can repeat every word in *Popeye*, but it's still considered... People say, "Oh, God, your big failure." It wasn't successful at the time because it wasn't *Superman*.

O: ***Of the projects you've been developing that you haven't been able to realize, which ones do you really want to get done?***

RA: There's not a filmmaker alive who has had a better shake than I have. I have never been without a project, and they've always been projects of my own choosing. My perception and general popularity is quite... People consider me some kind of a failure. I'm not a failure. My films may not satisfy a mass audience, but they were never made to do that. This big store, they sell shoes, and I make gloves. With films I do or am going to do, I never take into consideration, "Oh, this is really going to sell a lot of tickets."

O: ***But they last. People rediscover your films all the time.***

RA: Yes, they do, and that's very gratifying, but I still have to work every year to pay my rent.

O: ***What was the first movie you saw that made you want to make movies?***

RA: The first film that allowed me to look at films as more than just a novelty was David Lean's *Brief Encounter*. I was probably 21, and that just startled me. The person who had the most influence on my filmmaking was Norman Corwin and his radio writing. As to, "What director do you admire the most or have you emulated?," the truthful answer to that is... The directors who've probably had the most influence on me were probably names I don't even know, because I looked at a film that was really bad and I would say, "Hmm, I'm never going to do that." That's probably the most direct positive influence on the work I do. I don't even know who those directors are, but the other directors on my list would be probably the same as yours: Fellini, Bergman, Kurosawa, John Huston, David Lean. They float up there above anybody else, and it's very evident why.

O: ***You've done a lot of films that have taken on genres. Do you feel that you've laid to rest any genre clichés with films like* The Long Goodbye*?***

RA: No, they keep recurring. I'm not laying them to rest; I'm just moving around to another side, looking into the prism from a different angle, saying, "Oh, what happens if you look at it from over here?" Basically, I have to stimulate an audience and try to get them interested in what I'm interested in. That's not easy. ⌀

By Joe Garden
Originally Printed August 1995

"We're having sex. People don't just let anyone off the street do that."

Since ascending to John Holmes' vacated throne as the world's most famous male adult-film star, Ron Jeremy has become a ubiquitous figure in the world of lowbrow entertainment, his presence in TV shows, B-movies, and music videos inevitably serving as a visual punchline. Part of Jeremy's fame is attributable to the unlikely nature of his porn stardom: Short, unattractive, hirsute, Jewish, well-educated, solidly upper-class, smart, funny, and disease- and drug-free, Jeremy defies just about every stereotype about the self-destructive nature of porn professionals. But the other reason he's so ubiquitous is by design. As his workaholic schedule attests, Jeremy is an ambitious social climber on a relentless mission to win over the mainstream. That the mission seems doomed almost from the outset scarcely seems to bother Jeremy, who, having weathered changes in the porn industry as diverse as the arrivals of videotape and AIDS, now stands as a sort of public goodwill ambassador for the industry. Jeremy was quick to defend the professionalism needed to produce his oeuvre *in a 1995 interview with* The Onion A.V. Club.

The Onion: ***How has the adult-film industry changed in recent years?***

Ron Jeremy: Well, in the '80s, it was big features, a lot of money spent traveling around the world. They did shoots in Hawaii. It was a much bigger budget and better films in some ways. But then the market went video, so they decided to shoot directly onto video. It's a lot cheaper and simpler to shoot, but the girls are prettier. The sex is probably hotter.

O: ***Do you think that since the film quality has gone down, people are paying less attention to the details of plot?***

RJ: In some ways, yes, but it's changing a little bit. It's not quite the story lines of the old days, but it's getting a little bit better.

O: ***How did you get started in the porn business?***

RJ: I was doing theater off-Broadway in New York, and I got a license to be a schoolteacher. I still have a license, which is kind of funny, huh? And then I did *Playgirl* magazine in 1978. From there, I was approached to do adult films. I turned it down at first and missed out on a film called *All About Gloria Leonard*. Then I got into the business and did a film called *Tigresses And Other Man-Eaters*. That was my very first film. Samantha Fox broke my screen cherry.

O: ***Oh, really?***

RJ: Not the singer. The brunette one who was

an actress in porno. People get them mixed up. That was 19 years ago. I've done over 1,000 films. Me, Tom Byron, and a French actor named Jean-Pierre have all broken the 1,000 mark.

O: ***How would you say humor plays in pornography?***

RJ: Well, you take it to a certain point. Like, humor is great for a teaser for a play in the beginning. But when it gets down to the nitty gritty, you have to stop it, because you get criticized for it. See, people can't laugh and get a bone on at the same time. They say that the laughing has to stop when the sex begins. But humor is good to have in films. I feel that porno should be very light and carefree, and that plots should never be too dramatic. It's very hard to show a real love story in porno, because once you cut to the graphics, you've killed it. What you don't see in a film is more effective in a film than what you do see when you can use your own imagination. In making porno films, you can't do that. You have to show graphically. There's a lot of the filmmaking process you can't do. You make it light, carefree, up-tempo, fun little plots. That's the best you should do. Give me a good plot. Give me a good story line, but you shouldn't make it too dramatic. You can't have any deaths in it, can't have any killings. Your movie shouldn't have any shoot-outs, and it shouldn't have any I-love-yous in it, either, because it doesn't work. Now, the films are so soft and so white-bread, the ones made in America, that European markets don't even want to touch our films, 'cause they're too soft now. We can't show rape. We can't show coercion. When I directed the John Wayne Bobbitt film, I could not show any blood. Automatic rule. So we show her holding a penis, but it's obviously a dildo. It's very funny.

"I already shot a hologram technique. They shot me on hologram so I can now appear lifelike in your living room—isn't that scary?—with a girl. You know, we're the cheaper medium, so people experiment with us. In fact, we were the first to go CD-ROM with computers and all."

O: ***I didn't know that had to be taken into consideration.***

RJ: Oh, yeah. You have to keep it very soft, because they hold these films up against obscenity grand juries all over the country. Especially in the South, areas with a very strong Bible Belt. They tried to prosecute me in Tallahassee. Didn't work. But they've prosecuted people in Broken Arrow, Oklahoma; Dallas, Texas; and parts of Mississippi and Alabama.

O: ***How would you say the industry is changing with technology?***

RJ: Well, CD-ROMs. We've always been the leaders. People in porno have always been the leaders in new eras and new things—on tape, on CD. The first pre-recorded tapes were X-rated, are you aware of that? And all the major studios followed. The very first tapes to rent and bring home were X-rated. I already shot a hologram technique. They shot me on hologram so I can now appear lifelike in your living room—isn't that scary?—with a girl. You know, we're the cheaper medium, so people experiment with us. In fact, we were the first to go CD-ROM with computers and all. When it gets down to holograms, which will be the real future, there will be a little TV-set-type device which, with the use of light and laser, will put a lifelike scene in the middle of your living room in three dimensions. That will be the next step, but that might be 10 years away.

O: ***How has the AIDS virus affected the industry from your standpoint?***

RJ: Well, we're much, much more careful. Not everybody can get into the business. There's a whole big screening process with IDs and verifying and checking out where they're from, and if they are who they say they are, and getting a double AIDS test. Now, they have the DNA test as well as the regular test. There are three kinds of AIDS tests: There's one which is the same day overnight, another which is stronger, and the DNA, which is very strong. Now, DNAs are required. It's very strong, and you have to be keeping up. Some companies are now using all rubbers. I was very lucky. I was working when it was a more fun era, you know? AIDS has made it not as much fun to be a porn actor anymore. [Laughs.]

O: ***How has the new feminism affected the porn industry, the more sex-positive...***

RJ: Well, that would be a good thing if they were sex-positive. Right now, the National Organization for Women, which is called NOW, is divided down the middle on their attitude on pornography. Half the members think it's offensive and deserves government intervention. The other half find it okay. You know, it's women's rights to be in porno pictures, too. Censorship hurts everybody. If government gets in the way of porn, then they're going after *Ms.* magazine next. Andrea Dworkin, who's always been against porn and wants government legislation, writes erotic literature, but she feels her stuff is "artistic." And, as Gloria Leonard once said, "The difference between artistic and graphic is the lighting." Soft lighting, all of a sudden they think it's artwork. If it's hardcore lighting, then all of a sudden it's pornography. The other thing to keep in mind is that women have always been pretty big defenders of porn. Judge Ellen Greene stopped the multi-jurisdictional prosecutions around the country, making sure each district can only prosecute one at a time. Otherwise, the legal fees alone would cripple a company. And it was women on the Meese Commission who disagreed with its findings. Women, I find, are often very understanding. While they may find porn offensive and not like it, they feel it has the right to exist. They want to have the right to choose not to see it, whereas you don't want to be told by the government that you cannot see it. You don't want the government getting in the way of this, because it's a smoking gun that would start other things as well. We're kind of on the frontier. If they come after us, then everything else is next. R-rated films, any kind of violent

"Humor is great for a teaser for a play in the beginning. But when it gets down to the nitty gritty, you have to stop it, because you get criticized for it. See, people can't laugh and get a bone on at the same time. They say that the laughing has to stop when the sex begins."

films. It'll be back to TV's *Ozzie And Harriet*. You'll have to have two beds for married couples, and one foot has to be on the floor when you kiss.

O: ***What major events have really affected the industry?***

RJ: Well, it would shake up the industry if some performer turned out HIV-positive. When John Holmes died of AIDS, that was a big shake-up. Although he had not been in the business for years and had not infected or been involved with anyone in our business, it still didn't look good, because he was a former porn actor. Made us look pretty bad. Stopped people like me from getting laid as often. People think we're all just a bunch of walking viruses looking for a place to infect. [Laughs.] Walking pus-filled red dick. That was always a pain, you know. It's okay now, though. People know. There have been enough talk shows that the world knows the industry is very safe and very protected.

O: ***What advice would you give to people looking to break into the industry, either as an actor or as a producer? Should you just make your own?***

RJ: Basically, make your own, at least in an area in which it's legal to make one. Or just do it in your own home for personal use and then try to sell it as an amateur. A guy and a girl, shoot it nicely. Have a friend shoot it or something. Have nookie and then contact any of the companies that have their addresses listed on the videotapes or in the magazines. *High Society*, *Cheri*, get a copy of *AVN*. It lists companies you can send to. Send them a copy of the tape and see if they're interested. Or send your photo to the agents, say that you'll be coming soon to California, and give it a shot. A single guy hasn't a prayer. Not a prayer. If you go with a girl, then you can do it. Come to L.A., and they'll give you a shot together. And then, maybe if you do a good job, you'll work separately. But you have to come together with a girl. Whenever guys talk to me, I tell them they don't have a prayer. There are hundreds and hundreds of guys daily who call the agents and send in pictures of their faces, their dicks, and nobody can do a damn thing. It's worthless. The market is run on new women's faces. You can't have the same girls all the time, because the public wants to see new faces in women. It's a male-oriented public. If women want to watch videos, they'll watch Chippendale dancers. Or romantic videos, romantic movies. R-rated films. These cater to men. So a single guy has to go with a girl in order to get a job. Unless the guy is like Chippendale's material, with a phenomenal body, two DNA tests, and a dick to the floor. But that's very hard to come by. Most average guys need to come with a girl. It's like me asking Tom Cruise, "Hey, can I get into your films?" It kills me, 'cause guys always approach me on the street, and if they're going up to Tom Cruise or Arnold Schwarzenegger—"Hey, how can I be in one of your movies?"—the reaction would be the same. "What, are you nuts? There's a whole process involved." It's the same thing when guys ask me. In comparing their films to our films, it's just as difficult, if not harder. We're having sex. People don't just let anyone off the street do that. You can go get an escort, but this is different. This is public porn for the world to see. You have to be screened. It's a lot of work. If you go with a girl, you cut out a majority of the hard process. That's how I got started. That's how it was back in the old days, and that's still how it is today. New guys will have a hard time getting a job.

"Guys always approach me on the street, and if they're going up to Tom Cruise or Arnold Schwarzenegger—'Hey, how can I be in one of your movies?'—the reaction would be the same. 'What, are you nuts? There's a whole process involved.' It's the same thing when guys ask me."

O: ***How long does it take to film one sex scene?***

RJ: Eh, an hour. Yeah. Unless it's shot, like, Andrew Blake–style, with very soft, beautiful photography, shot on film, flowing camerawork, fancy lighting. Then it can take half a day. Most scenes, like Buttman-type scenes, John Leslie–type scenes, good, nice-and-nasty hardcore, maybe a little anal or whatever, an hour. It'll be edited to about 11 minutes in the scene.

O: ***I don't want to sound flippant when I ask this...***

RJ: Don't worry about it.

O: ***How big is your penis?***

RJ: Nine and three-quarters. They say 10 in some press, and I say fine. I'll keep the extra quarter-inch. They used to say that John Holmes was 14. He wasn't. He was 12. Which is still pretty massive! That ain't nothing to be shy about. In fact, he used to call me "Little Dick." I'd say, well, listen to this. I'd say, "Well, John, with you it's not sex, it's a pap smear. Once you hit bottom, where the fuck are you going to go?" We used to make jokes about that, you know. He'd call me "Little Dick," I'd call him "Pap Smear." ⌀

Mr. Show, Part III

By Stephen Thompson
Originally Printed September 1998

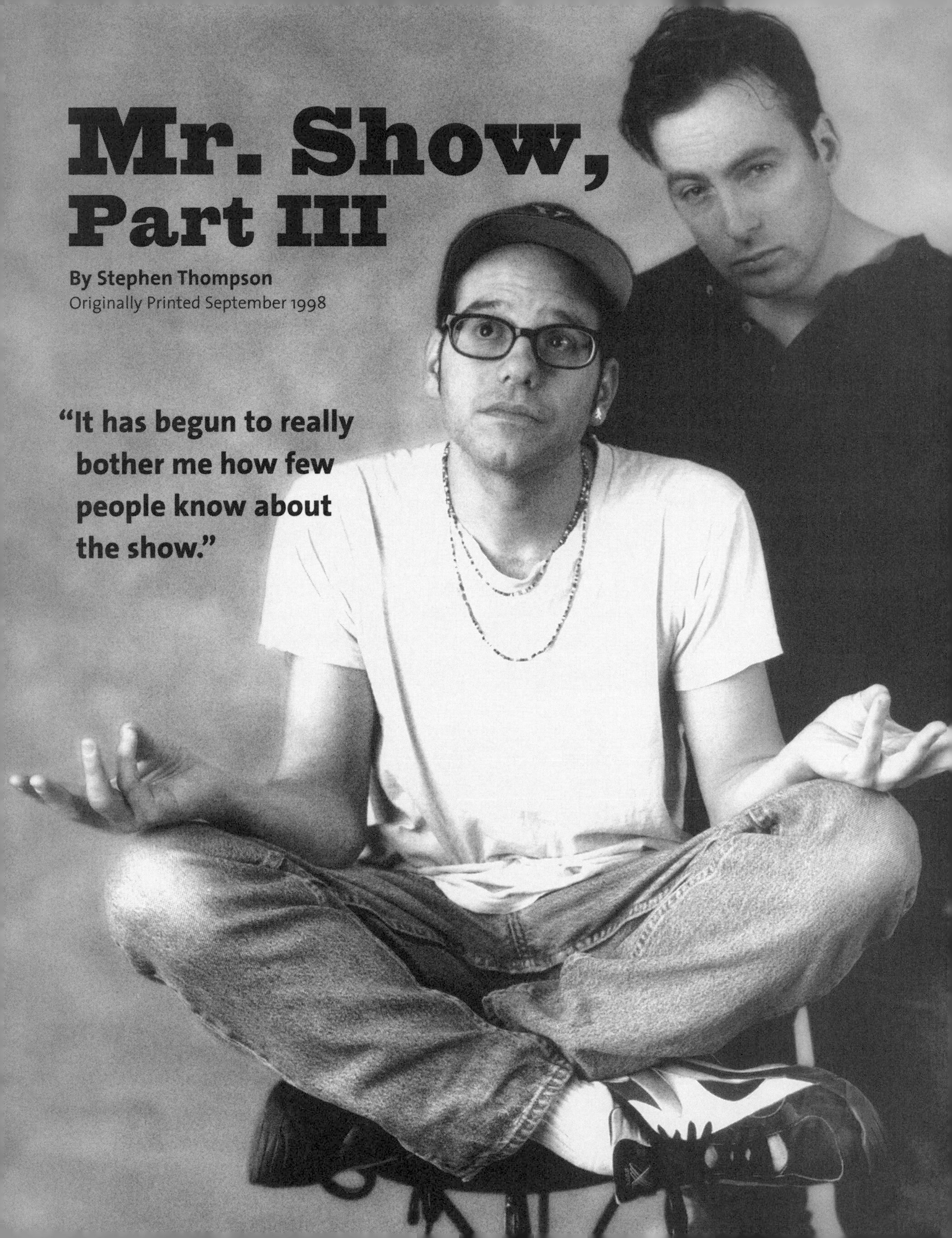

"It has begun to really bother me how few people know about the show."

By the fall of 1998, it had become an annual tradition for The Onion A.V. Club *to interview Bob Odenkirk and David Cross, the stars of and masterminds behind HBO's* Mr. Show, *a 30-minute, intricately constructed, satirical sketch-comedy series that was funnier than anything else on television. Having finally figured out how to manage their immense workload, the two spent much of the conversation venting the frustrations that accompany a tiny audience.*

The Onion: *The last time we spoke, about a year ago, Bob referred to your workload as "a fucking hellish bitch." Is the same true this year?*
David Cross: No. It's difficult now, and difficult in the home stretch, but it's not nearly as bad as it was last year.
Bob Odenkirk: It's a different kind of hell, in a way. We felt that last year's 10th show was not a good show. And with all the pressure coming down on us now, and all the different kinds of work we have to do at this point in our schedule... We're writing, we're rewriting, we're shooting, we're editing. Everything piles up. We don't want that last show to be the same thing last year's show was, where it was just us barely groaning it out. You can't do that to yourself too many times, where you just beat the shit out of your body for months. I've got to be really careful, because I got really sick a few weeks ago, and it was just from being run-down. Plus, my wife is pregnant. We're going to have a baby as soon as the season's over.
O: *She's holding it in until then?*
BO: I told her, you know, "I can't do it right now." I told her I could take care of the baby, but I couldn't love a baby right now. She could have it, but I'm just gonna barely tolerate it.
O: *Last year, you were going to do 13 episodes, but you ended up doing 10.*
BO: Right, and this year, we knew right away that we could only do 10.
DC: That's all we want to do.
BO: The show is so labor-intensive, and there's so much production in each episode, that it really limits how much you can do while keeping the quality up. One of our best episodes last year, maybe the best, was the ninth. But then the last one had some scenes that just weren't served very well. Not that anyone noticed, but we were really aware of how wiped out we were. We want to be steady on these 10, and focus on all of them and make

them all special, and not get so wiped out by the end. But maybe we won't be able to do that. We get so backed up every year. I don't think we could work more than we do. We work steady for months. We don't do other projects. We just write this show and try to maintain our standards, and that's life. This is what we can do, I guess.

O: ***If it's any consolation at all, it does bring a great deal of joy...***

BO: ...to a very small number of people.

DC: You know what? No consolation. I wish it was. I really wish it was. It means very little.

BO: I don't know how David feels about this, but it has begun to really bother me how few people know about the show. It didn't used to bother me. I used to say, "Hey, I don't care, as long as we're on the air." But now, I'm starting to really go, "We work so fuckin' hard, and I think our show is really special, and it just seems to be ignored."

"It's always best to do what you think is the funniest or smartest thing you can do."

DC: Well, I feel a little differently in the sense that... I don't think it's just blind optimism, but the nature of this kind of thing is that awareness will continue to steadily grow. I think that even if we stop and go away for three years, it's still going to grow and grow—slowly, but it will.

O: ***Years down the line, it could find a larger audience.***

BO: Well, yeah, we keep that in mind. You know, I've never in my life proceeded with a project because I thought it would please more people than the last thing I did. I've never had that as a motivation. But at the same time, part of me feels like it understands that motivation—that there's some legitimacy to going, "You know what? I just want to please more people." I wouldn't blame somebody for saying that and meaning it. I kind of understand that now. But at the same time, I don't think it's a good impetus for choosing any project, or a good way to proceed, because I think it's kind of false. In order to follow it, you have to kind of assume that what you think is funny will please other people, and that's never good. It's always best to do what you think is the funniest or smartest thing you can do. We just want to create something we can watch five years from now. That keeps us from indulging a lot of momentary impulses.

O: ***Yeah, you don't do a lot of topical stuff.***

DC: We disguise it. We don't call people by their names. We have familiar figures, but they're couched in something that will hold up.

BO: Yeah, but we're going to do something this year about property taxes in L.A. That's something where, 10 years from now, I'm still going to care about it.

DC: [Laughs.] That would be so funny!

BO: Because that extra 0.3 percent matters.

DC: You've got a kid now, you know?

BO: Yeah, America's got a kid now. Our audience has got a kid now, and they just bought a house in L.A. There are things that people are thinking about, and the point is, the price of bassinets has gone up, and we all want to know, "What's the deal?" ⌀

"The idea behind rock 'n' roll is joy." CHAPTER 6

"Guys! Lighten up! The image is heavy and everything, but you don't have to really be that... The idea behind rock 'n' roll is joy. It's joyful music. It's not a depressing thing."

Alice Cooper page 211

"I can still piss people off a little bit and make 'em cheer. I don't want to think I've lost my touch, you know."

Stan Freberg page 215

"When someone comes up and tells me that they love the music, I yell, 'Me, too!' And we just hug."

Andrew W.K. page 221

"If you go out and say, 'Oh, we broke up,' and then you feel like playing a show later on, all of a sudden you're like The Who. Who wants to be The Who? I want to be The Who in 1965, not The Who in 1999."

Tim Quirk (Too Much Joy) page 229

"I always have a fun time. It's a really nice crowd. I never have trouble, knock on wood. They're always fun, and they always love me, so it's really nice to meet with them and talk to them."

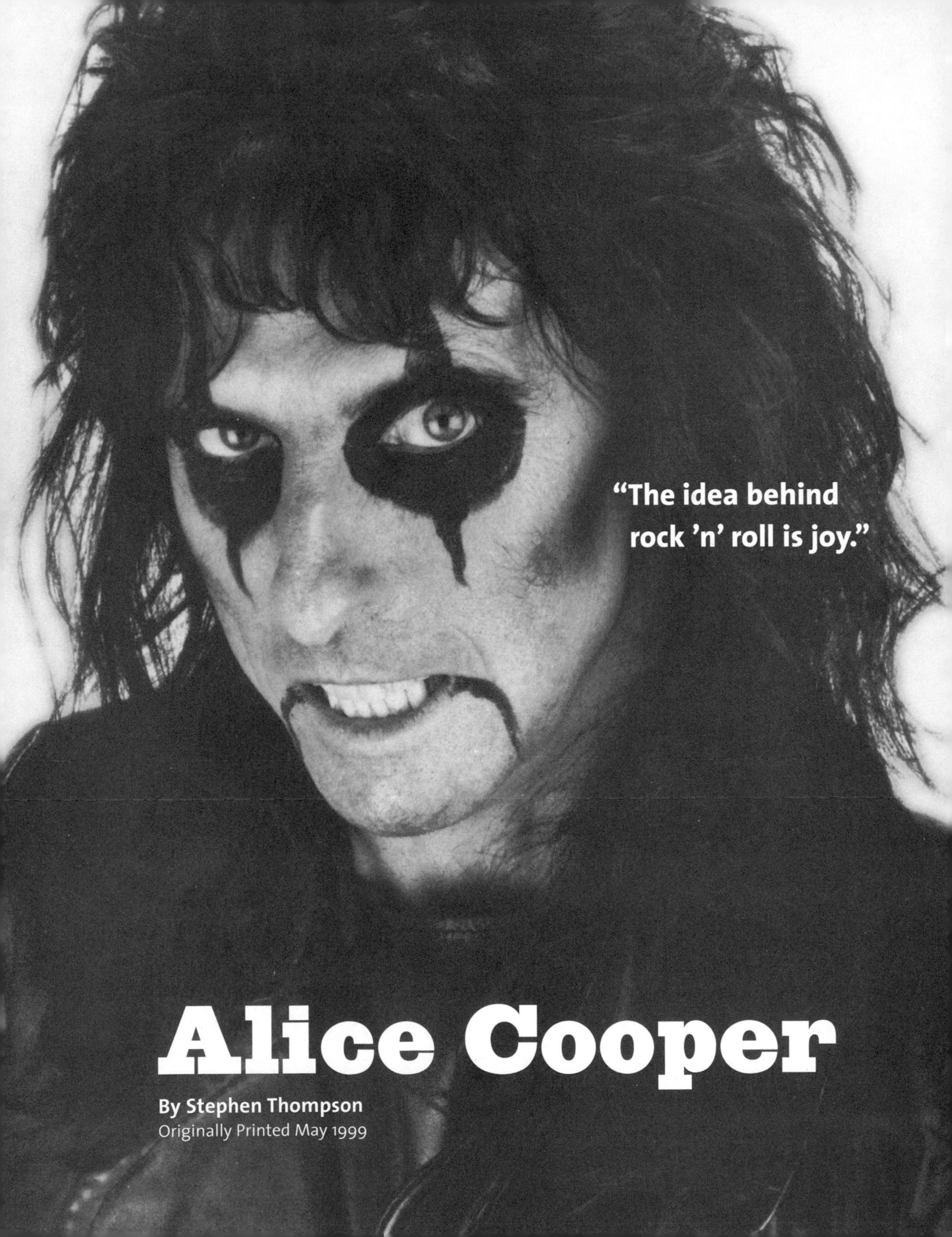

"The idea behind rock 'n' roll is joy."

Alice Cooper

By Stephen Thompson

Originally Printed May 1999

*Alice Cooper has received both credit and blame for influencing shocking, over-the-top rock acts from The Sex Pistols to White Zombie to Marilyn Manson. But many of Cooper's most popular contemporary descendants forget to emulate his rebellious sense of fun, heard in such timeless rock 'n' roll songs as "School's Out," "I'm Eighteen," and "Welcome To My Nightmare." Perhaps the first to build truly over-the-top theatrics into his live shows—his raucous sets feature blood and countless props, and generally end with a simulation of his own violent death—Cooper has always built his act on a solid foundation of catchy rock songs and a rare knack for showmanship. The cross-dressing, copious fake blood, and literal gallows humor raised some hackles in the '70s, and he's battled various forms of controversy on and off ever since. Shortly after the 1999 release of an elaborate, four-disc career retrospective (*The Life And Crimes Of Alice Cooper*), the singer and showman spoke to* The Onion A.V. Club *about his legacy, the secrets of shock, and his performance on* The Muppet Show.

The Onion: ***My first rock 'n' roll moment as a kid was seeing you on* The Muppet Show.**

Alice Cooper: Oh, that was a classic.

O: ***That seemed to take a lot of guts, for a somewhat controversial rock 'n' roller to do that show.***

AC: You know, at the time, I felt that the Muppets were... The reason they got away with everything was because it wasn't a black against a white; it was a green against a purple, you know? So nobody could really be insulted by the ambiguousness of what they were doing. It was these furry little things, and they were very hip. And I thought, you know, Vincent Price had done the show, and I looked around at everybody who had done the show, and they wanted me to do this Halloween episode. And I said, "Well, that's perfect. I watch the show all the time and I think it's probably the hippest show on television. I'd love to do that." We did it in London, and the funny thing was that when you're rehearsing—we were there for a week rehearsing that thing—you're rehearsing with the puppets. And you're talking to the puppets, not realizing that there's a guy down below you, and you're talking to his hand. So you're sitting there, and Kermit's going, "Well, Alice, um, should I move over here a little bit?" And I'm going, "Yeah, yeah, Kermit. I'll tell you what: The arrow's gonna come right through here, and I don't want it to get too close to you." And he's like, "Oh, I don't want to get hit with it." And after a while, I'm going, "What am I doing?" And Miss Piggy, you know, she'd literally flirt with you. She'd say, "Ooh, Alice, come over here," and that kind of stuff, and you would get so sucked into the character that it was like you were really talking to the character.

O: ***It's funny, because there are quite a few musicians today who are clearly influenced by Alice Cooper, but very few of them—maybe Rob Zombie and a few others—would do something like that.***

AC: Oh, it's the most fun thing, and if you can't have fun with your image... You know, I didn't let any guard down. I was still Alice, except for the fact that I was surrounded by all these creatures. And they wrote it so it was very funny. If it would have been *Sesame Street*, I wouldn't have done it, but it was the Muppets, and the Muppets were hipper than anybody. So I thought it was very cool, and it gives me all kinds of credibility with my 6-year-old. Besides, I thought that if Peter Sellers could do it, and if Vincent Price could do it, then Alice definitely belonged.

"As long as I'm sleek with long, black hair and can still do an hour and a half of high-energy rock 'n' roll, I'll keep doing it."

O: ***You're regarded as the father of shock-rock, and the man on whose shoulders the likes of Marilyn Manson stand. But most of those people seem to not be having any fun.***

AC: Boy, did you hit it on the head. The only person out there who's having any fun with this is Rob Zombie. And it's clear when you listen to his albums, and when you see his show, that he's having a great time. The other people look like they're just tortured souls up there, and you go, you know, "Guys! Lighten up! The image is heavy and everything, but you don't have to really be that." These guys are trying to live their lives the way their image is. The idea behind rock 'n' roll is joy. It's joyful music. It's not a depressing thing. You know, the big difference between an Alice Cooper show and a lot of the shows you're talking about—I won't specifically say anyone—is that I always left the audience on an upper. They walk away going, "Wow, I've got confetti in my hair and Alice has got a white tuxedo on, and he just did 'School's Out,' and balloons are popping." And then they remember back, and they go, "Wow, he did a thing with a baby carriage, and he did this, and then he got his head cut off. What a great night!" They always walked out with big smiles on their faces. Whereas I know a lot of people walk out of shows now, and they go, "Wow, my life is over." I don't know what they're going for. Are they trying to depress an audience? I guess that if you can make a buck with one emotion, you can make one with another. But to me, I liked the fact that people always came up to me—even now, 25 years later—and said, "The most fun I ever had was at your show where you came through the screen and did this and this and this." And then another guy would say, "You know, I never had so much fun at a concert as when the Cyclops came out and picked you up." And I'd just think back and think, "You know, those were fun shows."

O: ***I was going to ask about the Cyclops.***

AC: Yeah, I mean, it was a real Cyclops. This thing was 13 feet tall and it could pick me up. You could imagine how much fun the rehearsal was with that. But even the things that were dangerous were fun. The guillotine. To this day, I get nervous putting my head in that thing, because it's a 40-pound blade.

O: ***Is there a point at which you're ready to say, "Screw it. I'm just going to retire and play golf"?***

AC: You know, I do that every once in a while, even though I've never really cashed in my hand. I've never really said, "Okay, I'm out of this poker game." There was the time when I dropped out because of alcoholism, but I was fully intending to come back. But since then, since 1986, no. I haven't played my hand out yet. I keep thinking, "Gee, I wonder what the next album is gonna be about. I wonder what the next tour is going to be." As long as I can get an audience standing for an hour and a half, and as long as I'm not 300 pounds and bald-headed... You know, as long as I'm sleek with long, black hair and can still do an hour and a half of high-energy rock 'n' roll, I'll keep doing it.

O: ***Is anything shocking anymore?***

AC: Uh, CNN. CNN is more shocking than anything I can do. Audiences are pretty shockproof. It was easy to shock people in the '70s, but around 1978, I quit the shock business and said, "I'm just going to be in the entertainment business now. I just want the audience to walk away going, 'Wow. How did they do that? Wasn't that a great party?'"

O: ***Maybe fun is what's shocking right now.***

AC: Yeah, I guess so. Trying not to be shocking is shocking.

O: ***For people today who aren't really familiar with what you went through, what sort of censorship and controversy did you have to deal with?***

AC: Well, everything you did in the '70s was construed as being subversive on some level. Nobody in the band was gay, so the gay people thought we were making fun of them. And then the straight people thought we were trying to make everybody gay. And then, of course, the churches thought we were satanic, and nobody was satanic. We were anything but that. We were probably considered Communists, you know, and you couldn't find a more all-American band than Alice Cooper. We sat around drinking beer and watching football and baseball, and when people were calling for the end of the war, we were saying, you know, "Bomb them Commies!" So you couldn't find a more all-American, white-bread, Middle America band than Alice Cooper. We were everything that people thought we weren't. We would sit around on nights off, and people would think we had these wild orgies going on, and we were probably sitting around watching *Star Trek* and listening to Burt Bacharach.

O: ***You mentioned that you guys were anything but satanic. You're fairly outspokenly Christian.***

AC: Well, I mean, it's one of those things where I try not to put the two onstage, because they're different worlds. But at the same time, I always say, when people call me satanic, that it's probably the worst insult you can give me. I'm certainly not trying to be like that. The image has always been misconstrued, I think. I always go, "Hey! Alice is a character! Come on, guys." They really, truly expect me to live in this big gray house with a big cloud over it, like the Munsters. Of course, Rob Zombie's house is kind of like that. Rob Zombie's house really is pretty much the Munsters' house.

O: ***Where would rock 'n' roll be without Alice Cooper?***

AC: You know, I always figured that people would say, you know, "There would have been no Kiss and there would have been no this and that." I think somebody would have done a version of what I did. I don't know if it would have been exactly the same kind of thing, but definitely someone would have done some kind of version of it. It might have been a lot later. I mean, we were pretty far out on a limb when we came out as Alice Cooper. We knew that if this didn't happen, we were setting ourselves up for being the biggest bunch of jerks of all time—or some of the greatest geniuses. And it was really a matter of, "If this works, it's big. If this doesn't work, we are gonna be known as the biggest morons of all time." ⌀

"I can still piss people off a little bit and make 'em cheer. I don't want to think I've lost my touch."

Stan Freberg

By Stephen Thompson

Originally Printed September 1999

The career of satirist and comedian Stan Freberg has spanned more than 50 years. During that time, he's changed the face of radio and television advertising, perfecting the art of the humorous soft sell and saving or sustaining many of his clients' businesses. He's also widely credited with the creation of pop-music satire: Spike Jones wrote song parodies before him, but Freberg satirized music's style and performers, influencing countless comedians and songwriters in the process. He holds the distinction of being the last network-radio comedian, thanks to 1957's short-lived but fondly remembered The Stan Freberg Show. *And he recorded several best-selling comedy albums, the most famous of which is 1961's classic* Stan Freberg Presents The United States Of America, Vol. 1: The Early Years. *(A long-delayed sequel came out in 1996.) A broad sample of his recorded output, from such early favorites as "John & Marsha" to recent radio monologues and a new song, can be found on* Tip Of The Freberg, *a box set released in 1999. That year, Freberg spoke to* The Onion A.V. Club *about radio, advertising, satire, and music.*

The Onion: ***You've done many spots promoting radio and taught classes about the medium's power. How do you feel about radio today?***

Stan Freberg: I don't feel very good about it, frankly. At a local level, disc jockeys are doing a pretty good job trying to keep the medium alive, and there's a lot of interplay between listeners and hosts of call-in shows that we never had a couple decades ago, at least to the degree we have now. But the time is apparently past when we can do great drama on radio, except every once in a while on NPR. You'll have to excuse me: I just came back from Hawaii, so my brain is kind of fried. I was part of the faculty of an organization called Young Presidents' Organization, and I taught two different classes. One was called "Using Humor To Communicate," and the other was "Political Correctness: Just Another Form Of Censorship?" That received cheers from part of the audience and embittered silence from other people. I can still piss people off a little bit and make 'em cheer. I don't want to think I've lost my touch, you know. Among the things I played in this course was a thing I did 35 years before the term "political correctness" was ever invented, called "Elderly Man River." The wonder of that song is that the censor at CBS Radio didn't even realize I was putting him on. [In "Elderly Man River," Freberg sings

"Old Man River," but is interrupted by a CBS censor who instructs him to clean up the language. —ed.] He was only concerned that Jerome Kern's family didn't sue us for screwing around with the lyrics of "Old Man River." "He doesn't plant cotting / and those that plant them are soon forgotting." That's my favorite line. A guy at CBS Radio was always saying things like, "That family of acrobats you have on the show, the Zazalophs... What is that, Polish or something?" I said, "Probably, I don't know. We don't get into their ethnic background. The idea of having acrobats on radio is stupid enough." And he said, "Change their names to Jones or Smith. We don't want to offend any particular groups." So when I asked the man, Zazaloph, "What nationality is that, Czechoslovakian? Polish?" He said, "No, Swiss. This way we don't offend anyone." That's how we dealt with political correctness in 1957.

O: ***A lot of today's commercials employ a sarcastic, self-aware tone that seems to be building on your work. How do you feel about what you've started, and are they getting it right?***

SF: Most of the time, they don't get it right. The people now who do most creative work in advertising don't get it. I mean, first of all, they're not really trying to sell anything, and second, they don't care about the company. A guy came up to me one time after a speech and said, "As I see it, the whole idea is to get away with as much as you can get away with." I said, "No, that's not exactly it, fella." If that had been the case, I would have been in and out of advertising in about three days. You have to prove [the success of your method] to the client and the people spending the money, because in the end, it is their money. You have to prove that the Freberg way will sell their product better than if they just did straight advertising. Whenever I give a lecture or seminar, that's what I try to get across to people. I hear very few radio commercials that sound like I could have written them, or that they got the idea. The only really great creative work that I'm aware of is from my friend Jeff Goodby up in San Francisco. He did "Got Milk?," and he wrote the liner notes for the box set. Obviously, the man gets it. Plus, my son is just getting into that work now—Donavan Freberg, who was in the *Encyclopaedia Britannica* commercials. But I'm kind of sorry that I allowed [humor in commercials] to be unleashed, because there are so many crappy, bad attempts at humor in advertising, to the point that I hardly listen to radio. I dial over to the classical station, and even there, there's crappy stuff. I wish somebody would prove me wrong, but you have to admit that there's very little.

O: ***In television commercials, there's a pervasive sort of smug self-awareness.***

SF: A lot of television stuff is mean-spirited, and I think that's how political advertising got so mean-spirited, to where people are throwing things at the television set every time we have an election. The same people who produce commercials in radio and television are creating commercials for all the political candidates, and they took their cue from advertising. I once suggested that we need a moratorium on advertising for one year, and when I suggested that, I was talking to the American Association of Advertising Agencies. People got up in droves and left the room when I said that. I said, "Suppose Procter & Gamble stopped advertising soap for a year. Do you think anybody'd be any dirtier? No, sooner or later, if they needed soap or detergent, they'd stumble into the market and find by elimination the one that got them cleaner, got their clothes the whitest, and so forth, and they'd finally pick out the brand that they liked best, not influenced by any commercials." One woman yelled, "I don't like what he's saying, and I'm leaving," and she stomped up the aisle.

O: ***Do you regret helping any companies? Are there any companies you saved that you might have regretted helping?***

SF: There was a guy at Forest Lawn Cemeteries out here; Forest Lawn is the cemetery king in California. He was determined that he would hire Freberg to do some decent commercials for Forest Lawn that had a little element of humor, and I said, "No, thanks very much, but there's nothing funny about death, and I don't see how you can do that." But he persisted on and off for five years. Now, I hear Forest Lawn commercials that are attempting to do that, and I'm yelling at the car radio, "No, no, no, jeez!" So now I kind of wish I had done it, if only to save people from hearing those other ones. I don't know. I was turning down cigarette campaigns before it became fashionable. I wouldn't let CBS Radio sell *The Stan Freberg Show* to R.J. Reynolds and American Tobacco. The vice president of sales was yelling at me, "Freberg, are you crazy? I got these cigarette companies lined up!" For one show, I sponsored myself, because I was sustaining for 15 weeks with no sponsors. I was holding out for one sponsor to sponsor the whole show the way American Tobacco had sponsored Jack Benny, and the way State Farm Insurance later bought the whole *Jack Benny Show*. But those were the last days of the golden age of radio, I guess, and when that show went off, there were no more comedy shows emanating from New York or Hollywood. That's what makes me the last network-radio comedian in America. Big deal. That was one of the things that didn't help—that I wouldn't let them split the show up and I wouldn't let them sell me to cigarettes. But I managed, and in the last show I sponsored myself. [Sings.] "Stan Freberg, the foaming comedian / floats the jokes right down the drain." That was parodying Ajax the foaming cleanser.

O: ***You've talked about milestones, being the last network comedian. You're also considered one of the first to satirize songs rather than simply parodying them.***

SF: Yes, that's exactly right. Spike Jones was the only comedian who preceded me on records doing songs, but he did true parodies of the song and didn't have anybody saying, [adopts drunken voice] "Come on, you guys, stick some old rags in your mouth and let's sing it again from the top." In other words, I was the first guy to not only parody pop music, but to make editorial comments about it as I was doing it. Sinatra was a friend of mine—I did two tours with him in Australia, and he did a walk-on part in a show I did called *The Chun King Chow Mein Hour*—and he loved that song ["Sh-Boom"], because he loved the lyrics of Cole Porter, Ira Gershwin, and all the great lyricists over the years. He hated it that rock 'n' roll singers didn't have any enunciation. So when I did "Sh-Boom," he really loved that. In Australia, I preceded him, and he would always try to get there in time to hear me do "Sh-Boom" for the audiences. He'd stand in the wings and laugh.

O: ***Why do you think comedy records don't sell as well as they used to?***

SF: I don't know. My friend "Weird Al" Yankovic, a man who says that if it hadn't been for Stan Freberg there wouldn't be any Weird Al, was

"Weird Al" Yankovic On Stan Freberg

I discovered Stan Freberg as a pre-adolescent during my weekly ritual listenings to the Dr. Demento *radio show. I felt an immediate connection with his satirical music and warped sense of humor. As I became more familiar with his work, he became one of my all-time musical heroes. Today, whenever I'm asked about my musical inspiration, I always credit Mr. Freberg (along with Spike Jones, Allan Sherman, and Tom Lehrer). It was one of the greatest thrills in my life to cast him as a semi-regular in my short-lived Saturday-morning program* The Weird Al Show. *Stan played J.B. Toppersmith, the network tycoon who had ostensibly given me the show. It was so bizarre coming to work each day and getting to work alongside my hero. It was all I could do not to fall prostrate on the ground in awe-filled respect and admiration.*

totally influenced by me, but he does his own thing. He's a wonderful kid. He does his things in a unique way that's really not like what I did, and he has the advantage of doing videos, which didn't exist when I was kidding pop music. Still, you're right that comedy records do not sell all that much, although a *Time* story a few years ago, when I did *The United States Of America, Vol. 2*, had the headline, "Comedy Records Are Back." Al's new album is called *Running With Scissors*. [Laughs.] I love that title. Everybody can relate to that. The first time I met him, he dropped to his knees and kissed the hem of my sport coat. I said, "Yankovic, get up, get up. People are staring." I was on his short-lived Saturday-morning show on CBS [*The Weird Al Show*], and I played, of all people, the network censor. It was a part I was born to play, and my son and I did the puppets on that show. Those strange little puppets, Papa Boolie and Baby Boolie, were my son and me. I trained my son to be a puppeteer since he was a little boy. Off the subject, I saw my friend Buzz Aldrin being interviewed several times yesterday, because yesterday [July 20, 1999] was the 30th anniversary of the day we touched down on the moon. My wife and I flashed back to... Was it 30 years? We were at North American Rockwell, where CBS had asked us to come, because they had a whole crew there. Orville, the little space man from the moon, was a character I used to do. A producer at CBS had called me and said, "Do you still have that little space puppet?" And I said, "Yes, Orville comes out of a spaceship." He said, "NASA is gonna land on the moon, hopefully, and when they land the astronauts, by orders of the NASA doctor, they have to take a nap for four hours. We don't want to stare at Walter Cronkite for four hours, and we thought you could do something. Orson Welles is narrating a thing on space, and your friend Ray Bradbury has done something, and we want you to do some little pieces of varying length." And I said, "Oh, great, great." So my wife and I went out to North American Rockwell. And I stand there with Orville, and the guy's there with cue cards, and I'm changing the jokes up to the last minute, and we taped all this stuff, which they recorded in the CBS truck. While the astronauts were approaching the moon, we had just finished. So my wife and I hurry to the television set there, and they're deciding which one to put on first, and they said, "Why don't you go back to your hotel?" So we're at the hotel, and we've been up for, like, 30 hours, propping our eyelids open, and we hear Cronkite say, "Well, the astronauts are supposed to take a nap for four hours, so we'll be bringing you several things: a piece narrated by Orson Welles, some little satiric moments by Stan Freberg, and a... What's that? What's that? One moment... We hear that the astronauts want to forgo their nap and go right out on the moon." I yelled, "Oh, no, no! Take a nap, take a nap!"

O: ***And Buzz Aldrin is still your friend?***

SF: Yeah, 30 years later, you know, what's the difference? I told him this story, and he thinks it's hilarious. So now Cronkite is saying, "So, the astronauts all say they feel just fine, and the doctor says that if it's okay with them, it's okay with him. So we'll be staying live with the transmission from the moon." So for two hours, they stayed live on the moon, and all that stuff I did went on the floor. A week later, I was on *The Tonight Show*, and before I went to *The Tonight Show* to do that, the producer said, "Have you still got that little space man?" "Do I?!" He said, "Do you think you could do something on the moon landing?" I said, "I think I might be able to whip something up." So I compiled several little pieces and did this fairly long thing on *The Tonight Show*, which got screams of laughter, Carson beating the desk and all that. Now, that is what is known as "The Freberg Lost Footage," because some brilliant executive at NBC, after Carson was off and Jay Leno was on, needed space, so he said, "Well, what are all these tapes here?" "Oh, these are 10 years of *The Tonight Show*." And he said, "Do we really need those?" "Nah, let's degauss the tape." So they degaussed all those shows, including the ones I was on. My only hope is that somewhere, after you print this, somebody on the Internet will say, "Gee, I made a recording of that."

O: ***June Foray is still alive, and you're obviously still alive...***

SF: Yes, let me check my pulse.

O: ***But a lot of your team has died. As you continue to work, have you been rebuilding a team?***

SF: Well, it's been difficult. Fortunately, I was able to get my dear friend Peter Leeds on *The United States Of America, Vol. 2,* and Jesse White had had a stroke recently, but I still insisted on putting him in somewhere, so he was the one who didn't buy the jingle that Francis Scott Key had written that later became "The Star Spangled Banner." So Jesse was on that, just a few lines, but he's gone now, too. No, June and I are the only survivors of the Stan Freberg company of actors, though I've tried to use Lorenzo Music, the actor who is the voice of Garfield. He sounded a little bit to me like Byron Kane, who was a wonderful radio actor. All these people had some nerve to die on me. [Music died in 2001. —ed.] Gosh, it's amazing. And my son is coming along as a character actor. He's a wonderful actor, and he inherited my sense of humor and satiric outlook.

O: ***You've worked with some influential people.***

SF: Well, another one of my connections is that my wife, before she married me, worked for Peter Lawford. He was one of the Rat Pack, and she was his assistant when he did the *Thin Man* series at MGM. Later on, in New York, Peter Lawford came up and kissed her and hugged her and so forth. She introduced me as her new husband, Stan Freberg, and he said, "Oh, Stan Freberg, I was hoping I'd run into you so I could tell you this story." He said, "We were all at Hyannis Port, and all of a sudden Jack Kennedy came running in to where we were and said, 'Come quick, quick, this is that commercial I was telling you about.' And they all ran in, and it was my Chun King commercial with the Chinese people in the elevator. That's also in this box set. Imagine Jack Kennedy thinking that was so hilarious that everybody had to come into the den and watch it. Please don't forget to credit my dear wife, Donna Freberg. She married me right after she quit working for Peter Lawford in order to come to work for me, and we've been married now for 40 years. She's been my producer all these years. She's been my producer longer than she says she would have thought her patience would have endured. I drive her crazy. ⌀

Andrew W.K.

By Stephen Thompson
Originally Printed May 2002

"There's no wrong reason to like my music. There's no wrong reason to like anything. This music is freedom."

In the weeks that followed the March 2002 release of I Get Wet, *23-year-old Andrew Wilkes-Krier went from obscurity to omnipresence, becoming a media darling while making high-profile appearances on MTV and* Saturday Night Live. *A grinning populist with a stash of instantly ingratiating, wildly overdriven dance-metal songs—including the unstoppable single "Party Hard"—W.K. was alternately hailed as the savior of a depressingly dour rock world and dismissed as either a sideshow or an elaborate gag. But he's clearly dead serious about his music and its potential to inspire a world in need of passion and commitment. Shortly after the release of* I Get Wet, *W.K. spoke to* The Onion A.V. Club *about faith, strength, energy, the power of music, and the story of his life.*

The Onion: ***What was your childhood like?***
Andrew W.K.: Very good. Very solitary. Very fulfilled. In the neighborhood we lived in, there weren't a lot of kids. I started taking piano lessons real young, and I always had projects, so I was really entertained. I was a real serious kid, real intense, and there were a lot of things I was doing by myself that I took seriously, like organizing little pieces of paper, cutting out things from magazines, and filing them away. I'd set up these huge spread-out projects on my floor. I'd cut out those ads in comic books for, like, a million different T-shirts. I'd cut out each one of those designs and line them up. Stuff like that. Really intense, very serious, lots of drawing and planning things and working on things and looking forward to things. I lived in my own world, all the while taking piano lessons. The University Of Michigan had a good music school, and for part of the piano program, the advanced students would also teach. So you've got these enthusiastic piano teachers who were doing it because they enjoyed it. That was how I started music, and that's real important, because music to me wasn't... It wasn't like, "Hey, dude, you should get into music. Check out this tape." It wasn't, "Hey, you should play guitar so you can be in a band." It wasn't seeing something on TV or hearing somebody on the radio. It was based on literally just melody—just music without any other stuff attached to it. I ended up getting a very basic affection for music as it is. That's something that I guess is unusual, not that there's a right or wrong way to get into music. But music wasn't limited to what my friends showed me or thought was cool, or

what was on TV; it was all that and more. I could like any song by any band as long as I liked the melody, because there's no right and wrong when it comes to what you like. And I was just so fortunate to have parents who encouraged me to try things and do what I wanted. If you don't like something, you can always change your mind, but at least try. They were very supportive and unconditionally involved, and you can't trade that for anything.

O: ***You mentioned that you like things regardless of what anyone thinks. It's weird that*** **Rolling Stone** ***did a thing on you as part of its "Cool" issue, because it seems integral to your work that you don't care about being perceived as cool.***

AWK: That was interesting. What is cool? I say something's cool if I like it. So is that what's cool? I don't know. Cool is something that you allow yourself to do, and when trying is involved, sometimes it isn't the same. I'm happy to be thought of as cool, but I never was cool. Everyone thought I was this complete moron and complete dork for the majority of my school years. It's interesting, though: I was a loner kid who was very intense and serious and dorky and kind of nerdy and weird, but while I was given a hard time, I was never picked on the way other kids were. It's almost like there was an unspoken kind of respect, of "You know what? We're just gonna let you be, because you're doing your own thing." People didn't bother me. I mean, I did get picked on a lot in junior high, but I just dealt with it. I had my own little world where nothing could hurt me or bother me too much. I always had this place to return to. That's something I still have to this day, and it's just inside me. I guess people can find things like that in food, or in buying things and stuff like that, but if you can find it within yourself, you'll always be okay. So anyway, I was drawing a lot, drawing comic books and other things, all the while always playing piano. I would play piano for hours each day, practicing my scales and other things we were working on. We'd have these recitals at the end of the year, but all the while, I was making up my own songs from very early on. That's real easy to do on piano, because you have so many different sounds you can get out of it. You have that sustain pedal, and you can make it sound like a big, echoey place. I thought that was the coolest thing when I first started playing piano: I remember banging away on it with that sustain pedal held down the whole time, because it sounded like it was in a huge cave. I ended up getting a digital keyboard, which was so amazing to me—excitement to the point of delirium. I would sit for hours and hours playing stuff. That was when I started recording. It would be real basic songs, and I would sing and make up the words as I went along. In junior high school, with this keyboard, I recorded a whole tape called *The Mechanical Eyes*. I drew this cover, and my mom and I went and made color Xeroxes. And this one guy who played guitar used to come over, and we'd play together, and we considered it a band, but the idea of playing shows was unheard of. Eventually, we did form a real band with a drummer. That progressed, and when we started high school, we played a few real shows at this amazing place, this Unitarian church basement. It was a whole big thing where all these mind-blowing bands played and really changed my life. Seeing these weird, crazy punk bands that I couldn't even believe existed. I don't really know how they were able to play at these... The shows didn't last long, because there was always a lot of violence, and stuff would get broken, and the police would always come. I never imagined something could be so loud, that there could be screaming like that, and that

"Music, above all, is huge and magnificent and so much bigger than me or any one person."

they could be making this intense noise. I can't even describe how exciting and important it was, and from that moment on, I just became obsessed with these bands around my town. They all quit or got kicked out of school and were living in their own house at 15, 16, or 17 without their parents. Just living, stealing whatever they needed. All their equipment was stolen from other bands. The whole thing was so intense, so violent, so chaotic. I would just hang around on the outskirts hoping they wouldn't yell at me and tell me to leave and make fun of me. Which they did, but I couldn't stop hanging around. There are so many stories. When I was 17 or 18, I had a buddy who lived downstairs in this basement apartment. He had windows right on sidewalk level, and we piled a bunch of speakers into his windows at night. We had a real PA system this time, and we'd turn it up to 10. We'd plug the keyboard in and I'd just tape down as many keys as I could with books and tape. We completely underestimated how loud it was going to be. People from five blocks away were coming out of their houses thinking it was Armageddon. Within minutes, it was surrounded by police cars. It sounded like a gas line was exploding. We ran in the back, and the whole apartment building had crowded around his door, pounding on his door. We ran to his door and said, "Oh, sorry, I don't know what that was," and shut it off, and then split up for half an hour. There were a lot of other things happening at this point. There was a lot of mail fraud, forgery, vandalism, lots of stealing money from jobs, lots of stealing from places, like going into a bookstore, stacking up 20 books, and just walking out. I was basically just doing bad things. I had worked really hard to graduate high school a year early, and I spent that last year making fake gift certificates and putting them in envelopes. I'd forge a cancellation over the stamp to make it look like it came from Los Angeles, and then I would send it to somebody I knew, hoping they would take the gift certificates and try to use them and get arrested. It was really intense and bizarre, very solitary, and not spending a lot of time with friends. I was very angry, and I didn't care what people thought of me. I didn't care if what I was doing was bad or hurting people's feelings. I would feel bad about it just enough to not do something so crazy that I would go to jail, although I got close many times, and some of my friends did go to jail. My parents were very, very concerned. They only know probably about a quarter of the stuff I did. I ended up stopping all this stuff gradually, because all the while, I really, really loved my parents, especially my mom. I didn't love her more, but she really expected things of me. I knew that I had disappointed her already. They had me seeing all these child psychologists, and were very concerned that I was crazy. I ended up stopping because I knew how disappointed she would be if she knew all the money I was stealing, and how the reason I would get fired from a job wasn't because they had too many employees. I didn't care what someone thought of me, only what she thought. That was enough to stop, and now, looking back, it was for myself, too. So I had the good fortune of learning my lesson in the 11th hour rather than in the 13th, so I could still make the right decision when it counted. There is still so much we're leaving out, but we could sum it up as being... The best description would be calculated, intensified chaos and a solitary existence, yet with many amazing people around that I consider my friends. Then I moved to New York, not knowing a single person there. Not knowing what I was going to do, but it felt like the culmination of everything, from the piano lessons to all the hours spent working on mindless things, to all the dangerous stuff, to all the bands, to all the music, to all the wide world of options that were always present. It was culminating into this growing sense that I was going to bear down and start doing something. I didn't know what it was going to be, but there was a sense that I had to start making the most of each day. Like, I don't want to be sitting down for a minute. I used to just walk around the city for hours, just because it was better than sitting at home. But I had very little money. There was a lot of walking 80 blocks to work so I could save a dollar. Cooking everything at home if I could, and stealing money at that point, too. But there was definitely this excitement in the air. There was this sense of, "Wow, what can I do today to make the absolute most of this day?" That continued on, and I was always recording and becoming more focused on making songs and playing piano. I had this broken 3-track that I brought with me from Michigan, and I was getting better and better recording on that. That's when I decided that I was going to put all my energy and time into one thing, just to see what would happen. I didn't have any one plan. I just wanted to have something I could do every day, so I decided to make the most exciting songs I can possibly make, and to do everything I can to serve them and further their existence, which included playing shows, recording songs, making flyers, anything. I saved up all my money and borrowed a bunch of money from my mom to buy a computer that I could record on, and just kept working. I was playing shows, and all I could really do was play keyboard. I could kind of play guitar at that point, but it clearly was not my ideal situation. My ideal situation would have been to be in a band, but I knew I could play a show. I would be frustrated out of my mind, but I'd say, "Don't be a wimp." I used to carry this card in my pocket that had a list of things that I would think of and try to hold in my mind. The first one was "Don't be a fucking wimp." That took care of almost every situation I was in. If I was feeling depressed or whiny or discouraged, I'd pull that card out and say, "Don't be a fucking wimp!" That doesn't mean I'm not allowed to feel sad or have human emotions. But take a look around. Look at how good my life is. Don't be a fucking wimp! Snap out of it! Another one was "Never let down." Again, that's just to never stop trying. Life is too short. "Life is short," that was on there. This might be my one chance to do this, so aren't you going to make the most of it? It's better to regret what you've done than what you haven't. I say "No regrets," period, now. No regrets, no guilt, no embarrassment, no shame. Another one was "You'll only live once," which is tied in with that. And "No fear" was huge. However, I've updated that, because it's impossible to have no fear. You'll always have fear, but it's facing the fear. Someone who has no fear is not nearly as brave as someone who has fears and faces them. I believe everybody has fears, and to deny them is just putting up more walls. So all these things were just getting... The songs are what saw everything through. The shows I played were always like, if you had 50 people at the show, that was fantastic. That was a huge success. It was frustrating, though, because these songs were supposed to be played by a band. That's how I'd always envisioned it. I put ads in the paper to try and meet people, but that didn't work. Whenever I'd play a show, I'd talk to people, and I'd ask people on the street. If they looked cool, I'd say, "Do you play in a band, and would you want to?" That never really worked out. I ended up gradually meeting people who did help, and I'd make tapes and CDs of my songs and pass them out and put my phone number on them and just do everything I could. It eventually paid off with meeting people who helped me put together a band. I'm just so fortunate now to have this amazing band. I couldn't imagine a nicer bunch of people. They're kind, outgoing, hardworking, dedicated, responsible, smart... In every way, they are the perfect band. They're all at a point in their lives where they just want to do something the best they can, and know that the more they put into it, the more they'll get out of it. So I started recording in New York and continued in L.A., Michigan, Minnesota, and Florida. It was a lot of different people and a lot of different places, but all very necessary. There were a lot of engineers, and that's what we needed. The songs were good to go. We just needed all the best equipment and the systems to make them sound like they should sound. It was very work-intensive, to the point where some people didn't really enjoy working that way. It's very tedious, and it involves fine-tuning and stacking, where you're looking at each song under a microscope and every split second is important. There are no coincidences. There's no accident, like, "Oh, wow, that was cool. Let's keep that." Every melody line is composed of like 40 sounds combined. I did not want it to be the sound of a guitar and drums and bass playing. I wanted it to be the sound of the song playing, so you just hear one big, massive instrument grinding out this song. You can imagine it sort of all coming from one enormous source, where you just hear an infinite expanse of a million things all happening in perfect unison, all laid out in front of you. We spent so much time so that you don't hear thousands of hours of work. That takes thousands of hours of work, I believe, to achieve that. It's like a movie: When you're watching a movie, you're not thinking of the millions of dollars and thousands of people and lights and every other thing happening to light that conversation scene in a bedroom. I wanted to make satisfying songs that did exactly what you wanted them to do and did it again and again, and just kept paying off. That didn't punch you in the face, but instead just gave you a big, firm handshake and a hug. Instant gratification. Also, living a solitary kind of existence and having been hassled by people that I didn't feel similar to... It's very interesting, because I know a lot of people who feel left out, so the first chance they get, they want to leave someone else out and perpetuate that feeling. The people who didn't like me or didn't want me around, I always wanted to bring those people in. I wanted to make something that they would want to be part of. I wanted to make something that would make them happy about me and themselves and us. That's one of the most important things here: that nobody is turned away and nobody is left out and nobody is judged based on how they look or what they like or what they don't like or even why they like it. There's no wrong reason to like my music. There's no wrong reason to like anything. This music is freedom. It allows anyone else the freedom to do whatever they want, and it accepts that unconditionally. And it continues to just want to make you happy. All you need to know is, "Do I feel this in my stomach? Is this running through my veins? Does this go up my spine?

"No wonder people are tentative about believing in something: First, they're wondering if it's going to let them down, and second, they wonder what people are going to think of them."

Does this blow my mind to pieces? Does this affect me?" That is real. That is physical evidence, and you don't need to question it, or even understand. That's why I would never question why someone liked this or why someone's smiling or why someone is happy. It could be for one of a million reasons, some that people think I would think are bad or against me. Life's just way too short for me to qualify and quantify how this can make someone feel. Music, above all, is huge and magnificent and so much bigger than me or any one person. Someone says, "What if someone thinks you're just some kind of stupid joke?" And I say, "I don't care. I want to make them happy. If that makes them happy, if that's what puts a smile on their face, so be it." It's for everybody, for every reason. It's easy to get closed in. Somehow, for some reason, it's gotten cool to not have passion about something. It's gotten cool to be distant and detached from things, to have a seen-it-all, done-it-all, been-there-done-that attitude about things. No wonder people are tentative about believing in something: First, they're wondering if it's going to let them down, and second, they wonder what people are going to think of them. Which I only can attribute to the amount of information that's available and the things that are expected of people, and the way people are judged based on what they decide. It's just human nature, but being

"Being passionate takes courage, and the more you believe in something, the less possibility it has of letting you down."

passionate takes courage, and the more you believe in something, the less possibility it has of letting you down. The more you believe in it, the more it becomes your own. I just hope people have the strength to still give things a chance, and to say, "You know what? This isn't too good to be true. Maybe I haven't seen everything." It's easy to be overloaded sometimes, but I hope that we can look up to things in awe and not have to have everything at our feet. I hope that we can be amazed and excited and inspired by something without having to have everything figured out and put in our pocket. There's no one setting any limits on what you can enjoy, how you can enjoy it, why you should enjoy it, or what you should do except yourself. I look at what I have here as a miracle—that we're alive in the first place—and thank God for every breath I take, whoever He is or whatever it is. I'm doing this on behalf of everybody, on behalf of the thousands and thousands of people who've directly affected my life, on behalf of the millions that don't get a chance to do this, that don't have these things that I enjoy, that have to work just to get food. Even the saddest day is a miracle for me. When you have food, when you have a place to sleep, when you have friends and family and general health and safety, you have no right to complain. You're living life, and at that point it's up to you what you're going to do with it. Never concede this life, you know what I mean? I'm going to make all that I can of it for everyone else. This is not a return to the good old days. This is not a reaction to things that are bad now. It's not, "Things suck and we need to make them good again." This is forging ahead into uncharted territory. This is about working hard and inviting everybody into an unending, inexhaustible source of strength and energy. There's no rules, no limits, no, "Oh, you're giving too much of yourself away. You've got to take it easy." No! I'm doing fine! If we could make one person happy that day and I knew I could, why would I not do that? One guy in Europe asked me this question, and it was a really good question: "If you could change one thing in the whole world, what would it be?" And immediately, the first thing I thought of was to preserve all the forests and all the animals and all that. But then, that would cause a whole slew of problems. Imagine how that could backfire. Well, okay, at least I could wipe out poverty and hunger and disease. Well, again, you'd have huge population problems and more money problems created because of that. These huge ideas were just creating other huge challenges. All of a sudden, I just thought, "Well, you know what? If I could make a difference, or mean something, or change for the better the life of one person, especially a young person, even if it was just to make their day better... That is completely within my reach." It's within the reach of everybody to do something on a daily basis that helps anybody. Which makes somebody smile instead of frown. Which makes somebody feel better rather than worse. You know when you really like something, and you know that that thing you really love loves itself and loves you? It's a total bummer when you love something and go up to the person who's working on it, and you say, "God! This is so great! I love this so much!" And they're like, "Eh. Thanks, but it's no big deal." When someone comes up and tells me that they love the music, I yell, "Me, too!" And we just hug. It's that feeling that the people playing those songs are loving them just as much as you are while you're dancing, and that you could be up on that stage and playing those songs just as well. That is the point. The uncharted territory is that there is no line to be crossed. You don't have to hold back. This is our time. We have not lived and died yet. It has not all been done. It has not all been seen. I'm not religious. I never have been. My parents aren't, but we're not anti-religious, either. We were always just brought up with a very open understanding of who we were in a bigger picture. There was never any need to create a sense of guilt or shame. Oh, God. There's the other thing: No guilt! The idea of a guilty pleasure? That's as mixed-up to me as calling somebody a poseur. "You don't like this for the right reasons like I do." How awful. And the idea of, "I'm so ashamed for what I like." If you feel bad about liking something, then you don't really like it. Anyway, religion just puts up a bunch of walls that I don't need, but I have so much respect and admiration for those who have true passion and belief and dedication to having faith in something bigger than them, and look at it for inspiration. I have nothing against it, but at the same time, I think there's something to be wary of—for me, just in my opinion.

O: ***Who else do you like in music today?***

AWK: I like tons of stuff, really. Lots and lots of songs, because above all I like melody and rhythm. If it has that, especially if there's some sincerity and honest hard work and genuine passion put into it, I'm there. I love it. I just look at it as freedom: I have the freedom to like so many things and be excited about so many different things on all sides. A great song is that friend that will be there in the morning. You put it on first thing and it sets the day straight, it organizes things in your head, it makes you happy, it's comforting. And then you get home at night and it's there to put you to sleep. It's right there smiling and waiting for you. The minute you turn your back on it and don't want to listen to it, it's still there waiting for you. The minute you come back to it, it's there with open arms, never in judgment. And that's what this is, and that's what I am, and that's what we're doing. We will always be there. I will never let people down. I promise I will always do what I can. Have the faith to believe in this, and I will, too. In a world of confusion and pessimism, we can maintain some sort of clarity and truth. ⌀

"It was this really beautiful moment, and then I got arrested."

Tim Quirk (Too Much Joy)

By Stephen Thompson

Originally Printed March 2000

During the peak of its popularity in the late '80s and early '90s, the New York band Too Much Joy made its mark marrying slick rock to a healthy mixture of brattiness and earnestness. Consequently, its career highlights are all over the place: They include the catchy (and strangely sweet) pop single "Crush Story," the supercharged anthem "Longhaired Guys From England," the jokey college-radio staples "Drum Machine" and "Take A Lot Of Drugs," and an inspired cover of LL Cool J's "That's A Lie." But Too Much Joy faced a strange contradiction as its career progressed: Some felt the band lost its sense of humor as its musicianship and production values improved, while others dismissed it as a novelty act before hearing its slick, more musically accomplished later material. In 2000, singer Tim Quirk, who later formed Wonderlick with Too Much Joy's Jay Blumenfeld, spoke to The Onion A.V. Club *about his band's status, its infamous arrest in Florida, and its curious (and temporary) endorsement by Newt Gingrich.*

The Onion: ***Is Too Much Joy still together?***
Tim Quirk: Too Much Joy will never break up. It may never make another record and it may never play another show, but that doesn't mean we've broken up. It sounds funny, but it's actually true. I mean, I'm in California and the other guys are in New York, so it's tough to schedule dates. Our new idea is to do a Branson thing, pick one place to play, and have the world come to us. Only the people who are still really interested would actually do that. The thing is, if you go out and say, "Oh, we broke up," and then you feel like playing a show later on, all of a sudden you're like The Who. Who wants to be The Who? I want to be The Who in 1965, not The Who in 1999. I think in a way it's more respectable to keep going and sort of slow down.
O: ***What was the deal with Bozo The Clown?***
TQ: On the vinyl release of *Son Of Sam I Am*, we wanted to drop in samples from various things. We didn't have any samplers or anything, so we just directly scratched the stuff off the turntables onto our master tapes, and one of the things we did was off an old Bozo The Clown record. It was the perfect introduction to the song "Clowns," because he said, "And then I found something in one of my pockets. It was about as big as your shoe, but it was shaped like a rocket." We didn't make this shit up; Larry Harmon actually said this on the record, and it was sold to kids. It was

frightening. That was back before Biz Markie got sued, so you didn't need clearances for anything. You could do whatever the fuck you wanted, and we dropped it in. It was the type of funny thing that got mentioned in various reviews and interviews, but what we didn't know was that Larry Harmon was apparently kind of vain, and has kept a clipping service going for all these years. Whenever there's a mention of Bozo, he gets it. So he hears about it, and not only is he vain, but he's also very litigious, believe me. After this happened, I heard all the "Bozo sued me" stories, and there must be a thousand of them. I guess he's got a lucrative little sideline in licensing the name out. Anyway, his attorney sent a cease-and-desist letter to Alias [the band's label at the time] saying, "You can't print any more of those albums, and we're gonna sue you if you do." Luckily, it just so happened to be at the time when we were doing the deal with Giant, and part of the deal with Giant was that Alias couldn't sell any more records anyway, so my understanding for years had been that it just worked out nicely and we said, "We cease, we desist," and that was the end of it. But it turns out, I learned after the fact, that we actually had to pay him. I'm pretty sure it was $200. [Laughs.] We had to settle with him for $200, and then we had to cut it out of the Giant release. It's weird, because you'd think that would make the vinyl version actually worth something. But it's worth nothing.

O: ***How about the 2 Live Crew thing?***

TQ: Well, we were mixing *Cereal Killers*, which means the producer and the engineer were in the studio and we were all watching *Star Trek: The Next Generation* in the lounge. I guess a commercial came on, we flipped to MTV, and we found out that police in Florida had busted a record-store owner and then busted 2 Live Crew when they played a set. There were all these people giving these editorials about how it was censorship and it was wrong—which, duh, it is. It was like, "Hello, Florida, are you part of the country or not? What the fuck is wrong with you? How hard is it to read the Constitution?" But we're sitting there, and it seemed so hypocritical, all these people writing editorials in *Variety* and *Billboard* and shit, and everyone there already agreed with them. It's like, "You're not doing anything except making yourselves feel better." We were having this conversation around the TV and somebody, I'm pretty sure it was Sandy [Smallens, former bassist], said, "We should go down there and do a set of 2 Live Crew covers at the same club." And we all kind of laughed, because it seemed like a goofy idea, but our publicist was hanging out in the room. She heard that and went, "You guys have to do that." And she started getting really excited. I feel weird saying this, because there was always this perception that it was a publicity stunt, and in one sense, we probably wouldn't have done it if the publicist and the record company hadn't gone, "Yeah, we'll pay for it. Do it." There was certainly that aspect to it, but it wasn't the motivation. So we started talking about it some more, and the idea was to have a whole bunch of bands go down, like Red Hot Chili Peppers and Sonic Youth, Too Much Joy, and so on, and everybody would do one 2 Live Crew song, and the police would have to arrest 10 bands. They'd have to take 100 people to jail, and that would have been really cool. We sent out the press release, we sent out physical invitations to other bands, our manager was talking to other bands' managers, and all these people kept saying it was a great idea. So we booked the club and got the date, but no other band would commit. Two other bands had committed, but they were basically our level or smaller, and we really wanted the big names to come down. But there was a lot of this, "Yeah, yeah, see you there, man," and it just never materialized. We're like, "Well, do we call it off or just go do it ourselves? Oh, what the hell, these songs can't be that hard to learn." We did the same thing we'd done with "That's A Lie," where we turned rap songs into rock songs, so we played five 2 Live Crew songs and "That's A Lie" and "I Fought The Law" by The Clash and a few others, and we got a ton of press about it. We were going on all these talk shows and doing all these interviews with big-ass publications, being absolutely 100 percent sincere. I mean, I'm really proud to be an American, but not for any of the reasons that most people who say they're proud to be an American are proud to be Americans. I love the Bill Of Rights, but most Americans don't. And that's really true. I read this one thing in a newspaper once where they showed people the First Amendment and asked them where they thought it came from. More people thought it was part of the Communist Manifesto than thought it was part of the Bill Of Rights. That's just fucking scary. Anyway, I was getting kind of bummed out, because all these people were accusing us of being publicity whores. And I was like, "Don't they understand? This is really important. Nobody's doing anything. They're just writing editorials, and someone has to take action and show the world how dumb this is." So we went down and did it. And, look, we're little suburban kids, and the prospect of going to jail—even though you have ACLU lawyers behind you and you're not gonna spend too much time in there—is kind of scary. We spent the night in jail, and the hilarious thing was that there was this big holding pen with a TV, and we were heroes by the time we came in. Everyone was like, "You know Luther? Me, too, I'm down with him." One big convict stole Sandy's milk. Apart from that, it was relatively painless. It's weird: I had to transcribe the 2 Live Crew songs, and I'm here to tell you, they are crap. They have almost no redeeming value. They're just bad. They're dumb. They don't shine a light on anything, really; it's just poorly done and poorly made. What offended me the most about it wasn't the curse words or the way they talked about women; it was just the lack of any gleam of intelligence in it. It was just, "Hello, we're stupid, and if you buy our music, you are stupid." But that doesn't mean it doesn't have the right to exist. And actually, after spending a night in jail, I was like, "Wait a minute." After getting out, even though it was just for, like, nine hours out of my little ivory tower, I realized that everybody there was talking just like those lyrics I wrote down. In a weird sense, it became clear to me that while people thought they were offended by the language and the attitude and the cussing, I don't think they were. I think it was more like, "Oh my God, this is a segment of society that we ignore. It gets pushed into sections of our cities and our states and we don't have to deal with it, and that's the way we want it to stay. But once you get a record like 2 Live Crew becoming popular, and you start getting glimpses of this aspect of American life, you're like, "That's not us! Get it out of here. I don't want anyone to hear this." It wasn't like they were trying to outlaw bad language; they were trying to outlaw a subculture. I felt that pretty strongly in jail. It was important to me, and that's why I'm going on about it for so long. Also, I really think it was inspired. It was the type of thing Too Much Joy always aspired to. It was funny, but it made a serious point, and it wasn't something anyone else would do. We were successful a very small percentage of the time, but in that one instance, I think we nailed it.

"It was like, 'Hello, Florida, are you part of the country or not? What the fuck is wrong with you? How hard is it to read the Constitution?' "

O: *Did you guys really feed hamburgers to Steve Vai's vegetarian dog?*

TQ: Yeah, and I'm proud of that. People can do whatever they want, and I can make fun of them—that's America—but you cannot torture your pet. If you make a dog have a diet that's unnatural to a dog, that's torture. Dogs eat meat.

O: ***Did Steve Vai find out?***

TQ: If he ever read any of our press, I'm sure he did, but I don't think he really followed Too Much Joy's career very closely. Steve Vai was on tour with Whitesnake when we were at his house. But his wife, who used to be in Vixen, was there most of the time.

O: ***Did she ever object to you feeding the dog meat?***

TQ: We only did it when she wasn't looking. The only guy who knew was the administrator, the guy whose job was to run the studio. He was this nervous type. On a sitcom, he'd be

"It was the type of thing Too Much Joy always aspired to. It was funny, but it made a serious point, and it wasn't something anyone else would do."

the guy who was always going crazy that things were out of place, and then the wacky rock band would come in and do things behind his back. I think he's the only one who ever saw us, and we just looked at him like, "You can't do anything."

O: ***Now, you were detained by the Secret Service?***

TQ: Oh, yeah. That was a really weird night. It was in D.C., and there were Secret Service men all over the club. There were lots of rumors, like, "Who is it? Is it the Gore girls? Maybe it's Chelsea. Who's here?" We heard the prime minister of Bulgaria, we heard the prime minister of Bolivia. The crowd was talking about it, and everyone was talking about it backstage. So we come out onstage and, you know, we've got egos. It's sort of distracting when you come out and you expect everyone to be looking at you, and you see these guys stealing your thunder, wearing sunglasses in this dark club and little clips in their ear, standing with their hands behind their backs and their legs spread. I was like, "People have to look at me!" We open with "That's A Lie," and it's one of those things where we always try to tell a different lie during the song every night, to sort of make it site-specific, so this seemed like a perfect opportunity. When we got to the stop, I started riffing about how you could see these Secret Service folks all over the place, and there were lots of rumors about who they were there to protect. And I said, "A little-known fact about the Secret Service is that they're allowed to arrest anyone who threatens the president. But Secret Service men have no sense of humor, so I'm going to explain to you that this song is a joke and the reason it's funny is because it is called 'That's A Lie.' And we say many things that are outrageous, and then we say they are a lie, and you're allowed to make jokes about hurting the president. So, if I were to say something now..." And then I did this long, political drunken speech about voting for Clinton the first time and hating his guts now and basically wanting to kill him. "There's nothing you can do to me, because the band would then say..." And with absolutely perfect timing, they kicked in, and everyone says, "That's a lie," and we finish the song. It was this really beautiful moment, and then I got arrested. Well, not arrested, but detained. They had the decency to wait an hour and a half until the set was over, and then I got taken into a room and interviewed for close to an hour by a guy who was pretty cool and wanted me to not leave town. I was like, "We're on tour!" He's like, "Well, give me a number where you'll be tomorrow." I was like, "I'll be in Columbus, Ohio. I'm sorry I can't stick around." But I had this really long, intelligent talk with him where he was like, "Are you on drugs?" I said, "No." He goes, "You looked pretty crazy and drunk up there." I said, "I had a couple beers before I went onstage, but you see how much I'm sweating. I'm dead sober right now." He wanted to know if I'd ever considered suicide, if there was any history of mental illness in my family, stuff like that. It wasn't that hard to convince him that I wasn't a threat to Bill Clinton at that point. The one weird thing was, he goes, "Well, you did threaten to kill the president." I said, "No, I said I wanted to slap him silly." And he goes, "Yeah, you said that, and then you went on a bit longer." I went, "I did?" He goes, "You said you wanted to strangle him until he was dead." I was like, "Oh, I don't remember that. I guess I got a little carried away." [Laughs.] I really didn't remember that at all.

O: ***What was this about "Theme Song" being a GOP fight song?***

TQ: This is another true story. We have a diehard Too Much Joy fan who worked for the Republicans in 1994, when they took over Congress. He was working for the Republican committee to help get Congress re-elected, so he was constantly in meetings with Newt Gingrich and Dick Armey and the steering committee and all these people. There are a lot of these young, idealistic, ambitious people with lots of energy in Washington, and they get used by these old, evil scumbags. One night, Newt Gingrich was giving this rallying-the-troops speech where he was talking about how they were going to bring change. He was saying how some people said he was a destroyer, but that he wasn't a destroyer; it's just that sometimes you have to knock things down in order to build something newer and stronger and better. This guy, who's a big fan, got all excited and said, "Wait a minute, I have the perfect song for this occasion." He runs out to his car, gets *Cereal Killers*, runs back in, and starts playing "Theme Song." [The chorus: "To create, you must destroy / Smash a glass and cry, 'Too Much Joy.'" —ed.] And, according to him, everybody loved it and basically put it on repeat. They kept playing it and playing it and swaying arm-in-arm and throwing glasses into the fireplace and singing along with "Theme Song." So he came up to us at a show in D.C. one day and told us this story. I just looked at him and said, "That's beautiful. It's also bullshit. Get out of here." I walked away and he came after me, like, "I swear to you, it's true." I said, "Bring me proof." And he goes, "What do you want? I can get you a letter from Newt Gingrich." I said, "Okay, if Newt Gingrich writes me and says he knows the words to 'Theme Song,' I'll believe your story." Three or four months later, this guy comes backstage and hands us each a letter from Newt Gingrich, thanking us for helping them win the congressional elections in 1994, and specifically mentioning "Theme Song" and the line, "To create, you must destroy." We promptly leaked it to the press, sending them all copies with a little press release saying that Newt Gingrich probably hadn't listened to songs like "Take A Lot Of Drugs." Then Gingrich had to back out; he never said anything personally, but his office had to say, "No, no, no, he didn't sign that." But we had the letters with his signature and the seal. I think it got reprinted in *Time* or something, which was pretty cool. But, again, no one had really heard from us in a while. We were touring behind a new album, but the thing that gets us in the magazines is Newt Gingrich.

For more information on Too Much Joy, consult www.sayhername.com. Ø

Elvira

By Keith Phipps
Originally Printed April 1998

"I think I've become a little bit like the Easter Bunny or Santa Claus."

Since 1981, actress Cassandra Peterson has led a double life: After landing a job as the horror hostess at a Los Angeles television station, she developed the character of Elvira, a high-haired, deep-bosomed "Mistress Of The Dark" who mixes double-entendres, cheesy B-movie references, and a hint of menace. The character was a national hit, and a series of cameos, talk-show appearances, endorsements, videotapes, and guest-hosting jobs catapulted Peterson to stardom. In 1988, she starred in her first movie: Elvira, Mistress Of The Dark, *an entertaining, underrated film in the '80s-teen-comedy vein. While the years following its première haven't brought Peterson as many high-profile projects, she's kept her creation in the public eye with her talent, shrewd management, and likability. Her ongoing projects include a series of haunted houses, a line of toys and models, an award-winning microbrew (Elvira's Night Brew), books and a comic book, and a web site (www.elvira.com). In 1998, Peterson talked to* The Onion A.V. Club *about the state of Elvira, why she no longer represents Coors, and Federico Fellini.*

The Onion: ***To what do you credit the ongoing popularity of Elvira? It seems a lot of over the top characters disappear once their novelty has worn off.***

Cassandra Peterson: That's true. Hmm... I don't know. I'm as shocked as anyone. Every year, when I get more gigs, it's like, "Wow, you're kidding. It's still happening." One thing that certainly doesn't hurt is being sort of tied to a holiday. I think I've become a little bit like the Easter Bunny or Santa Claus: People expect me around Halloween. I think people enjoy the character and all that, but the longevity is hard to explain.

O: ***Well, it's a great character.***

CP: And the people don't see her all the time, all year 'round, because we're in the horror genre. And there aren't that many people around anymore who are tied to the horror genre. The Vincent Prices and the John Carradines have all passed away. It's nice to have one around.

O: ***The horror genre isn't quite as fun anymore. You seem to be trying to maintain the spirit of the fun of it.***

CP: Yeah. I lean more toward the B-movie side of the horror genre, not the *Scream* type of horror. I don't even classify those as horror films. I classify that as the evening news.

O: ***I saw that you made an appearance at some***

sort of Goth convention. Do you feel a kinship with the Goths at all?

CP: Oh, yeah, very much. I feel like Queen Of The Goths when I go to these things. Of course, my look has been around with a lot of other characters over the years—Morticia Addams and whoever—but I think we are definitely characters that started the whole Goth thing happening. The look, anyway.

O: ***The Goths seem to take themselves so seriously, though.***

CP: They do, you know? But I'll tell you, I've been to a few Goth conventions and Goth clubs, and I've had a lot of fun. I really have. Some do take themselves seriously, but then there are some who have a lot of fun with it. I was happily surprised to see, in the last few times I've appeared, that they really do have a sense of humor, most of them, and I had a great time. You're right that there are a few. Like, I remember when Siouxsie & The Banshees were out in the '80s. Now, there's a gal who takes herself seriously. No fun with the character there.

O: ***You never met her, I take it.***

CP: No, I didn't.

O: ***It seems like that would be an interesting encounter.***

CP: Yeah. She said kind of a negative thing about me in an article once. I was a big Siouxsie & The Banshees fan. She said I was [in dark monotone] "making fun of the whole movement." I'm like, "Hello! First of all, I was doing this about 10 years before you. Second, like, lighten up, okay?"

O: ***It's been 10 years since the* Elvira, Mistress Of The Dark *movie came out. What's your feeling on the experience 10 years later?***

CP: I still love the movie, and I think it really worked. It may not be the greatest movie ever, but it was Elvira, you know? And if you don't like it, then you don't like Elvira. We're trying to get another movie together—we have been for 10 years—and it's been going through development hell. Starting a project here, and then the place goes bankrupt, and starting another one, and they get a new owner... It's just been unbelievable, for 10 years. We're in the process of trying to make one that we just wrote, and trying to make it independently.

O: ***A lot of people probably don't know that you were in a Federico Fellini movie [1972's* Roma*].***

CP: Yeah, that's for sure. That was a lucky accident. I was over in Italy, starving, walking around with my friend, and I saw a bunch of lights and things going on. We walked over there, and we actually knew the assistant director. We'd met him in Las Vegas when I was a showgirl. His name was Stuart Birnbaum, and he was over there assistant-directing with Fellini. And he introduced us to Mr. Fellini, and [Fellini] said, "Oh, do you want to be in the film?" The next thing we knew, we were in the film. It was amazing. I didn't even speak Italian at that time, and Fellini would shout the directions in Italian, and then come over and tell me what they were in English. It was amazing. He was so nice, so accommodating, so friendly. I just loved him. And he'd always seemed like this weird, scary kind of guy. I was a big fan before I met him, and I was so intimidated by him. Then, once you got to know him, he was just this jolly, heavy-set Italian. So much fun. So sweet.

O: ***And you were the lead singer for an Italian rock band for a while, right?***

CP: That happened almost as a result of being in *Roma*. After the film, I was working at Cinecittà, which is the big film studio in Rome. I met some other people and got a little part in this movie, a little part in that movie, and ended up meeting a songwriter in one of the movies. The songwriter had some friends who had a band, and their lead singer, a woman from the United States, had just gotten married and left, so they were desperately looking for another singer. I auditioned and got that part, and traveled around with them for about a year and a half.

O: ***Did you do any recording?***

CP: They did. They had an album. It was so

dorky. [Laughs.] I was not on the album. I never recorded with them. It was kind of like covering pop tunes that were American pop tunes, but changing the lyrics to Italian. They just worked all the time, one or two nights here and there at nightclubs or in shows all over the country.

O: ***Before that, you were actually one of the youngest showgirls in Las Vegas.***

CP: Yeah, I think so. Maybe still, even, because I was 17 and had to get a signed thing from my parents. It was pretty unbelievable that they did it, but that was under severe threats from me.

O: ***It was the '60s, too.***

CP: It was the '60s; that's so true. And I had already been a go-go girl for three years. [Laughs.] It wasn't that big of a leap, you know?

O: ***I read something about an incident with someone trying to swindle you out of an appearance by promising Pamela Anderson Lee.***

CP: That was so weird. I was with Coors. I finally broke off my relationship with them... We left them, by the way. They did not fire me. They were just getting... You have to know Coors to deal with Coors. They would actually call me The Daughter Of Satan and stuff like that, you know? I was like, "Okay, well, this is pretty hard to deal with these people."

O: ***Well, they're a bunch of right-wing crackpots, aren't they?***

CP: Ooh, you can't even believe it. I guess some of the ad executives told us later that they held up an Elvira poster they made for one of the Halloween campaigns, which was one of the most successful campaigns they ever had... They showed the poster to the head guy at the time, a member of the Coors family, and he said, "I see demons there." I mean, how do you deal with that?

O: ***So instead they went with the wholesome, clean-cut image of Pamela Lee.***

CP: Yes, that's right. They went with somebody who was really, really wholesome. I have nothing bad to say about Pamela Lee or anything—I'm sure she's a wonderful person, and I've actually heard some very, very nice things about her—but, man, if you're going to switch, like, "Hello!" And that was fine if they went with Pamela Lee, or if they went with Ruth Buzzi. I didn't care. But then they called her "The Queen Of Halloween," and that really ruffled my feathers. Pamela Lee may be a lot of things, but she ain't The Queen Of Halloween, okay?

"At some point, when I do get really pathetic and I can't stay in the dress that well, I think the character could continue without me doing it."

O: ***Now, you were supposed to appear at some gay club, and they tried to offer Pamela Lee instead?***

CP: Yeah, I got a big appearance. They were paying me quite a bit of money in Denver; it's the biggest gay disco in America, apparently. I had an appearance there, and I was doing some other appearances in town, as well, so the timing worked out great. And a couple of days before I was to appear, somebody from Coors showed up and said, "If you'll take Pamela Lee instead of Elvira, we'll give her to you for free. We'll pay her fee, we'll pay her way out here, and you won't have to pay Elvira." And the guy there said, "What the hell would we want Pamela Lee for at a gay disco? What are you talking about?"

O: ***What kind of fan mail do you get?***

CP: Well, I actually have stopped looking at it. For a few years, I looked at it. And then the volume got too big to handle, and we gave it to a fan-club service that does it. So I don't really get to see all the goofy letters anymore. But I have some real doozies, I'll tell you. I was getting a lot of mail back then from, oh, like, prisons. Motorcycle gangs and stuff like that. I would get almost as much mail from policemen and firemen as I would from prisoners. That was always strange to me. Now, mostly we get hits on our web site, so I don't have as much direct contact. But one thing I have gotten is a huge collection of photos people have sent me of their Elvira tattoos. I have a huge collection of those.

O: ***Do you find that flattering?***

CP: Oh, yeah. I find it the sincerest form of flattery. If someone really likes you, they tattoo your picture on their chest, don't you think?

O: ***I couldn't say, really.***

CP: I also have a large collection of photos from people who painted their cars, their boats, their planes, their motorcycles with Elvira images. Also, a huge collection of pictures of people dressed as Elvira, which is really scary. I mean, kids, guys, girls, dogs, you name it. Those are pretty interesting. I've got a lot of artwork that people send me, also—pictures they have drawn of Elvira. Some are incredibly good, some really bad, some really, really bizarre and interesting. Those are things I get that I enjoy now, because, like I say, I'm not able to sit and read them all now.

O: ***Do a lot of people confuse you with the character you play?***

CP: Oh, yeah, definitely. In the beginning, I was getting a lot of pictures of people who were, like, the heads of satanic cults, who thought I was the High Priestess, you know? Plus, I go to a lot of monster and horror conventions, and those people sort of think that [Elvira is] me.

O: ***Do you enjoy doing public appearances?***

CP: Yeah, I do. I always have a fun time. It's a really nice crowd. I never have trouble, knock on wood. They're always fun, and they always love me, so it's really nice to meet with them and talk to them. I never mind that. I do a lot of appearances, so I pretty much get up in that drag maybe once a week. People think I hibernate after Halloween and don't do anything until the next October, but I work pretty steadily all year. Granted, Halloween time is really insane.

O: ***How has Elvira changed over the years?***

CP: Well, my hair has gotten higher. That's sort of the way I judge what year it was. I go, "Oh, yes, that must have been 1984, because my hair was medium high." At one point, it got kind of like a conehead, and I had to bring it down a little. It's become easier for me to be the character—not so forced. It's become second nature to me, and I know exactly what she would do, what she wouldn't do, how she would react, what she would say. It's so second nature that I never have to sweat about it before I do a show or an appearance.

O: ***It seems that, at heart, she's very sweet.***

CP: Yeah, deep down. Sort of like the hooker with the heart of gold: a tough exterior but a real soft spot underneath. I think that's why people like her, because there's a vulnerability about the character—not just this straight-ahead, horror, come-in-darling-let-me-drink-your-blood sort of thing. She has a sense of humor, and she's very vulnerable. I think that's why women like the character, too. She's not like, "I'm a sexy babe and look at me. I'm after your man." She's more accessible to women.

O: ***She's not really a vamp.***

CP: Not really. She tries to be, but she screws it up all the time.

O: ***I read somewhere that you've actually thought about retiring as Elvira...***

CP: Yes, I think about that every day. [Laughs.]

O: ***...and having somebody else play the character.***

CP: Yeah, we've thought about that. Some time, in the future... People always say, "When are you going to retire?" And I go, "Uh, last year." It's weird. I sort of intend not to do it too long, and then every year, there's as much work or more, or more opportunities, and I just keep doing it. I'm always thinking it's going to slow down, and it does not slow down. If anything, it's sped up. So I just keep plugging along. I'm going to be pretty pathetic here in a few years, but at some point, when I do get really pathetic and I can't stay in the dress that well, I think the character could continue without me doing it. I think there's enough merchandise and images of Elvira that are illustrations—in my comic book, and the pinball machine, and the books. All that stuff doesn't require that I be there to do it. I don't have to dress up and go anywhere to have those things around and keep Elvira's image in the public eye. So I think we could still do those sorts of things—cartoons, shows, books, records, and whatever—and just continue to do it. And eventually, we'll get someone else who could probably play the character and do appearances, just like Bozo The Clown. I hate to compare myself to Bozo, but that's just about the only comparison there is, where you have a camp and train all these people to be Elviras. Who knows? We have been approached by Universal, who asked about having an Elvira stroller—you know, one of the people who walk through the park. Right now, they have Frankenstein, Marilyn Monroe, Charlie Chaplin, and things like that. To get an Elvira would not be a bad idea. It wouldn't be me, of course. ⌀

CHAPTER 7

"Try and live your life and live in the world the way you'd like it to be."

"I don't want to live in a world where I am afraid of making the kind of art I want to make. The idea that I have to be afraid to do that is absurd to me. So one approach is that you try and live your life and live in the world the way you'd like it to be."

"I'm an inspiration, because I'm a product of the ghetto. I was born and raised in the ghetto. But the ghetto wasn't born and raised in me... That's the message I give to the kids now: 'What's slowing you down? Why can't you make it? You can make it if you want.' "

"People still believe in magic, and there's not one good thing about that. I believe in art. I think art should be in the place in our culture where religion used to be. Where magic used to be, there should be art."

"If you're pro-science, you're against superstition, and if you're pro-science, you're not spiritual. And if you're pro-science, you're in favor of people. ... So the fact that we are not spiritual people, the fact that we are material people, the fact that we believe in the real world permeates everything we do."

"I think that's the single most important contribution that I can offer: the strengthening of people's spirit and soul, the strengthening of families... I make intelligence cool. I make spirituality cool. If we can make one's devotion to God cool, then I think I did a great thing."

"In our purest sense, we were always attempting for subversion. We learned something from the hippies that, unfortunately, the punks at the same time didn't learn, and that is that rebellion is obsolete. In a healthy capitalistic world, rebellion is just something else to market."

"I find something a bit unnatural in the idea of being bound together in spiritual ideas with people. I'm sure that, in our natural state, we all believe something entirely different. I don't necessarily want anybody to believe the same things I believe."

"I woke up and I was 35. I used to be 31. I feel like this show has just aged me."

Mark Hosler (Negativland)

By Stephen Thompson
Originally Printed September 1997

"[Bono] said, 'We were just stealing from the thieves,' and I actually found myself yelling 'Fuck you!' to the TV set."

Negativland is most widely known as the musical act sued by U2 and Island Records for co-opting the Irish rock band's name, as well as extensively sampling its song "I Still Haven't Found What I'm Looking For," on 1991's U2 EP. *But Negativland isn't just some group of merry pranksters; its art is about tearing apart and reassembling found images to create new ones, in the process making social, political, and artistic statements. Those efforts got the band sued by the aforementioned behemoths, as well as by its former label, SST Records, for losses incurred in the Island lawsuit. They've also led to threats of litigation from Casey Kasem, whose hilariously profane* American Top 40 *outtakes were also sampled on the* U2 EP. *When Negativland's self-explanatorily titled concept album* Dispepsi *came out in 1997, the band members risked yet another legal challenge, this time from their most powerful target yet. Against that backdrop—the cola giant ultimately didn't sue—Negativland's Mark Hosler spoke to* The Onion A.V. Club *about why the group made an entire album satirizing a single corporate image, how advertisers have learned to take advantage of anti-advertising sentiment, and the ongoing parallels between his band and U2.*

The Onion: *Why Pepsi?*

Mark Hosler: Well... Because it tastes better than Coke! But why do you think? You've got the record. Why do you think Negativland made an entire record about one soft drink? As you were going through the record, did you get to a point at which you went, "All right, all right, enough with the Pepsi already"?

O: *Yes.*

MH: Good. You're supposed to feel that way. That's how I feel when I drive around or walk around anywhere in the United States and look at billboards and advertising. We could have picked anybody. We could have picked Nike. We could have picked Microsoft. Pepsi happens to have a lot of incredibly wonderful imagery associated with them that we could play with. They're very iconic in a really great way, and we happened to have a ton of their commercials. We collect stuff, and one of the things we ended up with in our archives was a lot of Pepsi commercials going back to when they started—from old radio ads all the way up to modern stuff. We had interviews with people who had worked on their ad campaigns. All kinds of Pepsi talk and cola talk. So we were working on this project that was dealing with advertising, and I suggested to the group that it would be a lot more interesting for us as an art project if we just focused on one company. We've got all this great stuff about this one company, so let's pick on them and hope that in the end, we end up with something that creates a much larger point of view than just one company. Surely, most people have a pretty good idea how corporations, through political action committees, have

"Here we have this ex-junkie homosexual wife-murderer advertising tennis shoes all over the United States, on every television set in every home."

bought and sold our political process. We've watched the passage of NAFTA and GATT and all these things that are creating a sort of de facto one-world government run by and for these corporations. In actual fact, Pepsi is more benign than most: As far as multinationals go, they just make sugary, salty things, not weapons. But it just seemed like a great area to play around in. I might sound like I'm being really serious and political in the way I'm describing this, but we tried really hard to make the record as open-ended as possible in terms of how you can interpret it. We tried not to make it sound like a finger-wagging piece of didactic agitprop. I sure hope to heck it doesn't seem that way.

O: ***In the CD sleeve, there's an essay on how Pepsi and Coke can save money. It's almost sympathetic.***

MH: We're trying to *help* them! You know, when you finish listening to our record, the one thing that sticks in your mind is the one thing all companies want you to remember when you see their ads. They want you to remember the name of their product. That's all. Advertising is not intended to brainwash you and make you go out and buy something; that's a really simple-minded way of criticizing it. I think advertising is just designed to make you familiar with this thing, so when you go to the store... Humans like to choose things that are familiar to them. It's just normal behavior. It isn't so literal that, when you see the ad, you're so stupid that you've been brainwashed to go down to the Safeway like a zombie and buy a six-pack of Coke or Pepsi. Though I am blown away at how successful Nike has been at getting their swoosh on everything. What's most disturbing is that we, the humans, have been tricked into being walking billboards for them. It has now become a very cool thing to wear the swoosh and have the "Just Do It" slogan on your car, on your baseball cap, on your shirt... My gut intuition is that this is a bad and disturbing thing, but part of me keeps thinking, "Maybe this is just *different*, and I'm falling behind the times."

O: ***What do you think of the way advertisers are becoming more aware of cynicism about the messages advertisers send? You're seeing more ad campaigns like Sprite's, that are saying, "Ignore the advertising. Obey your thirst."***

MH: Or the Miller Lite ads, where all the advertisements are about the process of creating an ad.

O: ***Do you think that, for people who have built an artistic existence around critiquing advertising, their statements are being co-opted?***

MH: Yes, we're fucked. [Laughs.] Basically, what they've done is, they have very cleverly adopted the language of their critics, and they've turned it into a new advertising style. It's very funny and amusing, and it comes off as real hip and reflexive and postmodern, and it's unbelievably cynical. It's extremely smart of them to do. When Pepsi hears what we've done, if they're really smart, instead of suing us, they should pay us a $50,000 licensing fee to use some of our record as an ad.

O: ***For the sake of argument, let's say Pepsi comes to you and says, "We want to use your record in an ad." What would you do?***

MH: Well, I'll tell you what just did happen recently. The advertising agency that handles the Nike account for all of North America approached Negativland. They wanted to hire us to do a series of radio ads for Miller Genuine Draft beer. They weren't asking us to be spokespeople or something; we're not that popular. But they wanted to use our cut-up, collagey, found-sound approach to make a bunch of ads. These guys are in their late 20s, they grew up listening to Negativland in college, and they think we're just great. These are the same guys who thought it would be cool to put William S. Burroughs in a Nike ad. And, relative to the world that they occupy, they *are* pushing the envelope. "Cool, here we have this ex-junkie homosexual wife-murderer advertising tennis shoes all over the United States, on every television set in every home." And I can see from their perspective how this is, "like, subversive, man." It's really interesting to me how these kinds of guys have talked themselves into this way of thinking. I know it makes sense to them. They approached us, and I think they thought they were giving us this great chance. I've even had friends of mine say, "Why didn't you guys take it? You could have done something subversive!" And my response is, "No, we couldn't." What has happened now in mass media and advertising is not only that they've adopted the style and the look of fringe culture; that has been happening for a long time. What they've now done is gone a step further: They've now taken the very idea that there is any dissent at all—it doesn't even matter what form it takes—and made it part of how they're going to sell something. I'm not sure where they go from here, and I'm not really sure where something like Negativland goes from here, either. But I do think that with this record, we were aware of all these things, and we were trying to push things that much further. We thought it would be an interesting approach to make something that actually is, to some degree, really obtrusive and annoying and obnoxious, because you keep hearing this one goddamn fucking product being mentioned over and over and over again on this record. I've been working on it for so long that my perception is skewed, but I do think the record is really fun to listen to, and we worked hard to make it fun. When you hear the CD, there's a lot of stuff going on: There are a bunch of layers to the concepts going on in the record. We're not offering up simple solutions, and it's very complicated, because as much as any halfway intelligent, progressive, left-thinking person could agree with some of what I'm saying, the fact is that we're so totally enmeshed in the kind of lifestyles we have in North America, with our cars and conveniences and TV sets, that it isn't so simple as to just say, "No, we're going to stop buying what they're selling."

"They've now taken the very idea that there is any dissent at all—it doesn't even matter what form it takes—and made it part of how they're going to sell something."

O: ***Is there a part of you that wants to get sued?***
MH: Absolutely not. We knew people were going to think that. For me, I don't want to live in a world where I am afraid of making the kind of art I want to make. The idea that I have to be afraid to do that is absurd to me. So one approach is that you try and live your life and live in the world the way you'd like it to be. I think, given the scale and the size of what Negativland does, there's certainly room for a lot more dissent than what we're offering. The really amazing thing to me is that, when friends of mine were seeing what we were working on over the last few years, their reaction would be, "Oh my God. What are you doing? You're going to be killed!" And I'd say, "You know, what if we were making this record called *Disclinton*, and we chopped up all

these political ads for Bill Clinton, and took his State Of The Union addresses and his press conferences, and did this whole thing on Clinton? Would any of our friends react with fear?" No. Of course not. They wouldn't. They would just think, "Okay, fine. It's kind of an obvious target, but fine. Go ahead, make fun of him." I think it's really telling, even though most of the folks I know aren't very aware of trademark law and copyright law, that they have an intuitive reaction that you aren't supposed to mess with these guys. That to me is very telling, and horribly tragic, but on the other hand, there's a sense that we have of, "Well, God, if everyone's so afraid to do this, someone has to." And I guess that means us, because either we're brave or we're crazy or we're stupid. But it certainly isn't because, "Gee, the publicity's great, and we sell lots of records," because that's never been the case. I will never, ever expect to do well off of this group. I'd like to scrape by and have the thing pay for itself.

"This is just a personal thing, but Negativland has claimed the Pepsi logo, and when I see it on cups and billboards, I feel like, 'That's promoting Negativland.' I think that's really interesting."

O: ***Has there been a truce with U2? I heard they apologized.***

MH: I don't think "apologized" is the right word. U2, their management, their publishing company, and their record label all agreed in principle that we should have our record back. However, Casey Kasem has never agreed to drop his threats to sue all parties involved if Island lets Negativland have its record back. That's a pretty bizarre ending to this whole story, but I think in the end they were embarrassed by all the bad press, and they were concerned about how bad they would look in our book [*Fair Use: The Story Of The Letter U & The Numeral 2*]. Which is interesting, again, considering the size of what we do. We're smaller than a pimple. We're a very little thing. Other than that, we've had nothing to do with them, except I kept thinking that maybe one day the phone would ring and they'd ask us to do a remix for their new album. The other funny thing is that, about a year and a half ago, when we were talking about what we would call our new record, at one point Don Joyce suggested that we should call it *Pop*. I guess we just continued to have some kind of weird synchronicity with these guys.

O: ***They've been out there touring and satirizing advertising...***

MH: Yeah, they just keep stealing all of our ideas. [Laughs.]

O: ***First they steal your song, "I Still Haven't Found What I'm Looking For"...***

MH: By the way, every time I hear that song on the radio now, I feel like that's *my* song. This is just a personal thing, but Negativland has claimed the Pepsi logo, and when I see it on cups and billboards, I feel like, "That's promoting Negativland." [Laughs.] I think that's really interesting. I never saw this as a side effect of doing the U2 single or doing the *Dispepsi* CD, but it's a peculiar little thing. When I'm in someone's car and I hear the beginning of "I Still Haven't Found What I'm Looking For," I get this little thrill, like, "I'm hearing my song." Isn't that weird? I forgot your question... Oh, U2's tour... Yeah, it's real interesting, because U2 is, in their own boneheaded, big-time way, grappling with some of the contradictions of trying to be an artist and having some integrity and doing work in a mass marketplace. I think they do a disservice to the issues they bring up, because they deal with it in a way that's so superficial and simple-minded. The effect of the advertising way of thinking on our brains and how we live on our planet is not the kind of thing to just make into an empty "ha-ha." I watched their television special with my mom, the one where Bono came on the TV screen and said, "We were just stealing from the thieves," and I actually found myself yelling "Fuck you!" to the TV set. I turned to my mom, who does not like to hear me swear. I thought I was going to be scolded, but she didn't say a word. I think she has a pretty good idea what we went through. [Laughs.]

Negativland's CDs are available from www.negativland.com, as well as through Negativmailorderland, P.O. Box 1154, El Cerrito, CA 94530. ⌀

By Stephen Thompson
Originally Printed October 1993

"I'm telling these guys, 'Why you gotta grab your crotch?' Then you see Michael Jackson grabbing his crotch 50 times. What's with him?"

*Born Lawrence Tureaud in 1952, Mr. T has survived the welfare struggles and Chicago ghetto of his youth, a lengthy bout with cancer, and a career filled with astonishing highs and depressing lows. He's been a bodyguard, a college-football player, a WWF wrestler, a movie star (*Rocky III*), a television regular (*The A-Team*), a commercial pitchman, and a frequent pop-culture punchline, but T remains world-famous after two decades in and out of the limelight. In this 1993 interview, conducted after the launch of his comic-book series* Mr. T And The T-Force, *the star spoke to* The Onion A.V. Club *about character, literacy, religion, and fame.*

The Onion: ***You've been active in literacy efforts over the years.***

Mr. T: I have. If I couldn't read, I wouldn't have gotten the part in *Rocky III*. If you can't read, the only thing you can do is enjoy the pictures, not the whole story. Reading is the key to knowledge. Knowledge is the key to understanding. So read on, young man! Read on, young lady! I'm an inspiration, because I'm a product of the ghetto. I was born and raised in the ghetto. But the ghetto wasn't born and raised in me. I come from a family of 12. I've got seven brothers and four sisters. I never robbed nobody, I never raped nobody, I didn't use drugs. That's the message I give to the kids now: "What's slowing you down? Why can't you make it? You can make it if you want." I love and respect my mother, and that's the message I tell the kids—white kids, black kids, whatever. They need to know that Mr. T is real, and that's the advantage we have. Batman, Rifleman, Superman, Iron Man, Tin Man, they might be nice guys, but they're not real. They can't go into schools. They can't go into the neighborhoods. But my record speaks for itself. I've been around for years, preaching the same message. I didn't just start doing this today. Not like some people that have a movie coming out, so they go visit kids in the hospital. You don't need that phony crap. All of these celebrities, they turn my stomach with their funny stuff. I've been going in the ghettos without the press, without bodyguards, talking to kids. "Get to reading, stay in school. You don't have to carry a gun." I know about peer pressure and all that, but I say, "Hey, they called me a sissy because I wouldn't join a gang. Who was calling me a sissy? Does it make me a sissy because somebody called me a sissy?" That's the same thing with race.

"Does that make you a nigger if somebody called you a nigger? Does that make you a honky or a redneck if somebody called you that?" No. They need a man like me to tell them. I'm tough and tender at the same time. I'm tough enough to fight them, and I'm not afraid of nothing. I'm not even afraid of death. But at the same time, it's not about fighting. I'm going to fight if you touch me or hurt me or do harm to my family. But if you call me a bad name, or whatnot, I'm too smart for that. That's the message the kids need to hear coming from me. I tell them, "If I fought every time somebody called me a name, I would never get out of jail. But I'm disciplined. I'm smarter than that." So I tell them, like my mother said, "Consider the source." When you see who called you the name, then you understand why they're doing it. Then you don't have to stoop that low. That's the message I try to bring to the kids, on the real side, because nobody brings it to them like Mr. T does. That's important. I'm not polishing it up, I don't pussyfoot around the issue. I call a spade a spade. I don't change my rap to the blacks, I don't change it to the whites. It's the same rap. It's steady, and it works.

"I'm going to say some basketball player or some football player is my role model? That's an insult to my mother, who scrubbed floors. That's an insult to my father, who picked up junk in the alleys and preached on Sundays."

O: ***You sound like you're running for president.***

MT: Nah. See, if I run for president, they'd be controlling me. Right now, I'm free. I can say it like it is. If I run for president, people will say, "No, Mr. T, don't write about drugs, you're the president." Politics, they make strange bedfellows, with deals and whatnot. I couldn't be a president. It ain't worth the headache or the pressure. The money's too low, and all that stuff. There's stuff that'd make me dangerous. I'm educated. Three things make a black man dangerous: the ability to fight, education, and money. If you get the education, you're gonna get money. I was dangerous from day one, because I'm intelligent. I get so insulted when I watch sports people ask athletes who their role model is, and athletes say it's this baseball player or this basketball player. How insulting to their mother and their father. How insulting to your mother, to say, "I like some other guy." Joe Louis was a nice guy, but not a role model. I learned when I got a little educated that Joe Louis wasn't educated. To call him my role model would be disrespectful to my mother, who scrubbed floors and had to go in the back door and sacrificed eating for me, and would knock on the neighbors' door so she could borrow a dollar until the welfare check came so I could go to school. I'm going to say some basketball player or some football player is my role model? That's an insult to my mother, who scrubbed floors. That's an insult to my father, who picked up junk in the alleys and preached on Sundays. See what I mean? Muhammad Ali was good in sports and everything, but he never fed me. Whoever's taking care of you is your role model. And this here, by you writing this, is gonna put something else on their mind. They're gonna say, "Oh, wow, I used to say a football player. I forgot about my mother." Sometimes you have to jar their memories. It takes a spiritually, morally strong guy like me to tell it like it is. I don't pull no punches. When I go to speak at the schools, they give me big standing ovations. I say, "By the time I leave, you're gonna wish you hadn't applauded for me. I'm going to tell it like it is, I'm going to call it like it is. Who breaks out the school windows, brothers? Any white folk coming in from the suburbs and breaking out the windows? Who's doing it?" But I hear, "Mr. T, you've been hanging around the white folks too long." See, if I come into a black neighborhood and say, "Thanks for watching my show," and give out high fives and all that, I'm not doing no good. I go out and see a kid grabbing his crotch. Ain't nobody telling them that. Where do they get it from? They watch MTV. I say, "If you wash up more often, you won't have to grab your crotch." I'm telling these guys, "Why you gotta grab your crotch?" Then you see Michael Jackson grabbing his crotch 50 times. What's with him? Dangerous stuff. Mike, you never say nothing to the 'hood. You owe something to the people. They buy your record, so tell the kids, "Hey, kids, don't fight." I know you don't talk that much, but you always say, "I love you." Say, "Kids, don't fight the races." They'll listen, because Michael's speaking. You're always talking about the hero of the world. How you gonna be the hero of the world, Michael, without telling the people not to fight? This is me, see? I'm just controversy. I can do that because I'm free. Nobody can tell me anything, no advertisers control me, and that's why I don't go to all the fancy parties. I'm a street guy. I don't dress up and all that stuff. People invite me to dinner because I'm Mr. T. I say, "Can I bring a friend?" So I find a couple of down-and-out people on the street, and I'd tell the guys, "This is my friend. I just met him." "What's your name, buddy?" "He needs a meal more than Mr. T do." I only eat once a day because I'm in training, and even if I'm not training, I really don't need all your food. I'm always conscious of the less fortunate. That's why I feed the hungry and I clothe the naked. And that's why I'm successful. I get so much because I give so much. That's what my father taught me. That's why I go to the hospitals. That's why I'm involved with the Make-A-Wish Foundation, the Starlight Foundation. A politician will say, "Vote for me, and whatever." They don't even remember you until the next voting time. But I'm giving people something. Is that wrong for me to tell a kid to stay in school, don't be a fool, don't get involved with drugs? I go to the library, and you can go to the library, too. You can study. I don't charge for going to schools. I've got to give something back. If I touch one kid in that community, that ghetto, that school, whatever, then my trip there wasn't in vain.

O: *You're working on another book, right?*

MT: Yeah, I'm working on my second book. The first book was called *Mr. T: The Man With The Gold*. This book I'm working on now is called *There Goes The Neighborhood*. Back in 1986, I bought a mansion in Lake Forest, Illinois, and then I cut down my trees and the neighbors got mad. How dare my neighbors get mad about my property? But the issue wasn't the trees, as if they don't cut down trees; the issue was that I was the only black man moving to a town of about 15,000 people. Stuffy people. Some of them were rich, some of them barely scraping. Actually, the really rich people didn't even say nothing. The people that got little houses, their house ain't bigger than my garage. So I'm sort of the black version of the

"Three things make a black man dangerous: the ability to fight, education, and money."

Beverly Hillbillies. My driveway's about a block and a half long, most unusual for a black man to have. I bought that house for my mother. All I've ever wanted to do since I was 10 years old, I told my mother, "Mama, one of these days I'm gonna be big and strong. I'm gonna be a football player and a boxer. I'm gonna buy you beautiful dresses, Mama, and I'll buy you a pretty house." It was the Lord's willing because it kept me away from the gangs and the drugs in the neighborhood. I had a higher calling. I was a poor black man, and I realized I've got to have a dream and a vision. Everything started as a dream. You gotta have insight, know what you want. You gotta have a plan. Like I tell anybody, if you fail to plan, you're planning to fail.

I've been planning ever since I was a youngster. You've got to start from somewhere. There's nothing wrong or demeaning in flipping burgers. It's more proud than selling drugs. I was born and raised on welfare, but don't make it your permanent address. It's not where you come from, it's where you're going. Some people, they want to live on welfare the rest of their life. That's their scheme. That's their con. How sickening and sad. That's the problems in the ghetto. It's a breakdown there. That's why we have so many illegitimate children, so many kids without fathers. Mothers having kids prostituting for them. That's what's going on. That's not stuff I heard about, it's the part I know. I always make my way back to the ghetto so I won't forget, so I won't lose touch with people. That's why my

"I wish that I could touch babies so that they could be healed. But the doctor told me, 'Mr. T, you healing them by coming here, putting a smile on their faces.' "

rapport is still strong after all these years. That used to be me and my family many years ago. I get more than I deserve. If I made do in poverty, $87 a month with my mother on welfare, why can't I make it now? We didn't starve. We spent wisely. Like I tell people in the ghetto, "If you can buy guns and bullets, why can't you buy food? You can buy heroin and crack cocaine, so why can't you buy bread and butter and milk? Why can't you pay your rent?" There's a lot of people in the ghetto who go out and get a fancy car and all that. The car costs more than their house. Meanwhile, your kids need shoes. That's not cool. It takes a man to tell it like it is. If I tell a kid to stay in school, the dropout don't want to hear me. If I tell a kid not to smoke, the tobacco industry is mad. Tell 'em you don't drink beer, the beer company gets pissed. I tell a kid don't do drugs, the drug dealers are mad. Stepping on toes. Can't no ordinary guy do this, because they're afraid, they don't have a backbone, they don't have the balls, they don't have the guts. They're worried, "What's somebody gonna say? I've got to check with my manager, I've got to check with..." So sickening. I don't check with nobody. I get up in the morning and this is my duty as a child of God.

O: ***Have you ever gotten any threats?***

MT: I don't worry about that. That's gonna happen. That means I'm touching a nerve. Like Dr. King said, it's not how long you live, but how well you live. I don't fear nothing. I don't carry a gun, I don't have bodyguards around me. What you gotta do, do it. If they're gonna get you, they're gonna get you. That's something I don't fear. I'm taught that my God can do anything but fail. That God plus one is the majority. I was taught that if God is for me, who in the world can stand against me? God is on my side, and that's all I need. I get up in the morning, I pray to God. I don't pray to the president, the governor, the mayor, no black caucus, no this and that. I pray to God and that's the end of it.

O: ***You're in a movie coming out called* Freaked. *What's the story behind that?***

MT: I play a very, very different role, because it was important that people see me in different things. I try to entertain as well as get a message across. It's a comedy, and I play a bearded lady. I'd get to the makeup trailer every morning, they'd put on makeup for two hours, a little bang on the top of my head, a barrette thing, and powders and makeup. Oh, boy, then they put the dress on me. Ain't life strange? Only in America. But it's fun. I like to do different things, so that's important. Like I say, I don't turn down nothing but my collar. I'm getting paid and making people laugh. I take a lot of pride in the work I do, because people pay to see me. They've got to get babysitters, park their car, get popcorn and candy. I've got to be conscious of that. I'm a blue-collar actor. I've got to be careful about the type of money I ask for, because I realize that thousands, hundreds, millions of people are getting laid off from their job. If I'm getting so much money off the people, I've got to give it back to the people. When they had Mr. T dolls, I went to the hospitals and gave dolls to the kids. My mother taught me there are some things money can't buy. Sure, I get clothes from gym-shoes companies and this and that. I got shoes that ain't touched the ground. I give them to the less fortunate people. I maybe wear two, three pairs of shoes the whole year. I don't need a whole lot of shoes to change into to try to impress somebody. Basically, I wear sandals, like Jesus. When it gets cold in Chicago, the snow way up to my knees, I still wear my sandals. But that's me. That's something that I try to do. People talk about being like Mike. No, I want to be like Jesus. I want to feed 5,000. I wish that I could touch babies so that they could be healed. But the doctor told me, "Mr. T, you healing them by coming here, putting a smile on their faces." I just show up unannounced and say, like Jesus said, "I come for the sick." The well don't need a doctor. ⌀

Teller (Penn & Teller)

By Stephen Thompson

Originally Printed May 1998

"People still believe in magic, and there's not one good thing about that. I believe in art."

Penn & Teller's act is hard to describe: Calling them magicians is almost an insult, because so much of what they do involves hilariously debunking and making fun of so-called magic shows. Calling them comedians glosses over the elaborate, fascinating, seemingly death-defying tricks they pull off with apparent ease. Penn & Teller's painstakingly rehearsed stunts and tricks, packaged with caustic humor, remain unique in a magic world that takes itself far too seriously. The duo's popularity has led to appearances on talk shows, a prime-time ABC special, a variety show on cable's FX channel, successful tours, and even a movie, 1988's Penn & Teller Get Killed. *In 1998,* The Onion A.V. Club *spoke to both Penn Jillette (whose interview appears next in this book) and the silent-in-performance Teller.*

The Onion: ***Ultimately, the two of you use your powers to entertain the people. Do you feel like you could be doing more for evil?***

Teller: [Laughs.] Uh, well, there are a lot of people who have taken care of that. I could be in the Senate. I think the powers we have are best used to stimulate the minds of the interested public.

O: ***Do you like the public?***

T: Immensely. And I don't understand performers who don't. You can see it in every aspect of our show: the fact that we get probably 15 people at various times up onto the stage with us and basically trust them not to screw up the show; the fact that, after every show, we hang out in the lobby and have people come up and say whatever they damn well please to us, or get autographs, or take pictures with us. We just like 'em. People come up to me on the street and make some little joke—like they'll say, "Excuse me, sir, what time is it?" And I'll say, you know, "5:15," and they'll say, "Hey! Made you talk!" And that's merely a way of saying, "I know your work and I like you." I couldn't be more pleased, because these are the people who are letting me do what I've always dreamed of doing for a living.

O: ***Are you tired of answering questions about how you're different from David Copperfield and Siegfried & Roy?***

T: Well, I don't frequently have to, because their audience and our audience don't overlap at all. People do not come to a Penn & Teller show to see a magic show. They just don't. They come to see weird stuff that they can see nowhere else, that will make them laugh and make the little hairs stand up on the backs of their necks.

O: ***Do people still believe in magic?***

T: Unfortunately, yeah. It's an embarrassing thing that, in a modern culture, people still fall for lines of bull that were invented in the caves. Look at the popularity of James Van Praagh, the guy who wrote a bestseller called *Talking To Heaven*. It has been on the *New York Times* bestseller list forever. And what is it? It's spirit-medium bullshit of the worst kind, and it's taking really serious advantage of people's grief and making money off of it. And people

"Everything that's evil about lying, once you put it in a frame on a stage, becomes virtuous and wonderful."

fall for it. So, yeah, people still believe in magic, and there's not one good thing about that. I believe in art. [Laughs.] I think art should be in the place in our culture where religion used to be. Where magic used to be, there should be art.

O: ***It seems like we've entered an era in which debunking magic is more popular than practicing it. You have the* Secrets Of Magic Revealed *specials...***

T: But what is that? That's the kind of thing that anybody could go to the library and read in the magic books. It's the kind of thing I loved as a kid. As a kid, I would go to the library and just sit for hours in the children's department, contemplating the diagrams of the old illusions. It's a fascinating thing to watch, which accounts for the fact that the show—which, as far as I can tell, has not a grain of wit or performance on it—is terribly popular. But that's confirmation that people love the concept of magic. They love the concept of lying turned into an art form: Everything that's evil about lying, once you put it in a frame on a stage, becomes virtuous and wonderful. People love measuring one view of reality against another. They love situations in which they can look at something and sort out for themselves where make-believe leaves off and reality begins. So I'm not surprised that that show is popular, because it's not in any way a dismissal of magic. It's a tribute to the fact that people are fascinated by magic. They're not fascinated by illusion, as Doug Henning would have us believe. Magic is a much tougher thing: It's not about watching a cartoon or a special effect. It's about seeing something that seems to violate all your previous experiences in the world, and coming to terms with that—whether it's coming to terms with it as poetry, or coming to terms with it as deceit, or coming to terms with it as technology. It's an incredibly vigorous kind of natural form to work in.

O: ***How did ABC respond to Penn & Teller tormenting children, drowning you, and making jokes about secular humanism before* Monday Night Football *[as they did on* Penn & Teller's Home Invasion*]?***

T: With remarkable support. They honestly did. I was absolutely stunned. I'll give you an example: Originally, we had placed the water tank [a bit in which a trick apparently goes awry, leaving Teller drowned] midway through the show, and then we would come back later, and you would see me alive and doing other stuff. We just thought that was an interesting placement. ABC said, "Look, couldn't you just leave Teller dead?" The only thing they seemed to care about, in terms of saying no, was the section of our polyester trick where we wrap the polyester around the kid's neck and try to strangle him. They wouldn't let us leave the mouse dead in the liquid nitrogen. We had to bring back the mouse. They care a whole lot whether a mouse is dead or alive, but Teller, who cares? But I was amazed and stunned, because I really expected a whole lot of serious prime-time censorship, and instead we wound up working with some very hip people there.

O: ***They were right, too, about the water tank.***

T: I think they were absolutely right. This may be the first time I've said that sentence in relation to a television activity. They were right.

O: ***What are the odds that one of you will actually be killed doing a trick?***

T: Um, I like to think none. Think back over what you may know of our career. We have run me over with an 18-wheel tractor-trailer. I have swung over bear traps on a trapeze. Nearly nightly, I swallow a hundred needles and six feet of thread and bring the needles up threaded without dying. It's kind of a specialty of ours to take elaborate, careful safety precautions, and make sure that you can never see them. We're incredibly prudent, and we tend to stand watch over each other to make sure the other guy doesn't get too out-of-control. In the case of, for example, the gun trick, we did the whole gun-safety course. When we were experimenting with it, we experimented very prudently, step by step by step by step. And I'll tell you, it was not a very pleasant action to be holding a gun up and pointing it at Penn's face, and I would assume he feels the same about me. [Laughs.] When we first did it, we had to have other people stand in as the shooters, because we couldn't stand the notion of pointing guns at one another's faces. So it's, I think, very unlikely. We're terribly cautious.

O: ***What do you want done with your corpse when you're dead?***

T: Um, it may not be entirely in my control. There are people I know who would like to have a grave to visit, and we already have a grave. But I think there are people who would like to know that my corpse is actually in this grave. Given my absolute druthers, I would certainly like to see that every part of my body is used for spare parts for science.

O: ***What do you and Penn disagree on? You seem aligned in every way.***

T: Well, you get aligned in every way by having every possible argument. Really, I believe the first six years we worked together, we did very little more than scream at each other all the time about every little thing. And, gradually, you come to accords about things. When an idea is developing, there will be disagreements every stage of the way. But that's the nature of how we work. We end up in the position that, if both of us can agree on it, then a large portion of the populace seems to be able to go along with it, because we've come at it from such opposite directions. ⌀

"If you're doing a trick like shooting .357 Magnums into each other's faces, you have brought up viscerally some important intellectual issues."

Penn Jillette (Penn & Teller)

By Stephen Thompson
Originally Printed June 1998

Shortly after getting off the phone with his uncharacteristically talkative stage partner Teller, The Onion A.V. Club *turned its attention to the characteristically talkative Penn Jillette.*

The Onion: ***How often do you get to use your fame and your act to advance your ideology?***
Penn Jillette: I would say every second. I think that's one of the reasons stand-up comedy got less interesting: People stopped speaking from their hearts and stopped saying things they really believed. You have people like Dennis Miller and Bill Maher, who brag that they make fun of both sides, who brag about a lack of strong convictions. And they're two very talented, very smart people, but I want to see more of their hearts all the time. I mean, if you're going to make fun of Monica Lewinsky, does that mean you think Bill Clinton is an acceptable president? If you're going to make fun of Monica Lewinsky, does that mean you think that being fat is a sin? If you're going to make fun of Monica Lewinsky, do you think that 21-year-olds who aren't perfectly attractive should be happy to blow anybody who asks them? I mean, what is the exact position? That's the stuff I want to know, because the jokes are just a little bit too easy. And we don't deal with anything political, but there are obsessions that Teller and I have. One is that we're pro-science, and, strangely, being pro-science is one of the oddest things you can do in show business. Which is very strange, because it was science that, oh, cured polio. We're not good at medicine; we're good at physics. We were good at physics in the 20th century, and in the 21st century, one would hope, we'll be good at medicine. When you're pro-science, that means you're an atheist, by definition, because religion... No matter how much they put "10 Top Scientists Talk About Why They Believe In God" on the cover of *Time* magazine, you kind of have to look and go, "How come these 10 top scientists are all teaching at community colleges?" [Laughs.] And how come this list is distinctly lacking any Nobel Laureates? What is that telling you? So if you're pro-science, you're against superstition, and if you're pro-science, you're not spiritual. And if you're pro-science, you're in favor of people. And I think if you're pro-science—although this doesn't follow completely logically; it tends to follow in terms of the culture—you're pro–civil liberties, because you have a limited amount of time on this planet,

and you know that other people do, too. So the fact that we are not spiritual people, the fact that we are material people, the fact that we believe in the real world permeates everything we do. It wouldn't necessarily permeate everything we do if we weren't in the field of doing tricks. When you are in the field of doing tricks, you are addressing every two minutes how one confirms truth, how we decide on truth. And if you're doing that, that's gonna come up a lot. You know, my feelings about politics, my feelings about rock 'n' roll, my feelings about art come up much, much less. My feelings about how one ascertains truth come up a lot, because we're doing tricks. If you're doing a trick like shooting .357 Magnums into each other's faces, you have brought up viscerally some important intellectual issues.

O: ***What do you want done with your corpse when you're dead?***

PJ: I guess I should make all sorts of jokes about giving it to friends and stuff, but I've already taken steps. I'm one of the people who has donated his body for any use at all. There are a lot of people who are organ donors, or they'll allow certain amounts of cadaver work. I have it so that if you have a biology class with first-year students, if they don't want to use a frog, they can use me. It doesn't have to be Harvard, it doesn't have to be nice, and they don't have to deliver me back to the box. If my life can be summed up by one student in one college learning one piece of anatomy from slicing up my corpse, I will be very happy.

"Mostly, the ACLU is a sexual thing for me. I guess it is for most people."

O: ***Or pulling pranks with it.***

PJ: Yeah, that's okay, too. I have all the joke answers, as well, but I chose to give you the straight answer, which is just to donate it straight to science. That's what everyone should do.

O: ***Have you done any lobbying for the ACLU?***

PJ: No, no. Mostly, I just have a crush on the president. I think Nadine Strossen is the hottest woman in the world, and when she comes to Vegas, I get to hang out with her, and it's just the best thing in the world. I want her husband dead. So, mostly, the ACLU is a sexual thing for me. I guess it is for most people. No, I don't do that lobbying thing, because it's so likely that if you do lobbying, you might find out you're wrong, and then, hey: You're Alec Baldwin. [Laughs.] You've been lobbying on the wrong side long enough that it would look really bad if you changed your mind. And I do, in fact, change my mind on positions a lot. I don't really think I'm qualified. I'm qualified to talk about James Van Praagh [who wrote a best-selling spirit-medium book titled *Talking To Heaven*] and Uri Geller [the self-proclaimed psychic who says he can bend spoons with his mind] and those people. I'm qualified to talk about people who are using magic tricks to sell spiritualism. I'm qualified to say that in the United States of America, the First Amendment is absolute. But I'm not really qualified to lobby. I'd kind of want to have a law degree, because I'm a sub-star. There are superstar-stars and sub-stars, and being a sub-star, I'm still visible enough that it's too easy to back me into a corner. If one is going to lobby, you should know everything about your subject. It just seems that the better way to address the issue is through what I do, which is the show. And if that comes up, there are things that I believe absolutely in my heart—like the cure for bad speech is more speech—and that comes through in everything we do. Skeptic organizations have wanted me to be a spokesperson and talk about the skeptics a little bit, and I just tell them that when there are truths to get out and important things to say, there are many different ways to do it. If you want to argue with me, any sort of how-to-win-friends-and-influence-people/what-do-you-think? type of stuff does not work. What you have to do to win an argument with me is, you have to yell facts that you can back up, and do it with absolutely no finesse. And if you get enough facts on your side in the right order, and I'm smart enough to understand them, and all of that comes together, then I do a 180 instantly. And I go, "Oh, you're right. We've saved some time here." If the ACLU sends me out on their dime and someone gives me a wonderful argument that I can't refute, I'll change my mind. And when you're working with an organization, you're really not supposed to do that.

O: ***Where would you be without [professional magician, skeptic, and debunker] James Randi?***

PJ: It's hard to say. I wouldn't be anything like I am. I hated Kreskin ["The World's Foremost Mentalist"] so much when I was a kid for his lying that I hated all magic and I hated all science. And it was Randi and Teller who told me I didn't have to. And if I hadn't been given that piece of information, I probably would have just stayed thinking that the idea of magic itself was evil. And I might have even gone so far as to think that scientists were just liars, because Kreskin used to present himself as a scientist. And I hated him so much—and this hate has not tempered in any way—that had Randi not come along... Magic is using a shotgun for target-shooting. It's taking the most dangerous and evil thing you can do, lying to people, and going out to a target range and shooting it in a safe direction that you've thought about very, very clearly. Doing stuff like Van Praagh and Kreskin is like taking a shotgun and going into a mall, and discharging it in people's faces and stealing 20 bucks from each one of them. It's the lowest thing you can do, and it hurts all of society in the same way that killing a smart person does. When you lie to a kid like that, that may be a kid who was going to get a good idea. And once Kreskin got a hold of your head, you weren't going to be able to get a good idea. It's a complete poison. Ø

"I make intelligence cool. I make spirituality cool. If we can make one's devotion to God cool, then I think I did a great thing."

KRS-One

Nathan Rabin

Originally Printed April 2001

KRS-One's booming voice and unmistakable flow are as much a part of the fabric of hip-hop as DJ Premier's scratches and Dr. Dre's sinister synthesizer whines. The Boogie Down Productions rapper—who was born Laurence Krisna Parker, but later named himself for an acronym signifying "Knowledge Reigns Supreme Over Nearly Everyone"—played a crucial role in bringing a social and political conscience to hip-hop, with socially charged works like By All Means Necessary, Criminal Minded, Edutainment, *and* Ghetto Music: The Blueprint Of Hip Hop. *As a solo artist, he's expanded the genre's thematic and musical boundaries, rapping on albums by artists as diverse as R.E.M. and Shabba Ranks and lecturing at college campuses nationwide. After a late-'90s hiatus that included a two-year stint as a music executive for Warner Bros., KRS-One returned with 2000's* The Sneak Attack, *his first record in four years and his first solo album on a label other than rap/teen-pop powerhouse Jive. In 2001, the rapper, intellectual, and activist spoke with* The Onion A.V. Club *about industry politics, respect, and the linguistics of hip-hop.*

The Onion: ***Do you think recent artists like Dead Prez, Mos Def, and Talib Kweli, who are socially conscious and clearly influenced by your work, are bringing a sense of balance back to rap music?***

KRS-One: Well, yeah, on the surface of it. Yes, they're bringing a great balance to hip-hop as a culture and to rap music. But it's more accurate to think that the people of hip-hop, those that participate in the culture, are growing up and seeing Mos Def. They are reaching for Talib Kweli and Jill Scott and Common and these people. They're reaching for them more readily now because of their own maturity. It's not gonna last. It's not gonna stay this way. But while it's here, artists like myself are enjoying it.

O: ***Why do you say that it's not going to last?***

KRS: Because hip-hop as a culture itself goes through stages. It grows—it's breathing, living. I've noticed that we usually start off conscious, then we wind up very highly sexual, and then we thug it out. Then things get a little funny again, with comedy and that kind of thing. Don't be surprised if you see a "Parents Just Don't Understand" coming out. That kind of rap may all of a sudden become very prevalent. People might wonder why that's going to be, but usually when the conscious rap comes about, comedy comes about, too, and usually when the gangsta rap is out, just to use that phrase or term, the sex comes out, too. We're getting ready to leave the sex and violence—which, by the way, won't disappear. It's just that the community of hip-hoppers is going to look at something different. This will now spur on a whole lot of artists to start thinking more consciously and making music that pertains to their self-worth.

O: ***You left Jive after* I Got Next. *What was the cause of that?***

KRS: We went in two different directions. I'm a staunch critic of Jive Records, as you know, but I'm also very respectful, because Jive supported me for 13 years, through some very controversial times. The guns on the covers of albums, the Malcolm X thing. And the head of Jive is a devout Jew. He's allowed me my freedom of speech, even when it went against Judaism and had a pinch of anti-Semitism in it, even though I'm not anti-Semitic. But when you're an intellectual and you're questioning religion, it can get pretty controversial. Jive Records gets my respect, but we went in two different directions. They started putting out Britney Spears and The Backstreet Boys and 'N Sync on the same label as me. They knew it, I knew it, we all knew that this was a disaster. It was an issue. Not so much that Britney... In no way to demean her art or anything, because I think she's very talented, but you can see where I'm coming from and see where she's coming from. What happened was, first I went to Warner Bros. and took an A&R gig there, because I wanted to study philosophy full-time with an emphasis on metaphysics. I thought that getting a job that was 9 to 5 would somehow help me out, give me the freedom I needed to study. But I learned that there were other things involved with that, as well. First of all, I'm not an executive. I didn't know that before, and I now know it. I also know that I'm freer as a hip-hopper than as an executive. Even as a black man, I enjoy more freedom as a hip-hopper than as a black man. That, too, is controversial to say, but it's the truth. By the way, my two-year stay at Warner Bros. was the best time of my life. Excellent company to work for. Time-Warner is the ultimate, and I was treated with high respect there. Just even thinking about it now makes me think about all the things I could have done there. But I would have had to give up rap. I would have had to give up hip-hop as a culture. Time-Warner would have become my culture, and it is a culture unto itself. It's like being Italian or Jamaican. Going back to the question, though, we just realized we had to go our separate routes. I also, creatively, was going in a different direction than Jive, because here I am wanting to save the world and uplift hip-hop. Jive was just interested in booty music and going platinum. All of that led me to pursue my own label. I didn't want to sign with another record label. What's the sense? Fifteen years of industry, and I'm going to sign another contract with Sony or MCA or RCA? My wife had, and has, a label called Front Page Records, which we used to do breakbeat albums on. So we simply took that label imprint, went over to Koch Distribution, and did a joint-venture deal with them.

O: ***What did your A&R work for Warner Bros. teach you?***

KRS: The single most important lesson I learned is that black people are the cause of black people's demise. I learned that at Time-Warner. Though I was treated with the highest respect from the owners of the company, which is obviously white people... Not obviously, but... [Laughs.] This is not a black-owned company. All the white executives there treated me as if they were my sons and I was their father, not the other way around. But, then, when I met with my black brothers, I say to you today very reluctantly, it was a disappointment. The attitude that I was confronted with on that level was ridiculous. They didn't want to speak to me. There were heads of A&R who didn't even want to speak to me. For the two years I was there, they never called a meeting with me to discuss things. I called many meetings that were ignored. Our head of publicity couldn't get it together with the artists I was signing. I had about a $5 million budget. They couldn't understand why I would sign Kool Herc, who was the father of hip-hop culture. They couldn't understand why I was talking to Chuck D and Public Enemy about signing to Warner Bros. They couldn't understand why I signed Kool Moe Dee, why I signed Mad Lion on the reggae side. They wanted artists who basically thugged it out and pimped it out, and it was a disappointment to me on that side. I never again will join in on the rhetoric that the white man is the reason people can't get ahead in corporate America. That's bullshit now, as far as I'm concerned. Maybe it was like that. Maybe in some corporations, it still is. But I know that at Time-Warner it ain't, and I was there from the highest level to the lowest level. And the problem is, black people are just constantly immature in their thinking, and we suffer as a people. You know, this is not about race in the sense that black people got to get something better than whites or Latinos or Asians. This is just basically that we keep complaining about what we don't have and what we can't do, and then, when we get in positions to do stuff, we fight amongst ourselves like savages. That was the single most important lesson I learned. It also opened my eyes to the reason black music looks the way it does on television and radio. It's always baffled me why BET looks the way it does. This is Black Entertainment Television. Why are we up there, then, looking like idiots? It's because black people are marketing black people like that. I commend the deal with Viacom purchasing BET. I hope Viacom cleans up and does some work. Viacom is a Time-Warner company, by the way.

O: ***Do you feel like people have a bias against older rappers?***

KRS: Just black people do. Just black executives have a bias against older artists. We don't respect our elders. Besides artists, we don't respect Frederick Douglass. We don't respect Martin Luther King. You look at every Martin Luther King Boulevard out here, and it's a crack block. That's not because of white people. That's because of black leadership. We just have that problem, and it's something that I am going to spend the rest of my life trying to conquer. So, yeah, when it comes to the artists themselves, you look at someone like myself. It's these black DJs that are like, "Aww, man, KRS. He always preaching. Aww, man." But you go to the white DJs, and they can rattle off my songs. It's so funny that, when Public Enemy was out, their whole audience was white. And they're like, "Farrakhan, don't say you understand until you hear the man," and "Fight The Power," or "Don't Believe The Hype," and it's white kids that are chanting the lyrics and benefiting from that kind of thinking. And black folk look at Public Enemy, and the best thing we could do is say of Public Enemy's last album, "Oh, his beats was wack." Regardless of the message, regardless of anything else, "Oh, Chuck could've came with a better beat. He should've got [DJ] Premier. He should've went to Dr. Dre." This is the extent of our respect for our older artists, and I think it's a shame. I think it's appalling, and I think it's one of the cancers of our race.

O: ***What do you think is the biggest problem with hip-hop today?***

KRS: The fact that everyone believes that all of hip-hop is rap music, and that, when you say "hip-hop," it's synonymous with rap. When you say "hip-hop," you should be thinking about breakdancing, graffiti art, or MCing (which is the proper name for rap), DJing, beat-boxing, language, fashion, knowledge, trade. You should be thinking about a culture when you say "hip-hop." I think that hip-hop should be spelled with a capital "H," and as one word. It's the name of our culture, and it's the name of our identity and consciousness. I think hip-hop is not a product. I think rap is a product, but when hip-hop becomes a product, that's slavery, because you're talking about people's souls. To me, that's the biggest problem.

O: ***What do you think is most encouraging about hip-hop today?***

KRS: That it is the only place where Dr. Martin Luther King's "I have a dream" speech is visible. When Dr. Martin Luther King said, "I have a dream... Let freedom ring from Stone Mountain," in his time, Stone Mountain was the Klan headquarters. Today, with the help of hip-hop, they're all hip-hoppers up there. And when I say hip-hoppers, I mean black, white, Asian, Latino, Chicano, everybody. Hip-hop has united all races. Hip-hop has formed a platform for all people, religions, and occupations to meet on something. That, to me, is beyond music. That is just a brilliant, brilliant thing.

O: ***Do you feel like the media pay too much attention to people like Eminem, Puff Daddy, and Jay-Z, who are seemingly in constant trouble?***

KRS: Yes and no. Yes, they pay attention, because they have to print controversy to sell, but those people pay more attention to the media than I think a conscious rap artist does. Eminem's publicity agent is obviously aggressive about getting him out there, and getting controversial stories out there. In a way, Eminem benefits from all of this, especially with the image he's portraying. If you're an outlaw, you want the media to print the fact that you got arrested for gun possession. You want the media to print that you slapped up your girlfriend, that you smoked a blunt and ran down the block. You want that, and I think the media have done a great service to Eminem and Dr. Dre, and so on. The real problem is not so much what *The New York Times* or *USA Today* or any of the major news media do. The real problem is with *The Source*, which claims it's "the magazine of hip-hop music, culture, and politics." Yet when you open it, the culture and politics is all about pimps and hoes. To me, that's incredibly damaging, because if hip-hop's own publication is saying that all we're about is bitches and hoes and pimps and guns and drugs, what do you expect more intellectual, more mainstream, more academic writers and journalists to take from this culture? These writers are looking at *Rap Pages* and *XXL*, who claim they're hip-hop on a higher level, but at the same time, KRS-One will never be on the cover of *XXL*. KRS-One will never be on the cover of *The Source*—unless, of course, I sell a million records. Then, of course, I can be on the cover. To me, that's the real problem. Hip-hoppers are not interpreting what hip-hop is, and when we do interpret it, we interpret it as something immature, unorganized, and outlaw.

O: ***Do you feel like the police are targeting rappers?***

KRS: Why, certainly. Just turn on the TV. I think BET and MTV are one of the main reasons why we have racial profiling in this country today, because police officers are human beings, as well. They themselves may disagree, they may think they're above that, but they're human. They go home, they have to buy their son or daughter the latest rap CD, they listen to it, and they listen to rappers confessing crimes, saying how they got away with murder. They listen to that. Any responsible man or woman with a family cannot respect that, and so if you watch BET and MTV, and then you put on a uniform and go out to patrol the street, you're like, "I know what you're about. You're really only about shooting guns, smoking blunts, and promiscuous sex." It's just hypocrisy on hip-hop's part to cry racial profiling when your race is on TV acting like fools.

O: ***It seems like, because there's such an image of what a rapper should be, rappers who don't conform to that image have a hard time getting their message across.***

KRS: That's because they want to play in an arena they're not supposed to be in. I've enjoyed much success. The IRS is always at my door, constantly. It's not that you don't make any money doing conscious rap music. You make a lot of money doing this, but if you're greedy and you're not satisfied with $500,000 a year, and you want $2 million a year, then you will suffer as a conscious rap artist. But if you're true to the upliftment of people and the unity of people, raising the self-worth of people, then you live within your means. But the problem is that we're looking at the grass on the other side, saying, "That's greener. I want to be in the thug market, but I want to be a conscious rap artist." It doesn't work like that. You can't expect to be on MTV and critique George Bush. You can't expect to be on BET or the cover of *The Source* advocating Jesus Christ or Buddha or Hindu Krishna or Moses. As a conscious rap artist, you have to play in the arena that you're supposed to be in. What is that arena? That arena is the college market. The conscious rap artist woos the college market, even though the college market is the wildest, most sexed-out, drug-driven market in the country, possibly the world. The conscious rap artist still has a high place in the university system. Obviously, you must know of my university lectures, my years of doing that. I'm not saying something that I've read, I'm telling you something that I've lived as a conscious rap artist: It's the university system that you really want to be at. On top of that, in terms of getting your record played, it's the mix-show level where you really want to be. So, yeah, it's hard to push a conscious rap artist in a gangster market. Then again, as a conscious rap artist, you should not want to be in a gangster market. You should be trying to establish your own market, create a place where you can be yourself and make some money and feed your family.

O: ***Do you feel like that's starting to happen, like some companies are marketing to a conscious audience?***

KRS: Oh, yeah. The whole world is conscious. It's just that we become conscious at times, and you become conscious when you lose a loved one. You wake up and say, "Man, it's real. I don't need this pimp gangster stuff anymore, I need something with a little more substance." And there is marketing for that. Deepak Chopra, look at him. He's probably the most successful self-help guru in the world. I don't think he's struggling for any marketing or exposure. You've just got to know where your audience is, and I do think there's going to be a surge of it, especially with the new administration, the presidency of George Bush. I think people are going to be reaching for this now.

O: ***What do you think has been your most important contribution to rap music and hip-hop culture?***

KRS: The defining of it. At least, I hope it is. It's so funny, a question like that, because what you think your contribution is is never what's told in history. They'll probably say something that I'm not even thinking about. But what I'm thinking about is, if I were to critique myself—step out of KRS objectively and look at him—I would say that KRS has introduced the concept of being hip-hop, not just doing it. The concept of rap as something we do, while hip-hop is something we live. The concept of living a culture. Don't just look at hip-hop as rap music, see it as a culture. My songs, in terms of "You Must Learn" or "Why Is That?" or "Black Cop," those kinds of songs make people question their environment. I think that's the single most important contribution that I can offer: the strengthening of people's spirit and soul, the strengthening of families, the unity of a husband and a wife. To me, that's most important. Without that, we have nothing. If a son doesn't respect a father, if a child doesn't respect a parent, then we're lost. And I think what I bring to hip-hop is that. I make intelligence cool. I make spirituality cool. If we can make one's devotion to God cool, then I think I did a great thing. I can rest in peace. ∅

Mark Mothersbaugh (Devo)

By Joe Garden

Originally Printed July 1997

"We saw Devo as something bigger than a rock band. We thought that was the most boring thing you could do. We wanted to be a clearing house for concepts and ideas."

*From its 1972 inception, Devo used a combination of herky-jerky, emotion-drained music, film, and elaborate live performances to present a vision of a de-evolving world. But co-leaders Mark Mothersbaugh and Jerry Casale meant the band to be more than just the musical equivalent of a conceptual comedy routine. Spreading their warnings about humanity's decline turned out to be easier than expected, thanks to powerful admirers (David Bowie, Brian Eno, and Neil Young among them) and the arrival of MTV, which turned Devo's 1980 song "Whip It" into a left-field hit. But as the '80s dragged on, Devo played to diminishing audiences, and its members began to pursue outside projects. Mothersbaugh founded Mutato Muzika and launched a successful career scoring commercials, TV shows (*Rugrats, Sliders, Pee-wee's Playhouse*), and films (*Happy Gilmore, Rushmore, The Royal Tenenbaums*). But Devo's legacy lives on: Its influence has been acknowledged by successors in rock and electronica, and the band itself occasionally re-forms to considerable interest. In the wake of one of these reunions, for the 1997 incarnation of Lollapalooza, Mothersbaugh spoke to* The Onion A.V. Club.

The Onion: ***Tell me about Mutato Muzika as an entity and an extension of Devo.***

Mark Mothersbaugh: Mutato Muzika is headquarters for Devo at this point. We're located on the beautiful Sunset Strip in West Hollywood, in a fluorescent circular green building that looks a little bit like a spaceship. That's where life after rock 'n' roll takes place. We're kind of like the subversive extension in the sense that a lot of our clients don't know that we were ever in Devo. That works to our advantage at times, because sometimes our clients have preconceived notions of what the music should sound like if they think you were in Devo. In this particular situation, we're able to work with full orchestras, with klezmer bands, with metal guitarists, with accordion players, with ethnic musicians and singers. Our client doesn't have it filtered through the Devo red hat.

O: ***What kind of commercials do you work on?***

MM: We do everything from regional to international spots. We were just asked to collaborate on some projects for McDonald's which would include doing in-store merchandising for them, creating albums' worth of music which would impart the message of Ronald McDonald and Barbie. Little do they know that it would be through the filter of Devo. Our subliminal messages would be fully intact and attached like antioxidants working their way into the system.

O: ***What kind of subversion do you plan to unleash upon a nation of underage hamburger consumers and Barbie fans?***

MM: Well, in general, we've done commercials for Hawaiian Punch, Toyota... I don't know, just about everybody: 7-Up, Hershey's, Nestle's. Nike. Fila. We have hundreds of clients. The one thing we found out early on was that you could insert subliminal messages into commercials without too much difficulty, without our clients being concerned about it or even noticing in most cases. A few times we even told them we did it, and they just laughed. They didn't care. It's strange. If it's something we kind of approve of as a product—certain computer products, for instance, or something that's healthy for people—we'll put in one kind of message. On something where it may be uninspired, sugar-coated crap, maybe we'll put in subliminal messages like, "Question Authority" or "Choose Your Mutations Carefully." We even did "Sugar Is Bad For You" once. I think sometimes subliminal messages hold a lot of weight. The very first Devo films were made on a budget of... The first one, *The Truth About De-Evolution*, was made for like $2,200. We put the words "Submit" and "Obey" in the film, and it won every film festival we sent it to. It did quite well. We would play it onstage before we would come out. There was no such thing as MTV in the mid-'70s. There was no way to show the stuff, so we would just string a sheet up and then show the film in front of us. Then we'd pull it down and play a set. It seemed to work every time. It seemed to program people perfectly to enjoy an evening of celebrating the downward spiral.

"We learned something from the hippies that, unfortunately, the punks at the same time didn't learn, and that is that rebellion is obsolete. In a healthy capitalistic world, rebellion is just something else to market."

O: ***I'm a bit embarrassed, because I believe I've been mispronouncing Devo [pronounced de-VOE] as Devo [pronounced DEE-vo]. Wherein lies the difference? Has it always been pronounced like that?***

MM: No, no. In the world dictionary, you're pronouncing it properly, because we are DE-vo. De-VO is a personal pronunciation that members of the band have used amongst themselves from the very beginning. It had a lot to do with the early imprinting of the contraction down into four letters. Before it was a band, we saw DE-vo, or de-VO as an art movement. We were tracking history as art deco, art nouveau, art de-VO. It's kind of like how "fuck" can mean something really great and it can mean something really bad. You can be fucked up, or "I just got fucked." You can get fucked and it can be good, or it can be bad. It's kind of the same thing with de-VO. You could say, "Those two people over there in the polyester double-knit body suits driving that gas-guzzling Cadillac are more DE-vo than we could ever be. Or you could say, "That young girl who just had surgery to her ears so they look like Spock's, and had a Pan-Pacific slant put to her eyes on purpose even though she's from Europe—she's very de-VO." So it has kind of more of a French feel when you're talking about high de-VO, and it has more of a hillbilly feel when you talk about low DE-vo. It's subtle differences that are absolutely meaningless to just about anybody other than half a dozen people who created the concept 20-some years ago.

O: ***You said Mutato was a subversive extension of Devo. Would you say Devo wasn't subversive?***

MM: In our purest sense, we were always attempting for subversion. We learned something from the hippies that, unfortunately, the punks at the same time didn't learn, and that is that rebellion is obsolete. In a healthy capitalistic world, rebellion is just something else to market. Even quicker than the hippies became hip capitalists, the punks became T-shirts and bumper stickers. We took our cues from the Viet Cong and the subversives during WWI and WWII in Europe, as opposed to from the hippies and the punks. In a certain context, when I say that Mutato has the ability to be more subversive than Devo, I think that, in the mid-'80s, people fixed a concept of what we were and who they thought we were based on misinformation that was generated by and disseminated by people who should have been working with us. I'm talking about record companies and magazines. You have to understand, during our career, that we were resisted vehemently by magazines like *Rolling Stone* and all the powers that be. Even MTV, soon after they got their payola structure established, cast us aside, even though originally we were the only band you would see on the hour every hour with a different video when it first came out. That was because nobody else was doing it besides us.

O: ***Is it true that Devo once opened for Sun Ra?***

MM: Yeah, in 1974. He almost never came out onstage, because there were fistfights between the audience and Devo. They were doing Tequila Sunrise out of a big 50-gallon vat and taking... What drug were they taking? Oh, the one you inhale. Laughing gas or something. It was Halloween in Cleveland, and somebody hired Devo as a joke. We were dressed in janitor outfits, and they were all dressed like hunchbacks and vampires, and permutations of lowest-common-denominator Halloween costumes. LCD horror. They ended up getting really pissed off at us and the music we were playing. At the time, we were a lightning rod for hostility. We would play a song like "Subhuman Woman" for seven minutes. We'd play "Jocko Homo" for 30 minutes, and we wouldn't stop until people were actually fighting with us, trying to make us stop playing the song. We'd just keep going, "Are we not men? We are Devo!" for like 25 minutes, directed at people in an aggressive enough manner that even the most peace-loving hippie wanted to throw fists. We were in a negative-energy vortex back in the mid-'70s.

O: ***When all these fistfights were erupting, were you guys able to hold your own?***

MM: Actually, the double-edged sword in some ways was that we were so insular. We started in Akron, Ohio, and there were just the five of us then. We did everything ourselves. We saw Devo as something bigger than a rock band. We thought that was the most boring thing you could do. We wanted to be a clearing house for concepts and ideas. That's where art de-VO came from. That's why we made films. We designed our own costumes, designed our own artwork and graphics. We designed every album cover that we ever had control of. The downside of doing everything ourselves and directing our own films and producing our own films and going out and getting the props and coming up with the concept and the ideas was that we didn't really collaborate a lot. At the time, everybody wanted to work with us. Bowie, Eno, Fripp, Iggy Pop. I stayed at Iggy Pop's house for a couple weeks. He wanted to record our first album before we did. I was like, "No, we want to do it first," and he was like, "Shut up, this would be so good for you." He was crazy during that time.

O: ***That must have been his drug-addled phase.***

MM: Oh, man, it sure was. I have tapes of Devo rehearsing in his living room in Malibu, and him grabbing the microphone from me and starting to sing wild shit over the top of our songs. It was a wild period. The insular part kind of made it hard for people to come in and take over anything. On the other hand, we missed out on plenty of opportunities. People like [Virgin Records head] Richard Branson flew me and Bob Casale down to Jamaica once, got us really stoned, and we were like, "Whoa!" In Ohio, we would sit around with enough pot to fill up a thimble, and we'd stare at it all day. Everybody would know for a week in advance that we were going to smoke this pot during the weekend. By Saturday night, everybody would be like, "This is that African stuff that's really hallucinogenic," and it was probably just picked off the side of the road in Mexico or something. We would finally roll this pencil-thin joint, and like eight people

"We'd just keep going, 'Are we not men? We are Devo!' for like 25 minutes, directed at people in an aggressive enough manner that even the most peace-loving hippie wanted to throw fists."

would all desperately try to get a little buzz off of this really bad pot. We'd all be like, "I think I'm high. Maybe I'm high. Yeah, I might have felt something. My throat's definitely feeling raw." It was that kind of thing. So Bob Casale and I go down to Jamaica, where we've never been before, and we have no money. We don't have a record deal or anything. Richard Branson gets us really high because he's got this big pile of pot on the table. We're there with all these South Africans who were a part of Virgin Records, and he goes, "What do you guys think of The Sex Pistols?" I go, "You know what? We just saw them last week. They came over to where we were staying in San Francisco 'cause we were both playing there on the same weekend, when they played their last show. It's a shame that they broke up." And he says, "Well, I'll tell you why. We have Johnny Rotten in the next room, and he wants to be the new lead singer for Devo. If you guys are up for that, we have the press from England here, and they're ready to take photos and do articles if you guys want to announce right now that Johnny Rotten is the new lead singer for Devo." Bob and I are like... This time, it's not like, "I think I'm getting high." It's like, "Oh, shit. What the fuck are they doing?" It was one of those horrible events where you realize you're sitting on the floor, and all these people are sitting around you, and I never realized how big Richard Branson's teeth were until that day. He's, like, staring at me with this big smile, waiting for me to say, "Yeah, Johnny Rotten can join Devo." Maybe you've been to school before, and in a situation where there's something totally absurd; it's a totally mundane normal experience that seems surreal and absurd, and you're fighting back laughter. You stifle laughter, and that just makes it worse, and then you can't help it. You're laughing so hard you can't stop. I'm in front of this guy who's a multimillionaire already, and famous because of The Sex Pistols and Mike Oldfield, and I'm going, "Oh my God, this is not the way to start a relationship." We couldn't stop laughing. It just made us pull the wagon trains even tighter when we finally got a record deal. That was our only defense. As it turned out, by the time we got with Warner Bros., they just wore you down through the pure *1984* double-think of everything. Warner Bros. had their own methodology of pummeling you and taking away your spirit. I remember going to visit [Warner Bros. head] Mo Ostin about six to nine months after audio cassettes became a big deal. Before that, people were just buying vinyl, but then audio cassettes were becoming the most sought-after item. They were paying us less money for an audio cassette, but there were articles in all the papers about how much cheaper it was to make an audio cassette than it was to press vinyl. So I went in and had a meeting with Mo Ostin, and said, "You know, Mo, I need to ask you something really important. Why is it that, in our deal, you have it so you're paying us substantially less money for every audio cassette that you sell than for every piece of vinyl, yet you make a bigger profit off every audio cassette?" He just smiled and looked at me like I was his dense, naïve son. And he goes, "Because that's the way it is." That was his answer. And I just left his office going, "Oh. Six fingers. Hold up your hand. I'm seeing six fingers." It was in some ways more appealing than being with the smaller pigs in the world who just sat there and bled you like parasites and vampires. At least he was totally up-front about it. He was totally unashamed that there was no justification except for power. ⌀

Alan Moore

By Tasha Robinson
Originally Printed October 2001

"I've seen a lot of things over the past 15 years that have been a bizarre echo of somebody else's bad mood. It's not even their bad mood, it's mine."

British writer Alan Moore was a comics fan from a very young age, and he was making a living scripting comic books by the time he reached his 20s. After winning awards for his V For Vendetta *series, a grim story about a poetry-spouting terrorist spreading anarchy in a fascistic future England, he attracted the attention of DC Comics, which recruited him to take over the* Swamp Thing *series. DC also gave Moore a launching pad for* Watchmen, *an intricately executed, seminal series that changed how literate comic-book readers thought about the superhero genre. Apart from* Watchmen, *Moore's greatest work to date is* From Hell, *a massive exploration of the Jack The Ripper murders that incorporates British history, Masonic ritual, and London geography in a fascinating and horrifying conspiracy theory. As the Hughes brothers' 2001 film adaptation of* From Hell *prepared to launch, Moore spoke to* The Onion A.V. Club *about his status as the Howard Hughes of comics, how the bad mood he was in 15 years ago has warped the comics industry, and why he worships a second-century sock puppet.*

The Onion: ***When you first started reading comics as a child and thinking about becoming a comics writer, did you ever consider the kind of deconstruction you've made into a career? Or were you just interested in imitating existing works back then?***

Alan Moore: I was 8. The deconstruction of comics was when the staples came out, for that age. I started out like any other child of that age, just purely obsessed with the characters. I wanted to know what Batman was doing this month, whether he was hanging out with Superman, or whether he was with the Justice League. Given a couple of years, I discovered things like Harvey Kurtzman's original *Mad* comic, which was reprinted in paperbacks that were available over here. I discovered Will Eisner's *Spirit*. These were an incredible jolt, because, for the first time, I was suddenly aware of the fantastic intelligence that could be invested in comics, given a talented enough creator. People like Kurtzman or Eisner were telling stories that could only be told in the comics form, but they were telling them with such style and power that I began to grasp what comics might be capable of. I started to realize how comics didn't need to be the way that the more normal comics that made up my reading diet always seemed to be, that you could do fantastic things. I certainly thought they could probably be made more realistic. I thought they could probably be given greater atmosphere, and that the writing could perhaps be improved. I didn't see why literary values shouldn't be transplanted to comics. But during those days, this was only on a very amateur level. I'd do sort of incoherent experimental comic strips for local arts magazines or local quasi-underground papers. Which were, I suppose, an attempt at learning my craft, but they weren't deconstructed; they were just messy. But, yeah, probably from an early age, there was a desire to do a different kind of comic book. I can't really claim to have any intelligent master plan. I probably didn't even realize that I was deconstructing superheroes until I was about halfway through *Watchmen*. Afterwards, it seemed a lot more obvious, but at the time we were just trying to do a cleverer-than-usual, more-stylish-than-usual superhero comic. But two or three issues in, it had become a sort of semiotic nightmare that I still get hounded by literature professors over to this day. It obviously, halfway through the telling, became a very different sort of animal.

O: ***Did that realization actually alter* Watchmen *in the writing? Did you end up changing the story midway through as you realized what you were doing?***

AM: We didn't. The basic plot was there from before we started work on it. And we knew that we were going to be treating these superheroes in a way that was probably a little more dark, and perhaps a little more naturalistic, than the way they'd been treated usually. I was writing the opening pages and, as is my custom, making tiny little thumbnail sketches to actually be able to envisage what the page would finally look like when it was drawn. I had two or three strains of narrative going on in the same page. I had a truculent news vendor giving his fairly uninformed commentary on the political state of the world, the likelihood of a coming war. Across the street, in the background, we have two people fixing a radiation sign to a wall. Sitting with his back to a hydrant near the news vendor, there's a small boy reading a comic, which is a pirate comic. And I think while I was doodling, I noticed that an extreme close-up of the radiation symbol, if you put the right sort of caption with it, could look almost like the black sail of a ship against a yellow sky. So I dropped in a caption in the comic that the child was reading about a hellbound ship's black sails against a yellow Indies sky. And I have a word balloon coming from off-panel, which is actually the balloon of the news vendor, which is talking about war. The narrative of the pirate comic is talking about a different sort of war. As we pull back, we realize that we're looking at a radiation symbol that's being tacked to the wall of a newly created fallout shelter. And finally, when we pull back into the beginning, into the foreground, we realize that these pirate captions that we've been reading are those in the comic that is being read by the small boy. This was exciting. There was something going on here. There was an interplay between the imagery, between the strands of narrative, the pirate narrative, the dialogue going on in the street. They were striking sparks off of each other, and they were doing something which I hadn't actually seen a comic do before. I think it was around those first three pages of *Watchmen* #3 that I started to realize that we'd got something different on our hands here. By the next issue, we had this incredibly complex kind of multifaceted view of time, where everything is kind of happening at once—at least in the mind of the central character. Which, again, opened up possibilities for new narrative tricks, which we pretty much kept up until the end of the series. But, like I said, it was purely while I was scribbling, doodling, writing bits of dialogue and crossing them out that I suddenly noticed these possibilities for things that could be done in a comic and nowhere else.

O: ***Is it true that you regret the effect that* Watchmen *had on the comics industry?***

AM: To a degree. Perhaps it happens in any medium, where anything of any kind of great proportion will have an adverse effect upon the medium itself. I think that what a lot of people saw when they read *Watchmen* was a high degree of violence, a bleaker and more pessimistic political perspective, perhaps a bit more sex, more swearing. And to some degree there has been, in the 15 years since *Watchmen*, an awful lot of the comics field devoted to these grim, pessimistic, nasty, violent stories which kind of use *Watchmen* to validate what are, in effect, often just some very nasty stories that don't have a lot to recommend them. And some of them are very pretentious, where they'll try and grab some sort of intellectual gloss for what they're doing by referring to a few song titles or the odd book. They'll name-drop William Burroughs here or there. Just like *Mad* comics, which was a unique standalone thing, it's almost become a genre. The gritty, deconstructivist postmodern superhero comic, as exemplified by *Watchmen*, also became a genre. It was never meant to. It was meant to be one work on its own. I'd have liked to have seen more people trying to do something that was as technically complex as *Watchmen*, or as ambitious, but which wasn't strumming the same chords that *Watchmen* had strummed so repetitively. The apocalyptic bleakness of comics over the past 15 years sometimes seems odd to me, because it's like that was a bad mood that I was in 15 years ago. It was the 1980s, we'd got this insane right-wing voter fear running the country, and I was in a bad mood, politically and socially and in most other ways. But it was a genuine bad mood, and it was mine. I've seen a lot of things over the past 15 years that have been a bizarre echo of somebody else's bad mood. It's not even their bad mood, it's mine. So, for my part, I wouldn't say that my new stuff is all bunny rabbits and blue-skies optimism, but it's probably got a lot more of a positive spin on it than the work I was doing back in the '80s. This is a different century.

O: ***Did you ever go through a traditional fandom period? Did you go to conventions, try to get autographs, try to meet artists, that sort of thing?***

AM: I actually attended the second British comic convention. It was nothing like the horrific conventions that exist at the present day. It wasn't a marketing exercise on behalf of the companies. I got to speak to people like Barry Smith and Frank Bellamy, and made a lot of really important friendships back then. Moving on a few years, the conventions were starting to get uncomfortably big and not so much fun, and I was starting to find something a little clammy about fandom. The whole idea that you could be a celebrity and be working

"I've become like the Howard Hughes of the comics medium. I hang around in a darkened room, eating ice cream in a negligee, or something like that."

in comics was an idea that had never occurred to me, because when I took on the job it was the most obscure job in the world. When the big turmoil about comics started in the middle '80s, and the conventions got bigger and bigger, and there was more television and press, that was the point where it all became a little much for me. I swore off public appearances. I've become like the Howard Hughes of the comics medium. I hang around in a darkened room, eating ice cream in a negligee, or something like that. Yes, it's nice at first to have lots of people telling you that you're a genius. Then you realize that they're almost certainly wrong, that they're all very young, hysterical, and sort of overwrought about something that was probably just a good comic story. There's something unhealthy about the relationship between celebrity and public that I couldn't really subscribe to. Everybody starts treating you as if you're on some different level, so you can't really communicate with them. I honestly think that the only possible communication is between equals. I started to feel very alienated and very strange. I didn't really sign up to be a celebrity, I only signed up to be a writer. That was the part that I was interested in.

O: ***Is celebrity itself the problem? Do you think it's possible for a creator and his fans to have a relationship if it's not...***

AM: It may well be possible. I know some people who manage it very well. But these days, everybody wants to be famous, and I think all too often, you'll see somebody who has maybe written one good book, made one good film, produced one good record, one good comic book. And all of a sudden, everyone's telling him that he's a genius, and he probably thinks, "Well, yes, I am. I always thought that I was sort of special, and, yeah, that's probably because I was a genius." He'll launch himself out onto the billows of fame, and he'll be washed up in the tabloid press six months later, when his bloated, heroin-sodden carcass bobs up to a beach somewhere. Fame does all sorts of unpleasant things to people. It tends to, in many cases, warp them. It doesn't necessarily make them happier. It's nothing that I'm very interested in. I figure that, for the number of people who read my work and get something out of it, I'm already having an untoward effect upon their minds and thoughts. Which I must admit I quite enjoy, in kind of a spooky, creepy way. But I don't want to colonize their imagination as some sort of idol.

O: ***With* From Hell *and* Promethea, *you get very deeply into the history of symbolism and magic. Are you trying to educate the masses, or is there a specific purpose?***

AM: Well, I do have a purpose. I am an incredibly vain person, but I am also, with *Promethea*, trying to educate people about something I am genuinely interested in, and which I generally think is of interest to a lot of people. When I was 40, I decided to become a magician, for various reasons. Most people get to 40 and have a midlife crisis, and that's just boring. They bore their friends by going around saying, "What's it all about? What's the point?" I thought it might be at least more entertaining to go spectacularly mad and start worshipping a snake and declaring myself to be a magician. It's been immense fun. And, more than fun, it's been illuminating. It certainly seems to have given me a lot of energy in my work. I'm probably doing more books now than I've ever done, even when I was young and sprightly. A lot of that is the new insights into my own creative processes, which I thank magic for. Because in some sense, when I'm talking about magic, I'm only talking about the creative process. Magic to me is something from nothing, which includes rabbits out of hats, the creation of the universe from a quantum vacuum, or how a comic comes into being from me sitting in an armchair with a completely blank mind. Any given creativity is magic. And by understanding magic, I have understood a little more about the processes by which I have been supporting myself for these past 20 years. Certainly, *Promethea* is a magical rant seemingly disguised as a superheroine comic. It's kind of a visionary odyssey, and I'm able to get over a lot of valid information. Not in terms of magic being a doorway to some strange mad dimension full of angels and demons and gods—although, yes, there is a lot of that. But I think primarily, magic is simply a new way of seeing the ordinary universe that surrounds us, and ourselves as creatures in that universe. I've certainly been impressed by some of the insights that I seem to have received from my imaginary friends. I mean, with the readership of *Promethea*, we've had some people who've got frankly bored with what I suppose must have come to sound like some sort of manic, ranting lecture from Charles Manson or somebody. But on the other hand, there are a lot of people who seem genuinely appreciative, and new readers who come to the book precisely because it is exploring things like Kabbalah and Tarot and notions of human history, the makeup of the human psyche.

O: ***When you talk about the way it's helped you and the way it could help other people in your situation, you make it sound essentially like a religion that you're preaching to other people in order to aid them spiritually.***

AM: No, I draw a sharp distinction between magic and religion. I see them almost as the spiritual parallels of say, fascism and anarchy in the political arena. To me, politics does not divide into right-wing and left-wing, in that capitalism and communism are both just two different ways of ordering industrial societies, which have not been around for a vast amount of time and probably won't be around for a lot longer. To me, the two poles of politics are fascism, which... from the original Roman concept, the symbol for it was a bundle of bound twigs. The idea being, "In unity there is strength." Religion is almost the political equivalent of that. Religion, strictly speaking, doesn't even have to be about anything spiritual. The Conservative Party is a religion in that they are bound together by belief. Almost any organization has its religious aspects. With magic, I worship a second-century Roman snake god who, on the best evidence that I can dredge up from that period, was some kind of elaborate glove-puppet that was being controlled by a second-century snake-oil salesman—basically a complete fraud, huckster, and showman. I find something a bit unnatural in the idea of being bound together in spiritual ideas with people. I'm sure that, in our natural state, we all believe something entirely different. I don't necessarily want anybody to believe the same things I believe, which is one of the reasons why I've adopted such a patently mad sort of deity. The idea of the deity is all I'm interested in, so that's fine for my purposes. Magic to me is more like anarchy. The roots of the word "anarchy" are an archos, no leaders, which is not really about the kind of chaos that most people imagine when anarchy is mentioned. I think that anarchy is about taking personal responsibility for yourself. I believe that fascism is about abandoning your personal responsibility to the group or to society. You say, "In unity there is strength," which inevitably will become, "In uniformity there is strength." It's better if all those sticks are the same size and length, because then they'll make a tidier bundle, which consequently leads to the kind of fascism that we saw in the '30s and '40s. All I would be urging people to do in *Promethea* is to use whatever system they happen to feel comfortable with, whether that be Christianity, or paganism, or Hinduism, or anything else, to explore the kind of rich world that I think all of us have inside us. It doesn't really matter which way you use, or which system you adopt. It's a territory I find very rewarding, very fulfilling, very human. To point out that territory to other people is something I feel happy about doing. To erect a huge church there and officiate over rituals, is not. ⌀

David Cross (Mr. Show, Part IV)

By Stephen Thompson

Originally Printed September 1999

"I woke up and I was 35. I used to be 31. I feel like this show has just aged me."

Though David Cross and Bob Odenkirk's Mr. Show *lasted only 30 half-hour episodes before fatigue and low ratings took their toll, it earned great reviews and a rabid cult following that continues to grow, even though its creators have redirected their attention toward movies, acting, and living comparatively normal lives. They reunited to make the* Mr. Show *feature-film spin-off* Run, Ronnie, Run, *and Cross has toured as a stand-up comic and appeared on occasional HBO specials. In the wake of the show's demise, and in conjunction with the 1999 special* David Cross: The Pride Is Back!, *Cross spoke to* The Onion A.V. Club *about his frustrating career path.*

The Onion: ***It seemed like 75 percent of Mr. Show's audience was people who were actually writing glowing articles about your show.***

David Cross: Oh, fuck, yeah. But I'm constantly surprised by the reaction. I was on the subway in New York last year, and this guy—I'm guessing 50, kind of a blue-collar, construction-worker-looking guy in his work clothes—was sort of looking at me. And I'm thinking that for some reason he doesn't like me, like he thinks I have an attitude or something. And then, after three stops, he turns to me and goes, "Hey, I think your show is the funniest thing on television." And I'm just, like, "Wow. That's fuckin' awesome."

O: ***I thought the show was actually pretty accessible.***

DC: I don't know, that was one of the complaints: that it wasn't that accessible, that it was very niche-oriented. It was certainly promoted that way, as this little underground secret.

O: ***"Watch Mondays at midnight!"***

DC: Yeah, if you can. If you can remember. "We're gonna tell you once and then not tell you again. In five months, watch that show you've watched Friday at midnight Monday at midnight. Gotta go, bye!"

O: ***What exactly happened to* Mr. Show*? Was it canceled, or was it a matter of workload?***

DC: It wasn't canceled. They would have been happy to have us do another season—they've got very little programming that's like it—but we just... To be fair to Bob, he was more willing to do another year of it, but I wasn't. I woke up and I was 35. I used to be 31. I feel like this show has just aged me. Not to take away from the benefits of doing the show, and the great times I had, and the creative outlet, and the fact that it's probably... I hope I'm wrong, but that show is kind of the thing that I do best. But I just couldn't take another year of not doing anything else. If we were just writing, or just performing, or just doing one thing, it wouldn't have been such a big deal. But after a while, it's like, you're there from roughly 10:30 in the morning until 8, and that's on average, and sometimes it's longer because you have to edit stuff. And you don't do anything else. A couple of times, I got offers to do tiny little parts in movies that I really wanted

"Some are definitely weaker than others, but we never did a bad, labored, sweaty, tired show."

to do. You want to do this thing, but you're like, "I can't be gone for 48 hours, man." There's nothing else. You don't see shows, you don't see movies, you don't do anything but sit in that unventilated room yelling at each other and making fun of everybody else. So, that's the reason. Plus, HBO wouldn't have given us any more money, which meant we would have basically been making very little money to, you know, work our asses off, and it would have been another year lost. And my career, the show, and show business are not the most important things in my life. When I'm talking to people, certainly in the last couple of months, people go, like, "Hey, man, I love the show." "Thanks!" "Is it coming on? I haven't seen any ads for it." "Oh, no, we're not doing it anymore." "What? Oh, dude. Dude! You've gotta do it!" "No, no. We've been working on a movie..." "But the show, man..." "But, no, this has allowed us to do other things, like, I actually biked to the store the other day and bought my own potatoes, which I haven't done in four years."

O: ***Do you feel that, career-wise, it was better to have your signature show be a limited-term thing that everybody can speak of fondly forever, sort of like* The Ben Stiller Show?**

DC: Absolutely, without a doubt. It's not even a question. The idea of doing 30 shows and not doing a bad one... Some are definitely weaker than others, but we never did a bad, labored, sweaty, tired show. Absolutely. And, in a cynical way, it's helped that it hasn't been that popular. I mean, we're not subject to the backlash that a lot of those popular shows are gonna have. I am wary of people looking at the next things that Bob and I do separately and going, "Well, that wasn't that funny. I wish they'd do the show again."

O: ***You're still working with Bob, right?***

DC: Well, we're doing a movie. We're doing a major, full-length movie, a totally different medium. We're able to expand things, take our sensibilities, put them in this totally different form, and get away with a lot more. We would not have been able to write that movie, or film it, or have a hand in the post- or preproduction if we were doing the show.

O: ***Are you going to continue working with him in the long term?***

DC: Oh, yeah, absolutely. He and his wife had a baby, and it's really mellowed him out quite a bit, but we're similar in a way. We wrote this movie with three of the other writers—Brian Posehn, Scott Aukerman, and B.J. Porter—and it looks like we're gonna start filming soon. Hopefully, it'll be out next summer. It shouldn't be too hard to do. It's fairly straightforward.

O: ***Is the studio planning a full-on release? It's not just going to play in New York and L.A.?***

DC: That's a decision they'll make later. The thing is, it's a relatively low-budget comedy, and those are the most bankable things you have for a studio. It's of very little cost to them, and all they've got to do is make three times the cost in gross to make money, and these kind of comedies usually do well for them. They know the show, they know us, they like us. We set a precedent with the show about working and having a creative say. We've got our creative freedom, which is paramount. Ø

"I don't want to stop playing. Why should I?" CHAPTER 8

"When you're 25, everybody's old. You think, 'My God, this guy is 35? He's ancient! He must be gonna die soon. He can't possibly last long.' Then you get to 35, and then, God help you, you get to 40, and you think, 'I don't want to stop playing.' Why should I? Actually, I'm getting better."

Lemmy Kilmister (Motörhead) page 285

"I know that all things come to an end, but I still enjoy doing the show... I don't have anything I really want to do that I don't have the time to do, so I haven't retired."

Bob Barker page 289

"I still think there's something for me to do that would be beneficial for me, both artistically and professionally. I'm going to keep plugging away at TV, in part because it keeps you in one place."

Andy Richter page 295

"I rolled with the punches, and I learned from them, and that's where I'm at right now. You know, no strings, just live and learn, and prosper from it."

Vanilla Ice page 301

"Most musicians complete their long journey to the middle because the forces that conspire against you—your agent, your manager, the rhythm section—whatever it is, it's weary, and you've got to constantly reinvest your enthusiasm for livin' large, Marge, so large you need a barge!"

David Lee Roth page 305

"If you'd asked me 21 years ago, I certainly wouldn't have guessed that I'd still be cranking out songs today. I still love doing it, and I have to assume that the American buying public will let me know when it's time to retire."

"Weird Al" Yankovic page 311

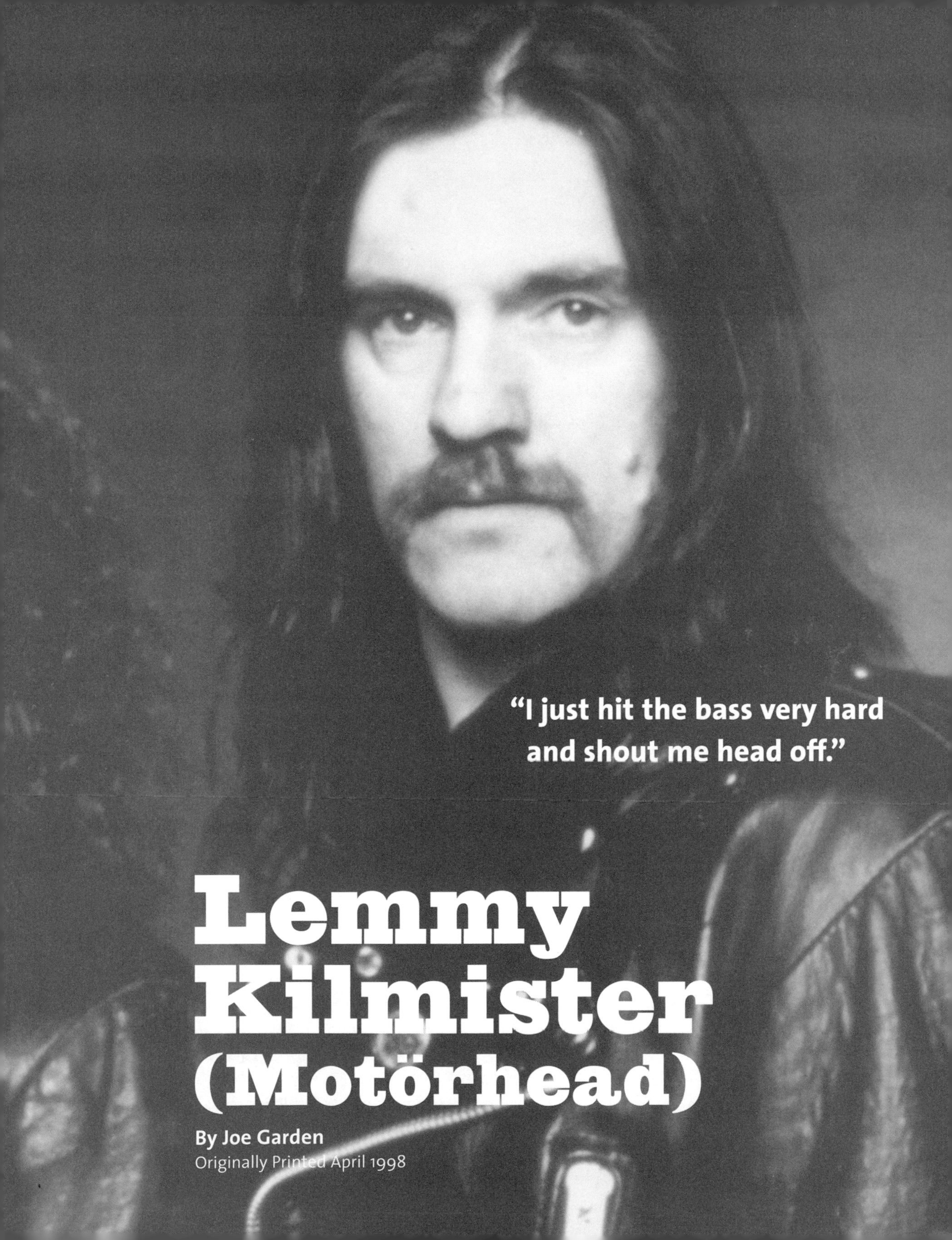

"I just hit the bass very hard and shout me head off."

Lemmy Kilmister (Motörhead)

By Joe Garden

Originally Printed April 1998

Even though its name is taken from the last song Lemmy Kilmister wrote for the British space-rock group Hawkwind, few bands have been as aptly named as Motörhead: If motorcycles could make music, there's little doubt what it would sound like. Motörhead's speed-driven intensity has served as an inspiration to metal and punk acts for years, but it might never have happened had Hawkwind not ousted Kilmister following his arrest for drug charges in 1975 in the midst of a Canadian tour. Returning to his native England, Kilmister created a band whose music matched its outlaw image, sparking a wave of British heavy metal in the process. In spite of label and lineup changes, internal drama, excessive lifestyles, and legal wrangling, Kilmister and Motörhead's mission has remained more or less unchanged to the present day. The title of a 1999 live album sums it up aptly: Everything Louder Than Everyone Else. *In 1998, shortly after the release of* Snake Bite Love, *Kilmister spoke to* The Onion A.V. Club *about his band's legacy.*

The Onion: ***Why do you think labels kept grabbing onto and then dropping Motörhead after releasing only one or two albums?***

Lemmy Kilmister: Labels nowadays don't seem to have any commitment whatsoever to the people they sign. They'll sign the band and then sack them halfway through the first album. It's obviously a tax wash: Lay out an advance, and then you can plead poverty at the next IRS audit. I'm sure that's what WTG [the Sony affiliate that released *1916* and *March Or Die*] was, 'cause they hired all these bands and then fired them all, right? Including Bonham. We went up to the label one day, and it was empty. All the staff had been fired except the secretary. That was it. That was all. It was major.

O: ***Did they at least make sure you got the money that was coming to you?***

LK: They paid us the advance. That's the thing, you see: They do that, then they include that with the IRS, and then they get it back from the record sales. Double-whammy. It's a license to print money, I suppose.

O: ***Do they still have the old catalog in print right now?***

LK: No, I think they sold it all, like the others did. Compilations coming. Wait for the next glossy box set. CMC actually shipped the first album, *Sacrifice*, before we signed. That is unheard-of nowadays, anybody having faith in the bands they sign like that. I'd go to bat for them any time. They've been great to us. I used to think it was hopeless. I used to think we were bloody doomed.

O: ***What precipitated your move from England to L.A.?***

LK: Well, I figured 44 years was long enough to live anywhere. Like, as Bill Clinton once so succinctly put it, it's time for a change, right? If you're English, you watched all these shows on TV all your life, and three-quarters of them are set in L.A. Then we went to play over here, and... It's the palm trees, you know? The palm trees are exotic to an Englishman. We have small, stunted bushes all pushed over one way with the wind and drizzle. It's quite a revelation when you come to California or Arizona or somewhere like that for the first time. It's sort of like living in Disneyland. It's great, but a lot nicer before they brought this no-smoking thing in.

"We worship 19-year-old women. We used to do it from afar, but we're getting a lot closer now. Almost caught one last week. Then, hopefully, later on, they worship us."

O: ***Are you still a smoker?***

LK: Oh, yeah. I go in there and smoke anyway. I don't care. My picture's on the wall in the bar. I've been going there since 1973. Throw my ass out for smoking a cigarette. Go on. It's not logical. Also, it's grossly one-sided. When we had the power, we always gave them no-smoking areas. Now we don't get any. The first thing you want after you buy a drink is a cigarette. The thing is, they haven't banned automobiles. [Coughs.] People are sitting at the sidewalk café on Sunset Strip doggedly not smoking three feet from the traffic, breathing in exhaust fumes. It seems like clowns to me. If you ban automobiles, I'll give up smoking.

O: ***Do you have any other drug of choice at this point, or is it just cigarettes and whiskey?***

LK: We don't talk about drugs anymore. We've already been hoisted by our own petard on a few of them. Kind of too controversial being in Motörhead, you know. We have four kinds of Starbucks coffee on the road. A lot of lemon cream slices, but that's about it.

O: ***What would the typical Motörhead rider contain?***

LK: A couple of bottles of bourbon, a bottle of vodka, a bottle of tequila. Bunch of Cokes. Bunch of beer. Bunch of cheese platters, you know. All that stuff. Two goats, a donkey, three *Playboy* bunnies (retired), and one *Playboy* bunny (current).

O: ***Do you usually write songs by starting out with the music?***

LK: Well, we're always panicked, because we're always under the hammer. We're very lazy in rehearsing. We pretend to rehearse, then we go to the studio, and we're trapped at the console with the producer glaring and people looking at their watches going, "Oh, we'd better order some more time." I wrote three different sets of lyrics for "Don't Lie To Me." I wrote four different sets of lyrics for "Joy Of Labour." I just couldn't get a couple of them to sound right, and I got 'em in the end. It's one of the best albums we've made, I think. We don't do much filler.

O: ***Leave the double-disc sets to The Smashing Pumpkins.***

LK: Good old Smashing Pumpkins. They've had their problems, haven't they? That was a shame, that guy. [Touring keyboardist Jonathan Melvoin died of a heroin overdose while on tour with the band. —ed.] It's always a shame. People won't listen to you. You tell them about heroin, and they won't listen. I hate preaching about it, because that's what it becomes, you know? I've seen a few people go under, including my girlfriend and a lot of my best friends. You try to tell people that, and they don't get it. They think they're the ones that discovered it for the first time. Part of the fascination is the ritual. A lot of rituals attached to heroin.

O: ***Do you guys have any tour rituals before you go out?***

LK: Yeah, we worship 19-year-old women. We used to do it from afar, but we're getting a lot closer now. Almost caught one last week. Then, hopefully, later on, they worship us.

O: ***Do you find that when you're on the road, the Motörhead fan base is staying young?***

LK: It's taking them longer to pick it up. It's difficult to get them to concentrate. The attention span is getting shorter, what with the MTV catastrophe. We just do the best we can. We do get a lot more young people than most bands our age do, because we came into the punk thing. I think we'll always be in a funny way linked with punk.

O: ***Would you consider Motörhead to have been a punk band?***

LK: If we had short hair, we would be a punk band, wouldn't we? We do mostly short songs that hit you in the face and run away. I always thought we had a lot in common with The Damned. We didn't know what we were doing, and we'd take our clothes off a lot, like [The Damned bassist] Captain Sensible. Only we didn't do it onstage.

O: ***You have a strong musician fan base. Any hard-rock band, and many punk bands, certainly owe a debt to Motörhead.***

LK: Yeah, Metallica really did it right. They came down to my birthday party and played there all dressed like me, with wigs on and bullet belts and black shoes and trousers. And they had the tattoo drawn on the wrong arm. They played 45 minutes of Motörhead songs, which is excellent of them. They interrupted their new album to come down at their own expense and do it. It's the best thing anyone ever did for me.

O: ***How did you come across the Motörhead way of delivery?***

LK: I just look up in the air, you know? That way, if the room is empty, I don't have to look at it, and if it's full, I don't have to look at all them ugly guys. I just hit the bass very hard and shout me head off. But we do good songs, and we haven't had any trouble. I play like hell on wheels, and I'm good at what I do.

O: ***At 25, did you think you'd still be rocking at 50?***

LK: God, no. I mean, I didn't think I was going to live past 35. When you're 25, everybody's old. You think, "My God, this guy is 35? He's ancient! He must be gonna die soon. He can't possibly last long." Then you get to 35, and then, God help you, you get to 40, and you think, "I don't want to stop playing." Why should I? Actually, I'm getting better. A lot of the bands carrying on don't get better. A lot of them are just doing it because it's all they know how to do.

O: ***What do you think is the future of Motörhead?***

LK: The future? Man, I'm not a swami fortune teller. I can't tell. All I know is I ain't going to give it up yet. We have enough success to keep doing it. We can make a living, so it's fine with me. I'm enjoying meself. ⌀

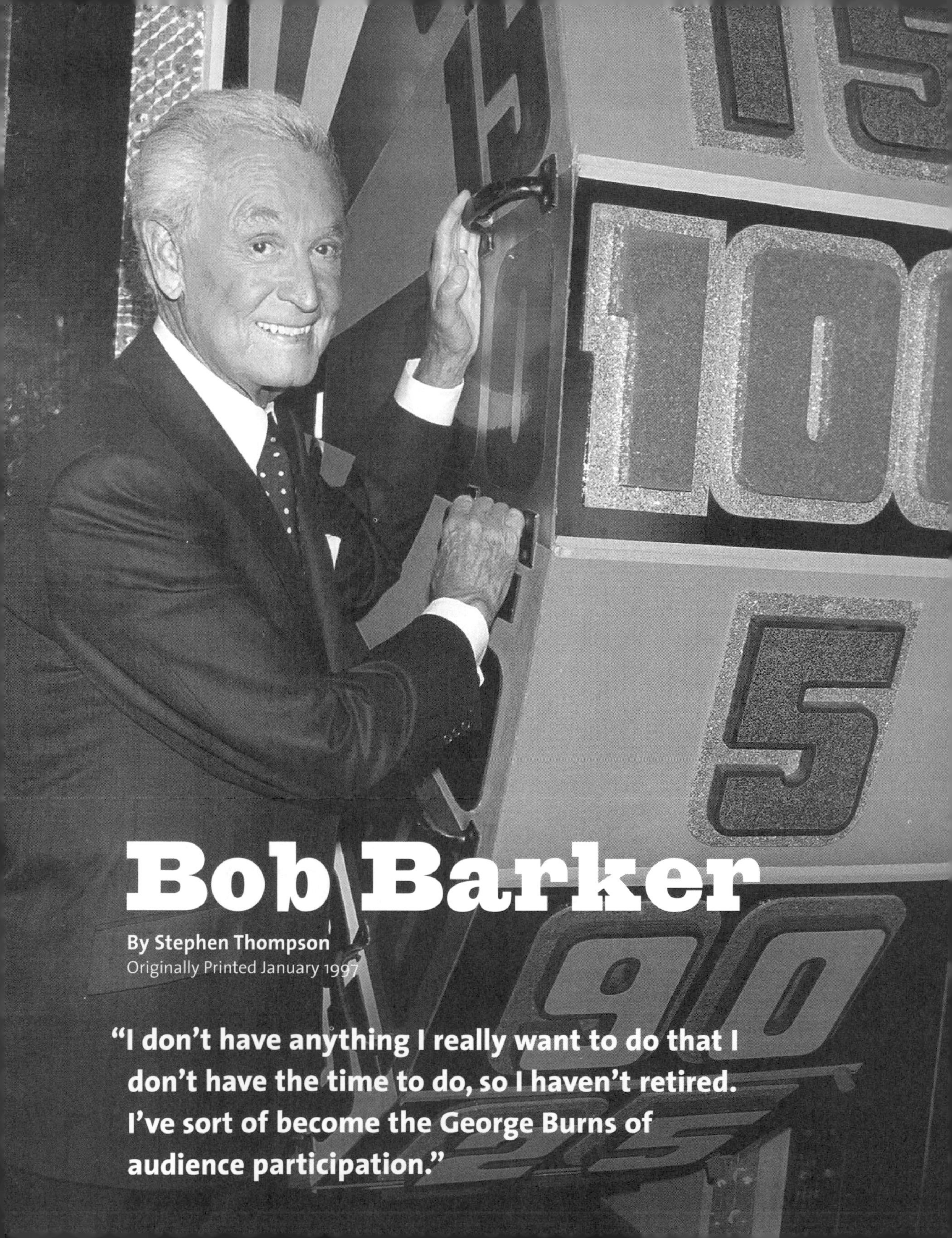

Bob Barker

By Stephen Thompson
Originally Printed January 1997

"I don't have anything I really want to do that I don't have the time to do, so I haven't retired. I've sort of become the George Burns of audience participation."

The Price Is Right has been a staple of American popular culture for decades, and Bob Barker has been the face of the venerable game show throughout its existence. Even before the show's 1972 debut, he was a household name, having served as host of the long-running Truth Or Consequences *for nearly two decades, and he's logged more hours on network television than anyone else in history. Barker has also branched out into movie acting (having turned in a memorable cameo in Adam Sandler's* Happy Gilmore*), and he's spent decades publicly campaigning for animal rights. In a 1997 interview, Barker spoke to* The Onion A.V. Club *about audience-inflicted injuries, his budding acting career, and why vegetarianism is the way to go.*

The Onion: ***How does someone get on* The Price Is Right*?***

Bob Barker: Well, all of our contestants are taken right out of the audience; it's the only show that does that. All the other shows preselect their contestants. One of our producers goes out and talks with everyone in the line while they're waiting to come into the studio. And then he comes in and talks to his assistants, and they decide who they think will be the most fun. And they choose the contestants from the people to whom he has talked. But these people are not told. They don't know they're going to be on until Rod Roddy says, "Mary Jones, come on down!" And that's how we get the spontaneous reactions. Now, we don't have a list of qualifications: He's looking for people who are fun, who are in a good mood. You know, sometimes someone is worried about something, and they're not as much fun as they might be another day, or they don't feel well, or what have you. And our contestants can be tall, short, fat, thin, old, young—we have all colors, all religions, and we have them from all over the United States. You know, the United States is a melting pot, and we want *The Price Is Right* to reflect that.

O: ***Do you ever have them screen out the people who might be too much fun, and might hurt you?***

BB: No, no. No, I take my chances, and have the bruises to prove it.

O: ***I remember you used to get a lot of Samoans up there...***

BB: I had another Samoan in Contestants' Row just the other day, a Samoan man, but he didn't win his way up onstage. But he was there with a group of Samoans, and there were some Samoan women among them, and had one of them gotten up onstage, I think I would have locked myself in my dressing room. [Laughs.]

O: ***What are some of the worst injuries you've ever sustained on the show?***

BB: Oh, they step on my feet, they kick me, they hit me. Women stand beside me and say, "Oh, I'm so nervous," and they give these little pinches on my arm that bruise. They really

"The United States is a melting pot, and we want *The Price Is Right* to reflect that."

hurt. I had one who was about five feet, four inches tall get under my chin and jump up and down. I think that was my most painful one. It's a dangerous job, and it's a wonder I've survived as long as I have.

O: ***Are you genuinely excited when someone wins a car?***

BB: Oh, yes. I'm delighted. I like to have them win. We've had shows where we didn't have any winners at all—and they were a lot of fun because of the people—but I love to see them win, of course.

O: ***Do you ever get to a point with a contestant where you just want to say, "Well, obviously the breath mints are cheaper than the cleanser, dumbass"?***

BB: No, I don't. For one reason, I don't know myself. I'm a terrible shopper, so I would not have the knowledge to feel that way about it. And I wouldn't, I don't think, if I did know, because it's a lot easier at home. When you're at home, you think, "Oh my gosh, that bid is too high," or "Oh, no, you should bid higher than that." You've got it all figured out, but when you get there, and there are lights, and there's the crowd, and there's the excitement, sometimes it gets a little tougher. In fact, many contestants mention that. I've suggested to many of them that maybe they should go home and call it in. And another thing: Maybe you watch the show a lot, and you think you know a lot of the prices, and you're looking forward to being on this show. And then, lo and behold, we bring out something you've never seen before. We have shoppers out deliberately looking for things that are new and different, because we want to keep people interested.

O: ***I was wondering about that, because you've been doing this show for 25 years, and you do know a lot of the games.***

BB: Well, and the people who come to the show know the games. There are people who fool around with the Internet who are *Price Is Right* aficionados, and it is amazing what they know about the show—the nuances, the little things about it that you would not expect viewers to pick up on. They don't miss a thing. I wear a ring on the ring finger of my left hand, and one time, because some soap got under it or something, I got a little rash and didn't wear it for a few shows. I got mail: "Where's Bob Barker's ring? What happened to Bob's ring?" They pick up on everything, which is very flattering, really.

O: ***You have a dedicated fan base.***

BB: We have a fan base now, we can hope, of all ages. And our demographics on the show reflect that. I had a contestant the other day who was 91 years old. We have young mothers tell us that their 2-year-old children like *The Price Is Right*, probably because of the excitement and the music and the jumping around and the running and everything. And, of course, we have a cult following at colleges and universities. Some of them actually schedule their classes so they can watch *The Price Is Right*, and they have it on at lunch in their cafeteria or wherever it is they're eating. They love the show, and they come to the show in groups when we're taping during breaks. And I don't just mean University of Southern California or UCLA or Pepperdine or schools around here; I mean the Ivy League schools and all over the Midwest and the South. We have groups of three, four, or even more come to the show. And when there are basketball teams or swimming teams or softball teams in town, often they'll come as groups.

O: ***How did you feel about* The New Price Is Right*?***

BB: Well, I was very disappointed in it. Our people were not associated with the show, nor was I. They wanted me to do that show, and I didn't want to do it five nights a week. I think a full hour five days a week and a half hour five nights a week is a little too much *Price Is Right*. And if I had done it, it would have been an awful lot of Bob Barker, too. I'd like to do *The Price Is Right* once a week at nighttime, for the full hour. But when I didn't do it, they got a whole different group, and they didn't consult with us about how to do the show. They took some of the games and made little changes here and there, and they tried to make it look nighttime and high-tech. And they destroyed the humanity of the show. Our show is a people show, and you'd never know it to watch that nighttime show.

O: ***Yeah, it was pretty pathetic.***

BB: No, no, it really was. The best thing about it is that it was not around long.

O: ***And [host] Doug Davidson is back on* The Young & The Restless *where he belongs.***

BB: That's right. [Laughs.] He seems like a real nice fella. I was on *Family Feud*: Our *Price Is Right* team played *The Young & The Restless* and, I might add, we destroyed them. But I was impressed with Doug's sense of humor and his general demeanor. I thought that he would possibly be a very good host. But it was not the right framework for him.

O: ***Having to be Bob Barker probably didn't help.***

BB: Well, you can't be Bob Barker. You can't be Art Linkletter. You can't be Ralph Edwards. You've got to go out and be yourself. And when you start trying to be someone else, you make a big mistake. If you start that, you're going to end up with a catastrophe.

O: ***What's Rod Roddy like?***

BB: Oh, he's fun. He's a lot of fun. He fit in from the moment he... Well, even during the audition, he fit in immediately. Some of the best announcers in Hollywood wanted that job, and we auditioned them. We had them work on the show for a week, and the moment we had Rod on the show, I said, "This is the guy." His sense of humor, and his interplay with me when I talk with him, and his little bits in the showcases: All of it just went well, and is still going well, and he's developed a loyal following of his own, too. He's a nice guy.

O: ***You've started to branch out into acting.***

BB: Well, it all came about quite accidentally. As a matter of fact, [my appearance in] *Happy Gilmore* was a direct result of *The Price Is Right*. It seems that Adam Sandler, fine young man that he is, had watched *The Price Is Right* ever since he was a kid. And when he started writing the picture, and they had this scene, he immediately put in Bob Barker. They didn't even consider anybody else. So they got in touch with my agent, and I said, "Well, I'm interested, but I want to see the script first." Keep in mind that for the last 20 years plus, I

"I was on *Family Feud*: Our *Price Is Right* team played *The Young & The Restless* and, I might add, we destroyed them."

have been doing karate, working out. I started with Chuck Norris for seven or eight years—and, of course, Chuck beat me up. Then, when Chuck got into pictures, I started working with Pat Johnson, who is one of the best-known choreographers of fight scenes and stunts here in Hollywood—and, of course, Pat beat me up. So I had not won a fight, and I'd been beaten up for 20 years. And when I saw the script, and I saw that I won the fight [with Sandler], I said, "I don't care what the money is. I want the role. Yes, I want to win the fight." So I did that picture, and I was delighted and surprised by the reaction to it, particularly among young people. I get letters about that picture to this day.

O: ***Are you pondering retirement at all?***

BB: Not really. I know that all things come to an end, but I still enjoy doing the show, and I've worked my entire life. I started doing shows of this type when I was in college. I got a job at a radio station, and at that time, every station large and small had a studio where they originated a certain amount of their own programming. I started out writing local news, and I did a sportscast. Then I was a staff announcer and a disc jockey. My wife heard the first audience-participation show I ever did, and she said, "Barker, this is what you should do. You do this better than you've ever done anything else." She didn't say I was good; she said I did it better than I've ever done anything else. And so, as early as that, she and I set out—now, this was before television—to get me a national radio show. So it's been my life doing radio, and then television. I still enjoy doing it, and I don't have anything I really want to do that I don't have the time to do, so I haven't retired. I've sort of become the George Burns of audience participation.

"I'm sure that every one of us has some things about him which are less than attractive. But the last thing in the world I would try to do is list them for you in an interview."

O: ***What is your life like outside of* The Price Is Right*?***

BB: Oh, I like to travel, but I don't. I like to read. I like to lie in the sun, which I'm doing right now. I excel at lying around in the sun doing nothing. I like to work out and stay in shape. I just enjoy the same things that every growing boy enjoys. [Laughs.]

O: ***Why should I become a vegetarian?***

BB: Well, in my case, I became a vegetarian out of concern for animals. It wasn't long after I became a vegetarian that I understood why so many people are becoming vegetarians—out of concern for their health. I immediately began to be able to control my weight much easier. I felt better. I had more energy. I think that if I were not a vegetarian, I probably would not be working now. It's really made a difference in my life. I've been a vegetarian for 17 or 18 years, and meat is repulsive to me now. Over a period of time, it becomes repulsive. I recommend it as a lifestyle, I really do, because the more you read, the more you find that eating meat is just not good for us. Beef sales are down, people have turned to fish and fowl—and, of course, fish and fowl are not good for you, either. The streams are so polluted that the fish are dangerous, and the things they do at these factory farms... The chickens there, you shouldn't eat a bite of it. And I think that, over time, there will be more vegetarians. I don't expect the world to be vegetarian in my lifetime, but I wouldn't be surprised to see it become more vegetarian in the not-too-distant future.

O: ***Tell me about your dark side.***

BB: My dark side?

O: ***We all see lovable Bob Barker on the television set. There's got to be the anti–Bob Barker who gets up in the morning and says, "You know, I don't want people to win on my show, and these people are idiots, and I don't want them to win some jukebox that's just going to be a big tax burden anyway." Do you ever wake up and feel like that?***

BB: Well, I've never felt those emotions, no. But I'm sure that I have many faults, and I'm sure that every one of us has some things about him which are less than attractive. But the last thing in the world I would try to do is list them for you in an interview. You'll just have to watch the show and figure it out. [Laughs.]

O: ***I just figured, why sidestep the issue? I thought maybe you'd just admit it.***

BB: Just flat-out ask the old man. See how senile he really is.

O: ***I thought the sun might be getting to you.***

BB: Yeah. When I was a kid, I was always in the sun. My wife loved the sun. We didn't know about sunblocks in those days, and they didn't talk about skin cancer. It was a misspent youth, I suppose, but in any event, my mother used to see me with Dorothy Jo, my wife, and she'd say, "Barker, you're going to addle your brain." I'm sure I'd have more brain cells had I stayed out of the sun. ⌀

For more information on Barker's work with animals, contact the DJ&T Foundation at www.djtfoundation.org.

“I did say, at a certain point, that I’m going to make my living by making people laugh, and part of that is shitting yourself.”

Andy Richter

By Stephen Thompson
Originally Printed May 2001

When Andy Richter started out as the co-host/sidekick on NBC's risky fledgling talk show Late Night With Conan O'Brien *in 1993, he was derided by critics as ballast—or, worse yet, an embarrassment. When he left the show seven years later, many of those critics wondered aloud how the show would maintain its greatness without him. Richter followed his departure from* Late Night *by appearing in movies ranging from Robert Altman's* Dr. T & The Women *to* Scary Movie 2 *to smaller, intriguing projects like the* Mr. Show *movie (*Run, Ronnie, Run*) and Louis C.K.'s Chris Rock–produced* Pootie Tang. *He even found his way back to network television, starring in the Fox sitcom* Andy Richter Controls The Universe *for Fox. After completing the show's pilot in 2001, Richter spoke to* The Onion A.V. Club *about his claim to fame, his crippling depression, and the embarrassment of shirtlessness on* Just Shoot Me.

The Onion: ***What do you want to talk about?***

Andy Richter: I don't know. Maybe questions that don't have anything to do with me. Those are always good. Just the stuff that isn't like, "Who was your favorite guest on the *Conan* show?" Or, "Did it bother you to not win staring contests?" Because I used to do college dates, and I actually had to stop doing them because it was just... David Sedaris, in one of his books, has a great thing about how, when you work in front of the public, you really want to view people as unique, special, and rare unto themselves. But, then, the more time you spend, the more you realize everyone's the fucking same. I used to do these college dates. I'd go and make a month's rent in one night, so it was kind of hard to say no, but I had to stop doing them because it got so sad, like, people in the Q&A part going, "Are you ever gonna win a staring contest? Ha ha ha!" And it's not their fault. That's, I guess, a relatively clever question if you're a fan of the show, but after the 10th time, it started to make me feel really sad. When I started, I thought, "I'll talk about the show, but I'll also try to throw in my personal take on my journey through show business." A lot of people basically do a one-sided interview. So I did that, and I found out more and more that, as I did it, nobody gave a shit what I thought. They just wanted to know, "Who's the Masturbating Bear? Who's in that? Who came up with that?" That was always another question: "Who came up with the Masturbating Bear?" Where do you go from that?

O: ***So now you do movies.***

AR: Yeah. It looks really good. I hired a publicist when I decided to leave the *Conan* show, which is a first. There was an NBC publicist who was very nice and very good to me and would get me lots of opportunities for stuff, but I didn't have my own. Now, I have my own publicist, so whenever I form a nicely rounded turd, they have to put something in the paper about it. I think by next month, there's going to be seven movies coming out that I'm in, but some of them are kind of a hiccup and you'll miss me. Still, it looks great in *Variety*.

O: ***Is there any discussion of a starring role, your own vehicle?***

AR: Yeah, there's been discussion about it. I know enough to not believe anything until there's a car waiting outside to take me to wherever it is. But there's been talk of it. I think it'll work, but I also have been kind of leery of jumping right into doing some shitty, retarded comedy that they just slap together with two guys who got fired from *Frasier* or something. I don't mind that the movies I've been doing have been small roles, because I'm interested in a career as a character actor. I'm glad that there's a feeling of an organic kind of growth and not just leaving the *Conan* show to go right into *Deuce Bigalow 2*. I'm excited to be in the *Mr. Show* movie. It's a really small part, but I'm excited to just be a part of that. Working with Barry Sonnenfeld [on *Big Trouble*] was really fun, too. I'm interested to see that. It's all been pretty fun. It's a weird thing, though, because... well, first of all, I'm a miserable fuck. I don't quite have the mechanical apparatus in my brain to actually enjoy anything.

O: ***Spoken like a true comedy professional.***

AR: It's been really fun, in a sense, to do all these movies, but with the good things in my life, I feel like, "Yeah, that's good, whatever. But what about these shitty things? What are we going to do about those, gentlemen?" It's a sickness that I try to change, especially now that I have a child. I don't want to create a miserable child. I'd like to have a child with the capacity for joy. But the thing about movies is, I realize now that the things that I've kind of... There are things from the *Conan* show that I didn't expect to miss. There's comfort in the consistency of working on the same thing. It's exciting to be in all these different movies, but it isn't that fun. It's a hotel room, and nothing is sadder than a hotel room. I have found, too, that movie sets, especially if they're not in L.A. or New York, are a hotbed of alcoholism. I did a movie in Florida, did a couple of weeks on it, and all the people had already been there. They're very nice people, but when I got there, there was this feeling of, "We've gone everywhere and tried everything that you could possibly want to do, and we've decided the best thing to do is go to the hotel bar and get bombed every single night. If you try and experiment and go and see the town, you're a fool." You work all day and get back to the hotel, and you don't want to look at those four walls or the TV, so you go to the hotel bar and juice it up. I don't worry about being an alcoholic or anything. It's just that I'm depressive, and it's like, "Oh, God, this is a load of laughs." Also, I'm still trying to plug away in television, which, in terms of my dream come true, isn't really... My dream is to be Peter Sellers, except without the borderline personality disorder. To be him, or to be, I don't care, Charles Durning or Ned Beatty. Just to be a character actor that works in movies for a long time and does good stuff.

O: ***You wouldn't flame out that way.***

AR: I hope not. There's always that possibility. I still think there's something for me to do that would be beneficial for me, both artistically and professionally. I'm going to keep plugging away at TV, in part because it keeps you in one place. Another thing from the *Conan* show is the freedom that we had, which wasn't because the people in charge trusted our artistic choices, but because they didn't give a fuck about it. It was the farm report to them, and it didn't matter what we did. I didn't realize how much I would miss that. With the pilot I'm working on, I've actually had, compared to some of the stories I hear, a really smooth ride. There weren't people who came in and said, "Hello, this is another person who can tell you what to do on your show." We didn't have that on the *Conan* show. One guy would watch in Burbank, if he happened to be in his office while we were rehearsing. He might call and say, "Don't let the priest fuck rabbits." But that was about it.

O: ***You talked about things you miss about being on* Late Night. *Do you miss the media referring to you as "a second banana with appeal"?***

AR: Oh, Jesus Christ, no. That second-banana shit. There's never any first banana. Where are the first bananas? "Today, President George W. Bush, the first banana of the nation..." There's a lot of shit in comedy that's par for the course, and you just have to take it. I did a guest shot on *Just Shoot Me* that has aired twice now. In it, I play a motivational speaker, and I didn't even realize... My wife said she read somebody online saying it was a rip-off of Chris Farley's motivational speaker, which didn't even fucking occur to me. I was like, "Oh, Jesus Christ." I just showed up and they paid me well, and I did what they told me to. In the script, I'm a recovering alcoholic, and then something that Laura San Giacomo's character says to me sends me off the deep end. I go on a bender and show up and tear off my shirt and drop my pants and run through in my underwear. I read that when the script first came, and I realized, "Oh, no, this is not considered, like, a Richter chestnut. This guy's gonna take off, and you can't get him in a show without having him take off his clothes." I took off my clothes a couple times on *Conan*, but the only reason I did was because, well, most of the time it was motivated. There were a couple of times it might have happened out of sheer comedy-writer laziness, and then me being weak and going, "Well, all right. If we don't have anything else, I guess I'll resort to that prop humor." Reading that script, I thought, "I don't want to fucking take off my clothes." But they bought me for this period of time, this is what they want, and there's no sense in fighting it. If I'd said, "I don't want to do that," it'd be like, "Well, you've done it before." But there's something inherently demeaning about it. If they'd hired

"It's exciting to be in all these different movies, but it isn't that fun. It's a hotel room, and nothing is sadder than a hotel room."

Rob Lowe to do a guest bit in the same part, and had him get drunk and tear off his clothes, the reaction wouldn't be comedy, because his is the kind of body that you'd want to see naked. The comedy inherent in me taking my clothes off is, "He should be ashamed of his body, but look at him! Look at fatty go!" Lest they think I'm not knee-deep in shame at all times, I'm not. I just have the ability to put it on hold for a laugh. That's another thing that's kind of irritating. You're a clown in a lot of ways. I did say, at a certain point, that I'm going to make my living by making people laugh, and part of that is shitting yourself.

O: ***What do you really think of Conan O'Brien? He seems like a huge asshole.***

AR: [Laughs.] Nice try. No, I think he's a brilliant man. He's a brilliant, brilliant man who I hope doesn't become as fucked-up as other talk-show hosts. Because there's something about that job that seems to make people weird. There's a part of doing that job that really makes him happy and is very fulfilling, but then I think that that fulfillment seems more substantial than it actually is. I said something once in an article, and he told me he found it very chilling: I said that having met David Hasselhoff 18 times is not going to keep the ghosts away when you're lying in a nursing-home bed. I still kind of feel the same way. But he's happy doing it. I just was by there. I was just talking to somebody about how glad I was to see him, and they were asking if I miss doing the show in front of the audience. I was like, "Hell, no. I don't miss performing for tourists, most of whom are mad that we're not Rosie. I don't miss that at all. They're despots, those studio-audience people." And Conan was saying, "I still love it. I still love dancing like a monkey in front of people who came in on a bus." He really, truly is a rare mind. He has a wonderful comedic mind.

O: ***He said that we should ask you about your homecoming crown.***

AR: Oh. Yeah, I was homecoming... No, it wasn't homecoming, it was prom. I was prom king. Which is actually saying I was the sixth most popular, because the five who were on homecoming were automatically disqualified from prom. Of course I have to look at it that way. It was really sort of touching to be nominated. To be king of anything is really great. Not a lot of people get to do that. But when they put the crown on me, it didn't fit my head, which isn't unusual because I have some sort of disorder that makes my head the size of a pumpkin. I looked inside the crown, and it was just a ricotta-cheese tub. They'd put velvet and fake jewels and white fur and dots of black on it with a marker so it'd look like ermine around it.

O: ***Are you the only person in comedy history who was popular in high school?***

AR: No, I don't think so. I don't think so.

O: ***People in comedy always say they were tortured geeks in high school, whether they were or not. It's almost reversed when you're an adult: You don't want to have been popular in high school.***

AR: I don't know what their problem is. It just doesn't occur to me to lie about that. There's plenty of stuff I lie about, but not that. I mean, I was always kind of funny, and people always tended to like me. I've always tried to be nice to people, so that sort of translates into popularity, I guess. It's not like my virulent virginity, which I could not get rid of, was a testament that I wasn't popular, or at least popular in the way I wanted to be. Also, my folks would let people drink at our house. That was a big key to it, too.

O: ***You set a record for the most money ever won on* Celebrity Jeopardy.**

AR: No, I didn't, actually. I think I was third. Some guy from *The Nanny* is first, and then Jerry Orbach is above me.

O: ***Does that make you smart, or are celebrities as a rule dumb?***

AR: Well, I refer to *Celebrity Jeopardy* as the short-bus *Jeopardy*, because it is a lot easier. Like, there was a whole column basically naming stores in New York.

O: ***Did you get to keep the money, or did you have to give it to some charity?***

AR: No, I gave it to the Southern Poverty Law Center. That's the deal. But you do get Sony merchandise. Someone had told me beforehand that they give you a catalog and you pick, I think it was $10,000 of Sony merchandise. You just pick out of the catalog whatever you want.

O: ***Is that whether you win or lose?***

AR: That's whether you win or lose—everybody gets that—so I was all amped up for that, like, "All right!" I love gadgets, and it's just like, "Sure, we could use another huge TV." But then I found out going into it... I think it was Jon Stewart who told me that now they send you a prize package, and that we were the first class of *Celebrity Jeopardy* people they did that with. It was still an incredibly generous package of stuff, but I was so... This is how fucking petty I am: I was outraged because I didn't get the thing that I wanted, and also because a lot of what they gave me was duplicates. It was the exact same TV I had, and then a DVD player... I had already spent way too much money on home electronics, so I wanted to be able to get more things that I didn't need, not the same things that I don't need and already had. I was so incensed that I went onto the web site and added up the retail prices of the things they gave me, and it was about $8,000 or so, and I was saying to my wife, "Can you believe it? Not even 10 grand." And she's like, "Calm down. This isn't very attractive, the way you're behaving."

O: ***How has having a baby affected your life?***

AR: It really has made me a lot happier. I'm not as miserable as I'm making myself out to be, but I do have... This is one of the things that's so great about *The Sopranos*: That guy understands depression. There are so many things there where you feel like, "Yes, exactly!" And one of the things is when Tony Soprano says, "My mother made it so that I have the inability to experience joy." I don't mean to say that my mother did that to me, but I understand that. There are times when I feel like, "Here I am on a beautiful beach, and look at that sunset, and what a great day it's been. Hmm... I don't know. I'm still not being carried away on a cloud of ecstasy." At the picnic, I don't look at the sky and see the clouds; I'm worried about the ants. Having the baby in my life has given me real palpable joy on a daily basis. A few times a day, I get the feeling of real joy, which is absolutely unbelievable and in some ways really transformative, and has completely shifted my priorities to where I don't... I want to do well with my career, but I don't really give a shit. I want to facilitate having a wonderful life with my family, and I happen to have stumbled on a racket in which there seems to be a relatively short line between the two points of where I am now and mad money. I don't want to do shit, and I'm not gonna do shit, but it definitely takes the edge off feeling like I've got to constantly be doing fulfilling work that's important, and I can't drop my pants and run across the set of *Just Shoot Me*. Absolutely I can. Ø

Vanilla Ice

By Stephen Thompson
Originally Printed May 1998

"Yes, we sold 15 million records and made a movie, but I was talked into a lot of things, like writing a slow song and wearing baggy pants."

Vanilla Ice's ubiquitous 1990 single "Ice Ice Baby" was the first rap song to top the pop charts, and his breakthrough album, To The Extreme, *sold more than 15 million copies worldwide. That success led to a movie deal (*Cool As Ice *came out in 1991), an appearance in Madonna's 1992* Sex *book, and a backlash the likes of which only come along once or twice in a decade. Critics and rappers assailed him, saying he falsified his biography (which played up a life on the streets inconsistent with the white Dallas suburb where he grew up) and co-opted and trivialized a black art form, capitalizing on white-friendly rap that couldn't be further from the genre's roots. Of course, the end was swift and brutal: His movie—a cheesy rebel-outlaw story that might as well have been made 40 years ago on another planet—barely lasted a week in theaters. His 1994 sophomore album, the gangsta-leaning, pot-celebrating* Mind Blowin', *didn't crack* Billboard's *Top 200 Albums chart. But in 1998, Vanilla Ice, whose real name is Rob Van Winkle, mounted a modestly successful comeback tour, selling out midsize venues across the country. During that tour, Van Winkle spoke to* The Onion A.V. Club *about drugs, posing nude with Madonna, being menaced by Death Row Records' Suge Knight, finding God, and reinventing himself.*

The Onion: *Is Vanilla Ice a character you're playing, or is that really you?*
Rob Van Winkle: Well, I mean, that's me, but I respond to Ice, Vanilla, Rob... Most people just call me Rob, but Vanilla Ice has been with me so long—since my breakdancing days—that I still respond to it.
O: *How many records have you sold?*
RV: Of every record that I've made? Over 20 million.
O: *And how many did* To The Extreme *sell?*
RV: Uh, 15 million of it. [Laughs.]
O: *I know you're doing a grassroots thing now. How do you feel about the idea of recapturing that mega-fame?*
RV: Well, for me, I hope it doesn't happen like that, because it wasn't what I expected anyway, in the beginning. With the mega-fame came the mega-downfall—you know, with the press and everything—and at a young age, it was very stressful to me. I never really got to enjoy the fame part of it, you know? I guess I kept my head on. I don't walk around like my shit don't stink. I race motorcycles and stuff. I don't walk around with bodyguards, and I

have a real recognizable face. Everywhere I go, people know me, and it seems like everybody trips out on the fact that I don't think I'm better than anybody else, or anything like that. You know how celebrities can be. I don't even mix with that crowd, man. That's not even me. I had tremendous success, but at the same time, it was being taken away. So I guess I stayed on the same level, you know? It's kind of paying off now, because what I'm doing now kind of fits that whole format anyway. I look out at my crowd, and I see a bunch of body-piercings and tattooed people going crazy, you know? That's basically the crowd I'm catering to. I guess they were the crowd that was in high school when "Ice Ice Baby" was big. I turned a lot of people in white America—and not just white America, but middle-class America—into hip-hoppers, you know? That hip-hop influence has carried over into some different rock bands and stuff, like Rage Against The Machine. Now you have rap mixed with the rock.

O: ***You have a tattoo of "A New Leaf" on your stomach. What does that represent?***

RV: Well, I turned over a new leaf about three years ago. Back in the early days, in 1990, with the success and having all my fame given to me and taken away at the same time... It was very stressful to me, and I turned to drugs as an escape route. It's one of my regrets, but at least I can say it with a smile on my face, because something good has come out of it, and that's the fact that I've found God. I found myself on the floor with an overdose one night; my friend was dumping buckets of cold water over me, trying to keep me alive. He thought I was dead, because I overdosed really bad. I woke up the next morning and realized that God had given me a second chance to live, but He said, basically, "If you fuck this one up, that's it." So I made a promise to God, right then and there, that I would never turn around and go back to those days. It's really, really strange, but God has been blessing me tremendously for the past three years—like, instantly, you know? I've got a beautiful wife and a baby girl who's seven months old, and things just couldn't be better for me right now. The past nine months, we've been going around, and all the concerts have been sold out. It's been off-the-hook.

O: ***How has the spiritual awakening changed your music?***

RV: Well, I'm not a preacher or anything. I'm a Christian, but I don't believe in religion or anything like that. I'm not a preacher: I do my music, and I still smoke a little green bud, but I don't do any other drugs or anything like that. I thank God for that. As far as my music goes, my music is still hardcore. It's going to be a shock for people to see me like this, because it's definitely a swing to a different side of what you'd expect. We're not traveling with a band right now, just my DJ [Zero] and Rod J and guys that have been with me forever. The show is just so tremendously different; it's like, every time we leave, the words everyone is saying are, like, "God, he shocked the shit out of me. It's not what I expected. It's awesome." That's really fueled me to keep going and doing what I'm doing now, and that's making this new record.

O: ***Is it true that you were in a grunge band?***

RV: Yeah, yeah. I still have it. It's called Picking Scabz. [Laughs.] They're pretty rough, man. I've been into this mosh-pit, stage-diving scene for about the past five years. It sounds tight. I play the guitar, drums, keyboards.

O: ***You used to just get slammed in the media.***

RV: Well, I was one of the only white kids doing what I did, coming up in hip-hop, in an all-black market. I think that had I been black, a lot of the criticism would never even have taken place, you know? But I probably wouldn't have had as much success, either. One hand washes the other. You never know what could have happened; all we know is what happened. They were enjoying taking punches at me, but you know what? I rolled with the punches, and I learned from them, and that's where I'm at right now. You know, no strings, just live and learn, and prosper from it.

O: ***I just saw your movie again. What did you think of all that?***

RV: Well, back in the day, man, I was manipulated a lot. My main thing is music, but back then, I was talked into a lot of different things. It's all in how you look at it, if you really want to look at it as being a success or not: Yes, we sold 15 million records and made a movie, but I was talked into a lot of things, like writing a slow song and wearing baggy pants and crossing over to this teen market, and doing the movie, and doing these little dolls and pins, and just making a novelty out of me, basically. It was my manager trying to suck any kind of dollar figure he could out of any type of market. I really didn't intend for that to happen, you know? I grew up playing black clubs and stuff like that, and I never even played a white club. I played the Stop The Violence Tour as an opening act for Ice-T and Stetsasonic and Sir Mix-A-Lot. Some people know I went out with Hammer and stuff like that, but I had a small record out on Ichiban [*Hooked*, which was remixed and released as *To The Extreme* on a bigger label], so I paid my dues. A lot of people think I was an overnight success, but I was an opening act for three or four years, and then I signed my contract with EMI. Then it kind of blew up overnight.

O: ***What happened with Suge Knight?***

RV: Ah, Suge Knight... Basically, he started Death Row Records with the money he got from me back in the day. He took some points off my record, *To The Extreme*. He more or less forced me into that.

O: ***Was he like a manager?***

RV: No, no. I didn't even know the guy. He just came with some papers one day and said, "Sign this," and kind of bullied around my bodyguards, and showed me that we were on the twentysomethingth floor, and that I'd better... I figured it out. I figured out his whole game, you know? He knew where I was at all times, and he wanted to show me that he knew where I was at all times. He showed up at restaurants. He showed up backstage at *The Arsenio Hall Show*, telling me, "All these people pay. If you want to live in my city, you gotta pay!" I was living in L.A., and I paid, I guess. But I'm still alive. I didn't go to the police, nothing like that. I didn't get any lawyers, or none of that stuff. A lot of people don't associate me with gangsta rap, but that is what sparked it off, in a roundabout way. [Laughs.] Death Row Records. Ain't that a trip?

O: ***What was the deal with Madonna? You were in her*** **Sex** ***book...***

RV: Well, like I said, there's a lot of things I regret, and that's definitely one of them. What happened with that was really strange, because we were kind of seeing each other at the time, and I just went over to her house on the beach. We were hangin' out by the pool, and all of a sudden she says, "We've got some guys coming over, and they're going to take some pictures. You don't mind, do you?" And I said, "No, not really. It's no big deal, I guess." I wasn't going out with her to look for any public awareness of it, or anything like that. And next thing you know, these guys are over there taking pictures, and she's taking her clothes off and saying, "Take your shirt off. Let's take some cool shots." And I'm just like, "Whatever." I'm going along with it, not thinking it's going to be any big deal. I didn't even sign consent or do anything saying she could use pictures of me. I haven't sued her or done any of that stuff, but... Next thing I know, I see this big-ass fucking book come out with a metal jacket on it, and it's like this big deal, you know? I don't know, man, it just kind of threw me into this slutty package, and I didn't feel like I wanted to be a part of it. That's one of the regrets, you know?

O: ***How did your new wife respond to that?***

RV: Uh... Not a good subject. [Laughs.] Not at all.

"I'm more belligerently enthusiastic and enthusiastically belligerent than I've ever been."

David Lee Roth

By Keith Phipps

Originally Printed June 2002

*When David Lee Roth calls himself "a song-and-dance man," it's not so much false modesty as truth in advertising from a man who sees nothing wrong with the job. As the frontman for Van Halen, he brought James Brown–like showmanship to hard rock, and fans responded to the mixture of Eddie Van Halen's guitar heroics and Roth's joyous, acrobatic frontman work. Unlike many titans of '70s rock, Van Halen thrived in the early days of MTV, thanks to colorful videos (largely orchestrated by Roth) and the integration of keyboards into its sound. But after the mammoth success of 1984, Roth released a solo EP that made him an MTV star in his own right, and deepened his schism with the rest of the band. Replaced by Sammy Hagar, Roth launched a solo career. Initial success in the '80s gave way to commercial indifference in the '90s, but Roth has still kept busy. After a highly publicized aborted reunion with a post-Hagar Van Halen in 1996, Roth released an entertaining autobiography (*Crazy From The Heat*) and restarted his music career as the head of DLR Band. Another frustrated reunion with Van Halen (following the group's split with its third lead singer, Gary Cherone) came to nothing. Roth's most recent work can be found on* No Holds Bar-B-Que, *a bizarre, self-directed video collection of musical performances, Osama bin Laden–hunting fantasy sequences, pirates, dwarves, and martial arts. Still awaiting commercial release, the video may be the most direct expression yet of Roth's odd inner world. Shortly before embarking on a tour with Hagar, in which he alternated sets with his old rival, Roth spoke to* The Onion A.V. Club *about staying energetic, rock 'n' roll rivalries, and his current reading list.*

The Onion: *If* Behind The Music *is to be believed, rock stars either mellow or die as they get older. You're not dead, so have you mellowed at all?*

David Lee Roth: I'm full of more rage at the planet around me. I'm more exuberantly, enthusiastically pissed off. I'm more belligerently enthusiastic and enthusiastically belligerent than I've ever been. I was born in Indiana with a banjo on my knee, and I think you're pretty well formatted by the time you're 12 years old; consequently, I'm a book-reader, I revere contact sports and history, both classic and popular, and I participate in these things constantly. You know, in the Bible it doesn't say, "Waddle forth and calcify." That sounds like a legal firm! [Laughs.] What happens is, I think, most musicians complete their long journey to the middle because the forces that conspire against you—your agent, your manager, the rhythm section—whatever it is, it's weary, and you've got to constantly reinvest your enthusiasm for livin' large, Marge, so large you need a barge! And whether it's Dr. Seuss or Sartre, you've got to deal with both. You mix it all in the bucket, whatever you do as an artist—and I'm a song-and-dance man, I'm show-people—and you don't know how it's gonna come out, but you've just gotta continually reinvest. And I do. Not a moment of my day isn't accounted for in some way. Don't get me wrong: Doing nothing means a lot to me, you've gotta average that in, and all work and no play makes for alarmingly predictable lyrics.

O: ***How do you stay fresh, then?***

DLR: My schedule changes according to the context. Obviously, when we're on the road, I own a Keith Richards Merit Badge and wear it proudly—you know, my hours reverse and it's a nocturnal existence. Great, bring it on, turn on the lights, camera, action. Here we go. A hard day's night. I'm talking to you here from the Mojo Dojo, which is my house in Pasadena, and I call it that because I started my first martial-arts lesson on my 12th birthday up here at the Buddhist temple on Raymond Avenue in Pasadena. To this day, Monday, Wednesday, and Friday at 7 in the morning, I train in Brazilian jujitsu, and then at 8:15, my Portuguese teacher comes over. She just left, and it's my last lesson before we go out on the tour. Two nights a week, I have a kendo instructor come here, who's in his 60s, and I have a kendo hall that I built in my house here. I take Spanish lessons twice a week, I read a book a week, I subscribe to 40 or 50 magazines a month, and there's never a lack of... "Okay, what community are we interested in this week? What are we gonna have for dinner? Let me count the ways." And on and on. I think very frequently, musicians become a victim of the very song they sing. I like all kinds of recreation. It's aggressive. I want to be part of everything. I'm not Scarface, but I'll just narrow it down. I want everything in New York and L.A.

O: ***In between is optional, I take it?***

DLR: Yes. There is a constancy of people and lifestyles and attitudes here. You can only be really flagrant and consistently colorful by disciplining the shit out of yourself. That make sense? New young artists say, "Why should I learn music? That's gonna be restricting. That's somebody else's rules." I tell them, "You gotta learn the alphabet, backwards and forwards. And then the choice is yours, 'cause last I looked, the Bible is written in the same words, the exact same alphabet, as my favorite pornography. Choice is yours."

O: ***How did this tour with Sammy Hagar come about?***

DLR: Let's do something unpredictable and yet patently obvious, once you hear about it. Go flip on CNN: What's more poignant than the word "unity"? And if two warring superguys—I'm an action figure—can actually make it happen for any length of time, then it's maybe some kind of action-figure metaphor. I don't think so. I think it's a lifestyle. I think there's an attitude and a point of view that transcends a list of songs, and I got more songs... I got more hits than Beethoven. And my music is familiar as Sears and Roebuck. It's as familiar as channel four on the TV set. Van Halen music when I was the quarterback, songs like "California Girls" and "Just A Gigolo" and so forth, are about young and impulsive. It goes way, way, way beyond just a cavalcade of tunes. And I think there are a handful of artists who have that specific lifestyle going well. You know, Jimmy Buffett, Grateful Dead, the Stones have it.

O: ***Where it's more than just music, but a way of life.***

DLR: Yes. It's a confirmation of sorts.

O: ***You were never sparing in your criticism of Van Halen after you left the band. Did any of that come back to haunt you when you befriended Sammy Hagar?***

DLR: Uh oh, did I hurt somebody's feelings?
O: ***I don't know, you tell me.***
DLR: There's no more rivalry backstage here than you would see... I don't know where. You know, you talk about the brawling rivalries in rock bands. The most I've ever seen is some open-hand slapping followed by tears, and then an elaborate great feeling followed by a commemorative T-shirt. We're not fist fighters by nature. The point here is music. The point here is show. The point here is something other than sports. I've always attached elements of the sporting credo, but I am not a football player or a fist fighter, and my intention when I go after somebody is purely antagonistic. I'm not a bully. Like, in this interview, I'm not gonna make fun of the Van Halens. I understand they're not doing too well medically and spiritually, so I'm not gonna beat up on them. I only wanna beat up on somebody my size or bigger, for entertainment value. I think you see the difference.
O: ***Do you have an opinion of [Hagar's signature brand of alcohol] Cabo Wabo Tequila? Have you tried it?***
DLR: I myself drink Jack Daniel's. I found it curious that Sam has had his club [in Cabo San Lucas, Mexico] for a decade and a half and he doesn't speak any Spanish at all.
O: ***So you have to translate for him?***
DLR: I have to translate that maybe there's a better kind of tequila. [Laughs.]
O: ***There's that rivalry again.***
DLR: Oh, of course there's a rivalry. Come on, if you got a hair on your ass, there's somebody across town that you're competing with. It might just be the jagoff in the computer terminal next to you, but you're competing! When vanity and rivalry disappear, all the lines go out of your stomach and you slow down and coast to a stop in the middle.
O: ***How did your video,* No Holds Bar-B-Que, *come about?***
DLR: A variety of ingredients, I think probably that you'd recognize instantly. Fritz Lang's *Metropolis*, Soupy Sales, Groucho, Kurosawa, Hugh Hefner, and on and on and on. But I've woven it together in a form that I think is much more appropriate for our national attention-deficit syndrome, or whatever it is we're having. As in, "Too hip, gotta go, golly, look at the time. Gotta go change the air in my tires, love to hang, bye."
O: ***Yeah, you don't really rest on one image for very long in that one.***
DLR: No, not at all. You're not interested. In this, you're entertained right along with your current state of biorhythms, which is frenzied. If you watch television and listen to radio regularly, if you spend any time at the local shopping mall, then your inner tempo is frenzied.

"I am the king of crosswalks around the world. I am the boss of public parks and mini-malls around the world. People will stop, literally, between the two white lines, and the first thing they're gonna do is that smile. The wraparound smile, babe... Are you smiling now?"

At least in the United States. And I tried to create a different type of television—it's not really a show and it's not really a biography. There's a lot of show-and-tell in there. I'm not really sure what it is. Perhaps that makes it pure. Like Picasso said, it's bound to go over some people's heads, so I created a version with a director's commentary. That'll come out on the DVD. You know, we're gonna sell it on the nation's highways and byways and at the shows and so forth, and the director's commentary certainly explains the impetus, the inspiration for each of the scenes. You know, I wrote and directed it, designed the costumes, and on and on and on. I don't know if it's gonna clarify for you what it is you're seeing, but it's even more entertaining with the commentary.

O: ***There's a lot of dance and electronic influences in some of the music. Is that a new direction for you?***

DLR: No. I was on the floor of Studio 54 probably a hundred times. I went to schools just up the street here, to the first high school in the United States to receive integrational busing. I went to junior high and high schools that were 95 percent black and Spanish-speaking. I can gang-sign the whole alphabet, I speak fluent Spanish and Portuguese, and as far as electronica and whatever, you hear in the background here what we're listening to. That's Timo Maas, the German kid who's doing the wheels of steel. Do I know how to dance? Oye! Miro! [Laughs.] And so, from there, I have a fascination for south of the border, anything rhythmic. Disco was solidly sent for me. I am a dancer by trade. So, you know, old-school Evelyn "Champagne" King and Candi Staton—tell me about that. I love imitating James Brown. [Yells.] I'm a black man trapped in a Jewish body, Keith, help me, baby! [Laughs.] So the logical leap is to electronica and the ProTools world, with big great computers and the bad boys who drive them. I listen to the stuff by weight. But I'm particularly good for hip-hop, trance, goth, electronica, Chemical Brothers, whatever you call that. Lots and lots of soundtracks, things like *Swordfish* and so forth. As well as south of the border, now that Brazil has caught up with digital sampling and the whole digital world.

"When vanity and rivalry disappear, all the lines go out of your stomach and you slow down and coast to a stop in the middle."

O: ***In the '90s, your type of music seemed to be eclipsed by something more dour. Do you feel that's swinging back the other way now?***

DLR: Well, self-tragedy is always a great way to dramatize yourself—ask any teenager. There's a better way to accomplish things than despondent oh-woe-is-me, but oh-woe-is-me gets you a seat on the cross-town bus faster than humor will, even good humor. If you want a cross-town bus seat, all you have to do is walk up to anybody and go, "Hey, man, kids are fuckin' dying!" They'll give you the seat. Try getting that same seat with five minutes of comedy. Try getting that same seat with general conversancy. Consequently, drama will probably take the precedent eye of the tribe. What has the most pathos? What is the most sincere and severe? That's what we generally give our prizes to. But it was Charlie Chaplin who built Hollywood.

O: ***When you left Van Halen, you planned to direct a movie, and that didn't happen. But did you ever consider acting in other people's movies?***

DLR: Not to any noticeable degree. You know, I entertain the same vision of, if Jack Nicholson calls me, desperate—"Dave, you gotta come down"—of course I would. Just like you would.

O: ***You're a natural for the camera.***

DLR: I'm a natural behind the camera. Perhaps you're beginning to discern that my attentions are more toward behind the scenes, more toward creating, producing, and directing what's going on here. It was a large part of what I did in Van Halen, and it's a large part of the resentment that they feel toward me. It's what I do here. When you look at the David Lee Roth *No Holds Bar-B-Que*, I'm not in a lot of that stuff. I'm not in a lot of the scenes. And if you saw the outtake footage, I'm probably not in two-thirds of it, because I was directing. I was working on the lighting, I was working on the recording, and so on. Which surprises people frequently, because we have the archetypic vision of a singer desperate to be in front of the camera at all times, as Madonna is perhaps accused of being. I spent so much of my time wearing the different hats and sunglasses: "Hey! Now we're a record producer. Hey! Now we're a video director. Hey! Now we're in the online bag. Hey! Now I'm a colorist." When I finally do pop in front of the lens, I'm glad and relieved to be there. In front of the camera and in front of the lens, there's no lawsuits, there's no agent, and there's most frequently no time limits. Do you follow my reasoning? And there's a longevity that's kind of built into it. I spend most of my time behind the scenes, and when it is time to perform, I'm genuinely delighted to do it.

O: ***The first draft of your autobiography was reportedly something like 1,200 or 1,500 pages long. Is that true?***

DLR: It is. The other half of it is sitting in my kitchen as we speak.

O: ***Will you publish that someday?***

DLR: Absolutely. A large part of going away is coming back, as Mark Twain said. It's no good unless you can show them a picture and tell them about it.

O: ***Any choice stories that you regretted having to cut from the first draft?***

DLR: Nothing off the top of my head. I think it's a continuum. It's not so much a series of accomplishments—good, bad, or in the middle—as it is the attitude maintained throughout. And I think that's what tickles people's fancy more than anything. Not a day goes by when somebody doesn't say to me, "You're that white guy," and then tries to imitate me right where they stand. I am the king of crosswalks around the world. I am the boss of public parks and mini-malls around the world. People will stop, literally, between the two white lines, and the first thing they're gonna do is that smile. The wraparound smile, babe... Are you smiling now?

O: ***Do you still enjoy touring?***

DLR: I love it. For many different reasons than why I ultimately signed up for this gig, obviously. What's the old expression, "Hell is in the eyes of others"? We look for ourselves for the first half of the game, by virtue of applause or selling tickets, or achievement through the support of others. But I do believe that if you make it past a certain point in time, you'll develop an inner resource of confidence, and by the time you get to the end of the daily race, if somebody stole the time clock in your race to the finish line, you don't need it. You know you ran good.

O: ***And you're at that point now?***

DLR: Yes. And I am enthusiastic for the road for other reasons. You know, I obviously have an intense fascination with music and performance. I'm dealing from a myriad of sources and inspirations and resources for my stagecraft. It's everything from *Seven Samurai* to Charlie Chaplin. It's everything from the Scarecrow from *Wizard Of Oz* to Led Zeppelin. [Laughs.] And it always has been, but why build it unless you're gonna fly it? Let's get airborne!

O: ***What are you reading these days?***

DLR: Right now, first thing in the morning, *The Art Of Worldly Wisdom*, by Baltasar Gracián, and that's just short little paragraphs—too-hip, gotta-go philosophy—but really, really practical. In the afternoon, I read *Shadow Warriors*. It's the new Tom Clancy book about the Special Forces. And in the evening, I'm working my way through an Andrew Vachss book called *Safe House*. You know, sex and violence. [Laughs.] I've always maintained, why do you have to read one book at a time? What is this, grade school? I read like I watch television.

O: ***Going back a bit, when you say you're pissed off, what are you pissed off at?***

DLR: I don't know. [Laughs.] I have rage. I'm probably the last person who should be pissed off at anything, if you could see where I'm standing and what I'm looking at right now. Palatial Wayne Manor, are you kidding? There's a brand-new Benz sitting up in the garage, and probably half a million screaming fans between now and Labor Day. I don't know, maybe I didn't get enough attention from Mommy. ⌀

"I've done a movie and a TV series, and someday I'd like to do a successful movie and a successful TV series. That would be nice."

"Weird Al" Yankovic

By Stephen Thompson

Originally Printed September 2000

When "Weird Al" Yankovic was a teenager submitting primitive pop parodies to Dr. Demento's radio show in the late '70s, few would have guessed that he'd be a venerated star 20-plus years, 10 studio albums, a feature film (1989's UHF*), and a children's television show (CBS's* The Weird Al Show*) later. But he's continued to thrive, selling platinum with 1999's* Running With Scissors *and serving as the subject of a comically tame VH1* Behind The Music *special. (Yankovic's most controversial life choice to date appears to have been his 1996 decision to parody Coolio's "Gangsta's Paradise," not knowing that the rapper hadn't given permission.) While touring to promote* Scissors *in 2000, Yankovic spoke to* The Onion A.V. Club *about the length of his career, the success of his side projects, and his clean-living ways.*

The Onion: ***Do you realize that you're four years away from being eligible for induction into the Rock And Roll Hall Of Fame?***
"Weird Al" Yankovic: No kidding. It crossed my mind a little while ago, but I think my chances are somewhere between Tiffany's and Milli Vanilli's. It would be cool. I just went to the museum for the first time a couple months ago, and I'm in there for, like, one second. They used the "Fat" video in a clip montage, which amounts to some sort of immortality.

O: ***How long do you see yourself doing this?***
AY: Oh, man, that's a tough question, because if you'd asked me 21 years ago, I certainly wouldn't have guessed that I'd still be cranking out songs today. I still love doing it, and I have to assume that the American buying public will let me know when it's time to retire.

O: ***At the same time, careers ebb and flow, and you've had low points where you might have thought it was time to leave. Had you done that, the world might never have known* Off The Deep End.**
AY: [Laughs.] Yeah, I've ebbed and flowed quite a bit, and I'm putting out albums at a much more leisurely pace these days. In the '80s, I was putting out an album virtually every year, I think mostly based on fear—that if I didn't, people would soon forget about me. Now, I've built up enough of a track record that some people will forget about me, but enough people out there are familiar with my body of work that I can wait two or three years and still come back without people going, "Weird Al who?"

O: ***Well, many generations of 12- and 13-year-olds have been indoctrinated. It happens every few albums.***
AY: That's what's really great for my record label. [Laughs.] My catalog gets rediscovered every time I put out an album. Some 12-year-old will pick up a copy of *Running With Scissors* and say, "Wow, this is really great!" And they'll go to the record store: "He's got other albums?!" Some of my most hardcore fans weren't even born when my first album came out.

"Weird Al" Yankovic On "Weird Al" Yankovic

What more can one say about "Weird Al" Yankovic—the man, the myth, the icon—that hasn't already been expounded upon in countless musical journals and pop-culture periodicals? His story is the stuff of legend. Raised in a humble home in Lynwood, California, and armed with that all-important bachelor's degree in architecture, Yankovic burst upon the cultural landscape in the early '80s, and soon the world was thrilling to his irreverent music videos and accordion-fueled ditties. Not content with merely being a sex symbol, Yankovic expanded his influence into every conceivable medium; his curly-haired presence was virtually inescapable as Yankomania swept the planet. With global domination under his belt, Yankovic was able to focus more energy back on his music, raising the bar impossibly high with each successive album release. After 20 years and 10 albums (considerably more, if you count the cheesy compilations), Yankovic continues to ruthlessly dominate the field of accordion-based rock parodies—and God help anyone who stands in his way.

O: ***What are you still looking to accomplish? You've worked in a lot of different media, with a TV show, studio albums, and a movie.***
AY: I don't think there are any new media I'd like to cover. I've done a movie and a TV series, and someday I'd like to do a successful movie and a successful TV series. That would be nice.
O: ***At the same time, those have a strong following.***
AY: That's true. *UHF* was an unqualified bomb when it came out—critics hated it, and it didn't have an impressive box-office opening—but it has gone on to achieve cult status. Among some fans, it's like *Rocky Horror Picture Show*, where they've seen it an insane amount of times and have memorized the dialogue. I wouldn't be surprised if they throw things at the screen while they're watching it.
O: ***Has there been any discussion of a modestly budgeted new movie?***
AY: Um, well, when I get off the road, I'll apply energy toward trying to be involved more in features and television. There are a few things being bandied about as we speak, but nothing I can really talk about. I've done a few cameo appearances in some really nice independent films: Mark Osborne, one of the guys who directed my "Jurassic Park" video, put out an extremely funny movie called *Dropping Out*. I do a little cameo in that. Judy Tenuta's got a movie called *Desperation Boulevard*, which is also very funny, and I've got a small part. After the dust settles from this tour, I would like to get more involved in that sort of thing.
O: ***Is there any dirt on "Weird Al" Yankovic?***
AY: I'm sure there is.
O: **Behind The Music** ***had nothing.***
AY: No, but they tried. They tried to dig up dirt, but there's very little to be had. There are probably a few library fines I haven't paid yet, but I'm a pretty clean-cut guy, overall.
O: ***What sort of stuff did they ask? What was the extent of their reporting?***
AY: It was a fairly long interview. They talked to me for about three hours and talked to my friends and people I've worked with. But as far as digging the dirt...
O: ***I think the extent of what they dug up was***

that* Polka Party *didn't do very well.

AY: Yeah, and the whole Coolio thing got blown out of proportion. So, four years after the fact, every single interview I do, I get, "So, what's this whole Coolio thing?" Ugh. "First of all, it was four years ago, and up until *Behind The Music*, most people had forgotten about it."

O: ***What's the worst thing about being Weird Al? What's bad about the job?***

AY: You don't ever want to listen to pop stars griping about how bad their life is, or about their lack of privacy, or blah blah blah. It's a nice job. It's a good gig. I'm glad I've got it. Sometimes it would be nice to have a switch where I could turn off the recognizability factor when I want to have a quiet dinner somewhere, but there are a lot more perks than downsides. I like what I do. ⌀

"You have to stand by what you did." CHAPTER 9

"I think you have to stand by what you did. One thing I will say: Some turned out better than others, but I did try my best on all of them. I never sloughed a picture."

"I'm trying to get my mind and my soul together. The only way I can do that is to be as honest as I can be, to try to be the best person I can be."

"It's not your average existence, for sure, being on the road since you're 15 and being verbally abused because you were being true to what you did. For playing rock 'n' roll, for chrissakes. I mean, we didn't hurt anybody. We were having a good time."

"Even though I was doing what was considered a B-movie, I thought it was *Gone With The Wind*. I thought it would win an Oscar. I think if you don't approach your work on that level, you won't achieve what you're looking for, whether it's great success or just acknowledgment, because you're half-stepping."

"Mistakes were made, so I learned by my mistakes. I won't make those again. I'll just make new ones, like us all."

"It was just songs that were written on the spot, you know what I mean? They came from the heart when I was with Phil. He was in love with me and I was in love with him, so the lyrics and all that came about with the relationship. That's what's so natural, and that's why I think those songs lasted, because they were so innocent and real."

"I made a lot of money, and I ended up buying myself an office where there were women. And I would always come on like a steam engine, telling them that they would all be stars. Lying through my teeth. It also gave me an opportunity to get a lot of pussy. That was really worthwhile."

"*Mr. Show* was so great, in that I feel like I finally got to do something really pure."

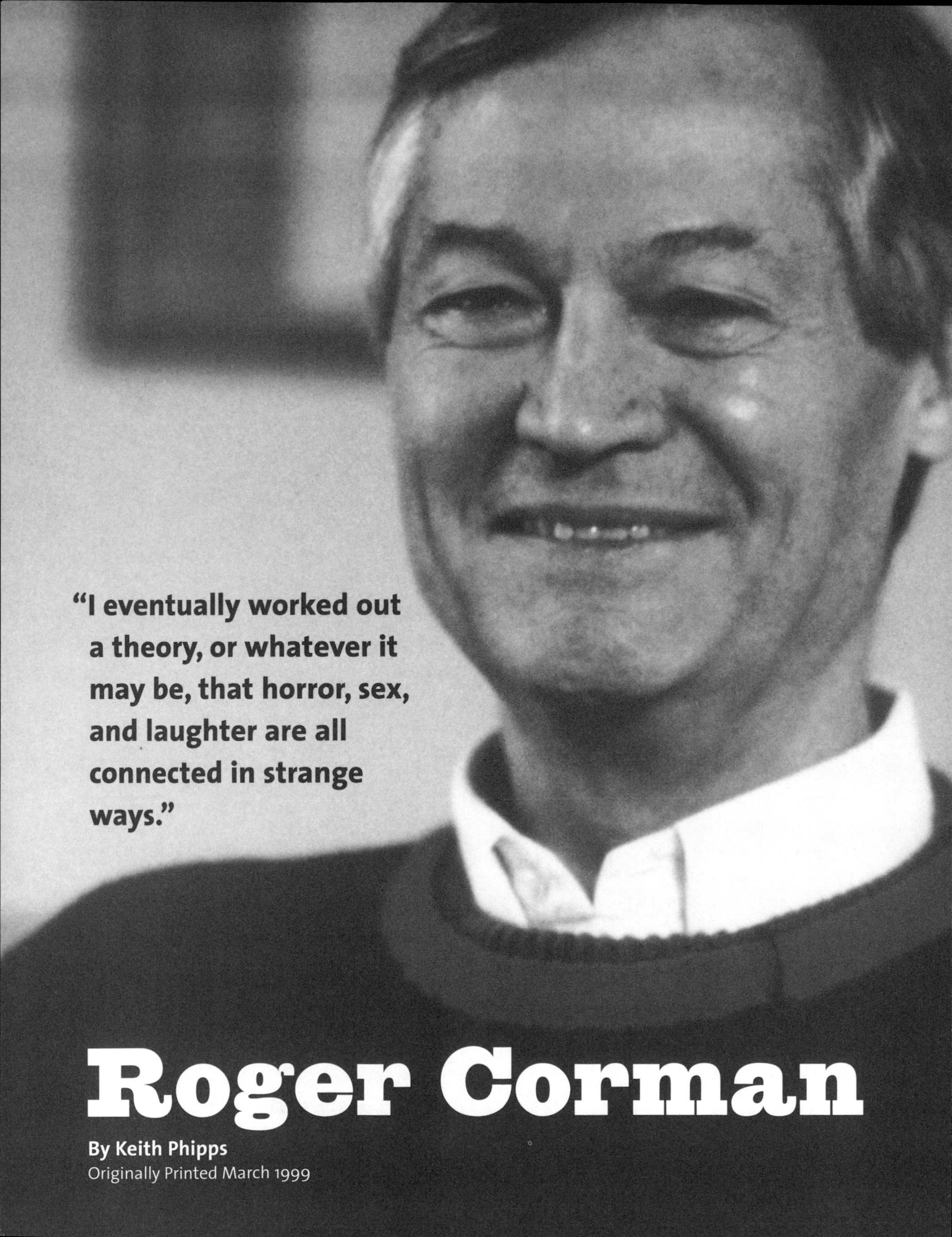

"I eventually worked out a theory, or whatever it may be, that horror, sex, and laughter are all connected in strange ways."

Roger Corman

By Keith Phipps

Originally Printed March 1999

To his eternal credit, Roger Corman started small and stayed that way. As a director and producer, Corman has been responsible for more than 400 films, almost all of them low-budget and many produced at breakneck speed with meager resources. His most notable titles include the original Little Shop Of Horrors *(which is famous for having been shot in two days),* Bucket Of Blood, The Intruder, *eight movies based on the works of Edgar Allan Poe,* The Trip, The Wild Angels *(a biker film, starring Peter Fonda, which anticipated* Easy Rider*), and a number of gangster movies, including* Bloody Mama, *which starred Robert De Niro. Corman also helped launch the careers of Francis Ford Coppola, Martin Scorsese, Jonathan Demme, Jack Nicholson, Peter Bogdanovich, James Cameron, Ron Howard, Joe Dante, and John Sayles, among others, and he stands out for his commitment to releasing worthwhile foreign movies and hiring female filmmakers, who typically couldn't get in on the ground floor anywhere else. In the early '70s, Corman mostly retired from directing and focused on producing films for New World, a studio that made some of the 1970s' most enjoyable B-movies, including* Death Race 2000, Rock 'N' Roll High School, Caged Heat, Big Bad Mama, Piranha, TNT Jackson, *and a number of films involving oversexed nurses. After selling New World in the early '80s and founding Concorde/New Horizons, Corman maintained his prolificacy, which he discussed, along with his past, in this 1999 interview with* The Onion A.V. Club.

The Onion: ***It's daunting to figure out where to start talking about your career, but your work does break down into distinct periods by decade. Are you proudest of any one period of your directing and producing work?***

Roger Corman: Probably the '60s. I started in the mid-'50s or late '50s, and I figure I'm most proud of the beginning of all that, when I was just sort of learning the process. I directed my last film in 1970, so I'd say for about 10 years from '60 to '70.

O: ***You've spoken before of making sure your films had a certain amount of political content. Do you feel that's also the period when you were the most political?***

RC: Probably, because at the beginning of that decade, I did a picture called *The Intruder* with a young actor, Bill Shatner, about racial integration in the American South. It won a couple of film festivals, got great reviews, and was the first film I made that lost money. I closed the decade doing pictures such as *The Wild Angels* (1966) and *The Trip* (1967), and a couple of other pictures which represented to a certain extent the counterculture and the changes going on in the late '60s.

O: ***What went into deciding to make* The Trip*?***

RC: Two reasons: One was that *The Wild Angels* with Peter Fonda, the first of the Hells Angels/biker films, was the biggest success AIP ever had. I'd done it about a year earlier, and it went to the Venice Film Festival and so forth. AIP asked me to do something else with

"They determined that a feature called *Roger Corman's Frankenstein* could be very successful, so they asked me if I wanted to do it. And I said, 'As a matter of fact, I don't want to do it. There are so many Frankenstein pictures out there. This would be something like the 50th Frankenstein picture, and nobody will care.' "

Peter that was contemporary, and both Peter and I were involved—he more than I—in the counterculture movement at that time. I had the idea of using the LSD experience and the counterculture movement within Hollywood as a metaphor, as it were, for what was going on in the '60s throughout the country.

O: ***Is there anything from the 400-plus movies you produced that you would not do now—or that you'd want to take back?***

RC: Not really. Some of them I'm less pleased with than others. But essentially, I think you have to stand by what you did. One thing I will say: Some turned out better than others, but I did try my best on all of them. I never sloughed a picture.

O: ***Do you object to the terms "exploitation films" and "B-movies"?***

RC: I don't object to the term "exploitation" in any way. That's what they were called, and I accept the word. B-movies, classically, meant the second half of a double bill of pictures that were made in the '30s to bring the audiences in during the Depression and give them two pictures for the price of one. So, from a technical standpoint, I never made a B-movie in my life. However, today the term "B-movie" is applied to low-budget films, so on that basis, I guess I did make B-movies.

O: ***In the '70s, exploitation films had more freedom in terms of the amount of sex and violence they could show. Do you feel that ultimately hurt exploitation films?***

RC: I think ours did not. I think some of the slasher films got overly bloody, and they really pushed beyond... I don't want to use the words "good taste." As a matter of fact, I once had a story conference where I said, "I don't want anybody to use the words 'good taste' around here." So I definitely don't want to use that, but I'd say they pushed beyond reasonable bounds in a number of the slasher films. And I think there was an audience reaction where at first it was welcomed, and then I think the audiences were turned off by them.

O: ***Around the mid-'70s, exploitation films generally stopped being as fun. They just became overwhelmingly about violence, and they lost their cleverness. Would you agree with that?***

RC: Yes. If someone cuts off an arm, someone later has to cut off a leg, and you just have to do more and more and more. You have to top the previous one until you have a screen that's essentially red with blood.

O: ***How do you feel about the state of exploitation films today? It seems as though most of them come out on video now. Do you think they'll eventually find the same audience, just in a different form?***

RC: They will find somewhat the same audience. It's unfortunate that most of these films no longer play in theaters. Occasionally, we will play one in theaters. What's happened is simply the domination of the market by the major studios, with a tremendous amount of money put into the films and an equally tremendous amount of money into advertising. We really can't compete.

O: ***What's the last movie you did that had a wide release?***

RC: We didn't have a wide release, but we came out the week before *Jurassic Park* with *Carnosaur.* And then we had an English semi-science-fiction film called *Shopping* a couple of years ago that had a reasonably wide release.

O: ***Do you see a connection between the decline of theatrical release for exploitation films and the decline of theatrical release for foreign and arthouse films in general?***

RC: Yes, I think. They're two completely different genres—although we participated in both ends of it—but they're both being hurt by the tremendous power of the majors.

O: ***Does the current indie scene excite you, or do you feel that the ease of making films has hurt their quality? The reason I ask is that your studios used to, and still do, function as an unofficial grad school for filmmakers.***

RC: I think what we do is good and we still do it. We very seldom will take someone directly out of film school and say, "You are a director." Generally, that person will work for us as an editor, sometimes a cameraman, and sometimes a second-unit director, so they get at least some practical professional experience before they move on to directing.

O: ***What about the crop of filmmakers who just jump right into making their own films independently?***

RC: I think it's very good. If you have the ability to do it, it's a wonderful thing to do. I think very few people, however, are really capable of coming straight out of film school and directing a feature. I think it's desirable to have at least a year or so—or, if you're really good, at least six months—of playing in the minor leagues before moving to the majors.

O: ***What made you decide to come out of retirement and direct*** **Frankenstein Unbound** ***in 1990?***

RC: Money. Universal had done some sort of market research, and they determined that a feature called *Roger Corman's Frankenstein* could be very successful, so they asked me if I wanted to do it. And I said, "As a matter of fact, I don't want to do it. There are so many

"I would go back now, at my age, only with something I really wanted passionately to do. And, at this moment, I don't have any such project. However, I could have one tomorrow morning, or just after I hang up the phone."

Frankenstein pictures out there. This would be something like the 50th Frankenstein picture, and nobody will care." And they kept calling me every six months or so. And then they kept coming up with serious offers of money, which were higher than I'd ever dreamed of, and I started thinking about it. So I said if I could find a new way to do a Frankenstein picture, I would. And then I remembered Brian Aldiss' novel *Frankenstein Unbound*, which was a new way to do a Frankenstein picture. Based upon the fact that it would at least have something new or original to say, I agreed to do it.

O: ***And nothing has tempted you back to directing since then?***

RC: No. I would go back now, at my age, only with something I really wanted passionately to do. And, at this moment, I don't have any such project. However, I could have one tomorrow morning, or just after I hang up the phone.

O: ***I can't pass up the opportunity to ask you about the making of*** **Bucket Of Blood.**

RC: *Bucket Of Blood* was my first attempt to combine comedy with horror. I had noticed that, in sneak previews and screenings, audiences would very often... I remember one film in particular, where they screamed at exactly the point I wanted them to scream. I thought, "That's perfect." It really worked. And then after they screamed, there was a little bit of laughter, and I thought, "That's not bad laughter. That's appreciative laughter. They understand what is happening and they're sort of laughing and going along with it." And from that I got the idea that horror is connected in some way with laughter, and I eventually worked out a theory, or whatever it may be, that horror, sex, and laughter are all connected in strange ways.

"I think some of the slasher films got overly bloody, and they really pushed beyond... I don't want to use the words 'good taste.' As a matter of fact, I once had a story conference where I said, 'I don't want anybody to use the words "good taste" around here.' "

O: ***How does that apply to some of your other films?***

RC: I thought that the way they're connected is in sort of a graph. In all three of them, you start building a little bit of tension, and you build tension higher and higher and higher, and then you smash that tension. In a horror film, the audience screams; in a comedy, they laugh; and in the sexual act, they obviously reach a climax. I thought, "This curve applies in all three, and there are some connections." So, first with *Bucket Of Blood* and then with *Little Shop Of Horrors*, and then with a third picture that wasn't seen that much called *Creature From The Haunted Sea*, I deliberately went for both comedy and horror. And also with *The Raven*, one of the Edgar Allan Poe pictures.

O: ***That's a favorite of mine, if only for the great cast.***

RC: That was very interesting, because I had three actors who were entirely different. Boris Karloff had been trained on the stage, for the stage, in a classical English way of acting. Peter Lorre had come out of the Bertolt Brecht/modified Stanislavsky improvisational school in Berlin. And Vincent Price had a little bit of both. It was amazing working with all three of them. Vincent could modify and work with Peter, but it drove Boris crazy. Boris was a good guy. He tried his best and he did a good job, but it was a major problem for him.

O: ***What you were talking about with comedy and horror would seem to make Vincent Price an ideal star for you. He can be very scary, but there's an over-the-top quality to his acting and his presence that makes him comic, as well. You did eight films with him, so you must have enjoyed working with him.***

RC: I enjoyed working with Vincent on every film. He was my first choice for *The Fall Of The House Of Usher* of everyone I could have. Obviously, I wasn't going to get the greatest stars. We didn't have that. But of everybody in the category we could look to, he was the clear and obvious first choice. I was delighted when he accepted. We worked together well on all of them because he was a very good actor, he was very intelligent, and he had that touch of humor that he could bring to it.

O: Rock 'N' Roll High School *was originally supposed to be* Disco High School, *right?*

RC: Right. That was my idea, and, luckily, Allan Arkush came to me and said... I made a deal with Allan to do it, and after he'd been working on it a few days, he came to me and said, "Roger, you can't blow up a high school to disco music. I want Rock 'N' Roll High." And I said, "Well, okay." And then it occurred to me that disco might be, and it turned out it was, a momentary phenomenon, whereas rock 'n' roll went on—not necessarily forever, but so far forever. The idea of the picture was mine, but it was Allan's idea to switch it. That idea was important.

O: ***There's no retirement in sight for you, right?***

RC: No. I have no plans. I would like to slow down a little bit, and I'm trying to give more authority to the people working with me and get less involved in the detailed work. But I have no intention of quitting. Ø

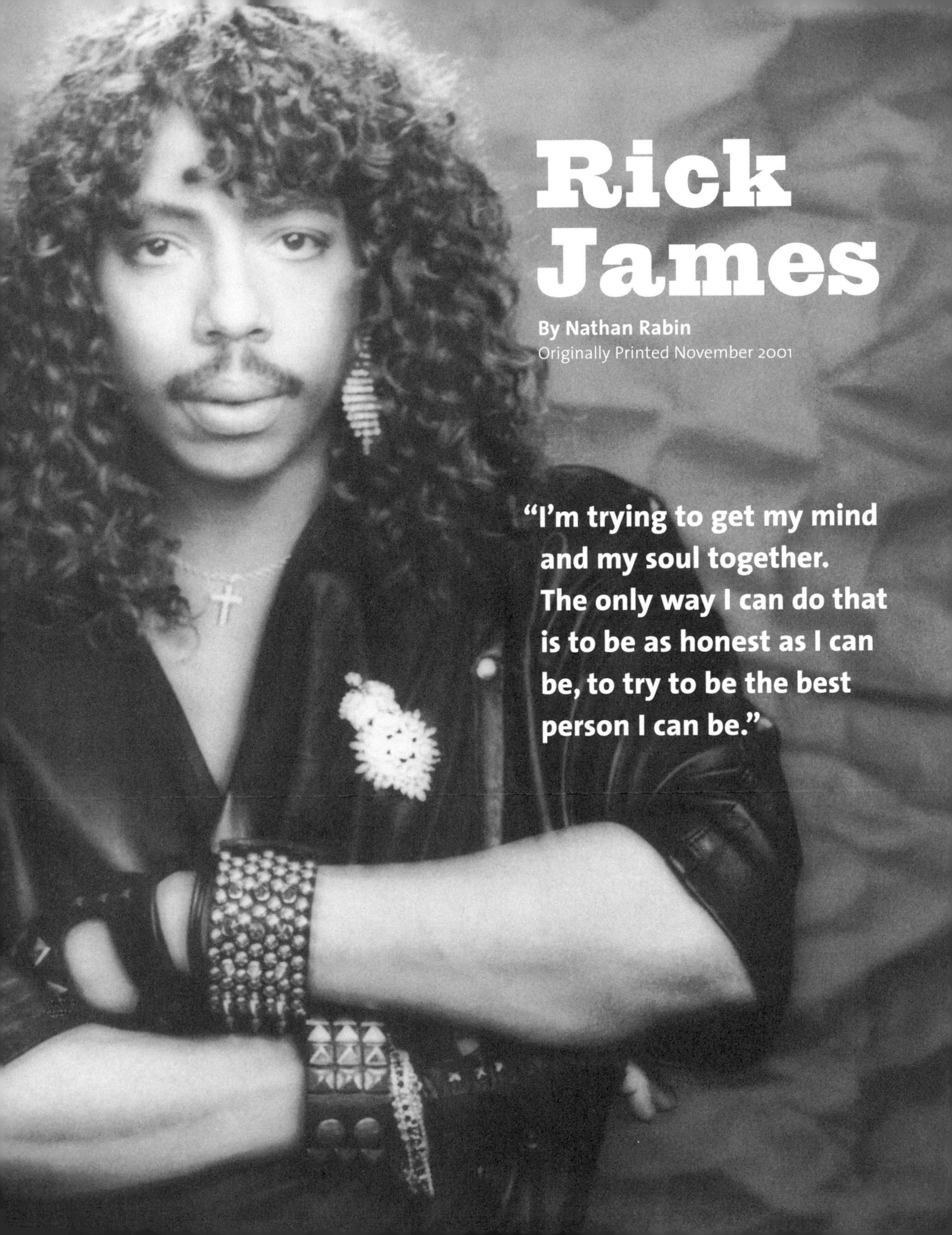

Rick James

By Nathan Rabin

Originally Printed November 2001

"I'm trying to get my mind and my soul together. The only way I can do that is to be as honest as I can be, to try to be the best person I can be."

The nephew of Temptation Melvin Franklin and the son of a numbers runner for the mob, Rick James ran away from home at 15 to join the Naval Reserve, then went AWOL two years later. While fleeing the military police in Toronto during the late '60s, James played in The Mynah Birds with future Buffalo Springfield members Neil Young and Bruce Palmer, but was forced to leave the country before the group could release an album. In 1977, he returned to America and established a reputation as a flamboyant performer and a gifted songwriter, musician, and producer. Throughout the late '70s and early '80s, James racked up a string of hits for Motown, both as a solo artist and as a songwriter, producer, and mentor for the likes of Teena Marie and the Mary Jane Girls. But by the late '80s, James' professional career had begun to take a back seat to his legendarily hedonistic lifestyle and Olympian appetite for self-destruction, and in the '90s, he suffered through the death of his mother, a stroke, and an extended stint at Folsom State Prison for drugs and assault. James has released only one new album in the past 13 years (1997's Urban Rapsody*), but has remained in the public eye through prodigious sampling of his work, the enduring popularity of his signature hit "Super Freak," and a memorable appearance on VH1's* Behind The Music. The Onion A.V. Club *spoke with James in 2001 about his aversion to explicit and sexist language, his notoriety, his friendship with Neil Young, and his appearance on* The A-Team.

The Onion: ***What led you to join the military at such a young age?***

Rick James: I'd quit school, and I was kind of running around doing nothing, smoking a lot of Mary Jane, and hanging out with my friends. I was going to get drafted, but I didn't really want to go into the Army. I was playing conga drums for an African culture group at a place called the African Center in Buffalo. There was a guy there who was teaching us Swahili, and teaching us about our heritage. In one of the classes, they told me that it'd be a good thing to join the Navy Reserve. Then I could stay in Buffalo and play for the African dance troupe, and I wouldn't have to go into the Army. So I joined the Navy Reserve, and much to my dismay, it turned out to be a big farce, because I missed a lot of meetings. That's something that you go to meetings for once every two weeks, or something like that. I can't remember. But they send you a sailor's suit, and the whole shit, right? You actually go to a reserve and have meetings, but you never end up going to the Vietnam War. So that's what I did, but what they didn't tell you was that if you missed meetings, you'd end up going to Vietnam. That's what happened. They were sending me to Brooklyn to wait on a ship, and I went AWOL in Rochester.

O: ***I guess the next step after that was when you joined The Mynah Birds.***

RJ: It was the first group I had in Toronto after going AWOL. I went into this club and started singing, and I ended up joining this band. The group ended up turning into The Mynah Birds, with Neil Young and a couple of guys who started Steppenwolf, Goldy McJohn and Nick St. Nicholas.

"It's like you motherfucking can't do a record without using profanity and motherfucking demeaning your own race. It really just started pissing me off after a while."

O: ***What kind of music did you play?***

RJ: We did blues, we did folk, we did a folk-blues type thing, and we did folk-rock type shit and R&B and country blues and shit. We did a little bit of everything.

O: ***Was that a happy period in your life?***

RJ: Yeah, because it was really innocent. It's like the old song says, "When you don't got nothing, you don't got nothing to lose." I didn't really have anything. I had a little room that I lived in with a bed and a record player. And I had this group, and we were all very happy to be living a very free life. It was in the village in Toronto, so it was a lot like Greenwich Village. Everybody who lived there knew each other, and it was like family.

O: ***Did you feel immersed in the counterculture of the time?***

RJ: Yes, totally. We had great people living there. Great musicians lived in Toronto. Joni Mitchell, she was coming up with us. We were all family. Joni and David Clayton-Thomas, lead singer of Blood, Sweat & Tears. People like that, and Neil, and Jessie Colin Young of The Youngbloods. It was like we were all coming up and learning together.

O: ***What was your relationship with Neil Young like?***

RJ: We had a great relationship. I found him in a coffeehouse playing acoustic guitar and harmonica, doing these songs that he had written, kind of like a Bob Dylan thing. When I came up from New York after seeing a lot of this old folk, I kind of flipped out and said, "Yeah, I want to get a folk artist in the band, someone that plays folk to add on to what we got." So I saw Neil in a coffeehouse playing one night, and I asked, "Would you like to join the band?" We got an apartment together, and he joined the band, and we were together for a couple years. Then I had to give myself up. We signed with Motown, and I had to give myself up to the Navy, because Motown found out I was AWOL, because the manager we got rid of had told them. They found out I was AWOL, and Neil and Bruce [Palmer] sold the equipment and rented a hearse and drove out to California and started Buffalo Springfield, and Goldy and Nick started Steppenwolf. I was in Portsmouth Prison, listening to them on my radio.

O: ***What kind of effect did living in Europe for most of the '70s have on your music?***

RJ: It gave me a sense of independence. It gave me a sense of the whole traveling-minstrel thing. I was over there singing and playing for a living. It was just playing a lot of Europe and traveling all around, learning that culture. I think all those culture-shock ordeals in my life have something to do with who I am now and what I write about, and how I translate it. I have a very fine love for classical music, I have a love for Indian music, sitar. I went to India, lived, and studied. I lived in Sweden and London. So I'm very familiar with Europe and its ways, very familiar with the European culture in Paris, and the French and the English and the Danes and whatnot, and Indian culture.

O: ***Your music has been sampled a lot, and you've collaborated with a lot of rappers. What was your first impression of rap music?***

RJ: Rap? Actually, Grandmaster Flash used to open for us a lot. I love rap. I love what they were doing, because there was a message to it. "The Message" is one of my favorite rap songs of all time. Sugarhill Gang, and all that kind of stuff. I was really into it in the '80s. Then, after it became so ridiculous, where they were talking about black women being bitches and hoes and all this bullshit, I kind of got out of it, out of a thing of enjoying it, and got into an animosity thing against it. But then it switched up again, and rappers became more intelligent about what they were saying and how they were saying it, and I got back into it. Even when they were talking so much smack, degrading black people and stuff, with all this "nigger" this and "nigger" that and "nigger" this... I'm so down on that word that I had trouble relating to it. I didn't want any more rappers fucking with my shit. Me and James Brown came to a thing together, where we didn't want anybody fucking with our shit who is gonna demean black people and shit. We were really pissed off at the time, the way they were translating our shit. Then, I was hearing this record on the radio called "U Can't Touch This," this big rap record. I called my accountants in a rage, telling them, "I thought I told you I don't want any more rappers using my shit." And then they explained to me how much money it was gonna make, and that there was no cuss words or anything in it, and I was happy to hear that. "U Can't Touch This" is the largest-selling rap record of all time, and I'm very proud about that, because it's like bringing back "Super Freak." It was financially lucrative, and it was a good thing, because they didn't degrade black people in it, and didn't get off anything that would be demeaning.

O: ***Was your primary objection to rap music that it's kind of derogatory?***

RJ: I don't like the derogativeness of what a lot of it says and the demeaning fact of how it puts the race. A lot of it, man, seems to be all about how women are hoes and bitches. Number one, my mother's not a ho and not no bitch, and she never was. And I'm sure a lot of them don't want to hear their mamas and sisters called hoes and bitches. I got tired of hearing shit like that. I just got tired of hearing all the ridiculousness. It's like you motherfucking can't do a record without using profanity and motherfucking demeaning your own race. It really just started pissing me off after a while. But I mean, there are a lot of rappers out there that I like and that I listen to. I think rap definitely has its place in the art world. I think it is an art form. But, just like any art form, you can misuse it.

O: ***Your album* Street Songs *just reached its 20th anniversary, and was re-released in a deluxe edition. Why do you think that was your most popular album?***

RJ: I think it was released at a big turn-around time for America and American black people. It was a renaissance. The '80s were a renaissance time for us. As you see, in the late '80s and the early '90s, black music totally changed. It was like a renaissance for us, a come-alive period for us after disco. After disco, funk bands became really, really popular, as opposed to disco artists, because disco was another mechanical form of music, and people were really tired of that shit. Although it was cool in the castles where it was played, it wasn't so cool in the minds of a lot of people in the street. So *Street Songs* came out and kind of took over, in a way, that whole thing that was lasting from disco. It kind of pushed shit back in the streets where it belonged: out of the castles and out of the discos and back into the street. I think people were excited about that, and people were dancing a lot in those days, and people were really happy. A lot of people were in college in those days, because I meet a lot of people now who all tell me, "Yeah, man, I grew up with 'Super Freak.' I was in college, high school, and 'Give It To Me Baby' opened up a lot of doors." I hear that a lot.

O: ***There's a theory that gangsta rap is so popular because people like funk, and that's where most of the popular funk comes from these days. Do you think that's true?***

RJ: Absolutely. People love funk, people love to dance. I don't think, a lot of times, the rap on top of stuff really means or meant anything. To a lot of kids, as long as the beat was low-down and filthy, they loved it. A lot of times, you could get up and say anything on top of it: "My asshole hurts," or "I got a hemorrhoid," or anything. It really didn't matter. And it would sell, because the beat was so funky. A lot of stuff looked like that. That's why I hate to have people call me a funk artist. To call me a funk artist really undermines me and everything that I've done.

O: ***Was it difficult reliving your past for* Behind The Music*?***

RJ: Not at all, because I look at my life now very therapeutically. I look at it as honestly as I can right now. I always have, but I didn't really expound on it vocally. As honest as I could be, that's as better as I can be as a human being. So, for me to talk about my life in past tense, the bad times versus the good times, I don't have a problem with that, because honesty is the name of the game for me right now. It's therapeutic for me. It just makes me a better human being.

O: ***Do you feel like the show gave you the opportunity to set the record straight?***

RJ: Yeah, set the record straight. And it's kind of a soul-cleansing thing. It's like going to see a psychiatrist. It's no different than that. If you're telling it the way it is and you're being really honest, you're going to get help. If you bullshit and lie, then you're not going to get any help. I'm trying to get my mind and my soul together. The only way I can do that is to be as honest as I can be, to try to be the best person I can be.

O: ***Do you think people have a lot of misconceptions about you?***

RJ: Of course, but people need to learn through me that, number one, people are always judging people, and all gossip is a lie. Number two, I hear people talking about me, they don't even know me, and it's ridiculous. I mean, when I created the Rick James character, when James Johnson created Rick James, he created a person that could stand the wave of all that bullshit. Because Rick James' attitude is, "Fuck you, I don't give a fuck what you all say about me, 'cause all of you are full of shit any-fucking-way. And all of you need to get a life. Because anybody that's gonna sit back talking about anybody's life needs to get a life." That's why we have soap operas. We have soap operas so all these fucking people out here who ain't got nothing to do from 10 'til 4, or whatever it is, can sit back and watch soap operas and look in the TV at everybody else's life.

O: ***Do you think that was a defensive thing, creating the Rick James persona to be so...***

RJ: Yeah, it was a defense mechanism, absolutely. It's a defense and an offense. It's a way that I could say, "Kiss my ass, fuck you," but the James Johnson part of me, if I let that seep in and that's who I am for real, yeah, it means something. I get hurt, yeah, and it bothers me. The Rick James thing is like, "Fuck you." It sounds really insane, I know, but it works. Probably because Rick can say, "Fuck all that, don't get upset over that shit." People talking shit, they don't even know you, man.

O: ***Your web site says you were working on a movie in the '80s. What happened with that?***

RJ: Well, I was doing so many drugs in those times that there were a lot of things that I was working on that I just kind of displaced and said, "Fuck it." A lot of things were happening in my life, and I was just going, "Fuck it." I was that way. If it didn't have much to do with music, I would get involved with it and then kind of drop it. Music was the only thing I was really interested in. Movies were fine, and I'd written a lot of those, and I hadn't written a book yet. I did that when I was in prison. So the book came about when I was in prison, but now times are much different, and my head is in a much different place. I'm concentrating on a lot of different things, like movies and musicals. A whole lot of things.

O: ***What do you remember about your appearance on* The A-Team*?***

RJ: Not much, because I was so fucked up. I don't remember a whole lot. I do remember George Peppard walking out on his scene with me because I didn't read the script, because I was up all night with a couple girls, getting high and having ferocious sex. By the time the limousine picked me up to take me to the set, I hadn't slept and I hadn't learned my script. They had to write big cue cards out for me. So George Peppard walked out, and Mr. T says to me, [adopts frighteningly accurate Mr. T voice] "Don't worry about it, Rick, fuck him. He's just mad because he ain't on the cover of a cornflakes box." Mr. T was cool. He just said, "This is your show, Rick, you do it the way you want." And he was right, but that was kind of a fucked-up situation. Not only was I loaded, but I forgot the shit. I hate it when I don't do a great job on something. I think I did *One Life To Live* after that, and I did read the script, and I did go to sleep on time, and I kind of redeemed myself.

O: ***So you think a big part of acting is remembering your lines?***

RJ: Well, remembering the lines. Acting is very hard, but I used to take it very lightly. A lot of my friends are actors, and one of my best friends, Eddie Murphy, he's one of the best. When I did his movie, *Life*, playing a gangster, he had to pull me through it. He took me through it, and I found that acting is a lot harder than people give it credit for. Now my head is, "Yo, these guys make all this money acting, and they fucking deserve it. Pay the piper." Acting's a fucking hard thing. Trust me. I don't ever look forward to doing a whole lot of it, personally. It's very fucking difficult, and it's a long and tiresome ordeal.

O: ***How would you like to be remembered?***

RJ: I don't know, man. Somebody who just stood up for what he believed in, and somebody who was down for his race and who wrote some funky songs and made people dance, and who was a pretty good fucking producer. That's all. I think my legacy is all in the music. When the planet gets totally destroyed and everything, and the music is gone, then all the legacies will be gone. Until then, the music will speak for itself. ⌀

"I went from being so low in the gutters to being so up there, going to number one and being able to turn around and say, 'Ha ha.'"

Joan Jett

By Joe Garden

Originally Printed February 1998

Rock stardom, of a sort, found Joan Jett at an early age. Joining The Runaways in 1975 at 15, Jett and the band attracted the attention of veteran producer, performer, and Svengali Kim Fowley, who saw potential in the spectacle and sound of underage girls playing loud, nasty rock 'n' roll. But the group's notoriety always outstripped its commercial success. When The Runaways broke up in 1979, Jett moved to New York and began a solo career, cultivating an image of independence that almost seemed like a response to Fowley's heavy-handed control. With her band The Blackhearts, Jett scored a massive hit with 1982's inescapable "I Love Rock & Roll." Follow-up hits and a leading film role in Paul Schrader's Light Of Day *helped turn Jett into an icon of female rock 'n' roll toughness, as well as a precursor to the likes of L7, Bikini Kill, and The Gits, with whom Jett would later perform. Though she hasn't released a proper studio album since 1994's* Pure And Simple, *she still tours regularly. In 1998, during one of those tours, Jett spoke to* The Onion A.V. Club.

The Onion: ***How did it affect your outlook on life to have been brought up in rock 'n' roll?***
Joan Jett: It's not your average existence, for sure, being on the road since you're 15 and being verbally abused because you were being true to what you did. For playing rock 'n' roll, for chrissakes. I mean, we didn't hurt anybody. We were having a good time. To this day, it blows my mind when I think about it, how weird people were. They couldn't handle teenage girls playing rock 'n' roll. They just couldn't handle it.

O: ***Did the abuse come from the audience or the promoters?***
JJ: Mostly it was from the press. The music fans you could get to, because they were fans. Obviously, some people are thick, and they're not gonna see what they don't want to see. If they just want to see pussy on stage, that's what they're going to see. If they are willing to be won over... And a lot of guys were. I've got to give them credit. People did come to the shows and say, "You know, I came to see you just because you were girls, but you rock!" Those kind of things made it worth it, because you were really reaching the people. But the press had this view of who we were, and that was it. They didn't want to give us any kind of life, because we were threatening. We were threatening to the status quo, and they just didn't want to have room for girls playing rock

'n' roll. It bothered them. First, people just tried to get around it by saying, "Oh, wow, isn't that cute? Girls playing rock 'n' roll!" And when we said, "Yeah, right, this isn't a phase; it's what we want to do with our lives," it became, "Oh! You must be a bunch of sluts. You dykes, you whores." Then it became a name-calling contest. Once that happened, we got pissed. We'd all fight back, and we were 16. We would swear. So it became a shouting contest, and the headlines were "Runaways Guttermouths." They completely got around talking about the music by making everything sensationalistic, talking about how much we smoked or how short our skirts were.

O: ***It must have been hard to wage a war against the press, because the press has the last word.***

JJ: Exactly. So there was nothing we could do. There were occasionally writers who were on our side. One U.S. writer in particular, Chuck Young, always gave us a fair shot. He used to write with this magazine called *Crawdaddy*. Some of the people in England gave us a fair shot, for the most part. We got our asses

"It's not like it's all fun and games, and all easy, and all accolades. Nothing is like that."

kicked all the time. It was definitely tough. The record company didn't really care enough. They weren't excited. I never really understood why they signed us in the first place. They didn't do anything except put the records out. To me, you've got to do a little bit more than that. If you're not going to do anything, at least help us help ourselves. Give us the money to do the right promotions. Whatever. Everything was a struggle.

O: ***Do you still get some of that reaction today?***

JJ: Well, I think at this point, a lot of people have made their mind up about me one way or another. I'm sure there's a certain segment of writers who won't ever give me the time of day, hate me, don't get me, don't think I'm good, or whatever. I guess that's fine. It's only an opinion. There are other people who do get it and can be objective. I could be wrong, but a lot of people, except for really young people, have made up their minds one way or the other.

O: ***Have young people been picking up on you, discovering you?***

JJ: I don't know how aware teenagers are of me. I think it really depends on the teenagers and how well-versed in music they are and what kind of music they like. Especially since I haven't had a lot of recent huge MTV hits or huge radio hits. I have had some radio success recently, but I don't know that it's necessarily things that teenagers would have heard. I don't know how much it filters down.

O: ***"I Love Rock & Roll" really catapulted you into the limelight. How did that change you and the band?***

JJ: It just changed the level at which we did things. Instead of traveling in a beat-up van, we were traveling in a tour bus or jets. It was definitely a mindfuck. I wouldn't change it for anything. The experience was incredible. A lot of it was really intense and scary and weird and nasty, and people treat you funny. You become a product, which is very strange. I went from being so low in the gutters to being so up there, going to number one and being able to turn around and say, "Ha ha." I mean, I didn't want to do that too much, and I didn't. But I felt it. You don't want to laugh too much, because you know it could all be over in a second.

O: ***And you don't want that to come back and haunt you?***

JJ: Right. You don't want to have bad karma. It's not that I want anyone else to suffer just because people were assholes to me, but I want people to recognize it. Also, you have to realize that shit is ultimately fleeting, and that people who don't have respect for you or don't like you aren't all of a sudden going to like you because you have a number-one record. It's not going to make any difference to them, and they might like you less. It really doesn't matter, and ultimately, you have to take it for what it's worth, which is that it was a really special record at a really special time. Not many people get to have a record that's number one for two months. That was great. I got to be on a lot of big tours, and I got to go around the world a few times. I think on another level, unless you're really cautious, it's easy to lose touch with everything because of the workload, because you're always on the move, because you're never home, because people blow smoke up your ass to your face and then turn around and say things behind your back. This is reality. It's what happens. When you're living that kind of life, you don't know how to live what would be more of a traditional sort of life, like cooking for yourself, or window-shopping. Those are the kind of things I've been learning how to do over the past several years. My life, since I was 15, has not been what most people's lives are. It's hard for other people to understand, because that's not their reality. To even talk to somebody about it, they can listen to you, but they may not be able to relate because they haven't lived it. How can they possibly understand?

O: ***You'll always have the people who say, "Yeah, it must be hard having a number-one hit and flying to shows."***

JJ: Believe me, I had a blast. I'm not complaining at all. Not at all. For the most part, I had a blast. But it's not like it's all fun and games, and all easy, and all accolades. Nothing is like that. That is the bullshit we get sold when we're young: that you grow up and you find a mate and you're happy ever after and you get a job and you retire and life is good, and that's not really what happens at all. Life is painful and it's joyful. That's the part that we finally realize getting older. ⌀

Pam Grier

By Nathan Rabin
Originally Printed February 2002

"We've got $20 million actresses today who are nude in *Vanilla Sky*, nude in *Swordfish*. So what did I do different? I got paid less, but that's it."

Perhaps the foremost icon of the blaxploitation era, Pam Grier began her film career in the early 1970s and quickly came to represent a new female cinematic archetype: sexy, strong, and perpetually willing to whoop some bad-guy ass. A military brat and the cousin of football player Rosey Grier, Grier made her debut in Russ Meyer's cult classic Beyond The Valley Of The Dolls. *While attending college (she majored in pre-med before switching to film) and working at American International Pictures, Grier caught the eye of B-movie maven Roger Corman, who paired her with writer-director Jack Hill for a series of popular action movies, including* Foxy Brown *and* Coffy. *When the blaxploitation boom ended, many of its key players were left scrambling for work, but Grier worked regularly in theater, television, and film, forming long-term work relationships with filmmakers like John Carpenter and Andrew Davis. In the mid-'90s, longtime fan Quentin Tarantino gave Grier's career a boost by casting her in the lead role of* Jackie Brown, *his follow-up to* Pulp Fiction. *Grier won considerable accolades for the role, including Golden Globe and Screen Actors Guild nominations for Best Actress. Since then, she's appeared in films like* Ghosts Of Mars, 3 A.M., Holy Smoke, *and* Bones. *Shortly before the 2002 video release of* Bones, The Onion A.V. Club *spoke with Grier about the blaxploitation era, race, gender, sex, violence, and her role as an icon of female empowerment.*

The Onion: ***You began your career doing beauty pageants. How did that begin?***

Pam Grier: I did it to gain confidence and raise money for tuition. My mother said it was one of the best ways to overcome my shyness and other things I had grown up with. I never went in thinking, "You're an African-American woman, so you're never going to win." I was just in it for the experience, and to show my brains and talent and help break stereotypes. It wasn't like, "Oh, I'll become a star. I'm beautiful." I never thought I was pretty. I couldn't even put on eyelashes or makeup. When you come from an environment that's military, and they don't stress that topic of aesthetics or beauty pageants and makeup, there are a lot of things you just don't have that city girls have. Not too many sisters at that time dreamed about becoming actresses. You're still a member of the Black Panthers, you're still trying to vote, you're still trying not to get run off the road or stopped or frisked.

O: ***Growing up, you didn't think of yourself as beautiful or striking?***

PG: No. We weren't taught anything like that in our family. We were taught that if our eyes worked and our legs worked, we were beautiful. We had so many kids in our family that if we all got in front of the mirror and were ashamed of browns and golds and yellows and whites, and we believed what society told us—that the darker people were less attractive and the lighter ones were prettier—we would have had sibling murders. My family, being half-rural and half-military, just came from a different place.

O: ***The first films you made were with Roger Corman.***

PG: Roger Corman was looking for an in-your-face, radical kind of natural actress who hadn't been pampered and frosted with wigs and blue eye-shadow. And one of my jobs happened to be at an agency where he was having trouble finding an actress. So people said, "You're tough and you're a military brat, you keep us in line. Why don't you go up there?" And I'm in film school, so I really have to sock away my money, and I don't have time. I don't want to be an actress, because I think that they have to be really pretty, and I'm not. So they say, "We can offer, like, $500 a week," and I'm saying, "I'm working three jobs and bringing home half that!" I guess they liked my attitude. The next thing you know, I'm doing a film in the Philippines, guerrilla filmmaking at its best, with a director named Jack Hill. He had a European sensibility to film, and so did I, and when it came to nudity, we're thinking about Fellini and Kurosawa and Bertolucci. You're not thinking about some sort of Victorian handicap called, "Don't show your breasts, it's considered indecent." The next thing you know, they're saying, "Ma'am, you're really a good actress. You're real. You're a natural, you're right there." So I had to learn and catch up with everybody, and I took it seriously. Even though I was doing what was considered a B-movie, I thought it was *Gone With The Wind*. I thought it would win an Oscar. I think if you don't approach your work on that level, you won't achieve what you're looking for, whether it's great success or just acknowledgment, because you're half-stepping. I went in doing the best work I could, which frightened them, because they didn't expect me to.

O: ***Shooting in the Philippines and doing your own stunts, were you ever worried that you might be seriously injured?***

PG: Oh, all the time, but since I was very athletic, and had run track in school, that helped. I was kind of a bouncy kid. I used to roller-skate into the sides of cars. [Laughs.] I had some flexibility, I loved speed, and for some reason, I did some of the stunts. But you're always in danger of something exploding, or leeches or cobras or snakes. You can get hurt at any time. But you listen and watch. These people live there, they understand the jungle of the Philippines, and they know what to do. If you're stupid and arrogant, you're going to get hurt. It's not the place to be arrogant.

O: ***When you were making* Coffy *and* Foxy Brown*, did you have any conception that you were creating a powerful new female archetype, this sort of iconic, larger-than-life figure?***

PG: No, not at all. You never know how people are going to respond. I just wanted to try to do interesting work. I was surprised and humbled by the legacy of it.

O: ***You were the first woman to play that type of character.***

PG: Yeah, well. I saw it in my real life, I saw it in the police force in Denver, and I saw it in the military. I saw women share the platform with men in my personal world, and Hollywood just hadn't wakened to it yet. Bette Davis and Katharine Hepburn changed the way they saw women during the 1940s, but I saw it daily in the women's movement that was emerging, because I was a child of the women's movement. Everything I had learned was from my mother and my grandmother, who both had a very pioneering spirit. They had to, because they had to change flat tires and paint the house—because, you know, the men didn't come home from the war or whatever else, so women had to do these things. So, out of economic necessity and the freedoms won, by the '50s and '60s, there was suddenly this opportunity and this invitation that was like, "Come out here with these men. Get out here. Show us what you got." And they had to, out of pure necessity. Out of necessity comes genius. Not to say that I was a genius, but I did the things I had to do.

O: ***Did you get a lot of feedback at the time about your film work?***

PG: The masses enjoyed it. They enjoyed seeing a female hero. And then some of the more conservative people said, "Couldn't you have done something else? Couldn't you have played a nun? Couldn't you play Mother Mary, or something more conservative?" And I said, "You guys are so fragmented that nobody's going to come. Nobody's going to see those movies." The way things are right now, they want to see action, they want to see heroes and heroines. And if you're not that, you're an art film, and if you were black, then you weren't going to be in that art film. If you were black, you may not get to do theater. So you're marginalizing yourself even further, and you're not going to get the experience or break down stereotypes. Although at the beginning, my ambition was never to break down doors. It was just to earn tuition for myself and work in an industry where women hadn't been allowed or invited. That's all I wanted to do, not thinking that I would make waves, change minds, excite people, incite people, turn people on, repulse people. We've got $20 million actresses today who are nude in *Vanilla Sky*, nude in *Swordfish*. So what did I do different? I got paid less, but that's it. And if you see it as an art form, what's the problem? You know what it's rated, and you know what you're going to see, because the critics tell you. If it offends you, don't go.

O: ***Other than the nudity, it seems like what bothered some people about your films was the violence. Did you ever have a problem with the violence in your early films?***

PG: No, not at all. I saw more violence in my neighborhood and in the war and on the newsreels than I did in my movies, so it didn't bother me. Coming from the '50s, things were very violent. We were still being lynched. If I drove down through the South with my mother, I might not make it through one state without being bullied or harassed. Unless you've been black for a week, you don't know. A lot of people were really up in arms about nothing, and if you challenge them, they go, "Well, maybe you're right." In the meantime, you have a headline writer who's made waves by asking questions and raising flags and saying, "Oh my God, Sam Jackson said the word 'nigger' 37 times in *Jackie Brown*!" And Sam said, "Well, there were 10 in the script, but I chose to say it more." He doesn't get attacked. Everyone else can maim, kill, and shoot, and they don't get attacked. At the time, I just said, "You guys just have to get real." I came from a very real place of no pretension, like, "Yeah, I'm sorry it's ghetto. I'm sorry it's lower-class." I wish I was Ivy League and I lived in the suburbs and my folks made $100,000, but that's not the real world. Either they accept my art and my sensibility, or they don't.

"I wish I was Ivy League and I lived in the suburbs and my folks made $100,000, but that's not the real world. Either they accept my art and my sensibility, or they don't."

O: ***A lot of your earlier films were attacked by the NAACP and other mainstream civil-rights groups.***

PG: Well, they would attack, but very minimally, and not very loudly. I mean, I hosted their awards show the year before it went to television, and my date was Freddie Prinze. I hosted the show, so if I was that horrific, why was I hosting the show? I was given keys to the city from every major black city in the country. I was meeting with mayors and raising funds. Of course, I was opening doors, and as you open doors and become bigger box-office, you have an opportunity to do *Lilies Of The Field*. Maybe I can do non-violent films. I'm still trying to do films about black women. Angela Bassett finally did a film about Rosa Parks, but look how long it took for that to get done. Why didn't somebody do Rosa Parks sooner? Why didn't they do Tina Turner then? There comes a point where you're "not valid." But as time goes by, and with education and academics and plain old consciousness, you kind of realize what went on, who did what, who got the limelight. Spike Lee got a lot of limelight by accusing Quentin Tarantino of giving 37 lines of "nigger" to Sam Jackson. When, in fact, that wasn't the case at all.

O: ***Do you think being known for action movies has hurt you in terms of getting other kinds of roles?***

PG: Not at all. I've done the best theater in the world. It's what you bring to the table. It's whether you can fill seats, you know? You got rappers filling the seats. That's all they care about. They don't care about me. They don't care if I'm gonna be naked and black. And whoever the critics are, whoever the naysayers are, they don't get it. This is a private industry. If you're invited to come to the party and drink from the fountain, it's a privilege. You can't tell them what to do. I don't see the NAACP telling them, "Well, why don't you make these films?" How come they don't go up to the black directors and tell them, "How come they aren't making these films?" You need to understand the dynamic. I tell young actresses today who are looking to get into films, "First of all, you are marginalized by the color of your skin." I tell actresses, "If you're too tall, if you're too fat, you're not going to work. I don't care how talented you are." It's a business, and sex sells. Sex, action, special effects, and violence sell. Yes, you can have art films about the triumph of the human spirit and all of that, but you'll have it done with a big-budget icon with a $20 million salary. You'll have Julia Roberts, you'll have Robert Redford, you'll have Russell Crowe doing those films, because if they're going to cost $90 million, they're going to make that movie for a public that's very large and mainstream. They're not going to make it for three or four million black people.

O: ***Do you consider yourself a feminist?***

PG: I consider myself conscious of how we're treated, and sometimes I can be a feminist. Sometimes I'm a little Republican, sometimes I'm a little Democrat. Sometimes I'm angry, sometimes I'm not angry. I'm not a total feminist, but I believe in rights for females. I believe that if we have to pay 100 percent for our college tuition, and then we get into the workplace and we're only given 70 percent of our counterparts' salaries, then we shouldn't have to pay but 70 percent of our college tuition. Maybe that'll stop the bullshit. Now, come on. I ask you, how would you like your mom, your wife, your daughter to spend $100,000 to go to Harvard or some state school, and go out into the workplace, and you know she's great, and men are getting paid $200 per week more than her? Would that piss you off? What if you lost your job and you stay home crippled while she goes out, and she thinks she's going to get a good job, but someone male with the same level of experience and the same level of education gets paid more than her? You're going to get pissed. Until you walk a mile in someone else's shoes, I don't want to hear it. See, that's the disparity that we have. That's what makes people say, "Why should I work so hard? I'm not going to get paid." When we have that so prevalent in the black community, that's what saddens me, because that's when we know we can't get films made that uplift. We have to have films about action and violence and special effects. That's the sad part, but you know what? It's not me doing it.

O: ***Is it true that you auditioned for* Pulp Fiction*?***
PG: Yes, I did. I went into Quentin's office, and there were all these posters of me up on the wall. I asked him, "Did you put these posters up because you knew I was coming?" And he said, "No, I actually was thinking about taking them down because you were coming." I was amazed that he was so interested in the style of that whole genre. Not only was it romantic, that type of genre, but we had his style of long scenes, because we didn't have the budget to cut, cut, cut. That style of shooting worked very well [on *Jackie Brown*], but it takes like a day or two to set up the whole scene before you can shoot it. But that's the brilliance of Quentin and his cameramen. They spent three days setting up the lighting for one scene so they could do it without cutting. It was incredible, because you had Robert De Niro and Michael Keaton with a sister at once. You have Batman and Raging Bull in the film with me, and Sam Jackson. And the fact that he would put a black woman in his film to make it interesting, you know, wasn't just hype. He did a really good job telling the story. So he brought his legacy. I was just invited to the party.
O: ***It seems like a lot of black actors and filmmakers who made action movies in the early '70s object to the term "blaxploitation" because they feel it's demeaning. Do you feel that way at all?***
PG: No, not at all. I'd be a hypocrite if I did. No, but everyone else can do violence. You know, Clint Eastwood, Sylvester Stallone, they can all do shoot-'em-ups. Arnold Schwarzenegger can kill 10 people, and they don't call it "white exploitation." They win awards and get into all the magazines. But if black people do it, suddenly it's different than if a white person does it. People respond differently because people come from different places.
O: ***Can you see a time when that isn't the case?***
PG: I will not be on this planet. I may come back in another form, and you know, I'll come back as a white man. If I get the chance, I want to come back as a white man and go to Ivy League schools. [Laughs.] Ø

Peter Frampton

By Nathan Rabin
Originally Printed July 2001

"Mistakes were made, so I learned by my mistakes. I won't make those again. I'll just make new ones, like us all."

An accomplished and sought-after session guitarist even before his good looks and catchy songs made him a household name, Peter Frampton first achieved fame with the late-'60s British rock group The Herd. Teaming with Small Faces frontman Steve Marriott, Frampton joined supergroup Humble Pie in 1969, then left two years later to pursue a solo career and serve as a session man on such seminal albums as George Harrison's All Things Must Pass *and Harry Nilsson's* Son Of Schmilsson. *But while Frampton's early studio albums were well-received, he didn't attain pop stardom until the release of 1976's* Frampton Comes Alive, *which became the best-selling live album of all time. The following year,* I'm In You *sold millions, but Frampton's career suffered from a combination of bad business decisions, questionable choices (such as starring in 1978's ill-fated* Sgt. Pepper's Lonely Hearts Club Band*), overexposure, and changing commercial tides. After struggling commercially for much of the past two decades, Frampton made a modest comeback in the late '90s, both as a prodigiously gifted guitarist and as a '70s icon. He made a guest appearance on a memorable episode of* The Simpsons, *won a Grammy, performed with Ringo Starr's All Starr Band, appeared in and composed songs for Cameron Crowe's* Almost Famous, *and was profiled on both VH1's* Behind The Music *and A&E's* Biography. *In 2001,* The Onion A.V. Club *spoke with Frampton about his rocky career and the fickle nature of fame.*

The Onion: ***Your press material says you were named the Face Of 1968 by the British press. How exactly did that come about?***

Peter Frampton: That was just because I was in a band called The Herd, and we had a hit, and we were a teenybopper band. I wasn't the lead singer of that band until management came along, and record producers looked at us all and said, "You'll sing." I said, "No, I do the backup singing. I don't do that, I'm the lead guitarist." They said, "No, no, no. You'll sing." So, being 17 at the time, I just went along with it. And the first thing I noticed was that I was being singled out as the cute one, I guess you'd have to say. All of a sudden, I was the face of '68. I was on the front cover of every magazine in Europe. It changed The Herd's image from a musical band into a teenybopper band. But we were very successful. And then I got fed up with it and left that band to form Humble Pie with Steve Marriott, who'd also been through a teenybopper-type thing with The Small Faces. But they had ridden out that storm by doing a very credible record album called *Ogden's Nut Gone Flake*, which was very well received critically. They got through the teenybopper thing, whereas The Herd never did.

O: ***Did it bother you that so much attention was paid to your looks?***

PF: Yes. Being screamed at is only fun for the first five minutes, in the scheme of things. You get frustrated by the fact that you're playing, but no one's listening. I've often seen that clip of Paul McCartney, when he was asked, "Will you ever play again live?" And he said, [adopts heavy Liverpool accent] "Not until they listen to us." That was never to be, so, yes, I can totally relate to the screaming stuff, which 'N Sync and The Backstreet Boys go through. But those chaps don't play instruments, so it's a little bit different.

O: ***Didn't you find it flattering?***

PF: Oh, yeah, but it gets old very quick. It's very fickle. Here today, gone tomorrow, especially with a teenybopper sort of thing. You're going to be popular with those teenagers at that time, and then it moves so quickly that you're out of fashion. I think on the A&E *Biography*, Alice Cooper said it the best. He said, "Peter got the big hair and the good looks, and as soon as you get screamed at, to the hardcore musical fans, there goes your credibility as a rock-god guitarist." There's no way that's going to happen when you're perceived along the lines of Donny Osmond. I hate to liken myself to that, but that's the dark side of the story, as far as I'm concerned. To even think that I was perceived in that genre blows my mind.

O: ***Did your early success prepare you at all for the success of* Frampton Comes Alive?**

PF: It did, but I don't think anybody can be ready for that sort of success. I was made aware straight away that there wasn't anybody up there with me. I was the only person there, because I had broken new ground. I'd sold more records than any other person in history with one album, at that point, in '76. It became a very scary place for me, because I didn't know whose advice to ask and lost my confidence in my own gut feelings about everything. I've since learned, over the years, that you have to look out for yourself. An artist has to be selfish; otherwise, he's not true to his own art. I think that threw me for a loop. For the first time, I was successful as a solo artist. I didn't realize at the time that management, the record companies, no one had dealt with anything like this before. It was the first time someone had taken record sales to the next level after Carole King's *Tapestry*, which was the biggest-selling record of all time up until that point. I was literally out there on my own and taking advice from people who didn't know any more than I did how to deal with the situation, in order to take full advantage of it and turn it into a long career, not one that was going to fizzle because it got so big so quick. This is all with hindsight, which is great, but at the time, it was like I was in the middle of World War III. There were things being fired at me left and right, where everybody wanted me for everything. And having taken, in the scheme of things, not that long—but, as far as I was concerned, most of my life—to get to that point in '76, I didn't want to turn things down. Everybody wants to be on the front cover of *People* and *Rolling Stone*. I didn't know then that too much coverage is death, overkill. We didn't realize that at the time. Mistakes were made, so I learned by my mistakes. I won't make those again. I'll just make new ones, like us all.

O: ***When you were making* Frampton Comes Alive, *did you have any idea that it would become the album you would be known for?***

PF: No, not at all. I was just following the same exact storyline that Humble Pie had already done, which was four or five studio records, and then a live record at the right time. The audience was at a fever pitch for Humble Pie, but they weren't seeming to buy the studio records as much as they were at the shows. It just didn't correlate. So we thought, "Let's give them what they seem to like to come and see." So we did, and it worked. I did that same thing at what I felt was the right time, and I guess it was, and bingo. No idea, and no clue of why. I only know the reason, my feeling of its longevity, is the fact that it was the best of Peter Frampton's four solo records, plus a number from a Humble Pie record, "Shine On." You add me in the live arena, giving just that bit more and the extra adrenaline, the extra excitement of "live." With those numbers, I feel that they are as good, if not better, renditions as the original studio ones. It sort of happened backwards to the way everybody else usually has success. You have a couple of studio successes, and then you make a live record, and nobody's really interested in the live record that much, except the devout fans, because everybody likes what they hear first. They don't want to hear a remix; they want to hear what they've heard, that's it. "What I bought, that's what I like." So when they hear it live, it's not the same. They're not going to rush out and buy that. Whereas me, hardly anybody bought my studio records, but when I put it together live, it went through the roof. Go figure. It's because I enjoy performing live so much. It's a wonderful feeling. It's my forum.

O: ***After* Frampton Comes Alive*, there were three million pre-orders for* I'm In You. *Were you intimidated by that much buildup?***

PF: Yes.

O: ***Was that a scary point in your life?***

PF: Yes, it was, because not only am I not going to be able to follow up this live record with another live record, but I'm following it up with a completely different animal. Also, following up the biggest record in history at that point... That's a lot of pressure right there. It was very scary at that point, and it wasn't an enjoyable album to make. I've learned from my mistakes, but that wouldn't have been the thing I would have rushed into doing as quickly as I did. With hindsight, I realized that's the one thing I allow myself when people say, "What would you change?" The only thing, which I can't change anyway. But, if I could have changed one thing, it would have been to take off at least 18 months before going into the studio and doing another record. And then, hopefully, I would have been able to wear jeans and a T-shirt on the front cover.

O: ***One of those things you did in the wake of* Frampton Comes Alive*'s success was star in* Sgt. Pepper's Lonely Hearts Club Band. *How did you become involved in that film?***

PF: We just thought it couldn't fail. This was going to be the biggest movie ever. And, of course, it wasn't. I was promised that Paul McCartney was going to be in the film, and I actually met Paul McCartney at a show in Philadelphia. We were playing there the next night, and I said, "I'll see you on the film set." And he said, "What film set?" I was talked into doing that and misled, so that's why. I think that both The Bee Gees and myself realized very early on that we'd made a bad choice. But then again, it played havoc with my career, there's no two ways about it. I'm not whining, because it's all in the learning process. We didn't know at the time that it was going to have that effect, obviously. Who's to say that, just because I'm number one on the charts, that I can also be in a big movie? There are a lot of people out there who love that movie. I don't know why, but they have seen it many, many times.

"Being screamed at is only fun for the first five minutes, in the scheme of things. You get frustrated by the fact that you're playing, but no one's listening."

O: ***It seemed like a weird idea to make a Beatles movie without The Beatles.***

PF: Whenever I'm with Ringo, people ask him, "What did you think of Pete being in *Sgt. Pepper's*?" And he says, [adopts Ringo Starr voice]

"We don't talk about that." [Laughs.] "He's a bloody idiot." Stuff like that. Doing the All Starr thing with Ringo was a great experience. I love working with Ringo.

O: ***Which do you prefer, being a frontman or a sideman?***

PF: I enjoy both, but there's something very special about being a hired gun, just being back there playing guitar and doing some backup vocals. I love that position. I would never turn it down. Like with David Bowie, that was wonderful. I enjoyed every minute of that, and all the sessions that I've done. I just really enjoy seeing how other people work and trying to tailor what I do to fit in with them, which is always a challenge. It's always a learning experience for me. I love working with other people. When I did Ringo's All Starr Band thing, I got to play for everyone. For Jack Bruce, I had to be Eric Clapton. For Gary Brooker, I had to be Robin Trower. For Ringo, I had to be George Harrison. I love that. And with Bowie, I had to be all those different guitarists, as well as play with him.

O: ***How did appearing on* Behind The Music *affect your career?***

PF: That and *People* and *Biography* all very recently—and before that, *The Simpsons*—brought up my visibility. And everybody went, "Yeah, Peter Frampton! Now, I thought he was dead. Didn't he die?" No, so it's wonderful when people come up to you and say, "You know, are you still in music? Do you still play?" "No, I'm a greengrocer, what do you think?" It was interesting, anyway.

O: ***Was it painful reliving parts of your past for* Behind The Music *and* Biography?**

PF: I think *Behind The Music* was more... We did so many reels of film for that. When I finally kick the bucket, they've got like a three-day special on me there, with the amount of film they did. It was more intimidating to do that than *Biography*, because *Behind The Music* has got an angle. It even admits as much. They want the dirt. Whereas *Biography* is the story as told by the people they interview, and by the research and everything, and by what I say. I thought *Behind The Music* was great, but *Biography* definitely told the story the way it happened, in a more drawn-out sort of way. People didn't just get sound-bites, they got actual paragraphs.

O: ***In* Behind The Music, *there's a formula for each act. No matter what your career happened to entail, you have to have the incredible success and then the crushing downfall.***

PF: Well, that's 25 to 35 minutes in. They call it the "Price Of Fame" spot. [Laughs.] The people that make it call it that. It's usually between 25 and 35 minutes in, bang!

O: ***Where was your "Price Of Fame" spot?***

PF: Well, I think it started with *Sgt. Pepper's*. [Laughs.] And the downfall, the downslide: The record company drops you, this, that, and then the clawing back to the above-ground afterwards.

O: ***How did you end up on* The Simpsons?**

PF: They just called me up. Bonnie Pietila, the casting director, called me up and said, "Would you like to be on *The Simpsons*?" And I said, "Are you kidding? Of course I would." Only a few people in the scheme of things have been on that show, and they're all big stars, so I said I was absolutely honored to be on *The Simpsons*. I said, "Give me an idea, what is it?" So she said, "Well, the story line is this: You, Peter Frampton, are headlining a Lollapalooza-type concert." There was deathly silence from my end, and I went, "Uh, Bonnie, the thing is, I wouldn't be doing that." Then there was silence on her end and I went, "D'oh, that's a joke!" [Laughs.] I said, "I got it, you want me to play the old, done-everything, been-there, done-this, crusty old rock star, right?" She said, "You've hit the nail on the head." So I said, "Oh, God, that'll be great, playing a grumpy old rock star." I threw myself into it. I did it in 50 minutes, the whole thing, because there were so many guest artists on it, with The Smashing Pumpkins and Sonic Youth and everything. They couldn't get us all together to read it, so I just went in and read my part. They asked me to ad lib a bit. The best part about it was when they animated my ad lib, which was the part when I come off… I think I've lost my pig at that point, and the button won't work, and I just walk right past Homer and I go, "Twenty-five years in this business, and I've never seen anything like it." It was just an off-the-cuff remark, and there I am, as a cartoon figure of me saying it. That was a real thrill.

O: ***I take it you're happy with the way the episode turned out.***

PF: Yeah, God, they show it all the time. I went to Australia with Roger Daltrey and Alice Cooper, and we did the British Rock Symphony over there. For the press conference in Sydney for it, the guy introducing us to the press said, "And, of course, on the end, the man that my son only knows as a character from *The Simpsons*, Peter Frampton." Halfway around the world, there's someone that knows me as this crusty old grumpy rock star. Which I thought was great. ⌀

"I think God saved me so I can show the kids what it was really about in the '60s."

Ronnie Spector

By Keith Phipps

Originally Printed September 1999

As a member of The Ronettes, Ronnie Spector was the voice behind some of the greatest songs of the '60s. Produced by Phil Spector, who romanced and married her, "Be My Baby" has one of the most instantly recognizable opening beats in rock 'n' roll, but the voice—part New York toughness, part tender vulnerability—drives the point home. Spector and The Ronettes followed that hit with many more, including "Baby, I Love You," "I Wonder," "The Best Part Of Breakin' Up," "Do I Love You," and "Walking In The Rain." But eventually, the hits dried up, and the Spectors' relationship turned worse than sour. Ronnie Spector's 1990 autobiography Be My Baby: How I Survived Mascara, Miniskirts And Madness *tells an unhappy story of abuse, and she's spent the past 15 years extricating herself from the situation, which she's understandably reluctant to discuss. In 1999, after a couple of failed comeback attempts and a guest spot on Eddie Money's 1986 hit "Take Me Home Tonight," Spector had something else to talk about: a new EP,* She Talks To Angels. *Produced by Daniel Rey and longtime fan Joey Ramone, it includes "Don't Worry Baby," the song Brian Wilson wrote for her, but that Phil Spector barred her from recording.*

The Onion: ***How was it to finally record "Don't Worry Baby" after all these years?***

Ronnie Spector: That was so great! I was supposed to do that 30-some-odd years ago. "Don't Worry Baby" was supposed to be the follow-up to "Be My Baby." I mean, Brian Wilson actually went home after hearing "Be My Baby" and wrote "Don't Worry Baby" for me. And, of course, he didn't get a chance to give it to me, because in those days Jeff Barry and Ellie Greenwich were writing my songs, and they didn't want anything to do with other people. "Don't Worry Baby" actually helped me in the '70s when I came back, to relax and stuff. I would play it over and over when I got depressed.

O: ***It's kind of odd, though: The lyric dealing with drag-racing, was that always there for you?***

RS: I knew that, too, but I didn't want to change a word. I left that in there on purpose because, really, it was a dedication to Brian Wilson.

O: ***Did you contact him to let him know you were finally going to do the song?***

RS: No. Other people did; he sure knows. As a matter of fact, about a month ago, he was in New York, and they invited me down to see his show. He actually sang "Be My Baby," and it freaked me out. I'm sitting there in the audience with everybody, grooving off his music, and all of a sudden I hear the drums going "bum-ba-bump."

O: ***It must have been a thrill.***

RS: It was! I went backstage after hearing him sing, which was an honor to me. Brian's been through a lot of tough times in his life, and when I got up to his dressing room, I just started singing "Be My Baby" to him, and he loved it. And then I sat next to him and put my head on his chest and started singing "Walking In The Rain," and he freaked. His body started shaking and then I got up and

"For me to get in the car and go to the grocery store and hear one of my songs, I have to stop and go on the side of the road with my car to hear it because I'm in shock."

sang "So Young." And he's like, "Oh, no, I love that song!" And then I went into "Do I Love You?" as I was walking out, and he was starting to tremble and shake. I thought I scared him. I thought he was going to have a heart attack or something. I said, "Oh my God, I've killed Brian Wilson," as I was walking out of the room, because he started actually shaking. So I sorta walked out of the room, and he just said, "Ronnie, you brought me so much love." I think for that moment, he actually became the old Brian Wilson. He was drug-free, he was the guy from the '60s with The Beach Boys all over again, just for those few moments that I sang. And I gave him like a little concert, because I know he's been playing my album for 30 years. That's all he listens to, and to hear me in person, without music, just singing those songs, it blew his mind.

O: ***What's your favorite of your old songs?***

RS: Probably "Be My Baby." I just love that song. I was in a restaurant the other day with my mother-in-law having lunch, and it came on. It never ceases to amaze me that it's still playing every day. I take my kids to karate class and I hear it in the car. The kids hear it, and it's like, "What?" I'm amazed that they're still playing it as if it were the '60s.

O: ***Did you have any idea that it would endure for this long when you recorded it?***

RS: Never. I mean, you never even thought about that. I never would have thought it would have gone into the year 2000, ever. Five years tops, you know?

O: ***Especially in the early '60s, when everyone still thought rock 'n' roll was a fad.***

RS: Exactly. In the early '60s, you were called one-hit wonders. That was it; you were in and you were out. For me to get in the car and go to the grocery store and hear one of my songs, I have to stop and go on the side of the road with my car to hear it because I'm in shock.

O: ***Why do you think people come back to it?***

RS: Because it was real, it was innocent, it was natural, the lyrics are pure. You know, "For every kiss you give me, I'll give three." It was just songs that were written on the spot, you know what I mean? They came from the heart when I was with Phil. He was in love with me and I was in love with him, so the lyrics and all that came about with the relationship. That's what's so natural, and that's why I think those songs lasted, because they were so innocent and real.

O: ***Who do you like who's working today? Is there anyone you're impressed with?***

RS: Today. Ugh. You know, so many people come and go, and before I get a chance to like them, they're gone. You know how you get a taste of a new group and then they're gone? They have the video bands, and the singers don't go out and learn how to perform live. The label spends half a million dollars to create this image of the band, and you go see them live and there's nothing happening. Stage performing is a dying art form, and I'm afraid with this technology and stuff that people are going to wake up one day and not know what rock 'n' roll feels like. You know, the sweat, the energy, the sexual tension. There's nothing like it in the world.

O: ***I can't imagine Whitney Houston working as hard.***

RS: Exactly. People like that, the Whitney Houstons, are obviously... It's for the money, for the glamour. I just saw her on one of these *Oprah* shows, and she's showing her outfits that she's wearing at her concerts, and that is not rock 'n' roll. What I do is peek out at the audience and see what they're wearing, and then I sort of slip into what I feel they... You know, you give to the audience. Today, people go up there and want you to admire them and look at their clothes and their wigs and their makeup, and it's not about rock 'n' roll at all.

O: ***Are you going to be touring?***

RS: Oh, yes. I don't know if it's going to be a big tour, but I know I'm doing San Francisco, all the "in" places. A lot of college stuff, so kids can see what rock 'n' roll was really about. I think God saved me so I can show the kids what it was really about in the '60s.

"You've got to have big breasts, casting huge shadows. Just so the women don't buckle at the knees."

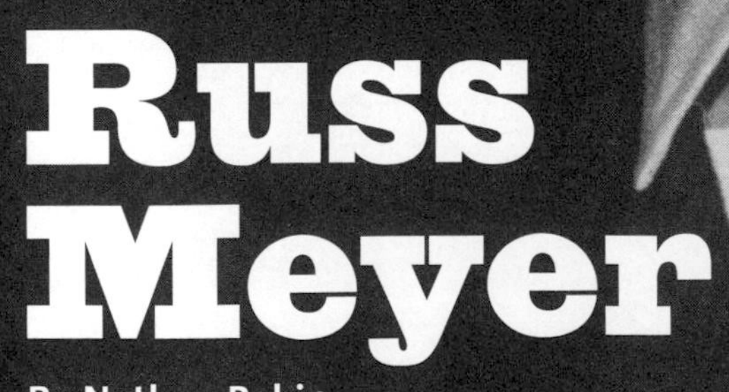

Russ Meyer

By Nathan Rabin

Originally Printed September 1998

*Equal parts cinematic visionary and filthy old man, director, cinematographer, producer, writer, editor, and photographer Russ Meyer is a unique figure in American film. Meyer's early movies (*The Immoral Mr. Teas, Eve And The Handyman*) were undeniably softcore porn, shot cheaply and quickly for a less-than-discriminating audience, but his artistry elevated his films above their disreputable peers. His early work was commercially successful, but Meyer ultimately built his reputation on two films: 1966's* Faster Pussycat! Kill! Kill!*—a demented proto-feminist tale of a group of big-busted, butch outlaws—and* Beyond The Valley Of The Dolls, *a hysterically over-the-top 1970 cult classic about the rise and fall of a female rock group, written by future Pulitzer Prize winner and frequent collaborator Roger Ebert. Bolstered by* Dolls' *runaway success, Meyer adapted Irving Wallace's anti-censorship novel* The Seven Minutes *for Fox in 1971. The result was an atypically chaste critical and commercial failure, and Meyer soon returned to making campy, over-the-top independent sex comedies. Meyer's last film was 1979's* Beneath The Valley Of The Ultra-Vixens, *although in 2001, he directed a softcore video featuring pneumatic muse Pandora Peaks. In 1998,* The Onion A.V. Club *spoke with the ever-candid filmmaking legend about The Sex Pistols, Elvis Presley, Roger Ebert, and, of course, the virtues of women with huge breasts.*

The Onion: ***What do you think is the key to the enduring popularity of* Faster Pussycat! Kill! Kill!*?***

RM: It's a little puzzling. Most of my films have women who have large breasts. It's not that the girls in that film are completely lacking in accoutrements. I suppose they like the idea of the women kicking the shit out of the men. More than anything else, I think that's the reason it's done very, very well.

O: ***Do you think it has a feminist sort of appeal?***

RM: Oh, yeah. Very much so. And Tura Satana [the film's star], without any question, is a feminist. Feminists love her.

O: ***Was that something you were thinking about consciously when you made the film?***

RM: No, I made another film prior to that in which I had men kicking the shit out of the women, so I thought, "Why don't we do one where the women kick the shit out of the men?"

O: ***How did you get your start as a filmmaker?***

RM: I was an amateur, but it was World War II.

I loved the war. I didn't want the war to end. I wanted the war to go on forever.

O: *You were a combat photographer?*

RM: Yes. I loved it. I landed in Normandy, and it went on from there. A lot of it had to do with me being able to take my product and find distributors: Without any question, they were very interested, and the press was always good to work with.

"I would always just kind of get young people, young women with big tits. You run into problems with women thinking, 'What is this fellow trying to do, trying to make some sort of pornographic movie?' And I would say, 'Yes, only with enormous tits. Yours are not large enough.' "

O: *How did you get from being a combat photographer to making films like* **The Immoral Mr. Teas?**

RM: I came back to the States and got a job with an industrial company. I made a lot of money, and I ended up buying myself an office where there were women. And I would always come on like a steam engine, telling them that they would all be stars. Lying through my teeth. It also gave me an opportunity to get a lot of pussy. That was really worthwhile. And I am still very much into that.

O: *That's been a motivating force in your career?*

RM: Very, very much so. Trying to get into their shorts.

O: *What have you been up to since you made* **Beneath The Valley Of The Ultra-Vixens** *in 1979?*

RM: I have this video thing that's very, very strong. I have a number of people working at my Los Angeles office, and now we have the European people going for it. There's no way that I'm going to stop.

O: *Do you own the rights to a lot of your films?*

RM: Absolutely. I'm just fiendish when people try to get into my shorts there, in that sense.

O: *How did your collaboration with Roger Ebert [who co-wrote* **Beyond The Valley Of The Dolls, Up!,** *and* **Beneath The Valley Of The Ultra-Vixens***] come about?*

RM: Tits. Plain and simple, he loves tits.

O: *He contacted you first?*

RM: Yes, he did. Because I got a lot of help from him from a standpoint of good criticism. It's still very much the same, but his wife really doesn't feel all that keen about me. She's afraid that he might get something in his shorts, and so on. Which I think is a good idea. I like the idea of him having a good time, and cheating on his wife and the whole thing.

O: *In a recent Malcolm McLaren biography, the author mentioned that at one point, you and Ebert were slated to write and direct the Sex Pistols film.*

RM: It wasn't really as rewarding as I thought it could have been. There was too much interference from the studio that we were working with, so it wasn't that keen a thing. That's all. It just didn't give me what I wanted, and Ebert felt the same way, that we were kind of pinned down.

O: *What did you think of Malcolm McLaren?*

RM: I think Malcolm McLaren needed at least one more lay in his life. I don't think he really understood much of what I was doing. Not that it was dreadfully important that he had to know, but he was obviously not in the same mold as me. He was always after me, trying to pick up anybody, even girls that were built like a willow, and so on. We weren't that keen on it.

O: *What did you think of The Sex Pistols?*

RM: I liked, what's his name...

O: *Sid Vicious?*

RM: Yeah. I liked him. I thought he had something going for him. His problem, though, was a little too much with the whipping and that kind of stuff. It didn't go in with me, particularly. [Changing the subject.] Kitten Natividad was always a great charmer in Britain when I was there, getting some things put together, trying to do a film with Darth Vader [actor David Prowse]. He was great. He would always be very cooperative. And we ended up looking for women, although he ended up looking more to me for women than him delivering to me, and then I'd get on his case about the fact that he wasn't really spending attitude on getting things to his advantage. But I think his wife had a lot to do with it. I think she'd like him to have a lot less to do with me than anything else. We made a film together, *Blacksnake!*, that was a failure. The women in the film were not terribly abundant, and that was one of the main reasons the film didn't work. I think we'll bring in Melissa Mounds and two or three other women... Melissa Mounds is close to me, and she has huge tits. That's what we'll use. One problem we had was that some people working on the film were gay. Not that it's wrong to be gay, but they were not all that tuned in to big tits, and so I had to lose their help.

O: ***What current filmmakers are you fond of?***

RM: I don't give any real particular thought about what current people are doing. I'm not that tuned in to that area. I'll catch a series of something, and I'll like it, and that's fine. I want to do a couple of really big, horny, large-breasted women, the kind of ladies I like, and that will be the next thing. I have one lady here right now, Ms. Mounds. She's very good. She'll put some sweat on your brow. She's very, very good from the standpoint that if you go on a tour with her, she'll be fucking you constantly. Unrelenting. Just every moment that you're free, she'll be sitting or lying on that bed, ready, legs wide spread open, pussy wet, ready to get everything you're ready to give her. That's the kind of lady that you need to have.

O: ***Are there any Hollywood actresses that you'd like to work with?***

RM: No. I would always just kind of get young people, young women with big tits. You run into problems with women thinking, "What is this fellow trying to do, trying to make some sort of pornographic movie?" And I would say, "Yes, only with enormous tits. Yours are not large enough." It's upsetting. All of a sudden, you have problems. But Melissa is very good. She has huge tits, and they're cantilevered. They must be cantilevered. They must be defying gravity.

O: ***So it's safe to say that you're not opposed to breast augmentation.***

RM: Oh, I think it's fine. If it does a good job, what the heck? It's very good. I would advocate it. When the woman is older and has the old man by the short hairs, then he can get his dick up. He can be doing something worthwhile.

"I made a lot of money, and I ended up buying myself an office where there were women. And I would always come on like a steam engine, telling them that they would all be stars. Lying through my teeth. It also gave me an opportunity to get a lot of pussy. That was really worthwhile."

O: ***What were your experiences like filming* Beyond The Valley Of The Dolls *for a major studio?***

RM: We had an enormous amount of women—a couple of agents would provide me with women—and by and large, I didn't have to go out and say, "Look, I'll give you a role." That was it. I would tell them, "I'll use you in the film, but you don't have to fuck me." And then they'd kind of breathe a sigh of relief.

O: ***When you're working on a project, do you***

usually start with actresses you want to use, or a script?

RM: It depends. I usually find a woman with big tits. That's all I really need to get started.

O: ***Then you find projects for them?***

RM: Well, I've had good writers. They've always been able to supply what I've needed. I've been away from it for a long time. But I'm getting ready. I've found a woman who is very giant in that area, and I think she's worthy of consideration.

O: ***So you'll be making a film sometime soon?***

RM: Yes. I like the whole idea of eating pussy, too. It's very good. Just get in there and chew right to the nub.

"We had an enormous amount of women—a couple of agents would provide me with women—and by and large, I didn't have to go out and say, 'Look, I'll give you a role.' That was it. I would tell them, 'I'll use you in the film, but you don't have to fuck me.' And then they'd kind of breathe a sigh of relief."

O: ***That's something you weren't doing earlier?***

RM: Not so much, but now I like it. But I can still whack away with my joint.

O: ***You're writing your autobiography right now, aren't you?***

RM: Yep. It's looking good. As a matter of fact, I'm here, at a young lady's place, getting a renewed ability to do things. We still have our military reunions, and the girls will go down and take care of some of my G.I. friends, sit on their faces and so forth. One just left now. She has big breasts, and she was going out to bring me some food. Which is a pretty good thought.

O: ***You used to be a photographer for* Playboy, *right?***

RM: Yeah, I've done that. It's just that I've got to find that kind of women, and *Playboy* really isn't coming up with it. The woman here, Melissa Mounds, whew! Big, big, big. Casting a long shadow.

O: ***You think that the women in* Playboy *don't have large enough breasts?***

RM: Yeah, by and large. I've taken [Hugh] Hefner to task many times. He says, "Look, you just bring someone around and I'll put them in my magazines."

O: ***You don't think it's possible to have breasts that are too large?***

RM: No, no. You've got to have big breasts, casting huge shadows. Just so the women don't buckle at the knees.

O: ***Of all your films, which is your favorite?***

RM: *Beyond The Valley Of The Dolls*. Ebert and I went for the big time. That was it. I had another friend who was doing some stuff for Elvis Presley, and knew women and so forth. I remember one of the first women sent to me by this man. Ebert was in the next room, typing away. Every production person at the time had a couch, the kind with a big hump at each end, so the woman could lay back and accept the dick comfortably. I remember, there was this girl—Elvis Presley had been whacking away at her—and he sent this girl over and put her in there. I told her, "Look, what I want you to do is to lie on the couch and put your pussy right up in the air." So I called Ebert, and I said, "Ebert, I want you to come in here and look at something." And he says, "I'm working on a script. I have no time for that." And I say, "Will you just get in there? There's something in there that I think you will find very, very interesting." And he went in, and all he did was turn back to me and say, "Hollywood!"

O: ***Did Elvis Presley ever visit the set of* Beyond The Valley Of The Dolls*?***

RM: Yeah, a couple of times. He was in and out, and that was it. He wasn't there for the purpose of nailing some girl. He had so many, he didn't need it.

O: ***What did you think of Elvis?***

RM: A charming, exciting, incredible man.

O: Beyond The Valley Of The Dolls ***is quite a cult film now.***

RM: A fact that both Ebert and I find extremely gratifying. But I have problems with Ebert now. His wife is always there. We just don't have the same communication and close friendship anymore. She realizes that Meyer is a bad influence. ∅

“*Mr. Show* was so great, in that I feel like I finally got to do something really pure.”

Mr. Show, Part V

By Stephen Thompson

Exclusive To *The Tenacity Of The Cockroach*

From 1995 to 1998, Bob Odenkirk and David Cross made 30 episodes of Mr. Show, *a remarkably funny and groundbreaking sketch-comedy series aired late at night on HBO. Thanks to a unique mixture of acting and writing talent, inspiration, and creative freedom,* Mr. Show *has already taken its place as a cult classic. But Odenkirk and Cross haven't had an easy time jumping through entertainment-industry hoops, with roadblocks ranging from indifferent network executives and shifting time slots to overwhelming exhaustion. With* Run, Ronnie, Run, *the* Mr. Show *movie, their most heated battles began in post-production, during a bruising (and mostly losing) dispute with director and longtime collaborator Troy Miller over creative control. Then, as the project neared its April 2002 release date, New Line shelved the film indefinitely. Odenkirk and Cross spoke to* The Onion A.V. Club *several times between November 2001 and February 2002, discussing* Run, Ronnie, Run*'s ever-changing release status, their frustrations with the finished film, and why it may all work out for the best in the end.*

The Onion: ***What is the status of* Run, Ronnie, Run*?***

Bob Odenkirk: It's shelved indefinitely. When it first looked like the movie was getting shelved, it was a very weird situation for me, because David and I had been campaigning to try to get the movie released. But even while I was doing that, I had mixed feelings, because I don't want New Line to release the actual movie that Troy Miller turned in. I want this recut that he did, using our notes. It is a much-improved movie: The way I would characterize it is that you don't pay for your laughs as hard. But I've got to say that not releasing it at all, even after campaigning to get it released, is such a fucking relief. It was like I had this terrible relationship for years, and when it was ending, I thought, "Oh, I'm gonna be so lonely and feel so bad," but when it ended, I felt so fucking *good.* All day and all night, I felt great. That's how I feel now about this choice they made. They've taken all this pain out of my life. I'm no longer arguing for a movie I don't really like, for a cut that's a little better but still isn't very good.

David Cross: We've kind of held each other's hands through this whole thing, and really been on the same page emotionally. I felt relief, but you had to go through all that fuckin' yo-yoing back and forth to get to that point. Eventually, you just go, "You know what? I'm done. I'm done, and I'm happy with being done. I don't give a shit. Fuckin' put it straight to video. I don't care." It's not fully our movie. I would care so much that I would do whatever I had to do—if I had to open up a shopping center with a chicken outfit on, I'd do that—to get the movie released. But it's not our movie. We're part of it, but it's not even close to *Mr. Show*. That's where you sort of pull back after a year and a half of getting aggravated, and having it really fuck with your head and interrupt your life. You forget what's fun and important and valuable in your life, and then you go, "Wait a minute. It's a fuckin' 86-minute comedy movie that's merely okay. What do I give a shit? It's not my fuckin' film. I didn't direct it."

BO: Now, this is the perspective that they granted us by shelving the movie. Throughout this process, we were faced with the choice of just quitting. We had that choice all along, and the fact is, you can't do that. We have friends who do that, and I just don't think it's responsible.

DC: Yeah, we didn't quit in the middle, we quit at the end. In the middle, we were still fighting to get input into the movie. It wasn't about the idea of releasing it. All the demoralizing frustrations were about having more involvement in the movie, and saying, "Guys, why don't you want our help? Look what we did before. We're not stupid guys. We're not fuckin' actors." But that shit is over. I can't go back in time and get dailies and make suggestions. Where we quit was working with a studio that doesn't know us, doesn't care to know us, and views us as fuckin' annoying actors. They don't give a shit. As much as you want to go into their office and say, "Hey, guys, we've got a bunch of fans! I just got off tour and I sold out everywhere!" They're like, "Huh? Who gives a shit? This is like *Joe Dirt*. How do I not market it like *Joe Dirt*?" And you just say, "Okay, forget it. I quit."

O: ***They wanted to market it like*** **Joe Dirt*****?***

DC: Well, because there was a similar wig, that's what our movie is like.

O: ***New Line is fat with hobbit dollars. How hard is it to put out a movie and see what happens?***

BO: Well, but they don't think it's a good movie. I mean, in their defense, they didn't like it that much. It isn't very well done.

O: ***Does a studio like each and every bad movie that comes out?***

BO: No, but they see a way to promote it, and they see our thing and don't see a way to promote it. It doesn't have a big movie star or a big TV star.

O: ***What about the soundtrack? The soundtrack has big names on it.***

BO: Not if you're the guy who runs New Line. You're 50 years old and you've never heard of anyone.

O: ***Don't they see the sales charts and see how Tool does?***

BO: No, they don't. Who shows them that? They've never heard of Tool. When you say Tool to them, they are completely mystified. We did it, and they were utterly mystified. They don't know what that means, or why it would matter to anyone. They're 50-year-old men who are billionaires, who live in fancy chalets, and to them, Mike Myers is an up-and-coming movie star. I mean, they are so fuckin' gone. They have never heard of Tool, man. Never heard of them. Numbers don't mean anything to them. We've said numbers to them. They don't count. They have to sort of know of it. You know what always happens with us? When we do get a break, it's because a personal awareness happens, usually through somebody's teenager. It happened at HBO, where some executive lady's son kept asking for the first four shows, and then word got around the executives that somebody was interested in our show—somebody that somebody knew. They didn't hear that a number of 14-year-olds like the show; they actually knew a 14-year-old who liked the show, and that was enough for them. You hear that shit all the time, man. Watch for that. It pops up all the time, and it's way more important than you can believe. People get albums, TV shows, and movies off some executive's 12-year-old, who goes, "Hey, Mom, I really like this guy. Get me this guy's album." "Hey, the kid wouldn't shut up about this guy, so I gave the guy a show." It's a testament to how out-of-touch executives are. Anyway, it's a relief, where we're at right now. I mean, we did our best trying to make a good product happen, and we couldn't do it. And that's life.

O: ***I would imagine that, in one form or another, that movie is going to come out. At some point, you'll be faced with the movie actually being released, at least on video.***

BO: Well, that'll suck.

O: ***Would you really be disappointed if it came out?***

BO: If it was not the new cut, yeah, I would. And I don't like the new cut that much, either. I would be very disappointed. I don't want it to come out, especially not straight to video with the original version. Because you look bad, and you watch the movie and go, "Yeah, I get why they put this on video. This isn't very good."

DC: Well, I don't necessarily agree with that. I think it's important to look at this, not through the highly subjective eyes we have, but in relation to movies that justify their existence. I certainly think it justifies its existence as a theatrical film, as well as a comedy. I don't think it's a terrible comedy. I mean, it's not the cool, groundbreaking, subversive movie that we thought it might be, but it's still funny, and I have no problem giving people the opportunity to see it.

BO: All right, I agree that I don't have a problem with people seeing it, but I just don't want to go through the hassle of talking about it and having to justify it, and having people go, "Yeah, I can see why this didn't come out."

O: ***Do you think that what happened with the movie will make it harder for you to make another one?***

BO: I don't know. It's probably going to make it harder. If I ran a studio, I would think twice about giving somebody who blew $8 million another couple million, wouldn't you?

DC: I'm not so sure I agree with that. I think people know the story. I don't think we're really to blame. I think they probably, understandably at this point, think we're difficult to work with, or...

BO: Sticky wickets.

DC: Sticky wickets. You know, I have no idea how other people involved in meetings we're not privy to are talking about us, but I think they know that we're capable of writing a comedy script and being good comic actors. We may not be able to jump right in and direct a film that we write, that we star in, that we get to cast.

"They're 50-year-old men who are billionaires, who live in fancy chalets, and to them, Mike Myers is an up-and-coming movie star."

BO: Listen, we keep running into this wall, and we've got to admit that it's there. It would be insane to not admit that it exists after hitting it so many times. Everything's okay now, though. I feel good.

DC: I can't wait to not talk about this anymore.

O: ***Reading back through the interviews we've done with you guys, there's a steady change in your attitude toward the industry and what goes on around you. How would you say you've changed from the beginning of* Mr. Show *to the completion of this movie? How are you different?***

BO: Well, for me, *Mr. Show* was so great, in that I feel like I finally got to do something really pure. I'm talking about the TV show, now. Just being able to do that once, and to really show people that we could do it and that it's worth doing... It's very relaxing to be able to say, "I did it once. I got to do something really strong one time." All the years before doing *Mr. Show*, I had that desire in me, and you just don't know if you'll ever get that opportunity to show people this idea that you have, or this sensibility that you have. It's weird: I'm doing a show called *NEXT!*, a pilot for a network on prime time, and I could never have done this first. Because, honestly, it's *Mr. Show*'s sensibility. That's my sensibility and David's sensibility, and that's what I write, so it can't really be anything else. And it's trying to apply that sensibility to topics that more people can relate to. I feel like it could work. People might really go for it. It's kind of smart-but-silly, you know? It's not as pure as *Mr. Show*, but because I already did *Mr. Show*, I'm okay with it. If I hadn't done *Mr. Show*, I'd be writing this stuff going, "Fuck, I don't really get to go all the way." But I already went all the way, and I did it for years, and it went great, and it was great. Now, I'm trying to do something else that is, on some artistic level, not as pure, but is an attempt to do other things that I haven't

"Listen, we keep running into this wall, and we've got to admit that it's there. It would be insane to not admit that it exists after hitting it so many times."

been allowed to do, like really reach a lot of people. On HBO, even its biggest shows are nothing compared to the audience you can get on a network. It's freeing to have done *Mr. Show*. Before, I had such a chip on my shoulder, and I know David would say I still do, but...

DC: I would say you exchanged one chip for another. But, you know, when I was listening to you and thinking about the question, one of the first things that occurred to me was that when we first met each other and I moved to L.A., I was very cynical—to a fault, I think. I guess I might have expected the cynicism to die down a bit, but it hasn't. It only got more resolved, to the point where I can't live in L.A. I might have expected that to dissipate a little bit with the success of the show—not with other people, but just with me, saying, "This is fucking great, it's unique, and now it's almost a little burdensome." We did this fucking amazing thing, and you know you're going to be compared to it, which is understandable. But it's a really tough thing to move away from. I can't possibly be prouder of anything. We worked so fucking hard and got our vision across. We did not compromise. It was great. Then you do something like fucking *Just Shoot Me*, and everybody knows you as the "chicken pot pie" guy, and you go, "Wait, but, no. What kind of weird existentialist hell did I enter?"

BO: It's just a great feeling to know you did *Mr. Show*, because if you're doing one of these sitcoms, you might be a little embarrassed, or feel like it's not really the smartest material. But you go, "Yeah, but I did *Mr. Show*. Everybody knows it, and there's proof of it." I don't want to compare myself to the greats, but you've got to believe that Eric Idle, when he was doing *Nuns On The Run*, was like, "Yeah, well, I did Monty Python."

O: ***But you guys killed yourselves on* Mr. Show*. You used to talk about how much it aged you, and how crushingly difficult...***

BO: It was hard, but we figured it out by the end. We could have done another season. Nobody seemed to give a shit. HBO certainly didn't.

DC: Tell him about how that happened.

BO: How we got moved to Monday at midnight?

DC: Just people... I got off the road, and everywhere I went, people were asking if there were going to be more episodes of *Mr. Show*. I'd tell them the very abbreviated story about how we quit, we were pissed off at getting moved to Monday at midnight just when we were building up an audience, and it was demoralizing and frustrating to work that hard and actually take steps backwards. Then we stopped doing it, both for personal reasons

and to work on the movie. And then, when we were done with the movie, Bob went and approached HBO about doing another season. They said "no," which you weren't surprised at, but I found shocking. We're the fucking cheapest show on TV.
BO: Yeah, but I think that they feel like they've found their audience. I mean, they're rightfully proud of *The Sopranos*, and *Sex And The City* has its audience, and the two cross over somewhat.
DC: I just think it points to their profound ignorance of how important the show is to a good number of people. There's a vast number of people I meet every motherfucking day, everywhere I go, that are fans who miss it.
BO: It's very hard. We had some great fans at HBO, but there were a lot of people at HBO who didn't like the show, or didn't get it.
O: ***You guys still like each other, right?***
DC: Yeah.
BO: Absolutely. We have a great time. We have bobanddavid.com, which we're trying to make like a magazine, where we get to write little fake articles and short comic pieces, and our friends will write stuff. We'll try to update that every two weeks to a month. And then we'll do another *Mr. Show* movie.
DC: People do ask me that when I'm on the road. "Do you and Bob get along? Are you still friends?"
BO: Yeah, David's in this pilot I'm doing.
DC: It's fun getting his sketches and making notes on them. Even that, or just talking, is still fun. There's maybe one person that I respect and have more fun with than Bob, and that's Chris Burke. Besides him, I really...
BO: Who's that? Oh, from *Life Goes On*.
DC: Yeah, he's a lot of fun. Sometimes he's not. Honestly, you're laughing at him.
BO: But you're laughing.
DC: You're laughing. There's few people I enjoy hanging out with and working with more than Bob.

"Everybody's your friend and happiness rains down from the sky." CHAPTER 10

"In America, everybody's your friend and happiness rains down from the sky... I talk to the multitude wherever I am, and that provides a living. I only tell them how to be happy, because happiness is the only thing I understand."

Quentin Crisp page 363

"I love the show, and I love the people. I love the stories we told. I mean, I'm angry about every single edit and line and costume change and rewrite, but that's part of the business. Ultimately, I wouldn't change anything."

Joss Whedon page 369

"I never regret anything. I don't believe in regret. It's just a big time-waster."

Michael McKean page 379

"I've been very fortunate, worked with a lot of news and TV people, too. I even worked with Ronald Reagan... I've been kind of blessed, I guess."

Billy Barty page 385

"I'm quiet. I'm peaceful. I'm 48 fuckin' years old. I got a great marriage. My wife is profound. I've had more poontang than fuckin' Frank Sinatra. I don't need to prove myself that way anymore."

James Ellroy page 391

"I'm 56, and people my age are always talking about getting up. I feel the same way I did when I was 22 years old... I'm better now than when I was 22."

The Unknown Comic page 395

"Now is the only moment you've got to work with. If you deliver excellence right now, that gives you the best shot at the best future you've got coming."

Robert Forster page 403

Quentin Crisp

By Keith Phipps

Originally Printed October 1997

"I talk to the multitude wherever I am, and that provides a living. I only tell them how to be happy, because happiness is the only thing I understand."

Though he was a supremely gifted writer, Quentin Crisp achieved a good deal of his fame simply by being Quentin Crisp. Born in England in 1908, Crisp was flamboyantly gay at a time when undisguised homosexuality was dangerous. His 1968 memoir The Naked Civil Servant, *which chronicles such dangers, has been turned into a play, as well as a movie starring John Hurt. In the '70s, Crisp moved to New York, where he continued to write while lecturing, acting in films as far afield as* Orlando *(1992) and* To Wong Foo, Thanks For Everything, Julie Newmar *(1995), and appearing in ads for Calvin Klein perfume and Levi's jeans. He died in 1999, while in England reviving his one-man show* An Evening With Quentin Crisp. An Evening *showcased his immense ability to mine the wit out of any subject. Two years prior to his death, as he was beginning work on his final book,* Dusty Answers, *Crisp shared that talent in an interview with* The Onion A.V. Club.

The Onion: ***More people probably know your name or face than know who you are or anything about your life, so maybe you could give us a short personal history.***

Quentin Crisp: Well, I lived in England all my life until I was 72, and then at last I had enough money to pay to leave it, so I came to America. I've always been American in my heart, ever since my mother took me to the movies.

O: ***Why is that? What's the difference between being American in your heart and being English in your heart?***

QC: Well, being English in your heart... England is very dreary, but I'm a people person. I would never go to a place and live there because the weather was good or the scenery was beautiful or the architecture was wonderful. I would only go because the people are kind, and in America, everybody's your friend and happiness rains down from the sky. And in England, nobody's your friend. So I at last could leave, and I came to America, and someone said the other day, "You came to America when most people decide to go into a nursing home." Which is true; I was already 72, but I couldn't pay my fare before that. I came first to America in 1977 at the invitation of a man who wanted to make my life story into a musical. But my agent said it was not to be, and it was never done. So I went back, but I'd seen New York, and I wanted to live there. Because everybody talks to you in the street. See, nobody talks to you in England. A vast, rain-swept

Alcatraz. So I came here then, and I lived in unaccustomed splendor on 39th Street until one of my spies found this room, by knowing someone who knew someone who knew the landlord. I've always lived in the same way. I lived in England in one room in a rooming house, and I live here in one room in a rooming house.

O: ***Why is that?***

QC: Well, because I've never found out what people do with the room they're not in. So I stay in one room, and it's easier to live there, to control it, to make it warm. It seems to me a convenient way to live, and it's cheap. Of course, England was much cheaper than America. But still I can manage. I've never worked since I've been here, that's another thing. You see, I have to work in England, but here you don't have to work. You can sort of enter the profession of being.

O: ***You never miss England?***

QC: Oh, I never miss England. No, someone said to me, "Don't you miss anything about England?" And I thought, "My gas fire." Here, there's no method of heating your room. Your room is only as warm as the super decides it should be. Today, for instance, I'm shuddering in my room because there's no heat. When I got here, I was writing a book, *Manners From Heaven* (1984). Then I... I sort of went... I don't know how to describe it. I talk to the multitude wherever I am, and that provides a living. I only tell them how to be happy, because happiness is the only thing I understand.

O: ***What do you usually tell them?***

QC: Well, I tell them not to do any of the things their mothers tell them—not to clean the place where you live, and not to wash the dishes, and all that. It's all a waste of time. I never spend my time doing anything I'll have to do again tomorrow. And I went recently to Los Angeles and told them how to be happy. Then I went to San Diego, which is wonderful, although California on the whole is a weird place—it's always burning or flooding or shaking or something. San Diego is always a cool summer, and I went there and told them how to be happy, and then I came back here. I go wherever my fare is paid. It's a strange situation, but people will pay your fare to get you to go and tell them how to be happy.

O: ***Well, probably not most people. You're one of the few people who could get paid to do that.***

QC: I don't know why.

O: ***Well, possibly because you've made a lifetime commitment to disregarding what people expect you to do, and what conventional morality would say you have to do.***

QC: That's right, yes. You don't have to do anything. I don't believe in convention at all. I do what I have to do to stay alive.

O: ***Was there a moment when you decided that there was no point in trying to fit in? When you realized that you had to wear your identity on the outside, that you couldn't be a closeted gay man?***

QC: People say to me, "When did you come out?" But I was never in! When I was about 6, I was swanning around the house in clothes that belonged to my mother and my grandmother, saying, "I am a beautiful princess!" What my parents thought of this, I don't know. But they bore it. And the real problem was not my sin, but my unemployability. So I went out into the world when I was about 22. I wrote books and illustrated books and did book covers, and I taught tap-dancing, and I was a model in the art school. I had no ability for any of those things, but what else could I do? You see, it may be true that artists adopt a flamboyant appearance, but it's also true that people who look funny get stuck with the arts. That's what happened to me. And then I came here, and I'd written several books before I got here—*The Naked Civil Servant* and so on. When I got here, I just went on doing the same things.

O: ***Would you say you're happy now?***

QC: And now I'm happy. I don't ever have to pay anything, and I don't ever have to wash the dishes, and I don't ever have to behave nicely. You can behave as badly as you like in America. Nobody notices.

O: ***Would you say you owe it all to the change in location? Because* The Naked Civil Servant *ends with such a tragic turn of phrase. ["Even a monotonously undeviating path of self-examination does not necessarily lead to a mountain of self-knowledge. I stumble toward my grave confused and hurt and hungry..."]***

QC: Yes, it has. It has made a wonderful difference.

O: ***Do you think the change in political climate allowing more freedom for gay people has had something to do with it, as well?***

QC: That's true, there is more freedom. You see, America believes in freedom. The English don't believe in it. They don't believe in happiness.

O: ***And you think Americans generally do?***

QC: Yes, it's written into the Constitution that you're allowed to pursue happiness. In England it would be considered a frivolous objective.

O: ***What's an average day like for you? What do you do on a day-to-day basis?***

QC: Well, I do two things. On a day like today, I don't go out at all, and then I can remain wrapped in a filthy dressing gown, doing absolutely nothing. And someone said, "I don't think you should say that. Couldn't you say you meditate?" So I meditate.

O: ***On a busy day, what do you do?***

QC: Well, I wake. I reconstruct myself, which takes about two and a half hours, and then I go out. You see, if you don't stay in some days, you can't recharge your batteries. In Manhattan, when you're out of the front door, you're on, and you have to be ready to smile and speak to people. Everybody who's been on television more than once wears in public an expression of fatuous affability. Because you may be addressed at any moment by somebody.

O: ***Do you get approached a lot?***

QC: More than most people. Not a lot, but every day someone notices me and waves to me, or stops and speaks to me, or asks me for an autograph, or photographs me.

O: ***Do you mind that?***

QC: I don't mind it. I don't know why people are so angry about it. I reviewed Mr. [Alec] Guinness' diary, which was a little book about 18 months of his life, and all he did was come up from his country home to London and eat expensive meals and go back again. And the only thing that ever annoyed him was being recognized. Well, he wasn't recognized by teenagers trying to tear off his clothes! He was recognized by middle-aged ladies saying, "Surely you're Mr. Guinness?" And all he had to say was, "Well, how charming of you to recognize me." I mean, it's not trouble. I don't understand why they're cross.

"It may be true that artists adopt a flamboyant appearance, but it's also true that people who look funny get stuck with the arts."

O: ***You've seen more of the country than just New York. What do you think of the rest of America?***

QC: Oh, yes, all America is much the same. I've been as far west as Seattle, and as far north as Detroit. When you're in Detroit, you eat in a restaurant which turns while you eat. And I've been as far south as Key West, from which you can go no further south. So I've really been all over America.

O: ***I recently saw a documentary about you where some gay-rights activists criticized you as being a sort of stereotype. How do you respond to that?***

QC: Well, I am a stereotype. I am an effeminate man. When I was young, I and the whole world thought that all homosexuals were effeminate. And of course they're not. You can just see which people are effeminate; that's the only difference. I became a prototype of the effeminate man, because I was conspicuously effeminate. But camp is not something I do, it's something I am.

O: ***The other thing they criticized, and this probably comes with camp, was your tragic demeanor. But you don't really seem to have a tragic demeanor anymore.***

QC: I don't think I have a tragic demeanor. I can't remember ever having a tragic demeanor. Although my life was tragedy. I was beaten up wherever I went, and people shouted at me and cursed me and threw things at me...

O: ***Those are things most people don't have to deal with.***

QC: You don't have to deal with anyone in America. They accept you the way you are. I

"The war was wonderful, of course. You were in danger, which was lovely, because you look your last on all things lovely every hour. And that's nice."

was on a bus going up Third Avenue, and a huge great man sat next to me and said, "Do you live here permanently?" And I said, "Yes." And he said, "It's the place to be if you're of a different stripe." I mean, it is.

O: ***There were bright spots to your time in England as well, right?***

QC: Well, the war was wonderful, of course. You were in danger, which is lovely, because you look your last on all things lovely every hour. And that's nice.

O: ***You recently popped up in a Levi's commercial.***

QC: Yes, I don't know how I did that. I didn't put on Levi's. I've never worn Levi's. I sat at a table, and you couldn't see my legs at all. I only said two words in the commercial. And then, when I was in Mr. Klein's advertisement, I went all the way to Brooklyn and went into a huge place where I thought we could film *The Charge Of The Light Brigade*. It was like an aeroplane hangar. And I found a square of paper and six very thin people standing on it. A man naked to the waist crawled on the floor between our feet. And I said to Mr. Klein, "What does it all mean?" Mr. Klein said, "Say that again." By mistake I'd written the copy.

O: ***Did they pay you for writing the copy?***

QC: [Laughs.] Yes.

O: ***And you've been in movies.***

QC: I've been in two real movies. I've been in *The Bride*. Mr. Sting played Frankenstein and Miss [Jennifer] Beals played the creature that he constructs for the monster. And then I was in *Naked In New York*, with Miss [Kathleen] Turner and the Karate Kid [Ralph Macchio] and Mr. [Tony] Curtis.

O: ***You were also in* Orlando. *You were terrific in that.***

QC: I don't really act. I say the words the way I would say them if I meant them. But I don't know how people act. I've never understood that. I asked a girl who came from America to England, when I was only English, and she admitted she had been to a drama school. And I said, "What did they teach you?" She said, "They taught me to be a candle burning in an empty room." I'm happy to say she was laughing while she said it, but she meant it. I've never learned to be a candle burning in an empty room. So I go on the screen and I say whatever I'm told to say.

O: ***You played Queen Elizabeth in* Orlando.**

QC: That's right. It was hell to do. I wore a bonnet so tight it blistered my stomach. I wore two rolls of fabric tied around my waist with tape, and then a hoop skirt tied around my waist with tape, and then a quilted petticoat, and then a real petticoat, and then a dress. I could never leave the trailer in which they were put on me without someone lifting up the whole lot and saying, "Put your foot down. Forward. More. Now the other one. That's right, now you're on level ground." I could never see my feet during the whole production.

O: ***How was your experience in* To Wong Foo?**
QC: That was very strange. Because nearly always, when actors are approached by the beauticians, they try to avoid the dabs that the beauticians put on their faces. They dodge them. But in *To Wong Foo*, when there was a pause in the filming, everyone was like a bird in a cage. "Me! Me! Look, isn't there something... Couldn't you put a bit of powder up there? Is my eyelash slipping?" And so on. They all wanted to be made up.
O: ***When that movie came out, all the actors who appeared on talk shows went to great lengths to demonstrate how masculine they were in real life. Did you notice that?***
QC: Yes, I never understand that. As soon as an actor takes a part as a homosexual, the press says, "What do your wife and children think of this?" And the actor never says, "Well, last week I was a murderer, and the week before that I was a child molester, and the week before that I was a lunatic. But now I'm a homosexual." [Laughs.] They all say, "Oh, they're behind me all the way. They approve of it." I don't know, but it seems very strange. They all object to someone playing a homosexual.
O: ***What do you think about the portrayal of gay people in movies today?***
QC: Well, I think it's much easier. You see, you don't have to be camp—you don't have to flap your hands and roll your eyes—because nobody does it anymore. See, the world was very feminine when I was young, and now it's very masculine. Because women have decided to be people, which is a great mistake. Women were nicer than people. When I wrote *Manners From Heaven*, I was interviewed by a woman who asked if I researched the subject. And I said, "Yes, I read all the books I could find about manners, and the extraordinary thing was, in all books up to the end of the Second World War, most were directed at how to comport yourself in the presence of the ladies." And I said, "And now there are no ladies." She said, "I don't think we're putting up with that, are we, girls?" And the girls said no, and I said, "Well, I thought you decided to be people." They said, "We are people." And I said, "But you can't be a person and a lady. If you're a person, you can open the damned door yourself." What matters is not whether you put your fork or knife together because you've finished your meal, or something like that. What matters is that you don't offend people or hurt their feelings by mistake by saying the wrong thing or doing the wrong thing.
O: ***A lot of people think New York is a rude city.***
QC: No, I think it's wonderful. People have all said that, but I find people so courteous and so generous. Free drinks in bars. Free taxi rides.
O: ***Well, a lot of it has to do with the fact that you're famous, too.***
QC: Well, I don't know. I've never not been famous. [Laughs.]

For more information on Quentin Crisp, consult www.crisperanto.org. Ø

"I designed *Buffy* to be an icon, to be an emotional experience, to be loved in a way that other shows can't be loved."

Joss Whedon

By Tasha Robinson

Originally Printed September 2001

Joss Whedon spent years in the screenwriting trenches before finally achieving popular success with his TV series Buffy The Vampire Slayer. *He started out in television, writing episodes of* Roseanne *and* Parenthood, *but after selling the original* Buffy *screenplay (which was filmed in 1992), he began working as a film writer and script doctor, doing uncredited touch-ups on* Twister, Speed, *and* Waterworld, *and writing drafts of projects such as* X-Men, Toy Story, Titan A.E., *Disney's* Atlantis, *and* Alien: Resurrection. *But Whedon came into his own with the television incarnation of* Buffy, *which ultimately grew from a cult classic into a cottage industry. As* Buffy's *creator, Whedon has had a hand in virtually all tie-ins, including the spin-off series* Angel *and a growing line of comic books. In 2001, heading into* Buffy's *sixth season amid plans for a BBC series spin-off and a Saturday-morning cartoon, Whedon spoke to* The Onion A.V. Club *about the* Buffy *phenomenon, his bitterness over his movie career, and the fans who share in his worship of his creations.*

The Onion: ***You're a third-generation television scriptwriter, possibly the first one. How did your family affect your career choice?***

Joss Whedon: At first, I was like, "I shall never write for television." I was a total snob. I never watched American TV; I only watched, like, *Masterpiece Theatre*. And I was like, "Television is lame-o, I am a film student, I shall never write for... They pay how much?" When I was just starting out, and I had no idea how I was going to become the brilliant independent filmmaker that I imagined myself to be, and I was staying with my father, I thought, "Well, I'll try my hand at a spec." You know, by selling a TV script, I could make enough money to sort of keep myself afloat. That was the first time I ever sat down and tried to write. I had always sort of written, but I had never studied writing or thought of myself as a writer exactly. I always assumed I would write whatever I made, but I never really gave it much thought. Then I sat down and really tried to write a script and found the great happiness of my life.

O: ***Was that in college or post-college?***

JW: Post-college. I started writing TV specs, and I was like, "Writing is fun, and there are some good shows out there! I was being a snob!" So I wrote a bunch of specs, I didn't get any work, and finally I landed a job on *Roseanne*. And having worked, now, in the movie and TV world, I'm still a complete snob, but it's reversed. I feel like film is a ridiculous hell, and TV is the greatest place in the world.

O: ***Did you ever have a day job that wasn't related to media or TV?***

JW: I worked at a video store. Actors wait tables, directors work at video stores. I did research for the American Film Institute, for the guy who was doing their Life Achievement Awards. Those were my two big, exciting gigs. I landed a job pretty young. I was, like, 24 when I started. I turned in my first script on my 25th birthday, and I looked much younger. When they found out I was 25, it was like, "Oh, you're no Boy Wonder. You're over."

O: ***Did you quit* Roseanne *when you sold the original* Buffy *movie script?***

JW: I wrote the *Buffy* script because I had way too much free time. I was on *Roseanne* for a year, and in the first half of that year, I wrote five scripts. I was a staff writer, the lowest thing you can be. And one of my father's older writer friends actually asked me, "Have they let you start to write a script yet?" I was like, "I'm on my fourth." Because there was such chaos, and almost nobody else there could do it. It was great. It was this vacuum of power, and I got sucked up. I got so much responsibility. But then my stuff kept getting rewritten, and in the second half of the year I just wrote one. I got shut out by the producers, basically, and I wasn't writing. I was coming in late, leaving early, and writing my screenplay instead, because they weren't using me, and it was driving me crazy, because I don't want money for nothing. So I said, "I quit." There was nothing for me to do there. So I had written *Buffy*, I hadn't sold it. I quit because I wanted to work harder, and I got a job on *Parenthood*, which ran for about 13 episodes. Which was a good show—good staff, good cast—that got eaten up by the network. So I had that experience, and after that I waned on TV and wanted to work more in the movies. And, after all the studios had "Loved it and passed on it!," [producer] Fran Kuzui started nosing around *Buffy*, and that started to take off.

O: ***What about your* Boy Meets World *direction credit? When did that happen?***

JW: [Laughs.] That never happened. I've never seen the show, but apparently it's on the Internet that I directed one. Boy has never met world. Let me put it this way: The episode of *Boy Meets World* that I never made, I'm still prouder of than *Alien: Resurrection*.

O: ***How closely were you involved with the making of the* Buffy *movie?***

JW: I had major involvement. I was there almost all the way through shooting. I pretty much eventually threw up my hands because I could not be around Donald Sutherland any longer. It didn't turn out to be the movie that I had written. They never do, but that was my first lesson in that. Not that the movie is without merit, but I just watched a lot of stupid wannabe-star behavior and a director with a different vision than mine—which was her right, it was her movie—but it was still frustrating. Eventually, I was like, "I need to be away from here."

O: ***Was it a personality conflict between you and Sutherland, or was he just not what you'd envisioned in that role?***

JW: No, no, he was just a prick. The thing is, people always make fun of Rutger Hauer [for his *Buffy* role]. Even though he was big and silly and looked kind of goofy in the movie, I have to give him credit, because he was there. He was into it. Whereas Donald was just... He would rewrite all his dialogue, and the director would let him. He can't write—he's not a writer—so the dialogue would not make sense. And he had a very bad attitude. He was incredibly rude to the director, he was rude to everyone around him, he was just a real pain. And to see him destroying my stuff... Some people didn't notice. Some people liked him in the movie. Because he's Donald Sutherland. He's a great actor. He can read the phone book, and I'm interested. But the thing is, he acts well enough that you didn't notice, with his little rewrites, and his little ideas about what his character should do, that he was actually destroying the movie more than Rutger was. So I got out of there. I had to run away.

O: ***How early on did it occur to you to re-do* Buffy *the way you'd originally intended?***

JW: You know, it wasn't really my idea. After the première of the movie, my wife said, "You know, honey, maybe a few years from now, you'll get to make it again, the way you want to make it." [Broad, condescending voice.] "Ha ha ha, you little naïve fool. It doesn't work that way. That'll never happen." And then it was three years later, and Gail Berman actually had the idea. Sandollar [Television] had the property, and Gail thought it would make a good TV series. They called me up out of contractual obligation: "Call the writer, have him pass." And I was like, "Well, that sounds cool." So, to my agent's surprise and chagrin, I said, "Yeah, I could do that. I think I get it. It could be a high-school horror movie. It'd be a metaphor for how lousy my high-school years were." So I hadn't had the original idea, I just developed it.

O: ***You joke a lot in interviews about how you wanted to write horror because you experienced so much of it in high school. Did you have an unusually bad high-school experience, or was it just the usual teen traumas?***

JW: I think it's not inaccurate to say that I had a perfectly happy childhood during which I was very unhappy. It was nothing worse than anybody else. I could not get a date to save my life, but my last three years of high school were at a boys' school, so I wasn't actually looking that hard. I was not popular in school, and I was definitely not a ladies' man. And I had a very painful adolescence, because it was all very strange to me. It wasn't like I got beat up, but the humiliation and isolation, and the existential "God, I exist, and nobody cares" of being a teenager were extremely pronounced for me. I don't have horror stories. I mean, I have a few horror stories about attempting to court a girl, which would make people laugh, but it's not like I think I had it worse than other people. But that's sort of the point of *Buffy*, that I'm talking about the stuff everybody goes through. Nobody gets out of here without some trauma.

O: ***You describe yourself as an isolated, solitary kid, and then you moved into writing, which is often a solitary profession. Did you have problems adapting to an environment where you have to work closely with large crowds of people for long hours every day?***

JW: You know, I had a lot of brothers, and then boarding school, 13 to a room. I definitely need my alone time. And when I'm writing, I'm happiest. My greatest joy is being alone with a story. But on the other hand, I enjoy people. I enjoy directing and making the show, and the people I work with are smart and funny. As long as I keep balanced, I'm okay. I need to spend more time alone than most people I know, and it's hard to... When you're producing a show, you're never alone. So to find the time to write, to really get away from everybody, it's difficult. But it's not like I can't be around people, like this insane recluse with a big beard.

O: ***Has your film degree come in handy, or did you walk out of school with a lot of useless abstract knowledge?***

JW: I walked out with unbelievably essential knowledge. I happened to study under the people that I believe are the best film teachers ever. Film hasn't existed that long, so I say that with a certain amount of confidence. The teachers at Wesleyan were brilliant, the most brilliant people I've been around, and there is not a story that I tell that does not reflect something I either learned, or learned but already knew, from my professors. In terms of production, the place was useless. In terms of connections, it wasn't the fast track to becoming a hotshot producer. But my... It was just an undergraduate degree, but I'm talking about an education, the most valuable thing I ever learned. Oddly enough, I never studied writing. I studied almost everything except writing. But I'd been around scripts my whole life. I'd seen my father's scripts, I knew the basic format, and I understood the basic style, the language, the rhythm.

O: ***Did you ever go to your father for writing advice?***

JW: I never actually said, "Father, what do I do?" But he has given me some great advice. In fact, I've actually said to my writers, "You know, my father said to me once..." and then stopped and said, "I can't believe that came out of my mouth." The best piece of advice he ever gave me—he's written sitcoms exclusively—was, "If you have a good story, you don't need jokes. If you don't have a good story, no amount of jokes can save you." I'm not really that interested in jokes. I like the more dramatic stuff. But that tenet of "the story is god" is the most important thing I could have learned.

O: ***When you saw the completed* Buffy *movie, it wasn't the film you wanted to make, and several years later, you re-created it as a successful franchise. Do you ever have similar thoughts about* Alien: Resurrection*? Do you ever want to go back and "fix" it?***

JW: Oh, yes, I have. Ohhh, yes, the fantasies. I've never had a worse experience in my life, and I've often thought of doing a lecture series on how to make movies based on just showing that movie, because I think they literally did every single thing wrong. The production design, the casting... There wasn't a mistake they left unturned. So I've often thought about it, because we'd been in talks about *Alien 5*. I love sequels, I love franchises, and I love big epic stories that go on and on. I used to love summer movies, before every single one of them was crap. So, yeah, I've thought about doing what I'd originally thought in *Alien 5*. And after I found out on the Internet that I was making it, just after I directed *Boy Meets World*... [Laughs.] I thought about what I would do, what I would want to do with that franchise. And I was like, "You know what? I think maybe I'd like to work on something that 19 people don't own and control." We have so many executive producers on *Buffy*—and they leave me alone, they're great, but I think I'd like to do something that isn't just somebody else's. Having said that, I'm now considering doing the *Iron Man* movie. But that's just because it's got that cool shiny suit. *Alien 5* was a longer shot. I mean, you have a body blow to recover from there.

O: ***Were you on the set for that, watching them take your script apart?***

JW: No, I wasn't involved at all. I only went to the set once or twice. I'd been on movie sets, and I tend to stay away from them, because people want rewrites. They see the writer, and they're like, "Wouldn't it be cool if my character..." "Gotta go, bye!" So I went once or twice, and I went after the première of *Buffy* [the series]. And the producer guy they had saw me, and said, "Hey, I went to the première of your show, and it was so weird. I said, 'Hey, they're playing it the way he writes it!'" I was like, "And what are they doing here?" That was my first sign that there might be trouble. I literally didn't see any of it again until I saw the director's cut, during which I actually cried.

O: ***Just over what they'd done to your script?***

JW: It was a single manly tear rolling down my cheek. About an hour into the movie, I just started to cry. I said, "I can't believe this." I was heartbroken.

O: ***How much of your writing made it into the final versions of* Twister *and* Speed*?***

JW: Most of the dialogue in *Speed* is mine, and a bunch of the characters. That was actually pretty much a good experience. I have quibbles. I also have the only poster left with my name still on it. Getting arbitrated off the credits was un-fun. In *Twister*, there are things that worked and things that weren't the way I'd intended them. Whereas *Speed* came out closer to what I'd been trying to do. I think of *Speed* as one of the few movies I've made that I actually like.

O: ***What about* Waterworld*?***

JW: [Laughs.] *Waterworld*. I refer to myself as the world's highest-paid stenographer. This is a situation I've been in a bunch of times. By the way, I'm very bitter, is that okay? I mean, people ask me, "What's the worst job you ever had?" "I once was a writer in Hollywood..." Talk about taking the glow off of movies. I've had almost nothing but bad experiences. *Waterworld* was a good idea, and the script was the classic, "They have a good idea, then they write a generic script and don't really care about the idea." When I was brought in, there was no water in the last 40 pages of the script. It all took place on land, or on a ship, or whatever. I'm like, "Isn't the cool thing about this guy that he has gills?" And no one was listening. I was there basically taking notes from Costner, who was very nice, fine to work with, but he was not a writer. And he had written a bunch of stuff that they wouldn't let their staff touch. So I was supposed to be there for a week, and I was there for seven weeks, and I accomplished nothing. I wrote a few puns and a few scenes that I can't even sit through because they came out so bad. It was the same situation with *X-Men*. They said, "Come in and punch up the big climax, the third act, and if you can, make it cheaper." That was the mandate on both movies, and my response to both movies was, "The problem with the third act is the first two acts." But, again, no one was paying attention. *X-Men* was very interesting in that, by that time, I actually had a reputation in television. People stopped thinking I was John Sweden on the phone. And then, in *X-Men*, not only did they throw out my script and never tell me about it, but they actually invited me to the read-through, having thrown out my entire draft without telling me. I was like, "Oh, that's right! This is the movies! The writer is shit in the movies!" I'll never understand that. I have one line left in that movie. Actually, there are a couple of lines left in that are out of context and make no sense or are delivered so badly, so terribly... There's one line that's left the way I wrote it.

O: ***Which is?***

JW: " 'It's me.' 'Prove it.' 'You're a dick.' " Hey, it got a laugh.

O: ***The only lines I really remember from that movie are that one and Storm's toad comment.***

JW: Okay, which was also mine, and that's the interesting thing. Everybody remembers that as the worst line ever written, but the thing about that is, it was supposed to be delivered as completely offhand. [Adopts casual, bored tone.] "You know what happens when a toad gets hit by lightning?" Then, after he gets electrocuted, "Ahhh, pretty much the same thing that happens to anything else." But Halle Berry said it like she was Desdemona. [Strident, ringing voice.] "The same thing that happens to everything eeelse!" That's the thing that makes you go crazy. At least "You're a dick" got delivered right. The worst thing about these things is that, when the actors say it wrong, it makes the writer look stupid. I listened to half the dialogue in *Alien 4*, and I'm like, "That's idiotic," because of the way it was said. Nobody ever gets that. They say, "That was a stupid script," which is the worst pain in the world. I have a great long boring story about that, but I can tell you the very short version. In *Alien 4*, the director [Jean-Pierre Jeunet] changed something so that it didn't make any sense. He wanted someone to go and get a gun and get killed by the alien, so I wrote that in and tried to make it work, but he directed it in a way that it made no sense whatsoever. And I was sitting there in the editing room, trying to come up with looplines to explain what's going on, to make the scene make sense, and I asked the director, "Can you just explain to me why he's doing this? Why is he going for this gun?" And the editor, who was French, turned to me and said, with a little leer on his face, [adopts gravelly, smarmy, French-accented voice] "Because eet's een the screept." And I actually went and dented the bathroom stall with my puddly little fist. I have never been angrier. But it's the classic, "When something goes wrong, you assume the writer's a dork." And that's painful.

O: ***Have you done any other uncredited script work?***

JW: Actually, my first gig ever was writing looplines for a movie that had already been made. You know, writing lines over somebody's back to explain something, to help make a connection, to add a joke, or to just add babble because the people are in frame and should be saying something. We're constantly saving something that doesn't work, or trying to, with lines behind people's backs. It's almost like adding narration, but cheaper. I did looplines for *The Getaway*, the Alec Baldwin/Kim Basinger version. If you look carefully at *The Getaway*, you'll see that when people's backs are turned, or their heads are slightly out of frame, the whole movie has a certain edge to it. I also did a couple of days of looplines and punch-ups for *The Quick And The Dead*, just to meet Sam Raimi.

O: ***Have you ever been asked to doctor a script that you thought was doomed from the start?***

JW: I've never taken a gig like that. There have been different situations... Like, *Speed*, I loved the idea so much that I was very anxious to come in and rewrite the characters. But I loved the plot. *Toy Story* was the greatest opportunity in the world, because it was a great idea with a script I didn't like at all. When you know the idea is solid... I've been pitched ideas, or seen scripts, where I've been like, "You don't need me. You need to not make this." There have been some terrible ones. But the thing is, for a script doctor, the best thing in the world is a good idea with a terrible script. Assuming they'll let you play with it, which they did on *Toy Story*. Because you have the solid structure and you can work the story into it.

O: ***Apart from the problems with getting respect and avoiding rewrites in film, what kind of differences do you find between writing for TV and writing for film?***

JW: I think every filmmaker should have to work in television. First of all, films wouldn't all be two and a half hours long, because you really learn about what you need when you're limited to 44 minutes. It's just a great, great training ground, to constantly be working. What you trade is the ability to control every piece of the frame, to really make everything work exactly the way you want. Yes, I have a great crew, we've been together so long, the cast gets it, and the writers are superb. But you sacrifice a certain precision. But you also have a higher chance of doing your best work and getting it out there, because there are fewer executives and stars and ridiculous people between you and getting it done when it airs in two weeks and you have to shoot it. I've been described as Ed Wood, and I've been assured that this is a compliment, because of the amount of work we have to get done in so short a time.

O: ***How about comic books? How does that compare?***

JW: Well, I get to be alone more, and the characters never say, "Oh, I don't think I'd say that in boldface," or "I don't think I'd wear this." They just sort of do whatever I tell them. It's different but similar, and there's a little more leeway. It's fun.

O: ***Do you prefer one of the three over the others?***

JW: At the end of the day, I would probably rather be making movies. I love television, because you get to see more of the characters than you'd ever see in the movies. You get to see 100 hours, 75 hours of a drama, and you just keep learning about the characters. That's really exciting. But at the end of the day, movies are my area. As long as I'm writing, I'm happy.

O: ***I attended your Q&A session at a comics convention last year, and many of the people who got up to ask questions were nearly in tears over the chance to talk to you. Some of them could barely speak, and others couldn't stop gushing about you, and about*** **Buffy*****. How do you deal with that kind of emotional intensity?***

JW: It's about the show, and I feel the same way about it. I get the same way. It's not like being a rock star. It doesn't feel like they're reacting to me. It's really sweet when people react like that, and I love the praise, but to me, what they're getting emotional about is the show. And that's the best feeling in the world. There's nothing creepy about it. I feel like there's a religion in narrative, and I feel the same way they do. I feel like we're both paying homage to something else. They're not paying homage to me.

O: ***Does knowing that you have fans who are that dedicated put extra pressure on you, or does seeing the show as something outside yourself make it easier to deal with?***

JW: You don't want to let them down. The people who feel the most strongly about something will turn on you the most vociferously if they feel you've let them down. Sometimes you roll your eyes and you want to say, "Back off," but you don't get the big praise without getting the big criticism. Because people care. So. Much. And you always know that's lurking there. It does make a difference. If nobody was paying attention, I might very well say, "You know what, guys? Let's churn 'em out, churn 'em out, make some money." I like to think I wouldn't, but I don't know me, I might be a dick. Once the critics, after the first season, really got the show, we all sort of looked at each other and said, "Ohhh-kay..." We thought we were going to fly under the radar, and nobody was going to notice the show. And then we had this responsibility, and we got kind of nervous. You don't want to let them down. But ultimately, the narrative feeds you so much. It's so exciting to find out what's going to happen next, to find the next important thing in the narrative, to step down and say, "That's so cool."

O: ***Are you ever surprised by your fans' passion for the show?***

JW: No. I designed the show to create that strong reaction. I designed *Buffy* to be an icon, to be an emotional experience, to be loved in a way that other shows can't be loved. Because it's about adolescence, which is the most important thing people go through in their development. And it mythologizes it in such a romantic way—it basically says, "Everybody who made it through adolescence is a hero." And I think that people get something from that that's very real. And I don't think I could be more pompous. But I mean every word of it. I wanted her to be a cultural phenomenon. I wanted there to be dolls, Barbie with kung-fu grip. I wanted people to embrace it in a way that exists beyond, "Oh, that was a wonderful show about lawyers, let's have dinner." I wanted people to internalize it and make up fantasies where they were in the story, to take it home with them, for it to exist beyond the TV show. And we've done exactly that. Now I'm writing comics, and I'm getting all excited about the mythology. We're doing a book of stories about other slayers, and I'm all excited about that, and it's all growing in my mind, as well. I think she has become an icon, and that's what I wanted. What more could anybody ask?

O: ***Do you ever feel a responsibility to society, to use your massive power for good?***

JW: Yes and no. I mean, I've always been, and long before anybody was paying any attention, very careful about my responsibility in narrative. How much do I put what I want to put, and how much do I put what I feel is correct? People say, "After Columbine, do you feel a responsibility about the way you portray violence?" And I'm like, "No, I felt a responsibility about the way I portrayed violence the first time I picked up a pen." It's a ridiculous thing to ask a writer. But you feel it, and at the same time, a writer has a responsibility to tell stories that are dark and sexy and violent, where characters that you love do stupid, wrong things and get away with it, that we explore these parts of people's lives, because that's what makes stories into fairy tales instead of polemics. That's what makes stories resonate, that thing, that dark place that we all want to go to on some level or another. It's very important. People are like, [whining] "Well, your characters have sex, and those costumes, and blah blah..." And I'm like, "You're in adolescence, and you're thinking about what besides sex?" I feel that we're showing something that is true, that people can relate to and say, "Oh, I made that bad choice," or "Oh, there's a better way to do that." But as long as it's real, then however politically correct, or incorrect, or whatever—bizarre, or dark, or funny, or stupid—anything you can get, as long as it's real, I don't mind.

O: ***One aspect of your fans' dedication is that they become very threatened by perceived changes in the show, like Giles becoming a lesser character as Anthony Stewart Head moves back to Britain, or the show itself moving to UPN.***

JW: Change is a mandate on the show. And people always complain. [Agitated voice.] "Who is this new guy, Oz?" "Where'd that guy Oz go?" They have trouble with change, but it's about change. It's about growing up. If we didn't change, you would be bored.

O: ***I've got a quote here from a recent interview with James Marsters [who plays Spike on*** **Buffy*****]: "Joss likes to stir it up. He likes a little chaos. He likes to piss people off. He likes to deny them what they want. He loves making people feel afraid." Do you agree with that?***

JW: First of all, if you don't feel afraid, horror show not good. We learned early on, the scariest thing on that show was people behaving badly, or in peril, morally speaking, or just people getting weird on you—which, by the way, is the scariest thing in life. In terms of not giving people what they want, I think it's a mandate: Don't give people what they want, give them what they need. What they want is for Sam and Diane to get together. Don't give it to them. Trust me. You know? People want the easy path, a happy resolution, but in the end, they're more interested in... No one's going to go see the story of Othello going to get a peaceful divorce. People want the tragedy. They need things to go wrong, they need the tension. In my characters, there's a core of trust and love that I'm very committed to. These guys would die for each other, and it's very beautiful. But at the same time, you can't keep that safety. Things have to go wrong, bad things have to happen.

O: ***What's your method for balancing humor and drama when you're writing the show?***

JW: We get bored of one, and then switch to the other. I thought we got very dramatic last year, and I was like, "We need more jokes this year!" Every year the balance falls one way or another. You've just got to keep your eye on it. All of my writers are extremely funny, so it's easy to make [*Buffy*] funnier. The hard part is getting the stuff that matters more. Our hardest work is to figure out the story. Getting the jokes in isn't a problem. We wanted to make that sort of short-attention-span, *The Simpsons*, cull-from-every-genre-all-the-time thing. "You know, if we take this moment from *Nosferatu*, and this moment from *Pretty In Pink*, that'll make this possible. A little *Jane Eyre* in there, and then a little *Lethal Weapon 4*. Not 3, but 4. And I think this'll work."

O: ***Does the writing itself come naturally to you, or do you have to set hours and force yourself to sit down and get it done?***

JW: It's like breathing. I'm not un-lazy, and I do procrastinate, but... Some of my writers sweat. The agony, they hate doing it, it's like pulling teeth. But for me, it comes easy. I don't rewrite, almost ever. I basically just sit down and write. Now my wife is making gestures about what a pompous ass I am. [Laughs.] And she's not wrong. But that's how it is. I love it, and I know these characters well enough that it comes a little more naturally to me.

O: ***Do you think you'd ever be able to completely let go of a*** **Buffy** ***spin-off, leave it totally in someone else's hands?***

JW: It's possible. A while ago, I would have said, "No." But now I'm working on what will be four *Buffy* shows and three *Buffy* comics, and eventually you sort of go, "Uh, maybe somebody else could do that other thing." Would I be able to not have any hand in it at all? I think I just said "yes" and meant "no." I don't want it to have my name on it if it doesn't reflect what I want to say. Because once you get to the position of actually getting to say something, which is a level most writers never even get to, and is a great blessing, you then have to worry about what it is you're actually saying. I don't want some crappy reactionary show under the *Buffy* name. If my name's going to be on it, it should be mine. Now, the books I have nothing to do with, and I've never read them. They could be, "*Buffy* realized that abortion was wrong!" and I would have no idea. So, after my big, heartfelt, teary speech, I realize that I was once again lying. But I sort of drew the line. I was like, "I can't possibly read these books!" But my name just goes on them as the person who created Buffy.

O: ***Are you ever worried about getting into a*** **Buffy** ***rut?***

JW: Yes. *Buffy* burnout big. I'm definitely eyeing some non-*Buffy*-related projects.

O: ***Besides*** **Iron Man*****, are there any other scripts on the horizon?***

JW: I have a script idea that I'm just developing, one of the things I really want to do, but it's still embryonic, so I don't want to say anything about it. Though I'm sure you can read all about it now on the Ain't It Cool web site.

O: ***And you'd direct that yourself if it ever actually became a film?***

JW: Yes. That's the next step. Part of the reason I made the TV show *Buffy* is because as a writer—even a successful one—in Hollywood, when you say you want to direct movies, they're appalled. They look like, "Do you kill babies?" I mean, they're just shocked. "What? You want to *what*?" "I'm a storyteller. I want to tell stories. I want to direct." "Uh, I don't get it. You want to *what*?" And people actually said to me, "Well, if you'd directed a video..." I'm like, just once, somebody please say to a video director, "Well, if you'd written a script... If you just knew how to tell a story..." I mean, the percentage of video directors who have actually told stories... Not that all writers can direct, or should, or want to. I'm sure a lot of writers want to direct because they're bitter, which is not a reason to direct. I want to speak visually, and writing is just a way of communicating visually. That's what it's all about. But nobody would even consider me to direct. So I said, "I'll create a television show, and I'll use it as a film school, and I'll teach myself to direct on TV."

O: ***Now that you've actually appeared on*** **Angel*****, do you have the acting bug?***

JW: I do and I don't. I've always had it, and I think it's part of being a writer and a director. It's knowing how you want things to be played. But I don't have the face—that's the problem—and I don't want the giant ego. I don't want to become Kevin Costner, singing on the soundtrack to *The Postman*.

O: ***What would you like to be working on right now that you don't have time for?***

JW: My movie. I really want to get rolling on it.

O: ***What would you like to be doing just in general that you don't have time for?***

JW: Well, everything. The things that people do when they don't write. Playing games, sports maybe. Drinking and sex are things I've heard a lot about.

O: ***If you had*** **Buffy** ***to do over from the start, this time knowing how popular it would get, would you do anything differently?***

JW: Not in terms of popularity. I mean, there were certain things on the show that I learned the hard way, but not really. I love the show, and I love the people. I love the stories we told. I mean, I'm angry about every single edit and line and costume change and rewrite, but that's part of the business. Ultimately, I wouldn't change anything. ⌀

"Everybody's going for the easy laugh now, and if they can't think of the easy laugh, they'll go for the vomit."

Michael McKean

By Keith Phipps

Originally Printed August 2000

For close to 30 years, Michael McKean has been a comedy fixture, alternating high-profile parts with countless supporting roles. He first gained national attention as Lenny Kosnowski on Laverne & Shirley, *where he teamed with close friend and collaborator David L. Lander. In fact, by the time* L&S *made its debut in 1976, McKean had already formed most of the relationships that would become significant to his career: He'd worked with Lander and Harry Shearer on the satirical radio program* The Credibility Gap, *roomed with Christopher Guest in college, and, through* L&S, *befriended both Rob Reiner and Penny Marshall. When the series wound down in 1982, the seeds had already been planted for* This Is Spinal Tap, *the beloved 1984 pseudo-documentary directed by Reiner and starring McKean, Shearer, and Guest as the members of a flagging British heavy-metal band. After* Tap, *McKean appeared in the cable favorite* Clue, *Guest's* The Big Picture *(which McKean also co-wrote) and* Best In Show, The Brady Bunch Movie, *Clint Eastwood's* True Crime, *and* Saturday Night Live. *He's also done voice-over work for numerous animated projects, been a guest on countless TV programs, and hosted Comedy Central's* Uncomfortably Close With Michael McKean. *In 2000, in the midst of one of Spinal Tap's periodic reunions, McKean spoke to* The Onion A.V. Club.

The Onion: ***We're talking on the occasion of*** **Spinal Tap*****'s 16th anniversary. Were you worried at the time that heavy metal was already too funny as it was?***

Michael McKean: You know what's really interesting: We had made this demo feature and showed it to some backers, hopefully to get them to put up money for it. We didn't have a studio, because the studio we were working for when we made the demo went out of business. We were shopping it around, and people said, "They've got to be more like Kiss. They've got to be more outrageous, with flame-throwers and everything." We would say, "No, no. The thing is, they're mediocre. The thing is, they're not even interesting." Some people thought we were attacking the least funny part, that we could have been much juicier. Or, at the time we were doing it, people were saying, "Why don't you do it about a punk band? There's nothing more happening than that." That would have been boring.

O: ***Punk hadn't parodied itself yet.***

MM: Or else it had made itself immune from

parody by just being, "Oh, yeah? Well, we already beat you to 'fuck you.' You're lagging now, bitch." That's kind of how we read that. This whole thing really sprang from... Chris had a character, a great cockney guitar-player rocker character, and the two of us roomed together in college and always talked about how great and funny rock 'n' roll was when it had pomposity that didn't pay off. You see it in

"I'll always write songs, and I keep thinking I'm writing songs for other people to sing, but I don't really do much about it."

all forms of music, but there was something about stadium rockers, when the stadium would go away and suddenly they're playing in little dives. It just struck us as funny. Then, you know the story, Rob did the TV special. We went on as Spinal Tap.

O: ***Rob Reiner has talked about literally taking the demo reel from studio to studio.***

MM: He absolutely did, and that's where he got comments like, "Why didn't you make this about a good band?" People really didn't get it at that level. One guy said, "You know what you need? You need something at the very beginning of the movie like the airplane's fin cutting through the clouds in the beginning of *Airplane*. That would tell us it was a comedy." And I said, "Well, that's a great gag, but if we started our movie like that, what's the point of view?" And he said, "It doesn't matter. You just gotta." They were afraid it wasn't enough like a comedy, that there was too much of people stepping on each other's lines and not waiting for jokes and all those things. I'm glad it stayed that way. I'm glad, when we delivered the final 84 minutes or whatever it was, that it still has that feel of something that really happened. We thought that was the funny part.

O: ***Over the years, I've heard any number of bands proposed as the real Spinal Tap. Who do you think is closest?***

MM: Well, there really is no one answer. I heard a rumor that Foghat or Foreigner or Journey, one of those bands... I think maybe Foghat, because I don't think it was anybody as big as Journey, where a girlfriend took over management of the band and was using astrology as a guide. This could be completely bullshit. In fact, the longer I think about it, the more likely it is. It just seems too perfect. But we got a lot of stories like that. Carmine Appice, who's this New York drum-legend guy, was in a band, and they had a drum riser in a bubble that rose from the middle of the stage hydraulically. And one night it didn't open, and he assumed that that must have inspired us. We didn't hear about it; we just wrote it in because we thought it was funny. That's how it always was. I never like to pin it down. I always thought that the rhythm of the name and the longevity of the band and the number of personnel changes made it closer to Uriah Heep than anything else. Status Quo, same thing. It's that rhythm, two words that are vaguely sort of higher-brow than the music.

O: ***With Uriah Heep, it's a Dickens reference, but they're playing the dumbest rock 'n' roll around.***

MM: Exactly, and Status Quo being, "Oh, it's fucking Latin, idn't?"

O: ***After* Spinal Tap, *there have been a lot of mockumentries. Outside of* Waiting For Guffman *and* Best In Show, *they've been very poor, for the most part. Why do you think that is?***

MM: You know what I like? I like *CB4* okay. It was pretty fucking funny, I've got to say. But a lot of it kind of falls short of the mark. Marty Short did things with a documentary feel on his TV show from the mid-'90s. It wasn't on for very long, but after the show had been taken off, they took a lot of the best sketches that hadn't been seen and put them together in a 90-minute special. *SCTV* always did that, too. They were always able to do that. Most of their stuff had the TV show as a frame, but they also had a real off-the-cuff thing going.

O: ***Do you think the problem is that most of them go for easy laughs most of the time?***
MM: Well, everybody's going for the easy laugh now, and if they can't think of the easy laugh, they'll go for the vomit. It seems like easy is the way we're going now. It's boring to me to do the jokes you would have thought of when you were 11, just to know that the audience is there.

O: Spinal Tap ***is legendary for having hours of unused footage. Were you part of the editing process?***
MM: We all looked at everything as we were shooting. We all looked at dailies every day. We knew there was stuff we never wanted to see after that day. The first assemblage we saw was probably around 15 minutes of some of the stuff that just happened to... We shot something that would at least work partially together, and that was scary. Then, more and more assemblages. I stopped going to those midway assemblages, and then we all saw the four-and-a-half-hour version, which was amazing. And we saw a lot of stuff we wanted to boot out, storylines that had to go. Some of that stuff resulted in a better movie. The removal of things gave us jokes we didn't know we had.

O: ***Is there anything you wish would have made the final cut, but didn't?***
MM: No. I remember there were some days when we got to work and it didn't work out. Because we didn't have a script, and we had hired some people thinking they could deliver something, and they couldn't. It only happened a couple of times, and they were people we didn't really know. Maybe they've become tremendous improvisers since, but at the time they were kind of scared by it, didn't know how to do it. But there were only a couple of those. Those were things I would have wanted to reshoot. I would have loved to have seen outside the bus from time to time. It was such an indoor movie, and I would have loved to have seen something more like... I mean, if you really think about it, the Graceland scene is the only real scene that's not under a roof. That would be the only thing, just to open it up a little bit. Maybe it would be a huge mistake, because there's that kind of claustrophobic feeling about the road that we tried consciously to catch.

O: ***When did you realize that*** **Spinal Tap** ***had a cult following?***
MM: Well, I don't know whether there was a moment when we knew that was the case. I guess when there was a theater in Boston that showed the first run of the film for over a year. That sort of tickled us, and we thought, "Oh my God, it's going to be that kind of movie. A midnight movie. Maybe it'll be something that'll have a little shelf life." That was the term we kept using while we were writing, because we wanted it to stay good and interesting.

O: ***Have you ever considered recording seriously on your own?***
MM: I have a lot of songs that don't really belong anywhere, don't belong in a Tap situation or in other things I've done. I'll always write songs, and I keep thinking I'm writing songs for other people to sing, but I don't really do much about it. I just sit around and play them here. That's just the kind of guy I am. I'm not interested in recording anything with me as the main vocalist.

O: ***How much is your singing voice like David St. Hubbins'?***
MM: It's pretty much become identical. I think if someone wanted me to play another rock 'n' roll personality, if I took that part, the big chore would be to have another voice and be a totally different kind of singer.

O: ***When you get recognized, what character do you get recognized as?***
MM: These days, mostly David St. Hubbins.

O: ***Have you aged into that character?***
MM: No, not really. I look like somebody else now. I look like somebody I can't quite place. I don't know, because I'm very white and I've gotten bigger. My hair has gotten thinner and I look really happy all the time, which I am. I

don't think I've aged into any character; I think it's the other way. Of course, last night we put the wigs on again and I looked in the mirror, and there's this guy, and he's gotten older, too. He needs more eye makeup than I do. I get that most of the time.

O: ***Did you get recognized more when you were on* Saturday Night Live?**

MM: Yeah, I did, but their ratings were way down. I think people who even watched the show didn't watch the whole show and didn't talk about it, because it was really not some of the better years.

O: ***The sense was that you were brought in as a ringer. Were you treated as a ringer?***

MM: Uh, no. I can't say so. I thought I was being brought in to play David Spade's dad.

"There was something about stadium rockers, when the stadium would go away and suddenly they're playing in little dives. It just struck us as funny."

They wanted me to do Clinton, and I hated doing Clinton. I don't think I did him well, and I was following the best Clinton of all, Phil Hartman, so I wasn't happy doing that. I don't think it was a marriage made in heaven. I have an interesting place in *SNL* history: I'm the oldest person ever to be hired as a regular, and I think I'm the only person who has been guest host, musical guest, and cast member.

O: ***It was weird, because in those years they had so many funny people—you, Janeane Garofalo, Chris Elliott—and I'm not sure why the show wasn't funnier.***

MM: Well, a lot of it has to do with how happy you are. Chris wasn't happy. Chris didn't like it, and Janeane didn't like it at all. But she always does point out that she had a couple of good shows, a couple of times when they had some good times. Amid the crabbiness, I had fun with everybody. I was pretty crabby myself sometimes. But I think it was kind of just wandering. It didn't know where it was going. The season after that, they got a lot of new people. They're very good, and the writing has generally gotten better. They still try and shove characters down our throats too early and make too much of them. I guess you've got to do that if you're going to keep producing feature films about those characters, but it seems to me that the chore at hand is to put on a really funny 90-minute show on Saturday night. You should be able to do it, but you can't always do it. That's the real dumb bottom line, and it's the truth. They can't all be gems. I thought they made some disastrous mistakes. I thought Norm Macdonald was great doing the news. I really did, because he was kind of insane, and that's what Chevy Chase had and most of the others had. Dennis Miller brought something else to it. He brought, "I'm doing the news and I'm really funny." Whereas Chevy and to some extent Dan Aykroyd, they played a part rather than just being, "Is it just me, or is the world going crazy?" And Norm had this other thing, which is, "Well, none of this makes sense to me." And that made me laugh. Anyway, it was an interesting period in my life, and it was a good thing to go to New York. It kind of turned my life in a couple of ways that really needed turning. I was a guy in my mid-40s and just divorced, and maybe I want to move to New York again, and what the hell's going on? "What's happening to my body, Mommy?"

O: ***If you're happy now, what's making you happy?***

MM: I'm married to Annette O'Toole, which was by far the smartest move I've ever made. That's working out extremely well, especially since she's working, which means I don't have to. I've never been in that kind of relationship before. She refuses to make me feel guilty about it. She's doing a show for USA called *The Huntress*. We've got good kids, too.

O: ***Work-wise, you're everywhere.***

MM: I try to stay busy. Since I've been married, I'll get a script and read it and go, "Yeah, okay, they want me to fly here and do this, and they'll pay me this. Hmm... Okay, I'll do that." And Annette will say, "What, are you crazy? This is not good." I'm just used to taking those gigs because, you know, you get a little extra change and get to go to another city. But she's right. There are certain knee-jerk jobs I don't take anymore because she won't let me. She's very frank about it, and it's great. It's nice having someone who's in my corner in the long run. She really thinks I'm good and convinces me that I shouldn't despair.

O: ***Is there any role you would take back?***

MM: No, because most of the films that I didn't have a good time doing didn't get much of a release anyway. I never regret anything. I don't believe in regret. It's just a big time-waster, and I could be swimming. ⌀

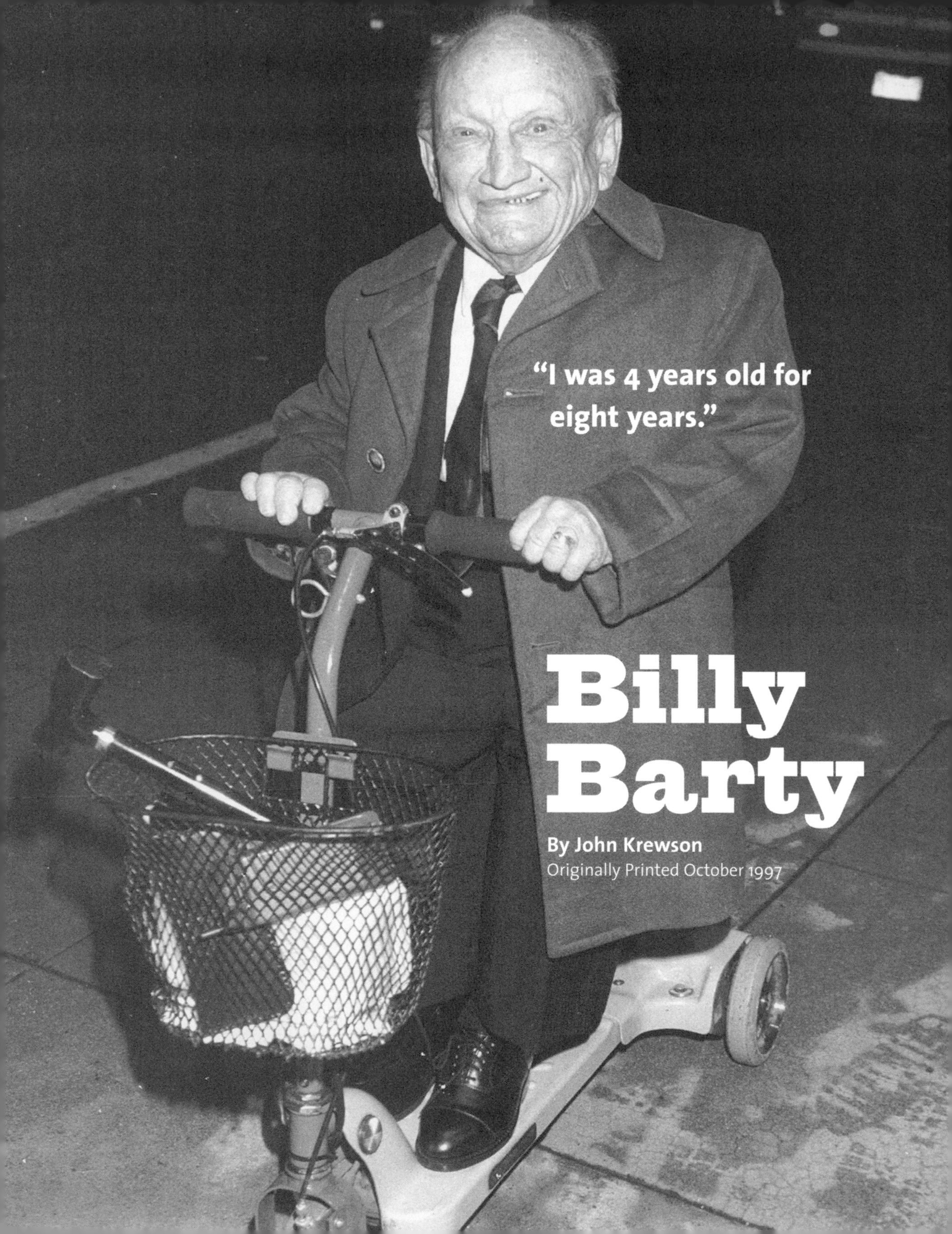

"I was 4 years old for eight years."

Billy Barty

By John Krewson

Originally Printed October 1997

For many years, Billy Barty was the most visible little-person actor in Hollywood, playing everything from Nazi spies to Liberace in a career that stretched from 1927's Wedded Blisters *to 2000's* The Extreme Adventures Of Super Dave. *Cast almost exclusively as a small child in his early roles, including a lecherous baby in Busby Berkeley's early films, Barty later made a point of avoiding typecasting. While he was always the first to crack a joke at his size, and his filmography contains its share of roles as circus performers, he sought to avoid parts he found condescending and lead America to a wider acceptance of people of short stature. In 1957, Barty founded Little People Of America, a non-profit advocacy organization that still champions the rights of little people today. A busy performer until his death in 2000, Barty spoke with* The Onion A.V. Club in 1997 *about the ramifications of short stature, his careers in baseball and vaudeville, quality children's television, and his celebrity golf tournament.*

The Onion: ***I heard you just had knee surgery. Did you hurt it?***

Billy Barty: No, no, just a matter of... What can I say? Time carries on, and it just deteriorated to where I had to get some new things put in, and they did some fiddling. So far, it's pretty good. It's just going to take a little time and patience. I had it done about three years ago, but then my ligaments and tendons were weak, so they knew something was going to happen, and it did happen, so they took care of it. I had an artificial tendon put in, a ligament put in, my Achilles' tendon fused to the knee... So I'm just recuperating and working on my golf tournament.

O: ***Do you golf yourself?***

BB: I used to, yeah. I was a good 21 handicap. I wasn't long, but I was down the middle. [Laughs.] And I guess I'm closer to the ground, so I one-putted a lot. That's why I like to play in scrambles.

O: ***Could you tell me about the Billy Barty Foundation?***

BB: Well, right! There's a lot of little people out there; there are considered to be about 1.5 million people of short stature in the United States, and what my foundation does is help with scholarships—we give away about 20 a year—and give medical advice and psychological support. Anyone can call and ask for information on the foundation and the golf tournament, which is celebrating its anniversary this year. A lot of them don't last 25 years. We started out with a little one-day tournament in Azusa, California, and now we're in Palm Springs for three days, playing at the Desert Dunes.

O: ***That's a famous course.***

BB: Yeah! Very nice! We have a great turnout. We give nice service, too, and the money goes

"It was amazing the respect that the children had for me. Because we're on the same level, practically. They're honest! Their mothers are, 'Oh, shut up,' but they're, 'You're a little man!' And if they say, 'You're a midget,' well, I correct them on that one—'I'm a little person!'—and explain it to 'em."

for a real good cause. So that's one of the things I'm working on, besides working with the Little People of America, which I started in 1957. That's international now, and we still have a lot of work to do. We're still trying to educate the public that the little people aren't all in circuses. They have legitimate professions, anything from doctors to lawyers to geneticists, you name it. So that's an interesting project. I'm quite involved in that.

O: ***When we called to set up this interview, you were off counseling someone who had just had a baby who was a little person.***

BB: Oh, yeah. It was quite a wonderful thing, 'cause a lot of people who give birth, you know, they're scared. Frightened. One out of 12,000 people born will be a little person. You know Steve Reed, a relief pitcher for the Colorado Rockies? He and his wife gave birth to a dwarf child. It was a beautiful thing; I just fell in love with this baby. It's a certain type of dwarfism we know about, so between the Billy Barty Foundation and the Little People Of America, we gave them the right doctors to go to and the right people to see, and he was completely thrilled. Then I told him how to pitch against the Dodgers, and he was a relieving winner. So I do that, and then there's my one-man show, which I'm putting together for the stage. Ninety minutes, showing anywhere, in any theaters we can book. I'll probably be ready to get back within the month, and we have a very good show, I think. It's a musical comedy, and it's going to be interesting. Who knows? We might be up there, in your area! That was great, traveling around doing vaudeville. I did that from when I was about 4 years old until I was about 17. That was working, in the early days.

O: ***You've been working in movies since you were about 10, haven't you?***

BB: Three! I'll be celebrating my 70th year coming up. Seventy years in the entertainment business, except for about five years when I got out of it to go to college. I'm writing my autobiography still. It goes back to when I started, when I was 3.

O: ***The first movie credit I found for you was in 1934, making you 10 years old or so.***

BB: Oh, no no no! Uh-uh. Nope. My first... What was it you got?

O: The Dog Doctor, *1934.*

BB: *The Dog Doctor*! I don't remember that one.

O: ***Well, they could be wrong.***

BB: No no no no! They could be right, sure, whoever they are. *The Dog Doctor*. Hmmm. But I started in 1927, when I was 3, in a movie called *Wedded Blisters*. Was a two-reeler. That's what they mostly did in those days. Called 'em that because they only used two reels.

O: ***You worked on a lot of movies early on in which you were a kid, a little boy, that sort of thing.***

BB: Oh, yeah! I was 4 years old for eight years. [Laughs.]

O: ***How did you spend the '40s and '50s? I couldn't find a lot on you.***

BB: Well, I didn't do a lot. I went to high school, finished high school in 1942, and went on to L.A. City College after that. Then I went on to L.A. State, which just a couple years ago gave me an honorary doctorate degree in germane letters. Majored in journalism. I was going to be a sportswriter or a sports announcer.

O: ***Did you ever call any games?***

BB: I used to announce a lot of the football games at L.A. City College. I did LACC in the first game ever televised in the city of Los Angeles, at the Rose Bowl. That was my big ambition when I went to college. That, and to be a football coach and a basketball coach.

O: ***Did you ever coach?***

BB: Yeah, I coached Little League. I played at L.A. City College in 1945, and I played basketball at L.A. State. I even played semi-pro baseball. [Laughs.]

O: ***You'd be a pretty hard man to pitch to, I'd imagine.***

BB: Definitely! I batted .500! One for two, and I had 45 walks! And seven stolen bases, even.

O: ***I'd think it would be maddening to find your strike zone.***

BB: It is! Like Eddie Gaedel at St. Louis [a little person the St. Louis manager brought out to protest changes in baseball's strike-zone rules]. But I played ball, and I proved that I could play second base, pitch, and run. Anyway, that's why I didn't get back into the entertainment business until about '47. I did a thing called *Three Wise Fools*, then one thing led into another, and I did a lot of TV shows. I ended up in 1949 in New York City, as the co-host of a children's show.

O: ***Was that any fun?***

BB: Oh, yeah. I had my own children's show out here for four years, from 1963 to '67: It was called *Billy Barty's Big Show*. We started out with a little half-hour show once a week, and wound up with an hourlong show that averaged 165 kids. Live, every day. It was amazing the respect that the children had for me. Because we're on the same level, practically. They're honest! Their mothers are, "Oh, shut up," but they're, "You're a little man!" And if

"Weird Al" Yankovic On Billy Barty

Billy Barty grew up, so to speak, in vaudeville, and his acting credits date all the way back to 1927—which, if you're doing the math, means he spent more than 70 years in show business. And, even though the sheer quantity of his cinematic output pales in comparison to, say, Ron Jeremy's, he left us with delightful performances in films such as Legend, Willow, *and* Foul Play. *Several decades ago, he also spent a chunk of his life touring with Spike Jones (one of my all-time heroes), where, among other things, he did a hilarious dead-on impersonation of a diminutive Liberace. He even had his own TV kids' show when I was growing up:* Billy Barty's Big Show. *Small children felt very comfortable around Billy, treating him like one of their peers. Due to his height (3' 9" by most accounts), he was invariably cast as "the little person" in TV and film projects. Especially near the end of his career, he was sensitive about taking roles that were specifically written for little people, which is why I was especially thankful when he agreed to play TV news cameraman Noodles MacIntosh in my 1989 movie* UHF. *The running gag was that every single one of Noodles' shots was extreme low angle. That's a joke that just wouldn't have played if we'd had to cast Jamie Farr or something. We gave Billy a single-card credit on the opening titles, even though he had a relatively small part and we weren't contractually obligated to do so, just because we were so happy to have him in the film. I wish I'd spent more time with him on the set. About all I really remember is that he was a total pro, and he was loved by everybody, and I think he was fond of the carrot sticks at the craft-services table.*

they say, "You're a midget," well, I correct them on that one—"I'm a little person!"—and explain it to 'em.

O: ***You were in a couple of Elvis movies. What was Elvis like?***

BB: He was fantastic. A delight. Friendly, nice, kind, courteous. He was worried about me all the time. He wanted to protect me. He was overprotective on *Harum Scarum*, because it was a rough deal. There were a lot of physical things going on in that movie.

O: ***I like the idea of Elvis trying to protect you.***

"Donald O'Connor to me is fantastic. I've known him since he was 8 and I was 9. We used to play in vaudeville together. Those days were fantastic. It's a lot different these days. I read scripts and I can't do 'em. I don't want to swear, I don't blow up 48 buildings, I don't have sex. What are you going to do?"

BB: Yeah, that was a thrill. And then, working with Burt Lancaster and Kirk Douglas [in 1986's *Tough Guys*]... It was a small part, no pun intended, but it was cute, and I was really honored to work with those two guys. Geniuses.

O: ***Did you get to hang out with them much?***

BB: No no no! I just worked a couple of days. Just a cameo. But I've been very fortunate, worked with a lot of news and TV people, too. I even worked with Ronald Reagan.

O: ***I would love to hear your take on Ronald Reagan.***

BB: Oh, he was wonderful. I even knew him in later years, you know. I've been kind of blessed, I guess.

O: ***You also worked on the Sid & Marty Krofft kids' shows of the early '70s.***

BB: Oh, yeah! They're out again. *Dr. Shrinker, The Bugaloos, Sigmund The Sea Monster, H.R. Pufnstuf*... Now, those are good children's shows.

O: ***Are you still working in TV much?***

BB: I just did a couple of things recently, like *L.A. Heat*, which goes over to Europe. I had a featured part in that, but I had to tell them, "Look, I can't walk, because I'm getting ready to go to the hospital," and they said, "Don't worry, we'll let you use your scooter." I said okay, so I drove the scooter all around. I was a crook on a scooter! Although I'll tell you, it's a different world in the entertainment business today. We gotta get our act together in the entertainment business. We got so much yuch-yuch. *Sesame Street* and all the friendly, instructive shows, that's one thing. And the Sid & Marty Krofft things are still good, like they were done yesterday, I think. It was a pleasure working for them. I know a lot of people who I really highly respect in the business. One of the greatest entertainers, to me, is Mickey Rooney. He does comedy, he does musicals, he can direct, he can write, he can do a little bit of everything. Mickey and I were in movies together back to 1929. He always pulls this line, he says, "Billy and I almost grew up together." Ba-da-bum! And Donald O'Connor to me is fantastic. I've known him since he was 8 and I was 9. We used to play in vaudeville together. Those days were fantastic. It's a lot different these days. I read scripts and I can't do 'em. I don't want to swear, I don't blow up 48 buildings, I don't have sex. What are you going to do? Besides, everybody probably thinks I'm dead now. [Laughs.]

O: ***You know, I'd pay to see a movie called* Billy Barty Blows Up 48 Buildings.**

BB: You would?

O: ***Sure. And I think all my friends would, too.***

BB: Okay! Write it!

O: ***You got it!***

BB: No, really! Seriously! The main thing is that you keep trying. Who knows? People ask me where I went to learn this stuff. I tell 'em I didn't go nowhere! You may not do it—I mean, it may not work out—but my thinking is that, as long as you try, you've done it.

For more information on the Little People Of America, consult www.lpaonline.org. Ø

"I'm quiet. I'm peaceful. I'm 48 fuckin' years old. I got a great marriage. My wife is profound. I've had more poontang than fuckin' Frank Sinatra."

James Ellroy

By John Krewson

Originally Printed November 1996

James Ellroy's prose is the equivalent of an amphetamine rush, so it's no surprise to learn that he spent his formative years devouring drugs and crime novels in equal measure. After distinguishing himself with superior detective and crime fare in the late '70s and '80s, Ellroy hit his stride with "The L.A. Quartet," the intertwined novels The Black Dahlia, The Big Nowhere, L.A. Confidential, *and* White Jazz. *After addressing national crime with the JFK-centered* American Tabloid *in 1995 (followed in 2001 by its sequel* The Cold Six Thousand*), in 1996 Ellroy turned to non-fiction with* My Dark Places, *which was equal parts autobiography, lacerating self-analysis, and detective story chronicling Ellroy's investigation into the 1958 murder of his mother. While promoting* My Dark Places, *Ellroy spoke to* The Onion A.V. Club *about his craft, his past, and the relationship between the two.*

The Onion: ***Are you recovered from writing this book?***

James Ellroy: I don't want to recover from writing this book. I feel very poised. I feel like I'm with my mother for the first time ever. I feel like I've confronted her, and the confrontation goes on. You've read the book. There is no closure. Closure is a preposterous concept worthy of the worst aspects of American daytime TV. It goes on. But my relationship to the event will continue to mutate. My relationship to my mother will continue to change as I revise my judgments of her, depending on what I learn about her. It goes on. I feel no less obsessive about my work and no less passionately committed to the life I have now, but I feel poised inside, which is a good thing to feel at 48. I'm grateful for the life I have. I lived bad for many years, and I've got a great life now. I've got the kind of life people only dream about.

O: ***Describe exactly how you lived bad.***

JE: Well, it's there in the book. I drank, I used drugs, I broke into houses and sniffed women's undergarments. I ate Benzedrex inhalers, jacked off for 18 hours at a pop, lived with my dad in a shitpad I described in the book. He laughed when nothing was funny and told TV commentators to fuck off and suck his dick. And I never felt terribly put down by any of this, which is interesting. I almost had an intransigent mental spirit. I always wanted things. How did I change my life? I wanted things. I wanted women and I wanted to write books. Whatever it cost and whatever it took, I would do it. And that's what saw me through. Shit, I lived bad. Now, I live in Kansas City. Now, I'm an uptight, rich, square-ass WASP motherfucker. Life is good, man.

O: ***You're kind of from white trash, though.***

JE: Well, interestingly, my father actually went to college, and my mother went to nursing school. They were too square and right-wing to be hip, too well educated to be white trash, too sexy to be square. They really didn't fit any mold. They weren't really hipsters. They were two of a kind, those two. They didn't fit on any of the pegs of the 1950s, that's for damn sure.

"You would have to be an absolutely disciplined, mentally controlled, systematic, meticulous worker capable of sustaining great concentration to write the kind of books that I write."

O: ***You have this persona about you yourself, the way you ask to be called "Dog." On book tours and in interviews, you've described yourself as a "knight of the far right."***

JE: I just do that to give people shit, especially in Leftist enclaves. It's just a shtick. White knight, far right. Rhymes. Death-dog-with-a-hog-log. And I've toned down that act for this tour. It's a very serious book for me, and I think the reviews reflect that so far. But I like to have fun out there. I like to go out and meet the people. I love to sell books.

O: ***Are you afraid that anything in this book—in which you reveal some ugly, hard things about yourself—is going to turn anybody off of James Ellroy?***

JE: It'll turn people on and it'll turn people off, and I figure that as long as more people are turned on than turned off, I'm doing fine. If more people are turned off than turned on, that's the way it goes. You know the boxing term, "He went out on his shield"? That's what I did with this book. Anything less than total candor was bullshit. I owed that to my readers, I owed that to myself, and I owed that most specifically to my mother. I've had some thrilling moments in my literary career to this point, and nothing comes close to giving Geneva Hilliker Ellroy, the farm girl from Tunnel City, Wisconsin, to the world. People have said, "Did you write this book to exploit your mother's memory and make money?" And there's a simple answer to that, which is, I got paid less than half of what I get paid for my novels. I spent just about the entire U.S. advance on the investigation. If I wanted to make money, I would have written another novel.

O: ***It's shocking to some people that you're happily married.***

JE: Well, people, particularly younger people with the rock 'n' roll sensibility—wearers of black, grad students, counterculturites, all that—like to think I'm a certain way. Look at the books. Look at how fuckin' meticulously they're constructed. You would have to be an absolutely disciplined, mentally controlled, systematic, meticulous worker capable of sustaining great concentration to write the kind of books that I write. The books are so dense. You cannot write like I write off the top of your head. It's the combination of that meticulousness and the power of the prose and, I think, the depth of the characterizations and the risks that I've taken with language that give the books their clout. That's where I get pissed off at a lot of my younger readers. I come on avuncular sometimes and say to a young guy, "Son, what are you doing? I'm your dad. I drank, I used drugs, I hate William Burroughs, I hate Hunter Thompson, I hate Charles Bukowski, I don't think any of 'em were worth a shit, and none of 'em can write, and William Burroughs is a misogynist cocksucker who murdered his mother." [Pauses.] His mother? Oops, Freudian slip. Murdered his wife. People can't take that. I get confronted with that all the time. I'm quiet. I'm peaceful.

I'm 48 fuckin' years old. I got a great marriage. My wife is profound. I've had more poontang than fuckin' Frank Sinatra. I don't need to prove myself that way anymore. I've got a woman I'm loyal to above all things, above my career. She's profound to me. I'm quiet. I live in Kansas City. I work. I'm not interested in popular culture. I hate Quentin Tarantino. I rarely go to movies. I hate rock 'n' roll. I work. I think. I listen to classical music. I brood. I like sports cars.

O: ***In your books, there seem to be two main forces at work: There's evil and weakness, and those two things oppose each other throughout your books.***

JE: I think there's a strong moral line in the books, and it's not a moral line you can attribute to any one character. It's just the overriding karmic zap that all my bad guys who fuck other people get. And my guys are essentially guys who discover their humanity a bit late in life, and learn the power of self-sacrifice and sometimes die and get blown up behind it. I find that to be a very moving part of the male drama. The great unspoken theme in noir fiction is male self-pity. It pervades noir movies. My guys are morally weak, and they reach toward a tenuous knowledge of self-sacrifice, and sometimes it's too late. I find that moving. It's not a life I'd want to live. But, then, I'm not completely my books.

O: ***Why the obsession with bad white men?***

JE: I think it all has to do with the world I first glimpsed the day my mother died. Men in suits, authority figures, darkness just around the corner. El Monte. White trash. L.A. County. Cops. Men cheating on their wives. Homosexual informants. Hophead jazz musicians, that kind of stuff. Black bebop players. Guys carrying beaver-tailed saps. Toadies for the right-wing establishment. I sensed it. My mind was a police blotter.

O: ***How did you go about applying that idea to*** **My Dark Places*****? One of the most striking things about it is that it's so similar in tone to your novels.***

JE: I needed to address that I've had some profound moral shifts in my own life. I cleaned up. I quit drinking, I quit doing drugs, I quit stealing, I quit breaking into houses, I tried to quit being a bad human being. I developed a conscience later in life than many. I call it the lost-time-regained dynamic. I can err on the side of being judgmental at the drop of a hat. ∅

"I don't believe it's Sinatra,
I think it's a friend of mine.
I'm going, 'Fuck you,
dickhead.' "

The Unknown Comic

By Nathan Rabin

Originally Printed April 2001

*Murray Langston's public profile has lowered considerably since his heyday, but for much of the '70s and '80s, he was one of television's unlikeliest success stories: an unassuming guy who found fame and fortune by covering his head with a paper bag and telling bad jokes. A veteran of numerous comedy and variety shows (*The Sonny And Cher Show, The Wolfman Jack Show, The Alan Hamel Show, *and many others), Langston got his big break when he appeared on* The Gong Show *as The Unknown Comic. The character took off, and Langston soon parlayed his fame into a series of television appearances, a feature-film vehicle (1984's* Night Patrol*), and a successful Vegas act. Before entering semi-retirement in the early '90s, Langston wrote and starred in the 1988 comedy-drama* Up Your Alley *and wrote, directed, and starred in 1990's* Wishful Thinking. *In 2001,* The Onion A.V. Club *spoke with the affable single father about his* Gong Show *fame, his famous friends, and the unique challenges of making a living with a paper bag on his head.*

The Onion: ***How did you get started in comedy?***
Murray Langston: I guess I started out in *Rowan & Martin's Laugh-In*. I was working as a computer operator. *Laugh-In* was a big, popular show, and Tiny Tim had made it big, so I just called up the show. I was very naïve and said, "How do I get in there? How can I get on that show?" They said, "Do something unusual, and call us." So I called back a couple days later and said I could do an impression of a fork. They had me on the show four times, as beautiful downtown Burbank's greatest impressionist.
O: ***What impressions did you do?***
ML: That's how easy it was. I did a fork, a tube of toothpaste. What else did I do? A grandfather clock, and one other one. Rowan and Martin did a bunch of jokes on me, stuff like that. Then it was the typical Hollywood story: After that, I didn't work for three years.
O: ***What did you do during that time?***
ML: I continued to do computer work. I was actually a computer operator at Universal Studios. I'd hang out around the studios and get to see John Wayne, Elvis Presley, and all these guys shoot movies. Then, after a few years, I started hanging out at a club owned by Redd Foxx and doing sketches. I was hanging out with guys like Cheech & Chong before they even made it. They were all trying to figure

out what the business was all about. I formed a comedy team with a guy named Freeman King, and at Redd Foxx's club, me and Freeman were seen by some producers, and they asked us to be on Sonny and Cher's summer show. So, for the next four and half years, I was on *The Sonny And Cher Show*.

O: ***What was that like?***

ML: It was total excitement. I was working with a different star every week, whether it was Jerry Lewis or whoever the stars were back in those days. The Jackson 5, all those people. You got to work with everybody each week. We'd always have either a musical star or an acting star on the show.

O: ***Was it at all strange, being a comedy professional and having to work with entertainers who weren't comedians by trade?***

ML: Yeah, well, I wasn't really a professional at that point, either. I was still getting off the ground. I was very naïve about the business. It's amazing how I was trying to hang out at Redd Foxx's club, and within months I was on a major television show.

"I thought it was flattering if anybody did anything resembling it, as long as they didn't do jokes. I didn't have any say. If anybody came out and started doing jokes as The Unknown Comic, I could file a lawsuit, but anybody putting a bag over their head for any other reason was a compliment."

O: ***Were you surprised that Sonny Bono found so much success, even after the show was over?***

ML: No, he was an ambitious guy. He just wasn't the nicest guy. To take Cher and make her the success she was and be part of it with his limited singing ability, the man had some knowledge and knew what he was doing. He went a long way with his talent. But he wasn't a sociably nice guy. None of us liked him on the show.

O: ***Of all the variety shows and programs you appeared on, which was your favorite?***

ML: I've got to say that my favorite time was the *Sonny And Cher* years, because it was all sort of new and it was the biggest show at the time. That definitely was a highlight. I got on the show, and all of a sudden my first sketch is doing a singing and dancing routine with Art Carney. I went, "Wow." I went from nothing to that, then doing things with Jerry Lewis and whoever else was on top of the world. It was a very exciting period of my life.

O: ***How did you come up with the character of The Unknown Comic?***

ML: This is the first time I'm being asked this. I had a really bad complexion, and it was cheaper than Clearasil. Actually, when *The Sonny And Cher Show* ended, I had a few dollars, so I bought a nightclub restaurant in North Hollywood. I specialized in ribs and later specialized in bankruptcy. I had the club for a few years, but it just drained me. Fascinating place, though, because people like David Letterman, the first place he ever worked in L.A. was my club. Debra Winger was one of my waitresses. A lot of guys started at my club.

O: ***Were people grateful to you for giving them opportunities?***

ML: I think everyone makes their own opportunities. I happened to be there. I don't think I was responsible for Letterman's career in any way. My place was just a place for him to work out. It was the first place Gallagher worked out.

O: ***Was he smashing melons at that point?***

ML: Yeah. Gallagher came from Florida with Jim Stafford. Remember Jim Stafford? "My Girl Bill" and "Spiders And Snakes"? He was a hit back then. He had his own summer show and a bunch of hit records. Gallagher was one of his best friends and was writing his act. He walked into my club one day, and I'm going,

"Jim Stafford!" Like I said, he was a big hit at this time. He says, "I'll get up and do a couple songs if you put my buddy on." I said, "Sure, who's your buddy?" The guy's name was Gallagher. He did the watermelon thing and floored the place. Stafford is making about $20 million a year now in Branson, Missouri. He's very, very successful. Anyway, so those couple years I had the club, I lost everything, and I was busted, broke. I had no money, and *The Gong Show* has been on the air maybe six months. And if you were in the union, which I was, and you appeared on *The Gong Show*, you got a few hundred dollars. I heard that everybody was going on who needed money—actors were making up these little bits—so I said, "Well, I could use the money." I said, "Well, if I put a bag on my head and tell a couple jokes, nobody will know it's me." I didn't want anybody to know it was me, because I'd just been on *The Sonny And Cher Show*. So I felt, if I just put a bag on and call myself The Unknown Comic, do a couple jokes, I'll get my couple hundred dollars. And that's all I meant to do. But what I did is, I came out and insulted Chuck Barris. I did a couple jokes and then said, "Hey, Chuck, do you and your wife ever make love in the shower?" And he said, "No." I said, "You should, she loves it." The audience loved it. So every time I'd come back... He kept asking, "You've got to come back and do something else. Insult me again." So every time I'd come back, I'd have to insult him at the end of it. But I was used to being an actor, a comedy actor, and to do stand-up was new to me. I never did stand-up before. So, from that point on, I had to try to figure out... I did about six or eight months when I was doing The Unknown Comic, did maybe 40 or 50 television shows like that. And all of a sudden, I knew I had something I could parlay. So I contacted Vegas and ended up going to the Sahara and started making some money, put a whole act together. I had a band called The Brown Baggers who had bags over their heads, had dancers called the Baggettes. I was getting paid, like, five grand a week, I think, but my show was costing me about six grand a week. But I had to do something, because I had no real act, and that's what I did. It took me about a year before I developed an act, and I could slowly let everybody go, and then I started making money. But in the beginning, that's what people wanted to

"To take Cher and make her the success she was and be part of it with his limited singing ability, the man had some knowledge and knew what he was doing. He went a long way with his talent. But he wasn't a sociably nice guy. None of us liked him on the show."

see, and the whole show was built around this bag character.

O: ***Did you want to distance yourself from the freak-show nature of* The Gong Show*?***

ML: No, not at all. On the contrary, I was trying to use it to the best of my ability. After all, the character I created was on that show.

O: ***You weren't bothered by the criticism* The Gong Show *received?***

ML: No. It's like any show. Critics try to slap success around, but how can you knock success?

O: ***Did you ever feel like* The Gong Show *went too far?***

ML: No. Not when you look at shows like *Jackass* today. I thought it was pushing the envelope because that's what made it a success, whether it's Jaye P. Morgan showing her boobs or those girls sucking on popsicles. It was definitely pushing the envelope, but that's the reason people watched it. They wanted to see how far it was going to go.

O: ***During the heyday of* The Gong Show, *did you ever get sick of being The Unknown Comic?***

ML: No, I always found it interesting. It was interesting to be in situations where people would be talking about me and they wouldn't know that I was him. That was fascinating. Then, sometimes, it would backfire. One time I was in a bar, talking to some girls and sort of flirting. I finally asked them what they did for a living, and they asked me the same, so I sort of sneaked it in. "Have you ever heard of The Unknown Comic?" And one girl goes, "Oh, I hate him." I just let it slide. I had one woman tell me that she met The Unknown Comic in Chicago and had sex with him, so there was a guy, and it wasn't me.

O: ***Were you concerned that any Tom, Dick, or Harry could claim to be The Unknown Comic?***

ML: Actually, they did. It became quite popular for a while. There was The Unknown Stripper,

"I came out and insulted Chuck Barris. I did a couple jokes and then said, 'Hey, Chuck, do you and your wife ever make love in the shower?' And he said, 'No.' I said, 'You should, she loves it.' The audience loved it. ... Every time I'd come back, I'd have to insult him at the end of it."

and they had a disc jockey that became The Unknown Disc Jockey on radio here. A lot of people were using it, but, no, I thought it was flattering if anybody did anything resembling it, as long as they didn't do jokes. I didn't have any say. If anybody came out and started doing jokes as The Unknown Comic, I could file a lawsuit, but anybody putting a bag over their head for any other reason was a compliment.

O: ***Were there a lot of Unknown Comic groupies?***

ML: I had no complaints. Oh, yeah, I had my share of groupies, I'll tell you. Major, major girl-groupies who would do anything I want with a bag over their head or my head. I had my series of legendary experiences in Vegas with women.

O: ***Did it seem weird to be famous for something that required anonymity?***

ML: And I did The Unknown Poster, remember that? With a bag over my head and a bag over my dick. It was actually a huge poster at the time, sold hundreds of thousands, but I never saw a penny. Me and Debbie Boone got ripped off. That was during the poster craze, after Farrah Fawcett. I did it after the Burt Reynolds pose, and it was in that *Playgirl* magazine, so I did the naked thing, laying down with a bag over my head and a long, long wine bag over my dick. It was very well received. But anyway.

O: ***Did you find it limiting, being The Unknown Comic? Obviously, there are certain types of humor you can't really do with a paper bag over your head. You can't do a whole lot of political material, I would imagine.***

ML: Well, yeah. When I do my show, I do an hourlong show, and only about 15 minutes is with the bag, so it never really became that limiting to me afterwards. I'm unlike a lot of comics in the business, though: I never had this drive to be really, really famous. I just enjoy working. I've done almost 800 television shows and movies. I've never had an agent or manager. I've always just done everything. I just coast along and do everything as it comes along. When things aren't happening, I go and make them happen. I literally retired for almost eight years to raise my daughter.

O: ***Being a creative person, was it difficult being out of the public eye?***

ML: No. Again, I just never had that drive to be really famous. What it was, too—and it really did affect me years ago, when I was just starting to make it as The Unknown Comic, and I got to personally know people like Rodney Dangerfield and Joan Rivers, and all these guys who were making it really big—was that most of them seemed miserable to me. I kept saying, "Here's a guy who's making millions, and he's not happy." I said to myself, "This is not necessarily what I need in life. I need to just concentrate on the important things." For me, it's all worked. I've been one of the most fortunate guys around. I'm happy 95 percent of the time, I have a great life, I have two wonderful kids, and I really, really enjoy my life every day. I'd watch these guys, and everything is a struggle. Who's stealing whose jokes, and blah blah this, and "Why can't I get ahead?" Everybody was always worrying. There wasn't a whole lot of happiness in that arena. Not to say that there aren't people who are successful and enjoy it, but I didn't know a whole lot of them back then. Even Steve Martin, who I knew well and had it as big as anybody could be, didn't strike me as a very happy guy, ever, with all the success he had.

O: ***Was that part of the reason you retired?***

ML: Well, the main reason was... I have this philosophy that change is growth. When you change things in your life, you can't help but grow, because you have to adapt to new things and acquire new knowledge. When I had a child—and I was 45 when I had my first child—it was like, wow. It was like a bomb exploded emotionally inside me, and it was a whole new set of things I had to learn about. I just thoroughly enjoyed it all. I enjoyed every diaper change, and every connection with having a child was new. Watching them feed their first bird, watching them do this, it's a whole new set of experiences. That's what I enjoyed a lot, and I would never change that. I wouldn't change those seven or eight years [of retirement] with my daughter for a TV series. It's just not something I would do. It's not that important, because a TV series is over and you're left with nothing, but a daughter, you've got that for the rest of your life.

O: ***Do you think you'll ever feel too old to put a paper bag over your head and tell jokes?***

ML: No, I don't think so. If I start tripping and falling, possibly. It's amazing, because I'm 56, and people my age are always talking about getting up. I feel the same way I did when I was 22 years old. But I'm sort of a health nut and an exercise person. I'm in great shape. I don't feel any of the aches and pains all these guys talk about. I'm better now than when I was 22.

O: ***If your life were an* E! True Hollywood Story*, what would the high and the low of it be?***

ML: I can't think of a whole lot of low periods. There must be a couple, though. The occasional breakups with somebody are low periods, I guess. But, like I said, I always try to take a negative and turn it into a positive. That's what I did with *Up Your Alley*. Some girl I was living with for two years left me, and I was either going to start drinking or do some-

"Kitty Kelley heard the story, the one who wrote the book on him. She heard the story, and she called me up and asked me about it and asked if she could put it in a book. And I denied it to her, because I wanted to save it for my book. My book is a lot more interesting, if I ever get it off the ground."

thing, so I made the movie. The movie turned out to be a nice little fun project. But the highs are my kids, no doubt about that. The highs in my show-business career would be *The Sonny And Cher Show*, becoming friends with Jerry Lewis, who is my idol, and partying all night with Elvis Presley. I partied all night with him. I've also been threatened by Frank Sinatra. He called me on the phone, threatened to break my legs.

O: ***What was the cause of that?***

ML: That was, ah, *Make Me Laugh*. I did *Make Me Laugh*, and I was doing a bunch of jokes. It wasn't as The Unknown Comic; it was as me, because I did it both as me and as The

Unknown Comic. And I did a joke where I was reading things out of a newspaper, because you're trying to make somebody laugh. I never did Sinatra jokes in my act, but I did one joke where I said, "Sinatra's gonna open up a halfway house for girls who don't go all the way." It wasn't a hard joke. I totally forgot about it. So I guess Sinatra saw a rerun six months later and he literally... I'm shaving, and

"I wouldn't change those seven or eight years with my daughter for a TV series. It's just not something I would do. It's not that important, because a TV series is over and you're left with nothing, but a daughter, you've got that for the rest of your life."

he calls me on the phone. Of course, you don't think Sinatra's calling you. So I pick up the phone, and he goes, "Is this Murray Langston?" I go, "Yeah." He says, "This is Sinatra, you cocksucker," and he starts cursing at me. "You ever mention my name, I'm gonna break your fucking legs," and all this shit. I don't believe it's Sinatra, I think it's a friend of mine. I'm going, "Fuck you, dickhead." He's going back and forth with me, and I'm laughing at him, and the more I laugh at him, the more he's getting pissed off. He's saying, "This is Frank Sinatra." The other thing is, I don't remember ever doing a joke on Sinatra. Finally, he screams at me, I don't know what he said. I said, "Yeah, if you're Sinatra, sing 'My Way,' asshole." That's what did it. He just yelled at me and hung up. So I got back to shaving, and a couple minutes later the phone rings again, and I pick it up. It's another voice that I recognize, saying, "Is this Murray Langston?" I say, "Yeah." He says, "This is Milton Berle. Do you recognize my voice?" And I recognized Milton Berle's voice. He says, "Look, Frank just called me. Apparently, you didn't think you were talking to him." I had to stop shaving, because I'd probably cut my throat at the time. Anyway, he tells me Sinatra's this and Sinatra's that, and he says, "I'm not blaming you. He's just a little crazy at his age." Anyway, it was funny, because he went through the agency and actually was trying... I found out through a lot of sources that he was really going to have somebody rough me up. I called up the producer of this show and I said, "You'll never guess what happened." And the producer says, "Yeah, Frank Sinatra called me." I said, "How'd you know?" "Well, where do you think he got your phone number?" I said, "You asshole." It was a big stink. What a jerk this guy was.

O: ***He was pretty old at the time, wasn't he? What was he going to do?***

ML: I know, but that's not the worry. The worry is, he had people around him who'd be glad to break somebody's legs for him. I went, "There's another idiot, this guy can't take a joke." If he would have just called me and said, "Excuse me, you did a joke on me, and I'd really appreciate..." And I would have said, "Oh, not a problem, man. I respect you." But he was such a vile person on the phone. And then Kitty Kelley heard the story, the one who wrote the book on him. She heard the story, and she called me up and asked me about it and asked if she could put it in a book. And I denied it to her, because I wanted to save it for my book. My book is a lot more interesting, if I ever get it off the ground. I've known everybody in the business. Robin Williams and I used to double-date, Debra Winger and I were an item back then. Actually, one time I dated three different girls who were in three different movies at one time. I partied all night with Lucille Ball, I used to date Lucie Arnaz. Got to party, spent Christmas with her. It's just a lot of interesting things that have happened in my life that were just fascinating, that I really enjoyed, that I can look back on. Again, being part of Jim Carrey and Robin Williams, all those guys and their early years when they were just starting out. It was fun. My life has intertwined with almost all these guys who are huge today. Jay Leno, Mavis [Nicholson, Leno's wife]. I used to date Mavis for years before Leno. So just the sexual part of my history is amazing, with a lot of the people I used to date back then. I had a great time. ⌀

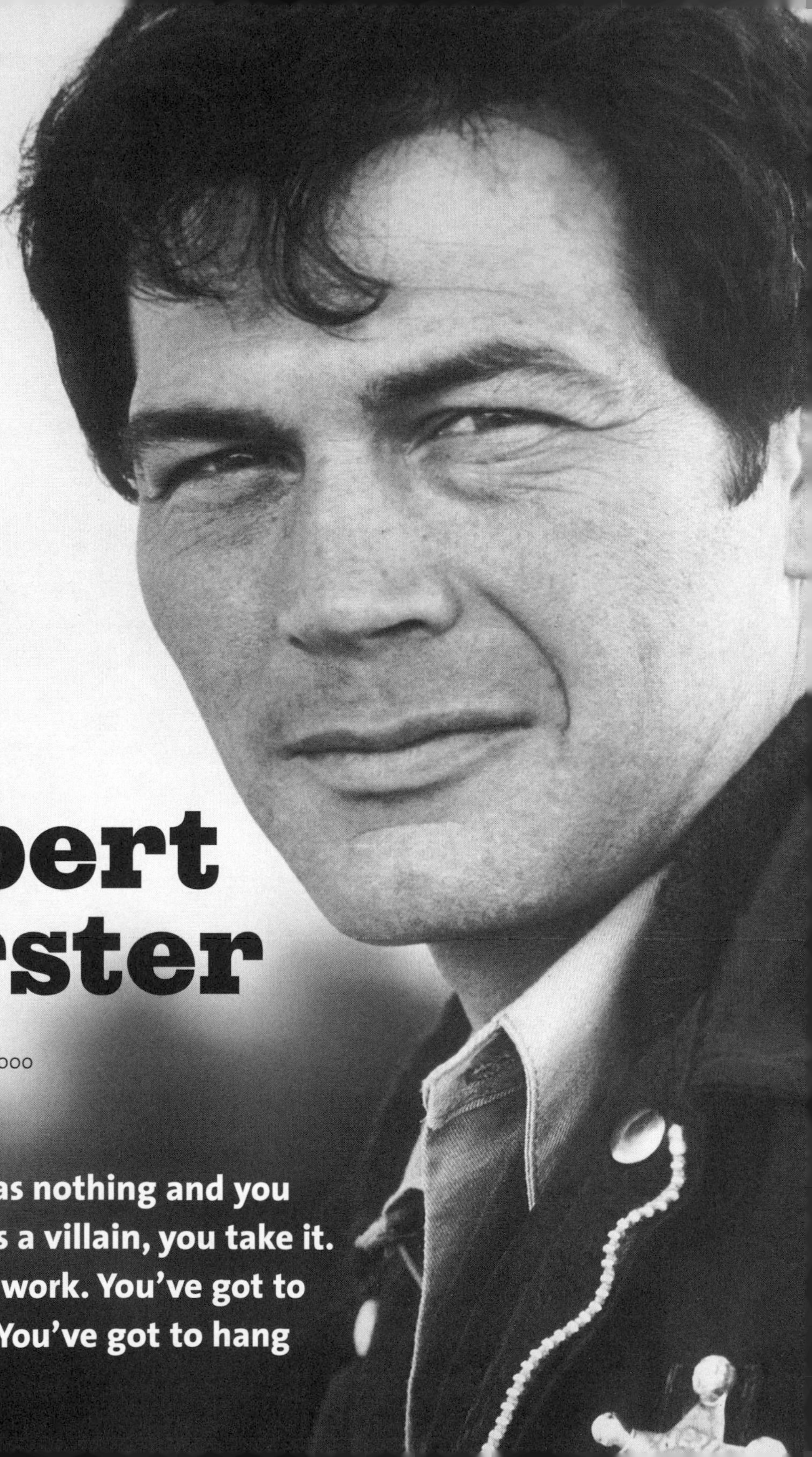

Robert Forster

By Keith Phipps

Originally Printed April 2000

"If you're cast as nothing and you get an offer as a villain, you take it. You've got to work. You've got to scrape it out. You've got to hang in there."

Robert Forster didn't become a household name until he appeared in 1997's Jackie Brown, *but he'd spent the preceding three decades earning the distinction. Forster was already an acclaimed Broadway actor when he won a major part in John Huston's 1967 film* Reflections In A Golden Eye. *After starring in Haskell Wexler's* Medium Cool, *a landmark work of* cinéma vérité *filmed in part amid erupting riots at the 1968 Democratic Convention in Chicago, Forster slowly slipped into failed TV series and B-movies, often proving the best part of films like* Alligator *and* Avalanche. *The '80s and '90s eventually reduced him to minor parts in* American Yakuza *and* Scanner Cop II, *but he made a comeback when longtime fan Quentin Tarantino cast him opposite blaxploitation icon Pam Grier in* Jackie Brown. *Forster's measured, subtle, Oscar-nominated performance in that film is no fluke: He's always been that good. In 2000,* The Onion A.V. Club *spoke to Forster about his busy schedule, his colorful past, his film roles, and his career as an inspirational speaker.*

The Onion: ***You've described your career as having "a five-year ascending first act and a 25-year descending second act." How would you describe the third act so far?***

Robert Forster: The third act is shooting forward and upward. It's pretty good.

O: ***What are you most excited about?***

RF: You know, during the period immediately following the [Oscar] nomination, I did a lot of stuff. I ran into Quentin after about a year. We were talking about it, and I was asking him, "How do you pick really good material? Because I've been working a lot." "Yeah," he said, "you've got to be careful about that, because sometimes an actor who hasn't worked a lot can be doing lots of things, and then everything comes out at once. Then you can't get away from the guy and people get bored real quick. Sometimes a guy has four or five things coming out at one time." I was ashamed to tell him I had eight different things that I'd worked on.

O: ***Not a lot of people know this, but you have a second career as a lecturer. Is that the right word for it?***

RF: Oh, it's a little less than a lecturer. I have one topic. Basically, it's a program I developed here during the last several years. There was a point at which, in that 25-year descending second act, I decided, "All right, you're not dead yet, Bob. You're not getting much work, but your creative life is not over. You'd better think up something to do." So I took lessons of my life, created stories around some of them, and went out and started doing this program. It's called "Interacting," and it's basically a stand-up act with positive stories instead of jokes. I continue to do it frequently. In fact, as soon as I finish with you, I'm going to do the Westwood Rotary big lunch. It's satisfying, occasionally they pay me, and I donate that to an actors' charity, so it's a triple-win situation.

O: ***When did you start?***

RF: Oh, gee, it's been six years now, maybe seven. I started out... I decided I would open this little actors' workshop I always told actors to look for. That gave me something to do on Wednesday nights, and after about a year of that, I realized that some of the things I was saying to actors probably had broader application. I ran into a magazine called *Speakers For Free*. I put myself in the magazine, and that's when I became a speaker. Not a lecturer, but part of this little program.

O: ***I don't want you to give your act away, but one item on the menu that intrigued me was "A Chilling Brando Story." Can you tell me what that is?***

RF: It's a story about respect. You want the story?

O: ***Sure.***

RF: This is my closer, by the way. It's four or five minutes long, so relax. In the same week in which John Huston gave me my very first acting advice, I met Marlon Brando. We were shooting starting at noon and finishing at midnight. I was playing a private, we were out on the drilling field, and there were lots of other guys dressed like me; we were drilling and doing Army stuff. Late in the afternoon of the fourth or fifth day of shooting, I hear a whisper, [voice drops to a whisper] "Marlon's here. Here comes Marlon. Marlon's on the set." Everybody looks. Yep, there he is, Marlon Brando. John Huston breaks the set up, he starts walking over there, and he turns back to me and says, "Come on over here, Bobby, I want to introduce you to Marl." I walk over, I'm introduced to Marlon, they blah blah for a minute. Marlon says to me, "When do you break for dinner?" I say, "In an hour or so." He says, "Well, come on over to my Winnebago and we'll have a little conversation." So we're sitting there in the Winnebago, and you know how they're set up: There's a couple of bench seats and a little table, and there's a picture window. The picture window looks out over everybody on the set. We're talking and Marlon's looking out the window a little bit. He turns to me and says, "Where's your dressing room?" I said, "Well, you know, I'm over there. I'm fine." I came from the theater, and I was used to dressing in the bathroom, if necessary. They'd given me a little corner with a drape on it where all the guys were dressing up as privates, and I knew it was a little bit of a loaded question. He's looking out the window a little bit more. He spots somebody. He gets up. He opens up the door. He points to the first assistant director, a big tall guy, and the guy comes running over. "What do you need, Marlon?" Marlon looks at him and he points at me. He says, "This actor hasn't got a dressing room. He's dressing with the extras." That's something I hadn't told him, something he determined on his own. I'm thinking, "Why is this guy putting the heat on me? I didn't ask him to." The first assistant is, "Oh, but..." as he's wringing his hands, and he's saying, "Marlon, I'm sorry, but there weren't enough Winnebagos because of the tennis tournament," or because it's Long Island or because of this or because of that. Marlon says, "But, by the way, when we go to Italy he'll have a great dressing room." And when we got to Italy I had a great dressing room. He dismisses the first assistant, but by now everybody on the set, though they couldn't hear what Marlon was talking about in front of his dressing room, they saw the body language of the first assistant and knew something was going on. Something was wrong, and now he's got everybody's attention. Now he points to the biggest guy on the set, one of the producers. I forget who it was; let's call him Phil. "Phil," he yells. He points, and Phil comes over. "Yeah, Marlon, what is it? What is it, Marlon?" "Phil," and he looks Phil straight in the eyes. I'm inches away from all of this. He says, "Phil, I'm very, very upset." And he eyeballs Phil for a long time, 12 or 15 seconds, enough time for sweat to start forming on Phil's upper lip. I'm thinking, "Oh, please, please, please don't let it be my dressing room he's so upset about." Finally, in answer to the question Phil and I are both asking ourselves—"What's he so upset about?"—Marlon says, "Phil, there's too many folks around here. They're making me nervous." "What do you need, Marlon?" "I need some tranquilizers, Phil." "Right away, Marlon. What kind do you need?" He tells him what kind he needs. He says, "I'll be right back." He starts to leave. Marlon says, "Phil. Phil." Phil comes back. "What is it, Marlon?" "Phil, there's no music in this Winnebago. I'd like to hear some music. A little classical music to make me feel better." "Right away, Marlon. Right away." He starts to leave. "Phil. Phil." Phil comes back. "Something with a couple of speakers, Phil." Phil leaves. Thirty minutes later, he's got a big guy with him carrying a big record player, two speakers, and a stack of classical records. The guy brings it in, he installs it in seconds, and he's out the door. Phil gives the tranquilizers to Marlon. "Anything else I can do for you?" "No, Phil, you did great. I appreciate it very much." "Anything you need, you just let us know, Marlon." "Phil, you did great, I appreciate it very much." He shoos Phil out the door, closes the door, sits back down, and watches Phil walk back to the other producers. We're waiting to find out whether we're going to work tomorrow or not. He watches them for a while, and then he turns to me and he says this: "You see, if you don't scare them, they will never respect you, all right?" I learned three important things. Number one, I learned that the word "respect" has polar opposite meanings. At one end of the meaning of the word, respect is the thing that people give you if you've got a hammer over their head. At the extreme opposite end of the meaning of the same word is the thing that people give you if they love you, if they're not afraid of you, and if they want you to succeed. Number two, I realized what passed for respect in Hollywood, and that's who's got the hammer. And number three, I realized that if I ever got any of this respect, I wanted it to come from the other meaning of the word, where you don't have to worry about getting stabbed in the back. I tell my children—and part of this program, by the way, is about parenting—that life is short. It's an arc: First you're born and you can't take care of yourself, then you can take care of yourself, and then for most of your life you have to take care of others until the very end, when you can't take care of yourself anymore. You've got to rely on the ones you've parented. "You'd better do a good job, Bob," I say to myself. I realized that life is a series of moments along this arc, moments at which you can deliver excellence, or less, if you desire. But if you do deliver excellence, you get that reward, and I've built up a metaphor during this program of what you get when you deliver excellence to any job of any kind: You get the reward of self-respect and respect from others and satisfaction. And this is the real McCoy. This is untransferrable wealth. You stick this in your pocket and it's like a little nugget that'll always be there. If you're ever wondering what to do right now, and if you're ever asking yourself, "What shall I do with this job that I've got right now?"... If I apply the simple formula that I'm going to do this job as good as I can, that and a little practice gives me excellence almost every time.

"During the years when I was trying to survive, I was doing dopey stuff."

And when you're delivering excellence every time, you get that reward I keep mentioning. If you happen to be getting that reward on a frequent enough basis, you know... Those in both religious traditions, the Eastern and the Western, talk about a path: the path of righteousness. If you're getting these rewards on a frequent basis, you're on that path. And if you're one of the ones who believe in a heaven, this is the path right to it. But if you're one of the ones who believe that inner peace is the best life has to offer, you know precisely what you're doing when you wake up in the morning. You're using your life and your life experiences to understand with, and with every action you create, you deliver that understanding. You're doing what an artist does: using his life to understand and deliver that understanding with every act you create. And if you're doing that, and you're getting those rewards on a frequent enough basis, you're making the best that you can out of the life you've got to live. End of program.

O: ***One thing about your comeback is that it came from the type of respect that you like: People loved your work and sought you out. It must have been rewarding to see what you've been teaching come through in your own life.***

RF: Well, you've heard of a 12-step program? I've got a three-step program. It's a whole lot easier to remember. Step three was during the period in which I was headed downward and downward. I kept thinking to myself, "This slide has got to stop." But I had an epiphany during that period, and the epiphany was the simple one, when you realize, "You know what? You're not dead yet, Bob. You can win it in the late innings. You've still got the late innings, but you can't quit. Never quit." That's step three: You're ready to die, you're waiting to die. Never quit, that's step three. Step two: You've got to have a strategy to get from where you are, which is in a deep hole, to winning it in the late innings. That's the obvious strategy. You deliver excellence to what you're doing right now, and I say excellence; I don't mean perfection. I mean the willingness to do the job as good as you can. If you're willing to do it as good as you're willing to think up to do it, that's what your mind is there for, and you deliver excellence right now, now being the only moment you can control or do anything with or be creative with. Now is the only moment you've got to work with. If you deliver excellence right now, that gives you the best shot at the best future you've got coming. That's step two. Step one: You've got to have a good attitude in order to deliver step two, because if you have a bad attitude, step two is precluded; you can't deliver excellence if you've got a bad attitude. Step one is to accept all things. "It doesn't matter that they're not giving you good jobs anymore, Bob. It doesn't matter that you don't get the Winnebago anymore, Bob. It doesn't matter that she doesn't love you anymore." Put it behind you, just like that. Your shoulders relax, you breathe easier. Suddenly you've accepted it, you've put it behind you, and you're not going to worry about that anymore, no more negativity about that. Put it behind you just like that. Acceptance gives you a good attitude. That's step one. Delivering excellence right now gives you the best shot at the best future you've got coming. That's step two. And it's not over till it's over, but then it's really over. Never quit. That's step three. And I promise, I use that in my own life and with my own attitudes for the years when I was doing lousy in hopes that I would have another shot at this career and do something better with it the second time than I did the first. And Quentin Tarantino came along and [*American Perfekt* director] Paul Chart came along, and then some others have come along, and guess what? We've got another shot at it.

O: ***A lot of actors who have comebacks don't want to talk about the lean years, but that's something you've been willing to do.***

RF: Well, what is there not to talk about? I've had children. I had four children, we all had to struggle to get up and get educated, and they all did their part, and we all did the best we could, and that's what a family and a parent are supposed to do.

O: *What are your favorite films of that period? You took some interesting films at that time, even if they weren't necessarily high-profile.*

RF: Oh... *Alligator*. It's a fun movie. *Peacemaker*, another fun movie. What are the pictures? Boy, you're talking to a guy who can't remember anything anymore. *Vigilante* was sort of an exploitation picture, but I met some good guys from it.

O: The Black Hole *seems like it must have been interesting, because it's such a big-budget film with a relatively inexperienced director involved.*

RF: When I did the picture, we had a script that did not have the last few pages. The script at the end said... I forget now how it was worded, but it made it clear that there was an ending that they were going to keep secret until they shot it. My assumption was, "Oh, boy, this is going to be a good ending. This is Disney, these guys know what they're doing, they're really gonna put something great out there." And when I saw the picture, I was really confused about what that ending was all about. So, with the exception of the ending, I liked the picture a lot.

O: *You also directed a film called* Hollywood Harry *which I had trouble tracking down. Can you tell me about the film?*

RF: Yes. *Hollywood Harry*. I went to Cannes with *Vigilante*, and that was the first time I saw how they sell movies. "Wow," I thought. "This is fun. I'm going to do this. How hard could it be?" I went home, got a writer I knew, and we got a sort of mediocre script together. I figured for half a million dollars I'd make a picture, probably sell it for a lot of money, get a house in Malibu. Well, it's not so easy to make a movie. I made it with a whole lot less, about $125,000. Eventually, I called up my daughter Kate, who at the time was 12 and wanted to act, and I said, "Do you want to work? Are you ready to work?" She said, "Yes, absolutely." And so I built a little picture around her and me.

O: *In the late '80s, you did three films in Spain with George Kennedy. How did that come about? Were they all filmed back to back?*

RF: No. One of those films I actually did. Two of those films are a Spanish actor who... Somebody told him he looked enough like me. He took my name and made, well, you see them. One is called *The Hopped-Up Nymphomaniac Of Rio Grande* or something like that, isn't that right?

O: *There's* Esmeralda Bay.

RF: *Esmeralda Bay* I did. That I think I did with George Kennedy. Name the other ones?

O: Satan's Princess?

RF: That's not a Spanish picture. That's just another dopey picture. During the years when I was trying to survive, I was doing dopey stuff. That one was made by a guy named Bert I. Gordon. His name was really Bert Gordon, but he decided to put an "I" in there so that his initials spelled "BIG." Aw, don't laugh at this stuff. This... [Laughs.] Bert I. Gordon, *Satan's Princess*. I've never seen it, but I know it's a horror.

O: *Then there's this thing called* Counterforce. *I think that's a Spanish film.*

RF: I did do *Counterforce*. That was a period where I played all the villains in the world. I played Noriega, Gadhafi, the guy that killed a kid and tossed him out of the airplane in the hijack picture. I can't remember what else, but that was a period in which I couldn't get any kind of jobs except terrorists and villains.

O: *How did you end up with villains? You don't seem like somebody who'd immediately be cast as a villain.*

RF: Listen, if you're cast as nothing and you get an offer as a villain, you take it. You've got to work. You've got to scrape it out. You've got to hang in there. ⌀